THE DISCURSIVE POWER

Imprimi Potest:

Joseph P. Zuercher, S.J., Praep. Provinc. Prov. Missourianae,
die 5 mensis Novembris, 1947.

Nihil Obstat:

Edmund J. Ryan, C.PP.S., Ph.D., Censor Deputatus,
die 7 mensis Junii, 1952

Imprimatur:

✠ Karl J. Alter, D.D., LL.D.,
Archiepiscopus Cincinnatensis
Cincinnati, Ohio,   die 20 Junii, 1952

Printed in the United States

by

The Messenger Press
Carthagena, Ohio

15.3.24

KLU

K63

F.8.

The Discursive Power

Sources and Doctrine of the *Vis Cogitativa*
According to St. Thomas Aquinas

George P. Klubertanz, S.J.

Assistant Professor of Philosophy

Saint Louis University

THE MODERN SCHOOLMAN

Saint Louis 3, Missouri

ACKNOWLEDGMENTS

I also wish to thank the following for their gracious permission to quote from their publications. To the Editorial Committee of the *Harvard Theological Review*, for permission to quote from "The Internal Senses in Latin, Arabic and Hebrew Philosophic Texts," vol. XXVIII (1935), by Harry Austryn Wolfson; to the Harvard University Press and the Loeb Classical Library, for permission to quote from Seneca, *Epistolae*, translated by R. M. Grummere; Sextus Empiricus, *Outlines of Pyrrhonism*, translated by R. G. Bury, and Philo, *Legum Allegoriae*, translated by Colson and Whittaker; to the Oxford University Press, for permission to quote from *The Meditations of the Emperor Marcus Antoninus*, translated by A. S. L. Farquharson; to the Pontifical Institute of Mediaeval Studies, for permission to quote from *Algazel's Metaphysics*, edited by J. T. Muckle, C.S.B.; and to the B. Herder Book Company, for permission to quote from the American edition of E. Gilson, *The Philosophy of St. Thomas Aquinas*.

TABLE OF CONTENTS

PART III

CHAPTER IX: :

APPENDICES

INTRODUCTION

Only a philosopher with strong antiquarian interests cares to know every little detail of the doctrine of St. Thomas. At first sight, the *vis cogitativa* might seem to be such a minor point, incapable of yielding any new philosophical insight.[1] In St. Thomas himself, the *vis cogitativa* appears to be insignificant, for he used it but little in his positive synthesis,[2] and only a little more in his discussion and polemic.[3] Modern writers on St. Thomas and on Thomistic psychology seem to take the same point of view; they devote very few paragraphs to the "cogitative power."[4]

1. This disparaging attitude is shared by some who know a good deal about the subject; for example, Max Horten, *Das Buch der Ringsteine Farabi's* (Beitraege, Baeumker, Muenster: Aschendorff, 1906, Band V, Heft 3), pp. 234-35. According to B. Hauréau, *Singularités Historiques et Littéraires* (Paris: Calmann Lévy, 1894), pp. 278 - 79, the whole business of faculties and impressed species is a bungled misinterpretation of Aristotle which is closely bound up with the wholly inaccurate biology of the Arabians. J. E. Combes, *La Psychologie de Saint Thomas d'Aquin* (Montpellier: Grollier, 1860), pp. 268 - 72, blames the whole theory of the *cogitativa* upon an undue influence from Averroes and an unchecked tendency toward sweeping generalisations.
2. This is clear from the fact that the longest single continuous text does not extend beyond two printed pages; texts a page or longer are not more than four. Compare the single article devoted to all four internal senses in the *Summa Theologiae* with the five articles on the will, or the eight articles devoted solely to the manner in which the soul knows bodily things.
3. The *Summa Contra Gentiles* deals with the *cogitativa* in book II, chapters 60 - 61, 70, 73, 75. On the function of these passages and the direction of the critique of Averroes contained in them, see below, chapter six, last section, *"Summa Contra Gentiles."*
4. Here is a list of representative Thomistic textbooks of psychology, with page references to their treatment of the estimative power and the *cogitativa*.
   Robert Edward Brennan, O.P., *General Psychology* (New York: Macmillan, 1937), pp. 224 - 35; *Thomistic Psychology,* (New York, Macmillan, 1941), pp. 131 - 32, 134 - 35, 142-43, 146.

1

This relative neglect of the *vis cogitativa* has a quite plausible explanation. Man is a being of many activities. Some of them are obvious; others extremely important. For example, man's sense activities are so evident that it requires an effort to ignore them.[5] Man's intellectual operations, on the other hand, are his specifically human ones; and so are of the first importance, both practically and theoretically. It can easily be concluded that economy of effort warrants us in getting rid of everything but the most obvious and essential questions in psychology.

In this streamlining of psychology and the theory of knowledge, modern students of St. Thomas and modern Thomistic writers have separated themselves more and more from the thinkers that study man in his concrete wholeness. An example will make this clear.

On the one hand, experimental scientists have been concerned with many obscure facets of human activity. They have been intensely concerned, in general, with the many inner processes that supervene upon elementary sensation.[6] In particular,

Joseph Gredt, O.S.B., *Elementa Philosophiae Aristotelico-Thomisticae,* 3rd ed. (Friburg: Herder, 1921: 2 vols.) 1, pp. 401-10.

Eduard Hugon, O.P., *Philosophia Naturalis,* 3rd ed. pars. 2 Paris: Lethielleux, 1922), pp. 255-56.

Vincentius Remer, S.J., *Psychologia,* 5th ed., aucta a Paulo Geny, S.J., (Gregorian University Press, 1925), pp. 114-15.

On these and similar textbooks, cf. Julien Peghaire, C.S.Sp., "A Forgotten Sense, the Cogitative," *The Modern Schoolman, XX* (1943), p. 123.

5. Some behaviorists write as if they meant to deny the reality even of sensation; it seems, however, that they are merely refusing to take the individual's experiences and feelings as worthy of scientific study; cf. Robert S. Woodworth, *Psychology,* 12th ed., (London: Methuen, 1940), p. 583.

6. For example, the studies of association and sensory perception.

More recent studies are summarized in "The Psychologists and the Nature of Man," *Proceedings of the American Catholic Philosophical Association* XXV (1951), 66-88. This article also contains material for notes 7 to 10 below.

Sometimes "Scholastic" psychologists fail to take account even of such elementary things as the distinction between sensation and perception, though this particular distinction would be readily as-they have studied the influence of the emotions, passions, and other acts of the sensory appetite upon intellectual operations. Thus, in the investigation of mental abnormalities, it has been proved beyond any doubt that the passions of the sensory appetite can intervene to distort the processes of intellectual cognition.[7] In normal situations, too, emotional attitudes influence intellectual adherence to opinions.[8] In trying to understand this relationship, men have discovered that the whole process of learning is shot through with appetitive factors: love, interest, fear.[9] Even the most exalted and abstract of human occupations are not immune from the influence of instinctive reactions.[10]

On the other hand, the average "Thomistic" account of knowledge has no place for an influence of appetite upon thought. Take the learning process.[11] According to many accounts, there are four steps. First in the order of time is sensation. Sensations are received and unified by common sense and transmitted to the imagination. By dint of frequent repetition they are impressed thereon. Finally, under the influence of the agent intellect these images or phantasms cause intellectual knowledge. In the meantime, of course, sensations and images also cause acts of the

---

similable, and perhaps even capable of some slight refinement, in terms of the Aristotelian distinction of sensibles into proper, common, and *per accidens*. For examples of passages where St. Thomas has treated of this distinction, see below, under the heading, *"vis cogitativa* and the *sensibile per accidens."*

7. Cf. Edmund S. Conklin, *Principles of Abnormal Psychology* (New York: Holt, 1927), pp. 63, 65 - 66, 75. Further references can be found in note 120, to chapter 9.

8. References below, chapter 9, note 119, section 2.

9. References below, chapter 9, note 119, sections 1, 3 - 5, and note 16, first paragraph.

10. Cf. R. S. Woodworth, *Psychology* 12th ed., pp. 371, 268, 270; even if the psychoanalysts have misinterpreted some of these facts, they are really there. Cf. from a different point of view, Joseph Maréchal, S.J. *The Psychology of Mysticism.*

11. This account is a summary of that given given by J. Gredt, *Elementa Philosophiae Aristotelico-Thomisticae,* vol. 1, pp. 401 - 10. It could be duplicated from any of the manuals referred to in notes 4, 13, and 19.

sensory appetite. In turn, the sensory appetite can account for
the *selection* of a particular sensation or image. But there is
apparently no way in which the sensory appetite can influence the
structure of knowledge, and particularly of intellectual knowledge.

Here are two accounts of knowledge. One explains it as a
clean-cut, almost mechanical process that could, at least theoretically, occur in isolation from any appetitive reaction. Its big
problems are the possibility of error, of influence from appetite,
of integration with the *whole* human person. The other account explains knowledge as a human process, that is vague and roundabout and is influenced by a host of purely subjective factors.
Its big problem is the possibility of truth, and so it is frequently
capitalized on by those who would remove any absolute from
man's grasp. I have heightened the contrast between these two
accounts, but one must honestly admit that the differences are there.

Two accounts of knowledge — how do they stand toward
each other? Perhaps the easiest thing to do is to ignore the
divergent account.[12] Another way to act, more common to thinkers
outside the field of what is known as Scholastic psychology, is to
conclude that St. Thomas and his close followers are simply out
of date, and that, at best, their philosophy must be modified.[13]

---

12. Some of the authors referred to have even written manuals of ex-
    perimental psychology; all of them make more or less use of ex-
    perimental data in other connections. So it cannot be the case that
    they are totally ignorant of the facts in question.
13. On the attitude of certain groups of modern psychologists, cf. Morti-
    mer J. Adler, *What Man Has Made of Man* (New York: Long-
    mans, 1937).
    It is perhaps more surprising to find so-called "Scholastic" phil-
    osophers in favor of a change. This is the attitude of Dr. Schuetz,
    "Die *vis aestimativa* s. *cogitativa* des h. Thomas von Aquin," *Goer--
    res-Gesellschaft zur Pflege der Wissenschaft* (Jahresbericht der
    Section fuer Philosophie fuer das Jahr 1883. Koeln: J. P. Bachem,
    1884), pp. 38-62. Similarly, in the related matter of the relation
    of the intellect to the phantasm, Dr. Rudolf Allers, "The Intellectual
    Cognition of Particulars," *The Thomist* III (1941), pp. 118 - 28.
    Among Scholastic manuals, the following are examples of those
    which reject the estimative and the *cogitativa* on "scientific" grounds.
    Cardinal Mercier, *Manual of Modern Scholastic Psychology,* tr.

But a more honest and scholarly approach is to re-examine the doctrine of St. Thomas; for perhaps the difficulty lies in the conception held by both groups of what St. Thomas really said.

A first step in this new evaluation is the study of the *vis cogitativa*. Why? Is not this merely one of four internal powers which all together make up but a small part of man's apparatus for knowing and doing? What advantage is to be gained from the study of a neglected power, provided that the remaining powers of man have been accurately presented?

Perhaps it is impossible to have a correct knowledge of three powers if the fourth is scarcely known, because the four powers may work together. Even more significantly, these powers may share in other complex activities of man.[14] It is obvious that a man is not just sensing, *or* imagining *or* thinking *or* willing *or* undergoing sense passions, one at a time. Several of his powers[15]

by T. L. Parker and S. A. Parker (London: Kegan Paul, 1928), vol. 1, p. 216.

Joseph Froebes, S.J., *Psychologia Speculativa* (Friburg: Herder. 1927: 2 vols.), vol. 1, pp. 32, 34, 174, 176 - 77.

Michael Maher, S.J., *Psychology,* 9th ed., (London: Longmans, 1925), pp. 92 - 96, 587.

14. It is sufficient to point out here that in the *Summa Theologiae* the *vis cogitativa* is spoken of thirteen times, the distribution including all three parts. This enumeration includes neither references to the same power under a different name, nor implicit references; for exact references, see below, chapter V.

15. Many modern psychologists, especially experimentalists, make light of "faculties." Their criticism, however, can well be said to be directed rather at the name, or at a particular presentation of the notion, rather than at the thing itself. Some very enlightening remarks are made by Robert S. Woodworth, *Experimental Psychology* (New York: Holt, 1938), p. 177; and L. P. Thurstone, *Vectors of Mind* (Chicago: University of Chicago Press, 1935), pp. 45 - 53. Charles Spearman, *Psychology Down the Ages* (London: Macmillan, 1937: 2 vols.), vol. I, p. 183, goes further to say that the notion of "faculty," correctly understood, is both useful and necessary.

This is not to say that philosophical and scientific psychologists should be doing the same work or arriving at the same conclusions. Experimental psychologists, for example, do not conduct analyses according to formal objects; they are much more interested in de-are in operation at any given time of his normal conscious life. If man were either sensing *or* imagining, and so on, perhaps it would be possible to understand him by studying each of his powers in isolation, and even by studying some of them. But if human operations can be *composite* even as *operations,* then the isolated study of the separate powers leaves us a long way from understanding man.

If St. Thomas thought that human operations are composite, then the study of the *vis cogitativa* takes on greater and greater significance. We shall see in the course of the textual analysis that St. Thomas repeats over and over again that the *vis cogitativa* acts as it does because it is in "union" or "contact" with reason. Upon this point he is insistent, far more insistent than he is about the working together of other powers. Once we have grasped the meaning of "contact" in the one case where it is most fully expressed and explained, we shall be able to notice the hints that St. Thomas drops in other instances, and be able to apply the explanation that we know he had in mind. If all this is true, then the key notion is that of contact, union, influence, composition.

Granted all this for the moment till it is proved by a textual study, we would naturally expect those who have written about the *vis cogitativa* to have stressed and explained this contact. Actually they have not done so, as we shall see by taking a brief look at the extant literature.

The older writers have comparatively little to say about the *vis cogitativa.* The great Commentators on St. Thomas, — Capreolus,[16]

---

tecting and measuring "capacities" like the "capacity for learning" or the "I. Q." Nevertheless, the possibility of such general capacities or factors logically presupposes the quite different and more ultimate distinction of powers. In this connection, it is interesting to see what an experimentalist, C. Spearman, has to say about the "G²" which he measured; cf. *The Nature of 'Intelligence' and the Principles of Cognition* (London: Macmillan, 1923), pp. 1 - 20. Compare also some interesting remarks by Mortimer J. Adler, *What Man Has Made of Man* (New York: Longmans, 1937), pp. 129 - 42.

16. Capreolus bases his discussion of the *cogitativa* on a work now considered doubtful, the *De Principio Individuationis.* Though he also quotes other texts, notably *Summa* I. 78. 4, the master text is the former. Consequently, he concludes that the object of the power

Cajetan,[17] and John of St. Thomas,[18] — touch just in passing on the idea of influence. Francis Suarez, S.J., maintained that the claims made for the estimative power and the *vis cogitativa* were beyond the scope of any sense power, and urged a return

---

is singular material substance: "quidditas substantiae materialis, et ipsae substantiae particulares possunt cognosci et percipi sensu interiori, qui dicitur vis cogitativa vel ratio particularis; talia enim objecta simul includunt substantiam cum accidentibus," *In IV Sent.,* d. 10, q. 4, a. 3, no. 10, in Joannis Capreoli *Defensiones Theologiae,* ed. Ceslaus Paban, O.P., and Thomas Pègues, O.P. (Turin: Cattier, 1900-1908: 7 vols.), vol. VI, p. 213; cf. also *in III Sent.,* d. 36, q. 1, a. 3 no. 1, ad. 4, vol. V, p. 434.

17. In commenting on *Summa* I. 78. 4, Cajetan expounds the argument, and refers back to the preceding article to show that there cannot be more than four interior senses. The rest of St. Thomas's statements seem clear to him. In commenting on III. 76. 7 (ed. Leonine, vol. 12, p. 189), he follows Capreolus, interpreting a passage which seems to differ from his own theory, in the light of the *De Principio Individuationis* and Averroes.

18. John of St. Thomas has two lengthy discussions, one on the distinction of the interior senses; the other on the question of expressed species. On the kind of knowledge the estimative has, there is nothing more than, "Ad hanc [aestimativam] pertinet cognoscere non solum sensibilia externa, sed etiam intentiones quasdam quae sensu externo non percipiuntur," *Cursus Philosophicus Thomisticus,* Philosophia Naturalis, p. 4, De Anima, bk. 2, q. 8, a. 1, 3⁰, ed. Beatus Reiser, O.S.B. (Turin: Marietti, 1930-1937: 3 vols.), vol. III, p. 242. On the *cogitativa* itself, these are typical remarks. "Id quod est aestimativa in brutis, quae naturali instinctu format illas intentiones insensatas, in homine dicitur cogitativa, quia cum aliqua collatione et discursu cogitat et format dictas intentiones, eo quod istae potentiae, [*that is,* cogitativa *and* reminiscentia] ex coniunctione ad intellectum modum quemdam discursivum participant," *ibid.,* 5⁰ p. 242. "Ex participatione intellectus, participantes ex coniunctione ad intellectum aliquem modum discursus circa singularia," *ibid.,* a. 1, p. 245. The very wording of *Summa* I. 78. 4 is recognizable. But what are these "intentions," and what is the "sharing and joining with intellect"? There is no discoverable answer. — John does not use the *De Principio Individuationis;* his key texts are the *Summa* article, and the *Commentary on the De Anima* of St. Thomas. In this he is followed by most Thomists.

to the Aristotelian theory of a single internal sense.[19]

In more recent times, there have been a few studies which deal explicitly with the *vis cogitativa* and related topics. An historical approach was taken by Domet de Vorges and Harry Austryn Wolfson. The former concluded that the estimative power is of merely an Arabian origin and should be discarded in favor of an explanation through "association of ideas."[20] Professor Wolfson implies that St. Thomas misunderstood Averroes,[21] and that he built up his own doctrine simply by confusing those of Avicenna and Averroes.[22] A critical and negative point of view was assumed by Dr. Schuetz. In what was intended to be a very carefully documented study,[23] he concluded that the *vis cogitativa* is superfluous and self-contradictory;[24] that it is of Arabian, not Aristote-

---

19. Cf. Frances Suarez, S.J., *De Anima*, bk. 3, c. 30, no. 7 (*Opera Omnia,* Paris: Vives, 1856: 24 vols.), vol. III, p. 705; no. 16, p. 708; c. 31, no. 18, p. 709; c. 9, no. 14, p. 650; c. 6, no. 8, p. 624.

    Among the authors of textbooks, a number follow these opinions of F. Suarez. Some explicitly base their position on his arguments and his authority, for example:

    John Joseph Urràburu, *Psychologia* (Paris: Lethielleux, 1896), part 2, pp. 750 - 51, 771.

    Tilman Pesch, S.J., *Institutiones Psychologiae* (Friburg: Herder, 1897: 3 vols.), vol. II, pp. 275, 286.

    Paul Siwek, S.J., *Psychologia Speculativa* (Rome: Gregorian University Press, 1932), pp. 148 - 49, 251.

20. Domet De Vorges, "L'Estimative," *Revue neo-Scholastique* XI (1904), pp. 433 - 54.

21. Harry Austryn Wolfson, "The Internal Senses in Latin, Arabic, and Hebrew Philosophic Texts," *Harvard Theological Review* XXVIII (1935), pp. 120 - 21.

22. *Ibid.,* pp. 121 - 22.

23. "Die *vis aestimativa* s. *cogitativa* des h. Thomas von Aquin," *Goerres-Gesellschaft zur Pflege der Wissenschaft* (Jahresbericht der Section fuer Philosophie fuer das Jahr 1883, Koeln: J. P. Bachem, 1884), pp. 38 - 62. Dr. Schuetz uses forty-eight texts of St. Thomas, while failing to make use of thirty others, among them the extremely important discussions in the *Commentary on the Ethics.*

24. According to Dr. Schuetz, the *vis cogitativa* has two functions, to perceive the useful and convenient, and to prepare phantasms, *ibid.,* pp. 43 - 45, and these two functions cannot be reconciled, pp. 45 - 49. He says that it is an impossible faculty, pp. 54 - 57.

lian origin; and that it essentially involves a mistaken interpretation of the νοῦς παθητικὸς spoken of in the *De Anima*.[25]
Expository and positive articles exist, though they are fewer than
might be expected. Rodolphe Hain, O.M.I., has two very short
articles on the *vis cogitativa*[26] and its animal correlate.[27] In such
brief compass, an explanation of "contact" from the text of St.
Thomas could not be given. Cornelio Fabro in two articles[28] tried
to establish that the *vis cogitativa* is the faculty of perception. He
seems to have been the first to group together the *cogitativa*, the
experimentum, and modern experimental data on perception. In
his view of the historical relationships, texts of Averroes can be
used to clarify those of St. Thomas. On the object of the *cogitativa*
and the nature of its *"contact"* or union with intellect, he has
little to say.[29] Rudolph Allers tried to apply the theory of the
vis cogitativa to modern problems, while confessing that the theory
itself was very obscure.[30]

---

25. *Ibid.*, pp. 39 - 42.
26. "De vi cogitativa et de instinctu hominis," *Revue de L'Université
    d'Ottawa* III, (1933), pp. 41* - 62*. This article spends most of its
    available space in proving that there are instincts in man.
27. "De vi aestimativa et de instinctu animalium" *Revue de L'Université
    d'Ottawa* II, (1932), pp. 98 - 114. This is mainly a re-presentation
    of *Summa Theologiae* I. 78. 4, with some illustrations from modern
    scientific studies of instinct.
28. "Knowledge and Perception in Aristotelic-Thomistic Psychology," *The
    New Scholasticism* XII, (1938), pp. 337 - 65, and "L'Organizzazione
    della percezione sensoriale," *Bolletino Filosofico* IV (1938), pp. 3 - 58.
    On C. Fabro's notion of the historical relationship between St.
    Thomas and Averroes, and the mistakes of interpretation consequent
    upon it, cf. below, ch. 9, note 56. On certain minor ambiguities, cf.
    G. P. Klubertanz, S.J., "The Internal Senses in the Process of Cogni-
    tion," *The Modern Schoolman* XVIII (1941), p. 20, note 22.
29. In these points C. Fabro seems to follow the lead of Cardinal
    Cajetan, if we can judge by his similar manner of passing over them,
    and his choice of references in other points.
30. "The *Vis Cogitativa* and Evaluation," *The New Scholasticism* XV,
    (1941), pp. 195 - 221. Dr. Allers intends to show that "feeling of
    value" is not the same as "awareness of value," and that the "act
    of appropriation of value" is due to the *vis cogitativa;* cf. especially
    pp. 214 - 221.

Of recent studies, that of Fr. Julien Peghaire, C.S.Sp.,[31]
deserves special notice, for it is by far the longest and most thorough.
His historical views, rather hinted at than expressed, are similar
to those of C. Fabro.[32] In discussing the nature of the union between intellect and *cogitativa*,[33] he relies on argumentation (very
sound, it is true), rather than on textual analysis. He has found
no texts to explain the "preparation of phantasms" by the *cogitativa*.[34]

In addition to these explicit studies, there are only the textbooks of "Thomistic" psychology already referred to,[35] a few
short notes in an edition of the *Summa*,[36] and some scattered re-

---

The obscurities he finds are the following: the relation between
intellect and the *cogitativa* is obscure, pp. 203 - 04; the "practical
syllogism" is very vague and obscure, pp. 205 - 06; no one knows
how the *cogitativa* discovers its "intentions," pp. 212 - 13.

31. "A Forgotten Sense, The Cogitative, according to St. Thomas Aquinas,"*The Modern Schoolman* XX (1943), pp. 123 - 40, 210 - 29. This
same article appears, in French, as chapter 8 of *Regards sur le connaître* (Montréal: Fides, (1949), pp. 309 - 94.

32. He does not seem to advert to the differences between the Thomistic
and the Averroistic *cogitativa;* cf. his treatment of the two writers,
ibid., pp. 210 - 11.

33. *Ibid.*, p. 140, where he gives an interpretation of the "union" and then
remarks, "St. Thomas refers to this interpretation."

34. *Ibid.*, p. 213, he says that this notion was left "to his [i.e., St.
Thomas's] disciples to develop."

35. Above, note 4.

36. "Editions de la Revue des Jeunes," Paris: Desclée.

J. Wébert, O.P., in his translation of *Summa Theologiae* I, qq.
75-83, "L'Ame humaine," (1928) speaks of the mysterious "rejail-
lissement ontologique (refluentia)" which the intellect has upon the
internal senses, pp. 358 - 59, commentary on q. 78, a. 4; also in Appendix II, pp. 381 - 82.

H. Noble, O.P., considers the *cogitativa* to be "la faculté maîtresse
des gens pratiques," in his translation of *Summa* II-II, qq. 47-56,
"La Prudence," (1925) commenting on 47. 3 ad 3, p. 243. In the
same passage he explains the estimative power in terms of an "en-
semble d'images innées."

marks in books[37] and articles.[38]

This is the scope of the writings on the *vis cogitativa*. Some very brief references have been omitted; it may also be possible that one or the other study has been overlooked. In spite of that, to one familiar with the amount of writing on the doctrines of St. Thomas, it cannot but seem strange that there is comparatively so little about the *vis cogitativa*.

Certain basic considerations are pointed out. Almost all writers agree that the estimative power is to be considered as the purely animal equivalent of the *vis cogitativa*. They agree that the difference between the two lies in some "influence" received from

---

37. André Hayen, S.J., *L'Intentionnel dans la Philosophie de Saint Thomas* (Bruxelles: L'Edition Universelle — Paris: Desclée, 1942). A. Hayen bases his interpretation of the *cogitativa* on his notion of "intentionality." According to him, this latter is a single analogous term. He contends that the elevation of the *cogitativa* is to be explained "par la présence intentionnelle de l'intelligence à la sensibilité," p. 181; an explanation which many readers will fail to find illuminating. A. Hayen argues from various texts using the term *"experimentum"* as if it were a univocal term, p. 178; for the contrary view, see below, chapter seven, *"experimentum."* On p. 179, Fr. Hayen translates *ratio particularis* as "C'est l'objet intelligibile," even though in all the texts which he quotes or refers to in his footnotes 8 to 13 this term signifies a potency or power.

   H. D. Noble, O.P., *Les Passions dans la Vie Morale* (Paris: Lethielleux, 1931), 1e partie, "Psychologie de la Passion," has a few interesting and very valuable, but general remarks. H. Noble's work does not enter into textual studies.

38. H. D. Simonin, O.P., "La notion d'"Intentio' dans l'oeuvre de S. Thomas d'Aquin" *Revue des Sciences Philosophiques et Théologiques* XIX (1930), pp. 445 - 63. This excellent article touches only indirectly on the *vis cogitativa;* it will be made use of below, chapter eight, "the estimative power — its opject."

   Rudolf Allers, "The Intellectual Cognition of Particulars," *The Thomist* III (1941), pp. 95, 163. Dr. Allers intends to point out certain obscurities in St. Thomas, for example, concerning the knowledge of the material singular thing, pp. 96, 128 - 63; concerning the intellect's dependence on the phantasm, pp. 118 - 28, and especially concerning the meaning of *continuatio,* pp. 106 - 08. It is this third point in particular which interests us here.

intellect. There is a rather general agreement on the key texts of St. Thomas.

Lacunae are strikingly evident. We have examined the articles and books to see whether they gave an explanation, based on the text of St. Thomas, of the "influence" which the intellect has upon the *cogitativa*. The earlier writers and the textbooks seem aware that there is a problem; many later studies point it out, but none solve it textually. This is not the only omission. Very little has been said by any of the authors about the object of the estimative and the *cogitativa*. There has been some discussion of the meaning of *intentio*, but no satisfactory solution. Finally, with the exception of J. Peghaire, the authors speak of the *cogitativa* only in connection with internal sensation. St. Thomas, as we shall see, spoke of it in many other connections.

Why these significant gaps? The chief reason seems to be the neglect of the historical approach to the study of the texts. How does this affect our problem? There is clear evidence that St. Thomas supposed his readers to be familiar with many things. For example, the word *intentio* has a technical meaning when used to designate the object of the estimative and the *vis cogitativa*. St. Thomas himself does not state this meaning; he contents himself with an example or two,[39] The only detailed exposition of the term is to be found in Avicenna.[40] Again, "contact" (*continuatio*) is a notion that frequently occurs in the texts that explain how the *vis cogitativa* operates. In these texts, there is not even an illustration or example. This term, too, is a technical one derived from Arabian Philosophy.[41] Once the ancestry is known, we are in a position to seek in St. Thomas himself for indications of the meaning. These indications are to be found in some of his critiques of Arabian teachings.[42]

Of course, the dependence of St. Thomas on the Arabians has not remained unsuspected; his frequent references to Avicenna

---

39. Cf. below, chapter eight, "estimative power — its object."
40. Cf. below, chapter three, "Avicenna."
41. Cf. below, chapter six, *"continuatio."*
42. For example, *Summa Theologiae* I. 88. 1. For other references, see below, chapter 6, note 32.

and Averroes would make this impossible. As we have seen, most
of those who have written on the *vis cogitativa* have made some
references to the Arabians; there have even been attempts to
write the history of the doctrines of the internal senses. But even
the most complete historical study, the scholarly work of Professor Harry Austryn Wolfson, restricts itself to a merely philological investigation. The rest of the historical references are very
sketchy, and frequently are chosen with a view to proving a
doctrinal point.[43]

This very situation underlines the necessity for an historical
approach. The arguments for it, drawn from the particular case
before us, are reinforced by general considerations. For an atten-
tive study of the sources of any thinker sheds some light on his
thought.[44] This is emphatically true of mediaeval thinkers. They
were vividly alive to a stirring intellectual milieu.[45] Their method

---

43. For example, Domet de Vorges shows that the estimative power
was invented by the Arabians, and gives this as a reason for reject-
ing it; cf. above, note 19. Cajetan uses history to substantiate his
interpretation of St. Thomas, above, note 18; so also C. Fabro, above,
note 28. The rest of the authors have only brief and scattered references to history.

44. To suppose otherwise would be to imagine that a philosopher lives
in an intellectual vacuum, or that, knowing the thought of others,
he can completely abstract from it in his own thinking. Some cases
are striking: imagine an historian who would treat Aristotle without mentioning Plato, or Plotinus without Plato and Aristotle;
Spinoza without Descartes, Hume without Locke and Berkeley, Kant
without Hume. On Descartes himself, and his dependence on Scholastic writers, cf. Etienne Gilson, *Etudes sur la rôle de la Pensée
Médiévale dans la formation du système Cartésien* (Paris: Vrin,
1930); in briefer fashion, cf. Joseph Maréchal, S.J., *Le Point de
Départ de la Métaphysique* (Paris: Alcan, 1923), cahier 2, p. 23.
The value of knowing sources is put in a more general way in
Etienne Gilson, *The Unity of Philosophical Experience* (New York:
Scribners, 1937), p. 59-60.

45. Cf. Etienne Gilson, *The Spirit of Mediaeval Philosophy* (New York:
Scribner's, 1940), pp. 1, 382-402. A summary glance at the titles of
the quodlibetal disputations held at Paris is sufficient to show both
the urgency of the matters discussed for those times, and the free
interchange of ideas among the masters; cf. P. Glorieux, *La Littérature quodlibétique de 1260 à 1320* (Le Saulchoir — Paris: Vrin. 1925).

of studying the authorities on all sides of every question was like-wise calculated to subject them to a variety of influences.[46] Further the mediaeval writers made no fetish of originality; ancient and contemporary thinkers, both great and small, were laid under con-tribution.[47]

All this is especially true of St. Thomas. The profound and exhaustive studies published in the last two generations have shown his keen awareness of the great philosophical questions.[48] Other studies show that he paid careful attention to the lectures of his contemporaries at Paris.[49]

---

46. Cf. M. Grabmann, *Geschichte der scholastische Methode* (Freiburg: Herder, 1909-1911: 2 vols.), vol. I, pp. 28-36, vol. II, pp. 13-24, 151-56, 199-220.
47. Cf. M. D. Chenu, O.P., "Authentica et Magistralia," *Divus Thomas* (Placentiae), XXVIII (1925), 257-85; Maurice de Wulf, *Histoire de la Philosophie Médiéval,* 6th ed. (Paris: Vrin, 1934-1947: 3 vols.), vol. II, pp. 407ff; Anton C. Pegis, *St. Thomas and the Greeks* (Milwaukee: Marquette Univ. Press, 1939); Etienne Gilson, "Pour-quoi s. Thomas a critiqué s. Augustin," *Archives d'Histoire Doc-trinale et Littéraire du Moyen-Age* I (1926), "La critique thomiste des Motecallemin," pp. 8-25; "L'avicennisme," pp. 35-44; C. Boyer, S.J. "S. Thomas et s. Augustin," in *Essais sur la doctrine de s. Augustin* (Paris: Beauchesne, 1932), pp. 138-65; H. L. Janssens, O.S.B., "S. Thomas et s. Anselme," *Xenia Thomistica* (Rome: Coll. Angel., 1925), vol. III, pp. 289-96; M. D. Chenu, O.P., "Notes de travail. I: La surnaturalisation des vertus. II. L'amour dans la foi," *Bulletin Thomiste* IV (1931-1933), 63*-99*; David Kaufmann, *Die Sinne* (Leipzig: Brockhaus, 1884), pp. 46-47, 8.
48. Ludwig Baur, "Thomas von Aquin als Philosoph," *Theologische Quartalschrift* CVI (1925), 249-66, CVII (1926), 8-38; Etienne Gilson, *The Spirit of Mediaeval Philosophy; Le Thomisme,* 5th ed. (Paris: Vrin, 1944); Pierre Rousselot, S.J., *The Intellectualism of St. Thomas,* tr. by J. E. O'Mahony (London: Sheed and Ward, 1935); André Brémond, S.J., "La synthèse thomiste de l'Acte et de l'Acte et de l'Idée," *Gregorianum* XII (1931), 267-83; A. Forest, *La structure métaphysique du concret selon s. Thomas d'Aquin* (Paris: Vrin, 1931).
49. *Supra,* note 47, and add: J. D'Albi, *S. Bonaventure et les luttes doctrinales de 1267-1277* (Tamines: Duculot-Roulin, 1922); M. D. Chenu, O.P., "Les réponses de s. Thomas et de Kilwardby à la con-sultation de Jean de Verceil (1271)," *Mélanges Mandonnet* (Paris:

The value of the historical approach to the doctrine of St. Thomas has been implicitly proved by the success of the studies using that method. In addition to this, its value in Thomistic studies has been asserted by very competent authorities.[50]

Vrin, 1930: 2 vols.), vol. I, pp. 191-222; P. Glorieux, "De quelques 'emprunts' de s. Thomas," *Recherches de Théologie Ancienne et Médiévale* VIII (1936), 155-68; E. Hocedez, S.J., *Aegidii Romani Theoremata de esse et essentia* (Louvain: Museum Lessianum, 1930); Anton C. Pegis, *St. Thomas and the Problem of the Soul in the Thirteenth Century* (Toronto: Institute of Mediaeval Studies, 1934).

50. Cf. Franz Cardinal Ehrle, *Die Scholastik und ihre Aufgaben in unseren Zeit,* zweite, vermehrte Auflage von Fr. Pelster, S.J. (Freiburg: Herder, 1933), pp. 37-54; P. Goudrault, O.P., "L'influence des études médiévales sur le progrès de la philosophie et de la théologie," *Revue Dominicaine* XXXIX, (1933), 3-16, 65-79; Gerald B. Phelan, "Presidential Address," *Proceedings of the American Catholic Philosophical Association* VII (1931), 27-40; Martin Grabmann, *Einfuehrung in die Summa Theologiae des hl. Thomas von Aquin,* 2nd. ed. (Freiburg: Herder, 1928), pp. 6-146; *idem,* "De Methodo Historica in Studiis Scholasticis Adhibenda," *Ciencia Tomista* XXVII (1923), 194-209; *idem,* "Commentatio Historica," *Angelicum* III (1926), 146-65; M. D. Chenu, O.P., "Pour l'histoire de la philosophie médiévale," *New Scholasticism* III (1929), 65-74; *idem,* "Apres dix ans," *Bulletin Thomiste* XI (1934), 1-3. Fr. Chenu has also some very penetrating remarks in various book reviews in the *Bulletin Thomiste* II (1925), 321, 332; IV (1927), 207; V (1928), 263, 332; VI (1929), 532, 616-23; XI (1934), 259; XIII (1936), 885-86; 893-95, and nos. 1497, 1498.

See also the briefer treatments, by way of introduction or incidentally, in the following: Fernand Van Steenberghen, *Aristote en Occident* (Louvain: Institut Supérieur de Philosophie, 1946), "avantpropos"; A. Forest, *La structure métaphysique du concret,* pp. 2-3; Jean Paulus, *Henri de Gand* (Paris: Vrin, 1938), pp. x-xiii, 5; Joseph Maréchal, S.J., *Le point de départ de la Métaphysique,* 3rd ed. (Brussells: L'Edition Universelle, 1944), cahier I, pp. 14-16; Etienne Gilson, *Le Thomisme,* pp. 6-7; *L'Esprit de la Philosophie Médiévale* (Paris: Vrin, 1932), vol. I, pp. 2-3, 11-20, 21-23; L. B. Geiger, O.P., *La Participation* (Paris: Vrin, 1942), pp. 18-26, 457, 163 note 1; Jacques Maritain, in a critical study of Henri Gouhier, "La Pensée religieuse de Descartes," *Revue de Philosophie* XXXII 1925), 81; I. T. Eschmann, O.P., "Bonum commune melius est quam bonum unius. Eine Studie ueber den Wertvorrang des Personalen bei

There remains only the question of the application of the
method. It is possible either to work back from the texts of St.
Thomas, or to work forward through preceding and contemporary
texts to study St. Thomas in their light. The former alternative
offers no help for research into the sources of oblique references.
Moreover, in our particular case where so little of the historical
matter has been published, the investigation into the sources of
some Thomistic texts would be so lengthy that we would lose the
whole thread of development. Consequently the task of patiently
wading through a large mass of texts imposes itself. It will be
necessary to gather all the texts that deal in any way with the
terms, the problems, and the authorities that St. Thomas speaks of.

Only after this work has been done will it be possible to determine which authors are involved in the development that led
to St. Thomas.

There are two reasons why all the texts found in this way
should be reproduced in this study. One practical reason is this:
a given document cannot be proved to be irrelevant except by the
presentation of some evidence from that writing itself. The second
is that some student may be interested in other aspects of the
doctrine of the internal senses; if the historical part of this were
very strictly limited to include only the relevant texts, such a
student would have to re-do a good part of the work, and such
duplication of effort is not at all profitable.

Thus this study of the *vis cogitativa* in St. Thomas divides
itself into three parts. The first four chapters present a brief history
of the doctrine of the internal senses, with special emphasis on
the *vis cogitativa* (if that term or any of its cognate forms are
used) or upon powers which have equivalent or similar functions
in psychologies where the *cogitativa* is not used. With regard to
the early Latin, Arabic, and Hebrew authors, the work of Professor Harry Austryn Wolfson has been utilized for a partial indication of sources (though it has needed completion in this mat-

---

Thomas von Aquin," *Mediaeval Studies* VI (1944), 62-120; there
are also some valuable remarks in F. Blanche, "Sur la langue technique de s. Thomas," *Revue de Philosophie* XXX (1930), 7-28.

ter), and in some few instances for the supplying of texts which otherwise would have been unavailable. An effort will be made to indicate how authors who have written in languages other than Latin became available to St. Thomas.

The second part, chapters five to eight inclusive, will deal with the doctrine of St. Thomas. This part will be introduced with a general indication of texts. The texts will then be considered in their context and in historical order, in so far as this is possible and practical. The textual study will aim at uncovering the thought of St. Thomas, just as it was. Questions of development of doctrine and modification will naturally be raised, and as far as possible solved.

The third part, chapter nine, will be an effort to present an integral and systematic account of the various points mentioned by St. Thomas in their historical and doctrinal contexts. This part will attempt to draw together the various threads of the investigation.

In the preparation and development of this study, I wish to make grateful acknowledgement of the valuable help and direction given me by Doctor Anton C. Pegis, president of the Pontifical Institute of Mediaeval Studies. I wish also to record here my gratitule for the less extensive, but very real help I have received from Rabbi Emil L. Fackenhein, Ph.D., with respect to chapter three; from the Very Reverend Louis-Marie Regis, O.P., President of the Institut Albert-le-Grand, on chapters six to nine; and from the Reverend Hugh Bihler, S.J., professor of experimental psychology, Woodstock College. I also wish to thank the University of Toronto for permitting me to print this adaptation of a thesis accepted by it in 1947.

PART 1

CHAPTER I

ARISTOTLE AND THE GREEK COMMENTATORS

A brief discussion of the Psychology of Aristotle has a three-fold relevance to an investigation of St. Thomas's doctrine of the *vis cogitativa*. *First*, there are to be found in the various writings of Aristotle a few vague hints scattered here and there which such a later doctrine might use as a point of departure.[1] *Secondly*, there are a number of points on which the psychology of the Stagirite was in need of completion,[2] or at least could well be so considered. *Thirdly*, it is a fact that the historical development of the Thomistic *cogitativa* took place in constant reference to Aristotle.

On the one hand, there are the *Commentaries* on Aristotle's *De Anima* of Averroes, St. Albert, and St. Thomas. All three of these *Commentaries* discuss the *vis cogitativa* or its equivalents in the course of their exposition of the "Philosopher." We could dismiss that as another instance of "fallacious paraphrase,"[3] but such a judgment is no longer in favor among modern scholars. There are after all various ways in which a text can be considered. We can restrict ourselves to a simple explanation of the terms and of the actually expressed thought. It is also possible to consider

---

1. Cf. A. M. Goichon, *Vocabulaires Comparés d'Aristote et d'Ibn Sînâ* (Paris: Desclée de Brouwer, 1931), p. 40; Harry Austryn Wolfson, "The Internal Senses in Latin, Arabic, and Hebrew Philosophic Texts," *Harvard Theological Review* XXVIII (1935), pp. 89-91.
2. Cf. St. Thomas Aquinas, *Commentarium in Aristotelis De Anima,* bk. III, lect. 6, ed. Angelo Pirotta, O.P. (Turin: Marietti, 1924), no. 667: "Ulterius autem quod iste motus aliam potentiam requirat, quam sensitivam, Aristoteles hoc non determinat."
3. This expression occurs in a strong condemnation of both the Arabian and the mediaeval Latin commentaries on Aristotle made by B. Hauréau, *Singularités Historiques et Littéraires* (Paris: Calman-Lévy, 1894), pp. 278-79.

not only what the author said, but what the reality was which he spoke about.[4]

On the other hand, such works as the *De Anima* of Ibn-Sina seem to have been written in conscious imitation of Aristotle. The great Arabian author made frequent reference to Aristotle in the elaboration of his doctrines on the internal senses; his method was followed by St. Albert and others. We shall see St. Thomas's own attitude in the course of this study.

These, then, are the reasons for a brief consideration of Aristotle. We shall treat, first, the backgrounds of the Aristotelian psychology in which the doctrine of internal senses was fitted. This will be followed by a second section, dealing with the suggestions and lacunae which gave the impetus to this further development.

BACKGROUNDS: "INTERNAL SENSATION";

POWERS OF THE SOUL

In his study of the sensitive soul, Aristotle passes from the consideration of the various senses: sight, hearing, smell, taste and touch,[5] to a consideration of the common attributes: motion, rest, figure, magnitude, number, and unity.[6] Of these common sensibles we are said to have an αἴσθησις κοινή— "a common perception."[7] This term, which is quite rare in Aristotlian usage,

---

4. On the ancient method of commenting — and so to a certain extent on the mediaeval method — "the dialectical treatment of positions," cf. Francis Macdonald Cornford, *Plato's Theory of Knowledge* (London: Kegan Paul, 1935), pp. 30-31. An instructive parallel can be drawn from the discussion of the Roman and Patristic method of commenting and the use of *eruditio* as given by Henri-Irénée Marrou, *Saint Augustin et la fin de la culture antique* (Paris: Bibliothèque des écoles Françaises, 1938) pp. 59-76, 125-28, 450-55, and *passim.*

5. *De Anima* II, cc. 6-12, 418 a 7 — 424 a 15.

6. *Ibid.*, III, c. 1, 425 a 14-30.

7. *Ibid.*, c. 1, 425 a 27.
   The phrase is thus translated by R. D. Hicks, *Aristotle De Anima* (Cambridge: University Press, 1907), p. 111. In the notes, p. 431,

is not explained at this point. But the meaning can be gathered
out of the further consideration.

After treating the common sensibles, Aristotle passes on to
two related points: the perception of the object of one sense by
another, and the sensible comparison of various sense objects among
themselves. We can and do say, for example, that "we *see* a sweet
object." This incidental (accidental) perception of the proper
object of one sense by another has its explanation in this, that
all the special senses form a unity.[8]

The same explanation is adduced for the fact that we can
know the difference between the various objects of the special
senses.[9]

Between these two discussions there is a passage which deals
with sensory awareness. It is very difficult to decide just what
Aristotle holds here, since what seems to be his solution is followed
by counter arguments. However, the question is decided very explicitly in the *De Somno*. Here it is said that there is a common
power accompanying the several senses, whereby we perceive that
we sense — κοινὴ δύναμις ἀκολουθοῦσα πάσαις.[10] The unity of sense,
which is somehow in the various senses, grounds the perception of
the common sensibles, sensory awareness, and the comparison of
the proper objects of these senses.[11]

---

he says "a common sensibility." G. Rodier, *Aristote, Traité de l'Ame*
(Paris: Leroux, 1900: 2 vols.), translates "la sensation commune,"
vol. I, p. 149. J. A. Smith, *De Anima* (Oxford: Clarendon Press,
1931), translates "a general sensibility."

8. Cf. *De Anima*, III, c. 1, 424 a 30.
9. *Ibid.*, c. 2, 427 a 1-5, 10-14.
10. *De Somno* 2, 455 a 12.
11. Cf. "Le sens commun, fond indifférencié de la sensibilité . . .", "il a
    trois fonctions: sentir les sensibles communs; constituer par son indif-
    férenciation l'unité du sensitif, ou comme nous dirons, de l'esprit perce-
    vant à travers la diversité des sens et des sensations spécialés; enfin,
    procurer au sentant la conscience de sa sensation," Octave Hamelin,
    Le Système d'Aristote, publié par Leon Robin (Paris: Alcan, 1920),
    pp. 377, 381; cf. Anthelme Edouard Chaignet, *Essai sur la Psy-
    chologie d'Aristote* (Paris: Hachette, 1883), pp. 374-75.
       Note that this is not the same as saying: "The common sense is
    the sense *of* the common sensibles." This latter statement is made

The *De Sensu* is likewise very explicit. "The general faculty of sense-perception is one,"[12] Aristotle tells us, and this is the power of the soul through which it perceives all that it perceives,

by John I. Beare, *Greek Theories of Elementary Cognition* (Oxford: Clarendon Press, 1906), pp. 277, 282-87; Clemens Baeumker, *Des Aristoteles Lehre von den auessern und innern Sinnesvermoegen* (Leipzig: Hunderststund und Pries, 1877), p. 62; Eduard Zeller, *Aristotle and the earlier Peripatetics*, tr. by Costelloe and Muirhead (London: Longmans, 1897: 2 vols.), vol. II, pp. 68-69; Friederich Ferdinand Kampe, *Die Erkenntnistheorie des Aristoteles* (Leipzig: Fues, 1870). p. 102; Clodius Piat, *Aristote* (Paris: Alcan, 1903), pp. 190-92; O. Hamelin, *Le Système d'Aristote*, p. 381.

It is strange to find so many writers making this assertion, since Aristotle himself points out that if there were a "sense of the common sensibles," then these would not be *common* any longer, but would be incidental sensibles for all the other senses. Cf. Marcel DeCorte, "Notes Exégetiques sur la Théorie Aristotélicienne du *Sensus Communis*," *New Scholasticism* VI (1932), pp. 187-214, especially pp. 189-90. In general agreement with M. DeCorte are G. Rodier, *Aristote, Traité de l'Ame*, vol. II, p. 360; Joannes Dembowski, *Quaestiones Aristotelicae Diversae*: I. De κοινοῦ αἰσθητηρίου natura et notione; II. De Natura et notione τοῦ θυμοῦ quatenus est pars ὀρέξεως (Regensburg: Dalkowski, 1881), pp. 9-20; Anthelme Edouard Chaignet, *Essai sur la Psychologie d'Aristote* (Paris: Hachette, 1883), pp. 374-75; an excellent treatment of this subject is to be found in G. A. G. Mure, *Aristotle* (London: Benn, 1932), pp. 109-112, and in J. Neuhauser, *Aristoteles' Lehre von dem sinnlichen Erkenntnisvermoegen und seinen Organen* (Leipzig: Koshey, 1878).

A subtle discussion, but irrelevant to our problem, concerns the *organ* of "common sense" (basic passages are *De Juventute et Senectute*, c. 1, 467 b 29-31 and *De Vita et Morte* a 5-23). An animated controversy was once carried on; cf. J. Neuhaeuser, *Aristotles' Lehre von den sinnlichen Erkenntnisvermoegen und seinen Organen*, pp. 110-18; C. Baeumker, *Des Aristoteles Lehre von den auessern und innern Sinnesvermoegen*, p. 86; J. Dembowski, *Quaestiones Aristotelicae Diversae*, pp. 50-63, 66; cf. also J. Beare, *Greek Theories of Elementary Cognition*, p. 327; E. Zeller, *Aristotle and the earlier Peripatetics*, p. 70; G. Rodier, *Aristote, Traité de l'Ame*, vol. II, pp. 333-34. M. DeCorte, "Notes Exégetiques sur la Théorie Aristotélicienne du *Sensus Communis*," says flatly: "le *sensus communis* . . . n'a pas d'organe," p. 202.

12. *De Sensu* 449 a 6.

though the various kinds of sensibles are perceived through different organs.[13]

The Greek commentators in this matter seem to follow Aristotle with hardly any variation and with very little amplification; Eustratius is a good example.[14] Themistius adds several illustrations: the foundation and the streams, the king and the messengers.[15]

When we consider the relations between the special senses and the common power of sensation, it becomes clear that this latter is not a power in the genus of accident, and much less a "faculty."[16]

IMAGINATION

Aristotle's first concern is to distinguish this from sensation.[17] In this detailed analysis, he denies that all animals have imagination;[18] but it seems clear that he is thinking of a developed and distinct one.[19] For at other times he admits that all animals have

13. *Ibid.*, 9-10.
14. Eustratius, *In Ethica Nocomachea*, ed. by Gustav Heylbut, (*Commentaria in Aristotelem Graeca,* Berlin: auctoritate Academiae litterarum regiae Borussicae, 1882-1907), vol. XX, 1892, p. 352, lines 27-29.
15. Themistius, *Paraphrasis peri psyches,* ed. Leonardus Spengel (*Themistii Paraphrases Aristoteles,* Leipzig: Teubner, 1866, 2 vols.), vol. II, *in III De Anima* c. 3, logos 5, p. 160, lines 12-22, 25-29; cf. also c. 10, logos 7, p. 220, lines 6-13.
16. Cf. "Chacque sens spécialisé plonge par ses racines dans le sens commun: par les racines, il n'est plus spécial, il est quelque chose du fond même de la sensibilité," O. Hamelin, *Le Système d'Aristote,* p. 381.
   For a detailed textual study corrobating these conclusions, cf. Edmund J. Ryan, C.PP.S., *The Role of the "Sensus Communis" in the Psychology of St. Thomas Aquinas* (Carthagena: Messenger Press, 1951), pp. 1-18.
17. *De Anima,* III, c. 3, 428 a 1-15.
18. *Ibid.,* and cf. II, c. 3, 415 a 10.
19. Cf. R. Hicks, *Aristotle de Anima,* p. 462, note on 428 a 10, and G. Rodier, *Aristote, Traité de l'Ame,* vol. II, p. 419, note on the same passage.

imagination, although in lower forms of sentient life, it is vague and indeterminate.[20]

After distinguishing imagination from intellect, knowledge, and opinion,[21] Aristotle arrives at a definition of it. It is a "movement resulting from an actual exercise of a power of sense."[22]

MEMORY

In the *De Anima*, Aristotle passes from sense cognition at the stage of imagination, and turns to intellect and appetite. However, in the two famous passages describing the ascending scale of knowledge,[23] memory is introduced as an intervening step. The main considerations concerning memory are to be found in the *De Memoria et Reminiscentia*.

The object of memory is the past;[24] hence, memory implies time. Consequently only those animals which perceive time are capable of memory. But the perception of time is a function of the primary power of sense perception. Therefore, memory belongs only incidentally to the intellect, directly to the general sensibility.[25] Again, the mnemonic image differs from the merely presented image in the same way that a painting considered as a likeness differs from that same painting in itself without that reference.[26] Finally, recollection (reminiscence) is a discursive or syllogistic process of arriving at the memory of a given object or act.[27]

---

20. *De Anima*, III, c. 10, 433 a 11, b. 30; c. 11, 434 a 3-4; cf. II, c.2, 413 b 20-24.
21. *Ibid.*, III, c. 3, 428 a 15-28.
22. *Ibid.*, 428 b 31 - 429 a 7.
23. *Metaphysics* A, c. 1, 980 a 28 - 981 a 19.
    Posterior Analytics B, c. 19, 99 b 30 - 100 b 5.
24. *De Memoria et Reminiscentia*, c. 1, 449 b 3 - 24.
25. *Ibid.*, 450 a 10-15. Cf. Themistius, *Paraphrasis* on this, ed. L. Spengler, vol. II, p. 233, lines 20-29.
    But in *De Anima* I, c. 4, 408 b 18 it is implied that the memory-image is in the sense-organs themselves; thus O. Hamelin, *Le Système d'Aristote*, "un trace laissée dans les sensoria par la sensation," p. 383.
26. *De Memoria et Reminiscentia*, c. 1, 450 a 25 - 451 a 15.
27. *Ibid.*, c. 2.

This in brief is Aristotle's doctrine on common sense, imagination, and memory.[28] Today we would be inclined to speak of these three under the heading "internal senses" or "internal sensation." These terms, it will be observed, are not to be found in the Aristotelian *corpus*.[29] What is the difference between the realities designated by these terms? To answer this question, it is necessary to look at the meaning of powers and their distinction.

POWERS AND THEIR DISTINCTION

Aristotle does speak of "powers" of the soul; it is somewhat disconcerting to see him using indifferently μόριον, ἀρχή, and διαφορά as well as δύναμις.[30] Let us see what the various terms are to which the designation "power" is applied. We have already seen that sense perception is such a term; others are: that by which the soul knows and thinks,[31] by which it originates local movement,[32] that by which the animal or plant is nourished,[33] that by which the animal desires.[34]

Are these parts or powers really distinct in one and the same soul? To suppose a distinction involves us in a quest for a

---

28. This discussion is not meant to imply that Aristotle's discussion in the *De Anima* had no sources; for indications of the Platonic origin of most of Aristotle's terms, and of some of the problems involved, cf. Hermann Siebeck, *Geschichte der Psychologie* (Gotha: Perthes, 1880: 1 vol., 2 parts), vol. I, p. 202 ff. If this were a study of Aristotle's doctrine in itself, these and similar historical considerations would have been highly important; cf. the careful use of the historical matter in Louis-Marie Régis, O.P., *L'Opinion selon Aristote* (Paris: Vrin; Ottawa: Instit. d'Etudes Médiévales, 1935), pp. 14-55, 75-88, 108-118, and *passim*. But as this is a study of Aristotle as a source, it is justifiable to use him in the way in which he served as a source, namely, with little more historical background than he himself supplied.
29. Cf. H. Wolfson, "The Internal Senses," pp. 69, 118.
30. Cf. R. D. Hicks, *Aristotle de Anima*, p. 550.
31. *De Anima*, III, c. 4, 429 a 10; bk. 2, c. 3, 414 a 29, b 19; bk. 2, c. 2, 413 b 25.
32. *Ibid.*, bk. III, c. 9, 432 a 15-18.
33. *Ibid.*, 432 b 22; II, c. 2, 413 a 25-30.
34. *Ibid.*, III, c. 10, 432 a 30 — 433 a 25-30.

principle of unity; this will then be a soul; consequently the question of parts will recur, and so on without end.[35] Experience shows that in animals and plants the soul is actually undivided,[36] and consequently the whole soul is homogeneous throughout the body.[37] Fortunately, for the purposes of this discussion it is not necessary to decide what Aristotle held on the distinction of intellect from the other parts of soul.[38]

In several instances of these discussions, Aristotle speaks of a distinction in place [τόπῳ, μεγέθει] as opposed to a distinction λόγῳ or τῷ εἶναι.[39] These latter terms are translated by R. Hicks as "logically,"[40] by G. Rodier as "logiquement,"[41] and by J. A. Smith (in the Oxford translation) as "by definition" and "in its being" respectively.[42] Aristotle's use of these words makes most of these translations unacceptable.[43] The best translation is "essentially" (perhaps "by definition" would be allowable), provided that we leave open the further specification as to whether this essential distinction be real or only of reason.[44]

---

35. *Ibid.,* I, c. 5, 411 b 5-20.
36. *Ibid.,* II, c. 2, 413 b 13-26.
37. *Ibid.,* I, c. 5, 411 b 20-31.
38. *Ibid.,* III, c. 4, 429 b 22-24.
39. *Ibid.,* II, c. 2, 413 b 13-26; III, c. 9, 432 a 18.
40. R. D. Hicks, *Aristotle de Anima,* p. 147, and text, p. 55. For a justification of his view, see p. 417, note on 424 a 25.
41. G. Rodier, *Aristote, Traité de l'Ame,* vol. I, p. 73, 199-201. It is difficult to see how he reconciles this translation with his explanation of τῷ εἶναι, which he says is the form or the notion considered in its indivisible unity, vol. II, p. 180, note on 412 b 11.
42. J. A. Smith, translation of *De Anima* 413 b 13-26, and 432 a 18 — b 2.
43. For example, Aristotle says that the concave surface of a socket (in a ball-and-socket joint), and the convex one of the ball are the same —τὸ αὐτό, that is they are not separate spatially, but only essentially —λόγῳ μὲν ἕτερα ὄντα, μεγέθει δ' ἀχώριστα *De Anima* III, c. 10, 433 b 21-25; cf. *ibid.,* c. 1, 425 b 26-30, and bk. 2, c. 12, 424 a 25; also *De Memoria et Reminiscentia* c. 1, 450 b 22-24.
44. This amounts to saying that Aristotle's terminology on distinctions is not always perfectly accurate or technical, and should therefore be translated by such terms as have the same openness as the Greek originals.

Perhaps the best way of considering this problem is from a different point of view.[45] In one passage,[46] Aristotle says that the definition of soul is like the definition of figure, and the different kinds of soul are like the different figures, triangle, square, and so on. According to this analysis, the different parts or powers of a definite kind of soul cannot be really distinct, any more than the triangle which is potentially in the square is really distinct from the square.

We have been discussing the Aristotelian notion of powers of the soul. In this discussion, the series of terms: common sense, imagination, and memory, has not occurred. The question now arises: are these three powers, and how are they distinct?

The definition of these three have been seen. Between the mere image as such and the mnemonic image there is a *formal* difference, as we have noted. Between sense and imagination, Aristotle seems to place a difference in *actuality,* τῇ ἐνεργείᾳ. [47]

---

45. Cf. G. Rodier, *Aristote, Traité de l'Ame,* vol. II, p. 199, note on 413 b 15.

46. *De Anima,* II, c. 4, 414 b 28-33.
    For a careful distinction between these "powers" and the modern notion of "faculty" cf. Hermann Siebeck, *Geschichte der Psychologie,* vol. I, part I, p. 202, and *idem, Aristoteles* 4th. ed. (Stuttgart: Fromann, 1922), pp. 77, 84.

47. *Ibid.,* III, c. 3, 428 a 9.
    On the meaning of this word, cf. L. M. Régis, *L'Opinion selon Aristote,* p. 65, note 1. According to the *Greek-English Lexicon,* by Henry George Liddell and Robert Scott, revised by Henry Stuart Jones (Oxford: Claronden Press, 1940), these are the meanings (pertinent to the present purpose) of the following words:
    δύναμις: capability of existing or acting, potentiality; power, faculty, capacity.
    ἐνέργεια: actuality
    ἔργον: deed, action, execution.
    According to Hermann Bonitz, *Index Aristotelicus* (Berlin, 1870) these are the Aristotelian usages:
    δύναμις: potentia 206a36
             vis 206b60, 207a45 ff.
    ἐνέργεια: motus et actus 251a22
    ἔργον: opera, negotium, actio 285b5-7.
           significet in actione et in opera cerni alicuius rei naturam, 285b32.

To understand the terms of these distinctions it is necessary to recall several statements made previously. Sense is really distinct from imagination, because the latter is a special kind of movement in sense (one caused by a previous sensation), while memory is a special kind of imagination (that is, an actual image known as related to its original source). According to this, it is impossible to find a common genus for these three: common sense is the sensitive power of the soul; imagination is a movement in this soul resulting from an act of one or more special senses, and memory is an imagination standing in a special known relation. Failure to realize this rather unusual arrangement results in difficulties.[48]

It is possible, though not in Aristotelian terms, to put common sense, imagination, and memory on a common basis. Suppose that we define *common sense* as the power found commonly and radically in the special senses, *imagination* as the power of having an actual image, and *memory* as the power of recognizing that a certain image refers to a particular sensible object in the past. Put in these terms, it is necessary to say that Aristotle did not hold a doctrine of three really distinct internal powers; but that, on the contrary, these three are for him one power.[49] It is

---

48. R. D. Hicks, *Aristotle de Anima,* p. 551, note on 429 a 31, gives a list of the problems that bother him. There is some ground for such confusion: first, these are several lists, one of powers, the other of activities, each arranged in an ascending scale, so that the stages correspond to a certain extent, yet not completely, and Aristotle gives no explicit distinction between them. Secondly, several words have various meanings; for example, the word φαντασία sometimes is "imagination," sometimes "image," αἴσθησις is "sense" or "sensation;" νοῦς means "intellectual soul," or "intellect," or "act of understanding" (not to speak of cases where νοῦς and its derivatives include φαντασία).

49. On these meanings of common sense, imagination, and memory, cf. G. Rodier, *Aristote, Traité de l'Ame,* vol. II, pp. 428 - 30.

Using similar ways of approaching this problem, other authors have concluded that these three are but one basic potency; for example, Franz Brentano, *Die Psychologie des Aristoteles* (Mainz: Kirchlein, 1867), p. 102; Jacob Freudenthal, *Ueber den Begriff des*

a significant historical fact that this conclusion was reached by
St. Thomas [50] and F. Suarez[51]; it seems to have occurred in a
vague sort of way to Roger Bacon;[52] to Cajetan it seemed at least
probable.[53]

Wortes ΦΑΝΤΑΣΙΑ *bei Aristoteles* (Goettingen: Rente, 1863), p.
53; George Grote, *Aristotle,* ed. by Bain and Robertson (London:
Murray, 1872: 2 vols.), vol. II, pp. 209-13; J. Beare, *Greek Theories
of Elementary Cognition,* p. 291; C. Baeumker, *Des Aristoteles Lehre
von den auessern und innern Sinnesvermoegen,* pp. 77-78; O. Hamelin,
Le Système d'Aristote, p. 382; G. Mure, *Aristotle,* seems to hesi-
tate between speaking of distinct powers, p. 117, and identification
of functions, note 1 of the same page.

One of the reasons for the disagreement of authors on this question is that some of them continue to regard Aristotle, not as a thinker
of the ancient Greek world, but through the eyes of later commentators. For example, Stanislaus Cantin, "L'âme et ses puissances
selon Aristote," *Laval Théologique et Philosophique* II, (1946), no. 1,
pp. 184-205, expounds the complete theory of the four internal powers
as St. Thomas gives them. S. Cantin gives only one reference to the
Aristotelian text; the rest are to St. Thomas, John of St. Thomas,
and Cajetan!

50. *In de Anima,* III, lect 6, ed. A. Pirotta, no. 667, text quoted above,
note 2, and discussed in chapter VII below.

51. Francis Suarez, S.J., *De Anima,* III, c. 30, no. 16 (Vives, 1856, 24
vols.), vol. III, p. 708. Fr. Suarez holds that internal sense is both
really and formally one potency, *ibid.,* c. 31, no. 18, p. 709, and his
main argument is that such was Aristotle's view.

52. Roger Bacon, *Opus Maius,* pars 5, Perspectiva, pars 1, dist. 1, ed.
John Henry Bridges (Oxford: Clarendon Press, 1897: 2 vols.),
vol. II, p. 9-10, "Sed textus Aristotelis Latinus non ostendit nobis
hanc distinctionem, nam non expresse fit mentio nisi de sensu communi et imaginatione et memoria. Quoniam autem non potest textus
Aristotelis propter perversitatem translationis intelligi ibi sicut nec
alibi, quoniam ubique Avicenna fuit perfectus imitator et expositor
Aristotelis . . . propter hoc sententiae Avicennae [adherendum est]."

53. See Thomas de Vio Cardinalis Caietanus, *Commentaria in De Anima
Aristotelis,* ed. P. J. Coquelle, O.P., (Rome: Angelicum, 1939: 2
vols.), c. 6, nos. 181, 187, pp. 169, 174-75. Cardinal Cajetan is not
very explicit on this matter; I follow the interpretation of John of
St. Thomas, *Cursus Philosophicus Thomisticus,* ed. Beatus Reiser,
O.S.B. (Turin: Marietti, 1930-1937: 3 vols.), vol. III, pp. 243-44.

POINTS WHICH ENCOURAGED DEVELOPMENT

Though Aristotle himself had not formally raised the question: are common sense, imagination, and memory three powers, and so did not elaborate any theory of internal senses, it seems almost inevitable that this question would some time have been raised. In answering this question, a later psychologist might have developed a three-power theory. At this level of development, there is nothing similar to the later estimative sense. Are there hints which encouraged development in this direction, or obscurities which demanded clarification? The points chosen for investigation are those made use of by Ibn-Sînâ and St. Thomas.

SENSE AS A POWER OF JUDGMENT

Aristotle says of sense in general that it is a judging power τὸ κριτικόν.[54] The Commentators, as Themistius,[55] repeat this phrase quite easily and without any development. The same general statement is made about the imagination.[56]

What then do sense and imagination judge? In the first instance, sense judges its proper object.[57] Aristotle states as a general principle that all knowledge is in some way judgment, and this he relates to his theory that the sense is a "mean" or "ratio" relative to the field of its proper object.[58]

In the second instance, sense judges about and between heterogeneous sensibles. The texts on this point have been referred

---

54. *De Anima,* III, c. 8, 432 a 15-18.
55. *Paraphrasis peri psyches* III, c. 4, logos 5, ed. L. Spengel, vol. II, p. 173, lines 6-8; cf. *idem: In Analytica Posteriora (Commentaria in Aristotelem Graeca,* vol. V, part 1, Berlin: 1900), bk. 2, c. 19, 100 a 15, ed. Maximilian Wallies, p. 63.
56. *De Anima,* III, c. 3, 428 a 1-5; cf. Simplicius *in Libros De Anima (Commentaria in Aristotelem Graeca,* vol. XI Berlin: 1882), comment on this passage, ed. Michael Hayduck, p. 208, lines 12-13, 17-18; cf. R. D. Hicks, *Aristotle de Anima,* p. 459, note on 445 b 10.
57. *De Anima,* III, c. 2, 426 b 8 - 10; cf. III, c. 4, 429 b 14-16; II, c. 5, 418 a 14; c. 10, 422 a 21; c. 11, 424 a 1-7.
58. This is stated with respect to each sense in *De Anima* II, cc. 5-12, and with regard to intellect, cf. *ibid.,* III, c. 4.

to above in the discussion of common sense.[59] Though this activity
or function is not the work of any special sense, it is still within
the field of sense as such.

In the third instance, sense judges the pleasant and the painful, and these functions in sense resemble affirmation and negation.[60] At this level the trouble begins. A being with sense-powers
does of course approach what is sensibly pleasant, and avoid the
sensibly painful. Has the comparison any further meaning? Simplicius finds no problem in following along the Aristotelian path.[61]
But John Philoponus remembers that pursuit and avoidance are
assigned to sensory appetite, and so assigns the judgment of the
pleasurable and the painful to the appetite.[62] This solution will
not fit into the Aristotelian framework, wherein appetite has no
cognitive function but is rather distinguished from cognition. Nevertheless, Philoponus's departure on this point is a reminder that the
relation between sense and appetite can bear investigation.

SENSE AND APPETITE

Aristotle insists strongly that appetite cannot be a distinct
part of the soul.[63] Wherever there is sense, there is also appetite.[64] On this, Simplicius follows Aristotle in detail;[65] some of
the other Commentators express this doctrine in the brief and
abstract form: perception and desire involve each other.[66]

---

59. *Ibid.*, III, c. 2, 426 b 8 — 427 a 16.
60. *Ibid.*, III, c. 7, 431 a 1-14, b 8-9; cf. *Ethic. Nicom.* VI, c. 2, 1139 a 21.
61. *In Libros De Anima,* ed. M. Hayduck, p. 265, lines 35-36, p. 266, lines
    12-14.
62. *Le Commentaire de Jean Philopon sur le troisième livre du "traité
    de l'ame d'Aristote,"* ed. by Marcel DeCorte, (Paris: Droz, 1934),
    p. 67.
63. *De Anima* III, c. 9, 432 a 18 — b 2.
64. *Ibid.*, II, c. 3, 414 b 1-5; cf. Themistius, *Paraphrasis peri psyches,* ed.
    L. Spengel, p. 47, lines 13-14.
65. *In Libros de Anima,* ed. M. Hayduck, p. 105, lines 12-15.
66. This is about all that is said by Alexander of Aphrodisia, *De Anima
    Liber (Supplementum Aristotelicum,* Berlin: 1887), vol. II, pars 1,
    ed. I Bruns, p. 73; cf. also Themistius, *Paraphrasis peri psyches,*
    ed. L. Spengel, vol. II, p. 220, lines 19-25.

This close joining of sense cognition and sense appetite raises a problem: stationary animals have at least the sense of touch, and so sense appetite; they have therefore the causes of motion, yet they do not move. This problem is solved by a distinction. Local motion is of two kinds: indefinite, and definite progressive motion.[67] The lower animals have an indefinite imagination, and so their desires will be indefinite; consequently, they will have only indefinite movements.[68] Perfect animals can sense at a distance;[69] they have also a definite imagination, and so a definite appetite; consequently they will have definite progressive local movements.[70] In this way the problem mentioned above is satisfactorily handled.

A second problem now arises. Actually, sensory appetite is aroused by objects which are neither sensibly painful nor pleasant at the moment. A stock example used by almost all the later psychologists is that of the sheep which fears a wolf, though there is nothing painful to the senses in the latter. This problem is not touched on in the Aristotelian writings directly; the solution would probably be in the same terms as those which are used in the discussion of "animal prudence" (*see below*).

A third problem is formally stated by Aristotle himself: appetites run counter to one another.[71] He seems to be considering the opposition of appetites in terms of different passions at different times, or at least with respect to different objects. For he says: "while that which originates movement must be one, namely, the power of appetite as such —ἓν ἂν εἴη τὸ κινοῦν, τὸ ὀρεκτικὸν ἢ ὀρεκτικόν— the things that originate movement are numerically many."[72] J. Smith[73] and G. Rodier[74] qualify the first part of this sentence by inserting the word "specifically"; R. Hicks[75] translates: "generi-

---

67. *De Anima* III, c. 1, 434 a 1-5; c. 9, 432 b 10-15.
68. *Ibid.*, III, c. 11, 434 a 1-7, c. 10, 433 b 30.
69. *Ibid.*, III, c. 12, 434 b 24-27.
70. *Ibid.*, III, c. 10, 433 b 26-30.
71. *Ibid.*, III, c .10, 433 b 5-13.
72. *Ibid.*
73. J. A. Smith, *De Anima,* tr. of 433 b 5-13.
74. G. Rodier, *Aristote, Traité de l'Ame,* vol. I, p. 207.
75. R. D. Hicks, *Aristotle de Anima,* p. 153.

cally the moving cause will be one." But it will be remembered
that Aristotle insists on the *real* unity of the appetitive potency.[76]
There is here one problem concerning appetite; this, though a
real problem, is not precisely to the point here.

Back of the problem of the unity of multiplicity of appetite
lies another in the order of cognition. After all, appetite is moved
by the cognized good. Now, how can one and the same sensible
object, actually sensed by one external sense, arouse conflicting
sense passions? — It is enough to point out the need for some
kind of development to handle these difficulties.

INTELLECT AND ACTION.

The intellect is both speculative and practical. As practical,
it has a reference both to a particular person[77] and to particular
things or acts.[78] This seems to be in partial conflict with the
proposition that sense alone attains the particular.[79] It is true
that by a careful analysis of δόξα and διάνοια one can go a long
way toward bridging this gap.[80]

Nevertheless, two problems remain. One is that it is not
clear how the juncture of sense and intellect (implied by these
two terms) can and does take place. The other problem is one
of textual interpretation. The first text which has historically caused
some developments is concerned with intellect and action, and cen-
ters in the "opinion about singulars, ἡ τοῦ καθ' ἕκαστα ὑπόληψις.»[81]
The second concerns the knowledge of particulars, and reaches

---

76. *De Anima* III, c. 9, 432 b 5-7, and c. 10, 433 a 21-22; cf. Themis-
    tius, *Paraphrasis peri psyches,* on the latter passage, ed. L. Spengel,
    p. 220, lines 6-12.
77. *De Anima* III, c. 7, 431 b 10-13, and *Ethic. Nicom.* 6, c. 5, 1140 a
    25-27.
78. *Ethic. Nicom.* VI, c. 7, 1141 b 14-15.
79. *De Anima* II, c. 3, 417 b 19-20, 23; cf. *Posterior Analytics,* A c. 31,
    87 b 28-31, 37-38; c. 18, 81 b 6-9; *Metaphysics* A c. 1, 981 a 15-20.
80. Cf. L. M. Régis, *L'Opinion selon Aristote,* esp. chapters 3 and 4.
    It is interesting to note that the Aristotelian διάνοια comes into
    the later Latin literature under the form of *virtus distinctiva* of
    Averroes; on this, see chapter three below.
81. *De Anima* III, c. 11, 434 a 18-19.

its crucial difficulty in saying: "Universals are from particulars. Of these it is necessary to have a sense, and this is intellect ἔκ τῶν καθ' ἔκαστα γὰρ τὰ καθόλου. Τούτων οὖν ἔχειν δεῖ αἴσθησιν, αὕτη δ᾽ἐστὶ νοῦς.»[82] The third text speaks of the knowledge of the contingent, a knowledge which is assigned to the "reasonable" part of the soul, τὸ λογιστικόν.[83]

Simplicius seems to have felt some difficulty in relating intellect to action. His solution can be thus schematized: action is due to appetite; appetite is due to imagination; if practical (desiderative) intellect is to lead to action, it needs the imagination.[84] Even here there is no explanation of the manner in which the imagination mediates between intellect and appetite.

THE PASSIVE INTELLECT

It is no exaggeration to say that the most bitterly controverted philosophical text is the fifth chapter of the third book of the *De Anima*. One of the remarks in this section, namely, that "the passive intellect is corruptible, ὁ δὲ παθητικὸς νοῦς φθαρτός,»[85] was at least for a time considered by St. Thomas to refer to the *vis cogitativa*.

The need for an interpretation of this phrase was felt already by Theophrastus, who says that the active and the passive intellects are somehow one, somehow two, and that the human intellect is a kind of mixture of them.[86] Alexander decided that the passive intellect is identical with the "intellect which becomes all things," spoken of just a few lines before; that this is the human intellect, which is perishable, and that the "active intellect" is a substance

82. *Ethic. Nicom.* VI, c. 11, 1143 b 5-6. On some aspects of the problems raised by this passage, cf. J. M. Le Blond, *Logique et Méthode chez Aristote* (Paris: Vrin, 1939), pp. 132 - 33, 138.
83. *Ibid.*, c. 1, 1139 a 13-16.
84. *In Libros de Anima,* comment on III, c. 10, ed. M. Hayduck, p. 306, lines 15-25.
85. *De Anima* III, c. 5, 430 a 25; on this text, cf. P. Alois Mager, "Der ΝΟΥΣ ΠΑΘΗΤΙΚΟΣ bei Aristoteles und Thomas von Aquin," *Revue Néo-scholastique de Philosophie,* XXXVI (1934), pp. 263-74.
86. Quoted in Themistius, *Paraphrasis peri Psyches,* ed. L. Spengel, p. 108, lines 19-21, 22-28.

distinct from man.[87] Themistius concludes that the passive intellect is not the intellect in potency, but another which he calls
a "common intellect"[88] or an "intellectual passion,"[89] something
due to the soul because of its being in the body. Philoponus says
that the passive intellect is the imagination.[90] Simplicius holds that
the passive intellect is corruptible as passive, and that its "corrup-
tion" is its passage into a better state when separated from the
body.[91] Sophonias puts all the differences of intellect mentioned
by Aristotle: agent and possible, theoretical and practical, true and
false, immortal and perishable, and the like, on the same basis, as
being a different aspect of the same intellect.[92]

When the Arabians and St. Thomas came to comment on
this passage, they knew at least some of these varying interpretations, and must have felt free to explain it as best they could.

ANIMAL "PRUDENCE"

That animals have some kind of "prudence" or practical
"wisdom" seems to have been realized from earliest times. Aristotle

---

87. Alexander of Aphrodisia, *De Anima Liber,* ed. I. Bruns, p. 90,
    lines 14-24.
    The interpretation of R. D. Hicks, *Aristotle de Anima,* pp. 507 - 08,
    and W. D. Ross, *Aristotle,* 2nd ed. (London: Methuen, 1930), pp.
    148 - 50, are quite similar to this. G. Rodier purposely avoids de-
    ciding this question, but he does seem to identify the "passive in-
    tellect" with the "intellect in potency," *Aristote, Traité de l'Ame,*
    vol. II, pp. 464 - 67.
88. Themistius, *Paraphrasis peri Psyches,* ed. L. Spengel, 3, c. 3, logos 6,
    p. 186, lines 9-18.
    This theory is similar to that of Marcel DeCorte, *La Doctrine de
    l'Intelligence chez Aristote* (Paris: Vrin, 1934), pp. 87-91, who in-
    geniously explains the "passive intellect" as "tout cet ensemble de
    fonctions allant de la sensation à la διάνοια, en passant par le
    mémoire et l'imagination, et impliquant le double travail de l'intel-
    ligence associée aux organs," p. 90.
89. *Paraphrasis peri Psyches,* ed. L. Spengel, p. 197, lines 26-29.
90. *Le Commentaire de Jean Philopon sur le troisième livre du "traité
    de l'ame d'Aristote,"* ed. M. DeCorte, p. 9, lines 36-37.
91. *In Libros de Anima,* III, c. 5, ed. M. Hayduck, p. 247, lines 17-19.
92. *Paraphrasis de Anima,* (*Commentaria in Aristotelem Graeca,* Ber-
    lin: vol. XXIII, pars. 1), ed. Michael Hayduck, p. 139, lines 16-18.

spoke of it in passing;[93] once only did he add that the apparently intelligent activity of animals is due to this, that they act by nature and for an end.[94]

The commentators repeat this statement of Aristotle, for example, Philoponus[95] and Simplicius.[96] Frequently they try to go a bit further, relating this expression to the doctrines of the *De Anima,* and *Metaphysics* A, c. 1. Themistius remarks that we commonly say that animals share in reason. But this means only that they share in the name, for what they do share is imagination, the superior power of sense.[97] The Greek commentary on the third book of the *De Anima* which goes under the name of Philoponus says that brutes act through some custom.[98] Simplicius states that in living things apart from man, "the ruler and leader of actions is the imagination."[99] With this text, there is a beginning of Stoic terminology in the treating of animal "prudence."[100]

---

93. E. g., *Metaphysics* A, c. 1, 980 a 28 - 981 a.
    Historia Animalium, VIII, c. 1, 588 a 21-32.
    De Partibus Animalium, II, c. 2, 648 a 5-8; c. 4, 650 b 24.
    Ethic. Nicom. VI, c. 7, 1141 b 27-28.
94. *Physics,* II, c. 8, 199 a 20-30.
95. *In Physica,* II, c. 8, (*Commentaria in Aristotelem Graeca,* Berlin: vol. XVI, 1887), ed. Hieronymus Vitelli, p. 137, lines 4-5.
96. *In Physica,* II, c. 8 (*Commentaria in Aristotelem Graeca,* vol. IX, Berlin: 1882), ed. Hermann Diels, p. 379, lines 18-19.
97. *Paraphrasis peri Psyches,* III, c. 3, logos 5, ed. L. Spengel, p. 162, line 27 — 163, line 9.
98. *In De Anima, III,* (*Commentaria in Aristotelem Graeca,* vol. XV, Berlin: 1897), ed. Michael Hayduck, p. 500, line 25.
99. *In de Anima,* III, c. 3, ed. M. Hayduck, p. 217, lines 5-6.
100. See e.g., Asclepias, *In Metaphysicam* A, c. 1 (*Commentaria in Aristotelem Graeca,* vol. VI, pars 2, Berlin: 1888), ed. Michael Hayduck: "the other living things, he says, have their ruler [τὸ κῦρος] in imagination and memory, just as the dog and the stag and the other animals discern the unsuitable from the suitable [τὸ ἀλλότριον ἐκ τοῦ οἰκείου]," p. 7.

CONCLUSIONS

We have seen that the psychology of Aristotle does not include a doctrine of internal sensory powers, at least as presented in the *De Anima*.[101] Nevertheless, his doctrine of common sense, imagination, and memory is capable of a development in the direction of a doctrine of three internal powers.

Further, there are some obscure passages and some lacunae in Aristotle's treatment of (1) sense as a power of judging good and evil; (2) the relation of sense to appetite; (3) the relation of intellect to action; (4) the problem of the "passive intellect;" and (5) animal "prudence." These points can, on the face of things, be generalized into two analogous problems: (1) the relation of sense to appetite and action; (2) the relation of intellect to appetite and action; in this second problem, sense must enter in, according to the Aristotelian setting, as somehow mediating between intellect and appetite.

These problems were inherited by the followers of Aristotle. They were not always seen in their full complexity; they seem at one period to have died out. In the Platonic view of man, the problems are either no problems at all, or are transposed to different terms.

Our next task will be to see whether these or related problems occupied later thinkers; whether there were any new data on them or on analogous problems; where and to what extent developments took place. This history of the dynamic of ideas will be treated in the next three chapters. Chapter two will follow the threads through the post-Aristotelian schools up to the re-entering of Aristotle in the Latin West. Chapter three will look at the rebirth of Aristotelian speculation in the Arabian world. Chapter four will see the influence of these Arabian-Aristotelian elements on twelfth and early thirteenth century Christians. Thus will conclude the first part of this study.

---

101. The reason for this qualification is that a theory of powers can be worked out of the *Ethics;* cf. L. M. Régis, *L'Opinion selon Aristote,* pp. 58-62.

CHAPTER 2

CONTRIBUTIONS OF POST-ARISTOTELIANS

Both in scope and in fineness of detail, the psychological analysis of the *De Anima* has remained unmatched for centuries. There are many reasons for this. One is that men of the intellectual calibre of Aristotle are rarely found. But the extrinsic reasons are also very important.

Shortly after the time of Aristotle, the Greek world was involved in a cultural and ethical breakdown that influenced the work of philosophers in two ways. The cultural breakdown lowered the general level of intellectual achievement above which great thinkers were able to raise themselves. A similar situation is found in the Roman world after the time of the barbarian invasions. The ethical breakdown stimulated thinkers to work on moral problems in accord with the needs of their time.

Again, early Christian thinkers were faced with practical needs. First, there was the hostility of the pagan world to overcome, and intellectual powers were bent to the task of explaining and defending the Christian religion. It is such an end which motivated the magnificent *City of God* of St. Augustine. These same thinkers were confronted with the great speculative and practical heresies. The solution of the questions thus raised was enough to absorb the energies of many great men.

In such circumstances, problems of speculative philosophy tended to be pushed into the background.[1] This is what happened in many instances to psychological problems. In St. Augustine, for example, the masterly psychological analyses of the *De Trinitate* have no proper autonomy as philosophical analyses — they serve the purposes of theology.[2] In other cases, the study of the soul is

---

1. On this point, some interesting remarks are made by Christopher Dawson, *The Making of Europe* (New York: Sheed and Ward, 1932) and Arnold J. Toynbee, *A Study of History* (London: Oxford Univ. Press, 1934-40: 6 vols.), vol. III, pp. 217-48.
2. On the reciprocal influence of psychological and theological con-

caught up into the movement of speculative and practical mysticism. Definite examples of these various utilisations of psychology will appear in the course of this chapter.

These historical circumstances themselves dictate the procedure to be followed. Complete exposés of the various thinkers would lead very far afield, while the mere enumeration of passing phrases and sentences would be a sterile and even an unfair method of presentation. The solution lies in a procedure that presents historically significant remarks in the framework of their doctrinal context.[3] In harmony with this plan, authors will be grouped more or less in accord with their general tendencies rather than in strict chronological sequence. Where doctrines lack significance, or repeat without notable development a thought already presented, they will be found in the notes.

THE STOICS

Stoic philosophy flourished from the third century before Christ to well within the Christian era. It is a movement of thought that borrows largely from Aristotle, yet has its own principles and its own original contribution. The Stoic psychology is for the most part to be found within the larger classification of physics (which is the Stoic first philosophy), and is to a certain extent determined by the ethical preoccupations.[4] Thus, on the one hand, we can

   siderations in St. Augustine's "trinitarian" psychology, cf. Michael Schmaus, *Die psychologische Trinitaetslehre des hl. Augustinus* (Muenster: Aschendorff, 1927), pp. 206-20; a more basic and general discussion is to be found in Anton C. Pegis, "The Mind of St. Augustine," *Mediaeval Studies* VI (1944), 56-61.

3. The nature of the investigation conducted in this chapter allows me to follow the lead of other researches when they exist. Generally, the references will indicate the sources of the opinions stated; however, it is not possible to trace every indebtedness. Sometimes, ideas acquired from others are not recognized to be relevant to a given problem till much later. At other times, original juxtapositions of doctrines will bring out points whose originality is very difficult to assess.

4. Cf. Ludwig Stein, *Psychologie der Stoa* (Berlin: Calvary, 1886-88: 2 vols., of which volume II is entitled *Die Erkenntnistheorie der Stoa*) vol. I, pp. 2-3.

see why the Stoics maintained that the soul was material,[5] and, on the other, why they paid little attention to the world of plants and animals.[6] Stoics insisted very strongly on the unity of the soul. Though they speak of powers, parts, or functions of the soul, it is always the same soul that acts directly by itself in various ways.[7] For this reason, though they usually enumerate eight powers of the soul,[8] the number varies from three to ten.[9]

It is this self-identity of the soul, both internally and with respect to its powers, that the Stoics refer to when they speak of "common sense."[10] Looked at as guiding principle and source

---

5. *Ibid.*, pp. 15-20, 87-88, 110-12; vol. II, pp. 106-08.
   Compare also Plutarch, *De Virtute Morali*: "νομίζουσι οἰκ εἶναι τὸ παθητικὸν καὶ ἄλογον διαφορᾷ τινι καὶ φύσει ψυχῆς τοῦ λογικοῦ διακεκριμένον, ἀλλὰ ταὐτὸ τῆς μέρος. ὃ δὴ καλοῦσι διάνοιαν καὶ ἡγεμονικόν ...," *Moralia*, ed. Gregory Bernardakis (Leipzig: Teubner: 5 vols.), vol. III, p. 149.
6. Edward Zeller, *Stoics, Epicureans and Sceptics,* tr. by Reichel (London: Longmans, 1892), p. 208.
7. Cf. L. Stein, *Psychologie der Stoa,* vol. I, pp. 119-33; vol. II, pp. 109-11; and Hermann Siebeck, *Geschichte der Psychologie* (Gotha: Perthes, 1880), vol. I, part 2, pp. 181-84.
8. Cf. L. Stein, *Psychologie der Stoa,* vol. I, pp. 119-33.
9. See Tertullian, *De Anima,* c. 14, PL II. 709-10; Nemesius, *De Natura Hominis,* c. 15, PG XL. 670. On this passage of Tertullian, cf. L. Stein, *Psychologie der Stoa,* I, p. 158.
10. This point is made, perhaps too emphatically, yet very clearly by Anthelme Edouard Chaignet. He says: "Ce n'est pas de ce nom de conscience, qu'ils avaient si heureusement trouvé, mais bien de celui du sense général, κοινὴ αἴσθησις, qu'ils désignaient la faculté qui accompagne toutes les autres facultés; ils se la représentaient comme un contact intérieur et intime, ἔντος ἀφή, par lequel nous nous saisons nous-même, et c'est à l' ἡγεμονικὸν qu'ils rapportaient l'acte vraiment solennel par lequel nous disons, *Moi,* τὸ ἐγὼ λέγομεν κατὰ τοῦτο,» *Histoire de la Psychologie des Grecs* (Paris: Hachette, 1887-1893: 5 vols.), II, p. 70. Chaignet identifies the quotations as taken from Stobaeus (*Sermones,* ed. Gaist., appendix 20. 9, vol. IV, p. 431) and Galen (*De Hippocratis et Platonis Placitis,* II, c. 2; *Opera Omnia,* ed. Carolus Gottlob Kuehn [Leipzig: 1823; 20 vols.], vol. V, p. 215). In the second quotation, A. Chaignet remarks: "Montrant par là, par ce geste et cette

of unity, the soul (and particularly its highest power) is called
the "hegemonikon." As a technical psychological term, this is
a Stoic invention.[11] In the majority of cases, it is used as a
synonym of *dianoia*.[12] The notion would seem to have points of
contact with that of the all-pervasive *logos*, and with the ethical
doctrine of living according to nature.

Because the soul is identical with all its powers, and therefore identical with reason, most Stoics tended to deny that animals
had sensation or a hegemonikon.[13] Others, notably Posidonius, admitted that a hegemonikon is to be found in all forms of life;
in plants it is in the root; in animals and man, in the heart.[14]

Those who denied a hegemonikon to animals had to find
some other guiding principle. In the earlier Stoics, this principle was
ὁρμή, impulse.[15] According to Panaetius, reason is the specific trait
of man, impulse of animals.[16] Seneca uses the term *impetus* on

---

démonstration toute physique, ajoute Galien, que se moi c'est la pensée,
l'âme pensante —δειχνύντες αὐτοὺς ... τὴν διάνοιαν εἶναι,» *ibid.*, p.
70, note 2.

11. A. Chaignet, *Histoire de la Psychologie des Grecs*, vol. II, p. 62,
note 1. Hermann Siebeck, *Untersuchungen zur Philosophie der Griechen* (Halle: Barthel, 1873), p. 257, suggests that the idea is partly
derived from the Aristotelian concept of a first cause of motion,
and that the term may be related to Plato's ἡγεμοῦν, *Timaeus* 41C.
L. Stein, *Psychologie der Stoa*, vol. II, p. 105, note 216, says that
the Stoics made the term popular; in vol. II, p. 108, note 219, he
tells us that Cleanthes is, as far as we know, the first to use this
word in this psychological sense.

12. Cf. A. Chaignet, *Historie de la Psychologie des Grecs*, vol. II, p. 62,
note 1; L. Stein, *Psychologie der Stoa*, vol. I, pp. 91-93; vol. II,
pp. 109-11.

13. Cf. L. Stein, *Psychologie der Stoa*, vol. I, pp. 91-93.

14. Cf. A. Schmekel, *Die Philosophie der mittleren Stoa*, (Berlin: Weidmann, 1892), pp. 258-59. The doctrine is explained in Galen, *De
Hippocratis et Platonis Placitis*, IV, c. 3, ed. C. Kuehn, vol. V, pp.
377-78.

15. See Galen, *De Hippocratis et Platonis Placitis*, IV, c. 3, ed. C.
Kuehn, vol. V, pp. 377-78.

16. Cf. A. Schmekel, *Die Philosophie der Mittleren Stoa*, p. 199.

occasion,[17] but the term *nature* is most common.[18] Since an animal always follows its guiding principle, nature, it is from this point of view a kind of moral ideal.

It is also possible to combine these notions differently and come to a very different result. Thus Marcus Aurelius combines the terms "impulse" and "soul" or "animal spirit."[19] Couched in these terms, the doctrine of the essential structure of sense life serves an almost opposite moral purpose. It is now the counter foil to reason, a life possible to man but essentially degrading.[20] A change such as this, however, seems to involve some kind of dualism or composition in the soul.

CHRYSIPPUS

Chrysippus was the leader of the Stoa about the year 251 B.C. Sextus Empiricus tells us that he is the only Stoic who took much

17. "Naturales ad utilia impetus, naturales a contrariis aspernationes sunt," Seneca, *Epistola* 121, no. 21, in *Epistolae,* tr. by Richard M. Grummere (New York: Putnam, 1917-1925: 3 vols.), vol. III, p. 408.

18. "Sine ulla cogitatione quae hoc dictet, sine consilio fit, quidquid natura praecipit," *ibid.,* and: "Quod illi ars praestat, his natura. . . . Cum hac scientia prodeunt; instituta nascuntur. . . . nocituri scientiam non experimento collectam. . . . Nascitur ars ista, non discitur," *ibid.,* nos. 6, 17, 19, 23; pp. 398, 406, 408, 410. Cf. also Cicero, *De Finibus,* iii, 16; *De Officiis,* i, 4. 11.

19. «Σῶμα, ψυχή, νοῦς—σώματος αἴσθησις, ψυχῆς ὁρμαί, νοῦ δόγματα,» *Meditations,* bk. 2, no. 16, in *The Meditations of the Emperor Marcus Antoninus,* ed. A. S. L. Farquharson (Oxford: Clarendon Press, 1944: 2 vols.), vol. I, p. 48; and "An obstacle to sense perception is injurious to animal nature; an obstacle to impulse is equally injurious to animal nature . . . ," *ibid.,* viii. 41, p. 161, as translated by A. Farquharson.

20. "To transpire . . . or to breathe . . . to be stamped by sense-impressions . . . or drawn by the strings of impulse . . . ," *ibid.,* bk. 5, no. 16, in translation cited, p. 103; "Τρία ἐστίμ ἐξ ὧν συνέστηκας σμμάτιον, πνευμάτιον, νοῦς, ἐὰν χωρίσῃς, φημί, τοῦ ἡγεμονικοῦ τούτου τὰ προσηρτημένα ἐκ προσπαθείας καὶ τοῦ χρόνου," *ibid.,* xii. 3, p. 236, and also vi. 28, p. 109.

interest in irrational animals.[21] For this reason it is helpful to look at his psychology in some little detail. The soul has two functions: representation and inclination.[22] It has four faculties, parts, or qualities: φαντασία, συγκατάθεσις, ὁρμή, λόγος.[23] These four terms are represented by the Latin *sensus, status* or *constitutio, impetus* or *appetitus,* and *ratio.*[24] All the parts of the soul are related to the principal part like the branches of a tree to its trunk.[25] The principal part of the soul is the guiding principle. In man it is reason,[26] in animals something like reason.[27] In the latter, it seems to be a blind tendency to live according to universal nature.[28]

---

21. "According to Chrysippus, who shows special interest in irrational animals . . . the dog makes use of the fifth complex indemonstrable syllogism, when, on arriving at the spot where three roads meet, after smelling at the two roads by which the quarry did not pass, he rushes off at once by the third without stopping to smell," *Outlines of Pyrrhonism,* tr. by R. G. Bury, i. 69 (New York: Putnam, 1933-1936: 3 vols.), vol. I, pp. 42-43.

   St. Thomas uses this little example in an objection which tries to show that brutes have choice because they show prudence; *Summa Theologiae* I-II. 13,2, obj. 3.

22. Cf. Emile Bréhier, *Chrysippe* (Paris: Alcan, 1910), p. 168.

23. Cf. *ibid.,* note 2.

24. For examples of such uses, cf. Cicero, *De Finibus,* III. 5. 16, and v. 19. 40; *De Officiis,* i. 4. 11; *De Legibus,* I. 10. 30; I. 17. 47; Also Seneca, *Ep.* CXIII. 18.

25. "Porro animae partes velut ex capite fontis cordis sede manantes per universum corpus porriguntur. . . . Totaque anima sensus, qui sunt eius officia, velut ramos ex principali parte illa tamquam trabe pandit futuros eorum quae sentiunt nuntios, ipsa de iis quae nuntiaverint iudicat ut rex," *Platonis Timeus, interprete Chalcidio cum eiusdem Commentario,* ed. *Joannes Wrobel* (Leipzig: Teubner, 1876), no. 220, p. 255. Cf. Galen, *De Hippocratis et Platonis Placitis,* II, c. 3, ed. C. Kuehn, vol. V, p. 219; III, c. 1; pp. 287-88.

26. Cf. L. Stein, *Psychologie der Stoa,* vol. I, pp. 173-75.

27. "Habent quippe etiam muta vim animae principalem, qua discernunt cibos, imaginantur, declinant insidias, praerupta et praecipitia supersiliunt, necessitudinem recognoscunt, non tamen rationalem, quin potius naturalem," *Platonis Timeus, interprete Chalcidio cum eiusdem Commentario,* ed. J. Wrobel, no. 220, p. 256.

28. Cf. E. Bréhier, *Chrysippe,* pp. 226-27.

This doctrine is a departure from the narrow limits of the ethical purpose of many Stoics. It was forced upon Chrysippus by the attacks of his opponents,[29] particularly of the skeptics.[30] Stoic doctrine early made its way into the Latin world. Cicero and Seneca exercised a very great influence upon succeeding ages. Besides these obvious channels, there were others, sometimes more roundabout. For example, Philo of Alexandria[31] and Plotinus[32]

---

29. Cf. L. Stein, *Psychologie der Stoa,* vol. I, pp. 173-75.
30. Cf. Victor Brochard, *Les Sceptiques Greces* (Paris: Imprimerie National, 1887), p. 256. From the argument that animals have such excellent perception and discrimination, the Sceptics concluded that because of the differences between animals and men the senses are unreliable; cf. Diogenes Laertius, *Lives and Opinions of Eminent Philosophers,* vii. 51, tr. by R. D. Hicks (London: Heinemann, 1925: 2 vols.), II, p. 493; and Sextus Empiricus, *Outlines of Pyrrhonism,* I. 36, tr. R. Bury, vol. I, p. 25. Hence, the Stoics, in their turn, had to argue that all sensitive beings receive the same impressions from the same objects; cf. Cicero, *De Legibus,* i. 10. 30.
31. For example: "Conscious life, ψυχή, is the power to grow, with the additional power of receiving impressions, φαντασία, and being the subject of impulses, ὁρμή. This is shown also by creatures without reason. Indeed, our mind contains a part that is analogous to the conscious life of a creature without reason," *Legum Allegoriae,* ii. 7, tr. by Colson and Whitaker (New York: Putnam, 1929: 10 vols.), vol. I, p. 241; "For the living creature excels the non-living in two respects, in the power of receiving impressions, αἴσθησις, and in the active impulse, ὁρμή, towards the object producing them . . . . the active impulse . . . . comes about by way of the mind's power of self-extension διὰ τὴν τοῦ νοῦ τονικὴν δύναμιν,» *ibid.,* i. 30, p. 167.
   On the concept of τόνος and its importance in the Stoic system, cf. L. Stein, *Psychologie der Stoa,* vol. I.
32. For the most part, Plotinus was opposed to Stoicism; yet, for example, in the refutation of Stoic materialism, see the use made of hegemonikon; *Enneads,* iv. 4. 7.
   There are also traces of Aristotelian sense psychology in Plotinus; for example: «Αἰσθητικὸν γὰρ κριτικόν πως, καὶ φανταστικὸν οἷον νοερόν. καὶ ὁρμὴ καὶ ὄρεξις φαντασία καὶ λόγῳ ἑπομενα,» *Enneads,* iv. 3. 23, ed. Emile Bréhier, (Paris: Les Belles Lettres, Budé, 1924; 6 vols.), vol. IV, p. 91, lines 31-33.

have traces of Stoicism in their works. Chalcidius,[33] Macrobius,[34] and Apuleius[35] transmit some Stoicism, along with their Platonism. Galen, an important source in his own right, also handed on much Stoicism and Aristotelianism, which he looked on as related doctrines, even though they are mentioned only to be refuted. Tertullian, too, has some traces of Stoicism.[36] Finally, the ascetical writers who borrowed so much from the ethical writings of the Stoics — St. Ambrose is a striking example[37] — also mention snatches of other doctrines.

GALEN

Galen, who lived from 131 to 201 A.D., was a physician with strong interests in experimental anatomy and physiology, as well as logic, ethics, and even physics. His teaching on internal powers of cognition is touched on only in passing. It is not an original

---

33. Chalcidius mentions the tripartite division of soul into reason, irascibility, and desire, ed. J. Wrobel, no. 182; and likewise into *species naturalis, species sensibilis, species ratione utens,* nos. 182, 223. This latter division seems to derive from Aristotle by way of Galen; cf. B. W. Switalski, *Des Chalcidius-Kommentar zu Plato's Timaeus* (Beitraege, Baeumker, Muenster: Aschendorff, Band III, Heft 6, 1902), p. 160.

34. Macrobius mentions the Platonic tripartite division of soul, *In Somnium Scipionis,* i. 6. 42-43, ed. Franciscus Eyssenhardt (Leipzig: Teubner, 1893), p. 504; he frequently speaks of the head as the seat of the soul, cf. *In Somnium Scipionis,* i 6. 81, p. 513; *Saturnalia* vii. 14. 23; vii. 9. 17-25, pp. 464, 442-43.

On the influence of Macrobius in mediaeval times, cf. Phil. M. Schedler, *Die Philosophie des Macrobius, und ihr Einfluss auf die Wissenschaft des christlichen Mittelalters* (Beitraege, Baeumker, Muenster: Aschendorff, Band XIII, Heft 1, 1916).

35. Cf. *De Dogmate Platonis, Opera Omnia,* ed. G. F. Hildebrand (Leipzig: Knobloch, 1842: 2 vols.), i. 13, 18; vol. II, pp. 200, 201, 210.

36. In *De Anima,* c. 15, PL II. 711, Tertullian says that we must accept the hegemonikon.

37. Cf. J. T. Muckle, C. S. B., "The De Officiis Ministrorum of St. Ambrose," *Mediaeval Studies* I (1939), pp. 63-80.

doctrine;[38] to all appearances it is merely a summary and sharpening of Aristotelian teachings. But it has all the effectiveness of a summary. In addition to this, there is an original element in the localization of these powers.

In general, Galen asserts, against the opinion of the Stoics, that the soul has its seat in the cerebrum. The soul does not act directly on the body, but on an intermediary, namely "spirit" or breath, πνεῦμα.[39] Even merely practicing physicians should know this much about it,[40] although much more is to be said about the physiology and mechanics of this spirit.[41]

In addition to the external senses, "the remaining power of the soul, that is, the hegemonikon, is divided into imagination, reason, and memory."[42] These three functions are localized in the front, middle, and posterior ventricles of the brain, respectively, in the sense that their spirit-instruments are located there.[43]

A question about the "seat of the soul" seems to presuppose a strongly accentuated interaction dualism.[44] A question about the localization of powers, on the other hand, can be based on observation. In fact, the Galenic localization has some scientific basis,[45] naturally very incomplete and to some extent faulty. A doctrine of intermediaries between soul and body seems to depend on an effort to "soften" an interaction dualism.

To divide the functions of the soul into parts, as Galen does,

---

38. Cf. Harry Austryn Wolfson, "The Internal Senses in Latin, Arabic, and Hebrew Philosophic Texts," *Harvard Theological Review* XXVIII (1935), pp. 72-73.
39. Galen, *De Locis Affectis,* III, c. 9, ed. C. Kuehn, vil. VIII, pp. 173-75.
40. *Ibid.,* pp. 176-77.
41. Galen, *De Usu Partium Corporis Humani,* VIII, c. 14, ed. C. Kuehn, vol. III, pp. 673-83.
42. Galen, *De Symptomatum Differentiis,* c .3, ed. C. Kuehn, VII, p. 56. Greek text in Appendix II, no. 1.
43. Galen, *De Locis Affectis,* III, c. 9, ed. C. Kuehn, vol. VII, p. 173-75.
44. Galen himself strongly approves of the Platonic doctrine on the soul.
45. The theory that the seat of sensation is the brain is due to the discovery of the nerves by Erasistratus and Hierophilus in the third century B. C.; the work was completed and the theory elaborated by Galen himself (130? - 200 A.D.),

implies some common basis of division. If, as seems historically to have happened, the three parts (imagination, reason, memory) do in some way derive from Aristotle, they are not handled in an Aristotelian way. In Aristotle, intellect is non-sensory, while imagination and memory are sensory. What about the "reasonable part of the soul"? In Aristotle, this phrase has many meanings. In Galen, as in the Stoics, *dianoia* seems to be equivalent to *logos*, and both words mean "reason," and are roughly equivalent to the Aristotelian *nous* or intellect. If this is the base, then Galen has either materialized reason, or spiritualized imagination and memory. His reference to the hegemonikon and his use of the term *dianoia* lead us to suspect that with the Stoics he has materialized reason. However, the other alternative is theoretically possible, and in fact was the supposition under which the division was adopted by others, as we shall see in a number of instances.

NEMESIUS AND ST. JOHN DAMASCENE

The *De Natura Hominis* ascribed to Nemesius (supposed to have been Bishop of Emesa in the first half of the fourth century) transmits the Galenic theory[46] (that is, the localized tripartite division of cognitive powers). In the translation of Burgundio, the three powers receive the names of *phantasicum, excogitativum,* and *memorativum,*[47] which shall be translated as imagination, cogitative, and memory." In the Galenic statement, the three powers were simply designated. Nemesius advances the theory by explaining just what the three powers are. To the second power, the cogitative, there belong:

---

46. Cf. Werner Wilhelm Jaeger, *Nemesios von Emesa* (Berlin: Weidmann, 1914), p. 4, 21; cf. B. Domanski, *Die Psychologie des Nemesius* (Beitraege, Baeumker, Muenster: Aschendorff, Band III, Heft 1, 1900), pp. 74-99.

47. "Phantasticum quidem tradit excogitativo ea quae apparent; excogitativum vero vel discretivum assumens et diiudicans transmittit memorativo," *De Natura Hominis,* c. 12; Gregorii Nysseni (Nemesii Emeseni) περὶ φύσεως ἀνθρώπου *Liber a Burgundione in Latinum Translatus,* ed. Carolus J. Burkhard (Vienna: 1896-1902), c. 12, part 3, p. 15.

judgments and statements and acts of flight and impulse, but especially the understanding of intelligibles, and virtues and sciences, and the theoretical aspects of the arts, and the part of the soul which takes counsel and chooses.[48]

There is good ground for seeing, in this set of functions, a summary of various designations or offices applied by both Aristotle and the Stoics to the intellectual principle.[49]

How does Nemesius understand the three-fold division? We need but recall that he was violently anti-Aristotelian in his conception of the soul; his Platonic dualism led him to assert the spiritual nature of sensation. The three powers, then, are three equally spiritual functions of a spiritual soul, all three using, as their organs, a part of the brain and the "animal spirit" within it.[50]

When the *De Natura Hominis* was translated (in 1058 and again in 1159) it was likely to meet favorable acceptance, because of its affinity with the Platonic spiritualism of the Augustinians.

The Galenic theory as amplified by Nemesius had another way of influencing the development of psychology. The passage, from which the quotation given above is taken, is to be found in an almost word-for-word fashion in the *De Fide Orthodoxa* of St. John Damascene.[51] This eloquent and prolific writer, who lived in the last quarter of the seventh and the first half of the eighth centuries, has the unusual distinction of having influenced three different cultures. He was a powerful figure in the Greek world of his day. His *De Fide Orthodoxa* had a notable influence in the

---

48. *Ibid.*, c. 11, pp. 13-14. Latin text in Appendix II, no. 2.
49. Cf. the discussion of H. A. Wolfson, "The Internal Senses," pp. 80-81, which is concerned with the parallel passage of St. John Damascene referred to in note 51.
50. "Organa autem eius [imaginationis, vel phantasmatis, vel imaginativi, etc.] sunt anteriores cerebri ventres et qui in eis est animalis spiritus," *De Natura Hominis,* tr. Burgundio, ed. C. Burkhard, c. 5, part 3, p. 3; "Organum autem et huius [memorativi] est et posterior ventriculus cerebri . . . et qui in eo est animalis spiritus," *ibid.,* c. 12, p. 15; "Organum autem et huius [excogitativi] est medius cerebri ventriculus et animalis spiritus qui est in ipso," *ibid.,* c. 11, p. 14.
51. *De Fide Orthodoxa,* II, c. 19, PG XCIV. 937-38.

Latin West after its translation about 1150.[52] This same work
was also "influential in the early history of Arabic philosophy."[53]
As we shall see, the Galenic influence, reinforced by the authority
of Nemesius and St. John Damascene, seems first to have come into
the Latin world through translations from Arabic works.

ST. AUGUSTINE

We have seen that in the psychological doctrine of the Romans
there was a heavy charge of Stoicism. We have also seen that
some of the early Christian Latin writers kept a certain amount
of the same philosophy. In others, there is very little philosophical
doctrine at all; in Lactantius, for example, there is predominantly
an attitude of puzzlement about "inextricable questions."[54]

---

52. For his influence on St. Albert the Great, cf. Dr. Arthur Schneider,
    Die Psychologie Alberts des Grossen (Beitraege, Baeumker, Muenster:
    Aschendorff, Band IV, Heft 5-6, 1903), p. 155, note 1. For a
    definite influence on this point on Alexander of Hales and Jean de
    la Rochelle, cf. chapter four below.
53. H. A. Wolfson, "The Internal Senses," p. 80.
54. "Quidam sedem mentis in pertore esse voluerunt. . . . Alii sedem eius
    in cerebro esse dixerunt . . . potius in summo tamquam in arce
    corporis habitare. . . . Sensus omnis . . . membra in capite sint lo-
    cata. . . . Hi vero aut non multum aut fortasse non errant. . . . Sive
    etiam mentis locus nullus est, sed per totum corpus sparsa discurrit,"
    De Opificio Dei, c. 16, in *Opera Omnia,* ed. Samuel Brandt and
    Georg Laubman (CSEL, vol. XXVII, Vienna: Tempsky, 1893), part 2,
    fasc. 1, pp. 52-53; "Sequitur alia et ipsa inextricabilis quaestio, idemne
    sit anima et animus an vero aliud sit illud quo vivimus, aliud autem
    quo sentimus et sapimus," *ibid.,* c. 18, p. 57.
        On Lactantius and his attitude, cf. Étienne Gilson, *La Philosophie
    au Moyen Age,* 2me éd. (Paris: Payot, 1944), pp. 107-09.
        In another way, Gennadius, the probable author of *De Ecclesiasticis
    Dogmatibus,* in that he seems to show an acquaintance with the
    Greek philosophers of the type that might be found in one of the
    common collections of "opinions of the philosophers"; cf.: "Anima-
    lium vero animae non sunt substantivae, sed . . . cum carnis morte
    finiuntur atque moriuntur, et ideo nec ratione reguntur nec vivunt,
    sicut Plato et Alexander putant, sed ad omnia naturae incitamenta
    ducuntur," c. 17, PL LVIII, 984-85.

St. Augustine offers a strong contrast to the other Latin writers of the Silver Age. Though his background is Platonic,[55] his great psychological analyses are remarkably original. Throughout a long and active life (he lived from 354 to 430 A.D.), St. Augustine found time to write a very large number of works, remarkable as well for the penetration of thought as for the beauty of their style. He is the greatest single influence, outside of the Bible, on the molding of European thought.

In speaking of powers of knowledge, St. Augustine seems to have been the first of Latin writers to use the term "internal sense,"[56] and he means by it a real sense power. "Internal sense" is the source of sensory consciousness and appetite,[57] and is the judging and guiding power of the animal.[58]

55. On the Platonic background of St. Augustine in psychology, cf. Etienne Gilson, *Introduction à l'étude de Saint Augustin,* 2me éd. (Paris: Vrin, 1943), pp. 57-58, 74, 310, and *passim;* on the modifications St. Augustine made, cf. e.g., pp. 62, 280-81, esp. 310-23. W. Ott, in an article "Des hl. Augustinus Lehre ueber die Sinneserkenntnis," *Philosophisches Jahrbuch* XIII (1900) pp. 45-59, 138-48, especially in the first section, draws up a number of parallels between St. Augustine and Plotinus, and also points out differences.
56. Cf. H. A. Wolfson, "The Internal Senses," p. 71.
57. "Custodiebam interiore sensu integritatem sensuum meorum," *Confessions,* i. 20, CSEL XXXIII, part 1, p. 28; "Atque ita gradatim a corporibus ad sensientem per corpus animam atque inde ad eius interiorem vim, cui sensus corporis exteriora nuntiaret, et quousque possunt bestiae," *ibid.,* vii. 17, p. 162; "sensu autem interiore et corporalia per sensus corporis sentiri, et ipsum corporis sensum," *De Libero Arbitrio,* II. 4, PL XXXII. 1246; "Sensum illum interiorem de istis corporis sensibus judicare, cum eorum et integritatem probat, et debitum flagitat, quemadmodum et ipsi corporis sensus de corporibus judicat," *ibid.,* c. 5, col. 1247.
On the meaning and function of "inner sense" in St. Augustine, cf. Bernard Kaelin, O.S.B., *Die Erkenntnislehre des hl. Augustinus* (Sarnen: Ehrli, 1921), pp. 32-33.
58. "Magis nos arbitror ratione comprehendere esse interiorem quemdam sensum, ad quem ab istis quinque notissimis cuncta referuntur. Nam aliud est id quo videt bestia, aliud quo ea quae videndo sentit, vel vitat vel appetit: ille enim sensus in oculis est, ille autem intus in ipsa anima. . . . Hic autem nec visus nec auditus nec olfactus nec

He seems likewise to have been the first to develop a special meaning for *cogitatio*. In classic times, *cogitare* normally referred to intellectual operations, particularly when these were concerned with things to be done. In Silver Latin, it begins to mean on occasion "to imagine."[59] In an extended passage in the *De Trinitate*, St. Augustine speaks of the created trinity (an image of the uncreated Trinity) of phantasy, memory, and cogitation.[60] The third term of this group means: to make an assertion about corporeal images, involving a combination or separation of those images.[61]

---

gustatus nec tactus dici potest, sed nescio quid aliud quod omnibus communiter praesidet," *De Libero Arbitrio*, II, c. 3, PL XXXII. 1244.

59. The common meaning of *cogitare* is "to plan, intend." With the accusative of person, it means "to think, imagine;" e.g., in Tacitus, *Or.* II, Pliny, *Ep.* iv. 2.2; Quintilian, Seneca, and Cicero use it rarely. Cf. Charlton T. Lewis and Charles Short, *Latin Dictionary* (Oxford: Clarendon Press, 1897), p. 360.

60. "Jam vero in alia trinitate, interiore quidem quam est ista in sensibilibus et sensibus, sed tamen quae inde concepta est, cum jam non ex corpore sensus corporis, sed ex memoria formatur acies animi, cum in ipsa memoria species inhaeserit corporis quod forinsecus sensimus, illam speciem quae in memoria est, quasi dicimus ejus quae fit in phantasia cogitantis," *De Trinitate*, XI, c. 7, PL XLII. 933; "Atque ita fit illa trinitas ex memoria et interna visione et quae utrumque copulat voluntate. Quae tria cum in unum coguntur, ab ipso coactu cogitatio dicitur. Nec jam in his tribus diversa substantia est. . . . Sicut autem ratione discernebatur species quae fiebat in sensu formato ut esset visio (alioquin ita erant conjunctae, ut omnino una eademque putaretur) ; sic illa phantasia, cum animus cogitat speciem visi corporis, cum constet ex corporis similitudine quam memoria tenet, et ex ea quae inde formatur in acie recordantis animi; tamen sic una et singularis apparet, ut duo quaedam esse non inveniantur nisi judicante ratione, qua intelligimus aliud esse illud quod in memoria manet, etiam cum aliunde cogitamus, et aliud fieri cum recordamur, id est, ad memoriam redimus, et illic invenimus eamdem speciem," *ibid.*, c. 3, col. 988-89. On the meaning of "phantasia" in these passages, cf. *ibid.*, c. 5, col. 990; IX, c. 6, no. 10. On the nature of this trinity, and the relation between *cogitatio* and memory, cf. B. Kaelin, *Die Erkenntnislehre des hl. Augustinus*, pp. 23-31.

61. In addition to the passage quoted in note 60, cf. "Sed hinc adverti ali-

It is possible that this Augustinian meaning of cogitation explains how the Arabic term *fikr* used by Avicenna, which according to Professor Wolfson represents the Greek φαντασία λογιστική or βουλευτική (διανοητική),[62] came to be translated as "cogitative

quando manifestius potest, aliud esse quod reconditum memoria tenet, et aliud quod inde in cogitatione recordantis exprimitur, quamvis cum fit utriusque copulatio, unum idemque videatur: quia meminisse non possumus corporum species, nisi tot quot sensimus, et quantas sensimus, et sicut sensimus, ex corporis enim sensu eas in memoriam combibit animus; visiones tamen illae cogitantium ex iis quidem rebus quae sunt in memoria, sed tamen innumerabiliter atque omnino infinite multiplicantur atque variantur. . . . Cogito autem [solem] sicut volo currentem et ubi volo stantem, unde volo et quo volo venientem. Quadrum etiam mihi cogitare, in promptu est. . . . Hae autem formae rerum, quoniam corporales atque sensibiles sunt, errat quidem animus, cum eas opinatur eo modo foris esse, quomodo cogitat intus, vel cum iam interierunt foris, et adhuc in memoria retinentur, vel cum aliter etiam quod meminimus, non recordandi veritate, sed cogitandi varietate formatur," *De Trinitate,* XI, c. 8, PL XLII. 994-95; "Quapropter dum conjuncta cogitamus, quae singillatim sensa meminimus, videmur non id quod meminimus cogitare; cum id agamus moderante memoria, unde sumimus omnia quae multipliciter ac varie pro nostra voluntate componimus. Nam neque ipsas magnitudines corporum, quas numquam vidimus, sine ope memoriae cogitamus. Quantum enim spatii solet occupare per magnitudinem mundi noster obtutus, in tantum extendimus quaslibet corporum moles, cum eas maximas cogitamus. Et ratio quidem pergit in ampliora, sed phantasia non sequitur. Quippe cum infinitatem quoque numeri ratio renuntiet, quam nulla visio corporalia cogitantis apprehendis," *ibid.,* XI, c. 10, col. 997-98. On this last passage, St. Augustine excuses himself for having failed to remember the "four-legged flying things (locusts) of the Old Testament;" cf. *Lib. Retractationum,* II, c. 15, PL XXXII. 636.
  W. Ott, "Des hl. Augustinus Lehre ueber die Sinneserkenntnis," p. 47, translates *cogitare* as "vorstellen."
  Cf. Robert G. Gassert, S.J., "The Meaning of *Cogitatio* in St. Augustine," *The Modern Schoolman* XXV (1948), pp. 238-45.
62. On the meaning of the Arabic *fikr,* see H. A. Wolfson, "The Internal Senses," p. 91; and A. M. Goichon, *Lexique de la Langue Philosophique d'Ibn Sînâ* (Paris: Desclée de Brouwer, 1938), no. 521, p. 280; cf. *ibid.,* no. 524, p. 281, on *Mufakkira;* also see these two numbers in A. M. Goichon, *Vocabulaires Comparés d'Aristote et d'Ibn Sînâ* (Paris: Desclée, 1939), p. 25.

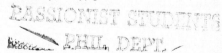

power." The doctrines of course are not the same; but there is enough similarity between them to make it possible for a translator to use a form of the root *cogitare* to designate a sense power under the control of reason.

It is necessary to remember that St. Augustine, in this trinity of phantasy, cogitation, and memory, is not speaking precisely of internal senses; though the first and third terms indicate powers, or better, a power of the soul, the second designates a special kind of action or activity. However, it would easily be possible to develop this inner trinity into, or confuse it with, a doctrine of powers. Such a development or juxta-position is made all the easier in that in St. Augustine this trinity is joined with a theory of the grades of forms, which has some resemblance to a theory of degrees of abstraction.[63]

A passage of St. Augustine, in itself of less intrinsic importance, was much more influential than any of the preceding analyses. It is a medical theory[64] of localization.

> There are three ventricles (as it were) of the brain, one in front, near the face, from which all sense comes; another in the rear near the neck, from which all movement comes; a third between the two, in which it is proved that memory flourishes, lest, since motion follows sense, man may fail to join together what must be done, if he should forget what he did.[65]

---

63. "In hac igitur distributione cum incipimus a specie corporis et pervenimus usque ad speciem quae fit in contuitu cogitantis, quatuor species reperiuntur quasi gradatim natae altera ex altera : secunda de prima, tertia de secunda, quarta de tertia. A specie quippe corporis quod cernitur exoritur ea quae fit in sensu cernentis, et ab hac ea quae fit in memoria, et ab hac ea quae fit in acie cogitantis. . . . Visiones enim duae sunt, una sentientis, altera cogitantis : ut autem possit esse visio cogitantis, ideo fit in memoria de visione sentientis simile aliquid quo se ita convertat in cogitando acies animi, sicut se in cernendo convertit ad corpus acies oculorum," *De Trinitate*, XI, c. 9, PL XLII. 996.
64. Cf. *De Genesi ad Litteram*, VII, c. 12, PL XXXIV. 362.
65. *Ibid.*, c. 18, col. 364. Text in Appendix II, no. 3. W. Ott, "Des hl. Augustinus Lehre ueber die Sinneserkenntnis," says that this localization is based on intermediaries.

The source of this teaching is unknown to me, and it is diffcult to see how it is to be harmonized with the normal Augustinian psychology. However that may be, it was precisely this paragraph which St. Isidore of Seville put into his *Libri Differentiarum* with the introductory remark: "as Augustine says."[66] We shall find this doctrine appearing again, occasionally by itself, at other times in combination with the Galenic localization.

BOETHIUS

Boethius, who lived from 450 to 524 or 525, has a position of importance in the development of the mediaeval philosophies that is greater than the intrinsic value of his work. Part of his significance lies in his strategic historical position. In many matters, he is the immediate source of Aristotelian teachings. For example, he gives a rather simplified version of the three kinds of soul according to Aristotle: vegetative, sensitive, and rational.[67]

Another part of his significance lies in the kind of synthesis that he attempted. A notable example of this is pertinent to our purpose. In a short passage enumerating the powers of knowledge, Boethius added the Platonic (and even neo-Platonic) "intelli-

---

For other instances of St. Augustine's use of medical theories in the discussion of sensation, see *De Musica* VI. 5. 15, PL XXXII. 1171; *De Genesi ad Litteram,* VII, 15. 21 and 17. 23, PL XXXIV. 363, 364; *De Div. Daemon.,* 3. 7, PL XL. 584-85.

66. *Libri Differentiarum,* II, c. 17, no. 51, PL LXXXIII. 78.

67. Cf. "Quibus vero sensus adest, non tantum eas rerum capiunt formas, quibus sensibili corpore feruntur praesente, sed absente quoque, sensibilibusque suppositis ante cognitarum sensu formarum imagines tenent, memoriamque conficiunt, et prout quodque animal valet, longius breviusque custodit. Sed eas imaginationes confusas atque inevidentes sic sumunt, ut nihil ex earum coniunctione et compositione efficere possunt. Atque idcirco meminisse quidem possunt, nec aeque omnia. Amissa vero oblivione memoria recolligere ac revocare non possunt. Futuri vero his nulla cognitio est. Sed animae vis tertia quae secum priores alendi ac sentiendi vires trahit, hisque velut famulis atque obedientibus utitur, eadem tota in ratione constituta est," *Commentaria in Porphyrium a se Translatum,* I, PL LXIV. 71; CSEL XLVIII. pp. 136-37.

54

gence" to the (Aristotelian) series of sense, imagination, and reason.[68]

> Sense looks at man himself in one way, imagination in another, reason in another, intelligence in still another. For sense knows figure constituted in its subject matter; but imagination judges the figure alone without matter. Reason transcends this also, and weighs in a universal consideration the very species which is in singulars. The eye of intelligence is loftier still. For, going beyond the ambit of the universal, it looks at the simple form itself with the pure summit of mind.[69]

This interesting experiment in the combination of Aristotelian and Platonic notions was soon to be put into the context of a systematic discussion of the progress of knowledge.

Three works "On the Soul"

The *De Statu Animae* of Claudianus Mamertus was the first in a series of works *"On the Soul."*[70] Claudianus, who was born about 473, was an inhabitant of Vienne. He deals with the powers of the soul very briefly, and scarcely of set purpose. The powers, according to him, are: memory, *consilium*, and will;[71] or again:

---

68. Cf. É. Gilson, *La Philosophie au Moyen Age,* p. 302; M. D. Chenu O.P., "Notes de Lexicographie philosophique: Disciplina," *Revue des Sciences Philosophiques et Théologiques* XXV (1936), pp. 691-92.
69. *De Consolatione Philosophiae,* book V, prosa 4, nos. 18-20, ed. Adrian Fortescue (London: Burns Oates and Washburn, 1925), p. 150. Text in Appendix II, no. 4. Cf. Prosa 4 and 5.
70. Cf. É. Gilson, *La Philosophie au Moyen Age,* p. 151.
71. "Memoriam, consilium, voluntatem, quibus humanae animae confit unitas, videre possimus, quamlibet rationali atque irrationali meminisse commune sit," *De Statu Animae,* I, c. 20, in *Opera,* ed. Augustus Engelbrecht (CSEL, Vienna: 1885), p. 71; "In memoria esse hominis pecudisque confinium. . . . Sed quoniam animae belluarum etsi imagines locorum naturaliter retinent, ipsius tamen substantiae suae scientiam non habent, in recordatione corporalium rerum quas per corporis sensus hauserunt, necessario remanent, et ratiocinandi non habentes oculum, non dicam supra se aliquid, sed ne se ipsas videre non possunt," *ibid.,* c. 21, p. 71.

memory, cogitation, and will;[72] this latter trinity is based on St. Augustine, with some modifications. Claudianus's most important contribution lies in the identification of the soul with its powers and apparently even with its operations.[73]

Cassiodorus, 490-583, of an important Italian family, spent about the first half of his life in political activity; removed from his office, he entered a monastery. About 450, while still a layman, Cassiodorus wrote a *De Anima*. Though the works of Boethius were in circulation by this time, the *De Anima* of Cassiodorus descends mainly from St. Augustine and Claudianus Mamertus.[74] He mentions one group of powers, similar to those of St. Augustine, composed of imagination, memory, and cogitation.[75] There is another list of the natural powers of the soul,[76] which shows a pronounced syncretism in terminology and doctrine.

> The first [power] is the sensible, in both parts. It gives us the sense of intelligence by which we sense all incorporeal things in a varied imagination. It also makes the bodily senses active.[77]

Note here the extremely generic uses of "sense" and "imagination." These may have some relation to the usage of "sense" by St. Augustine already noted.[78]

---

72. Cf. the title of c. 24: "Quia non est aliud anima, aliud memoria, cogitatio, vel voluntas, cum haec eadem una sit anima," *ibid.,* c. 24, p. 84.
73. "Tu enim cum dicis aliud esse animam, aliud animae cogitationem, melius fortasse dixisses illa de quibus cogitat cum de se non cogitat, non esse anima, ipsam vero cogitationem non esse nisi animam. . . . Haec autem dilectio, quod est anima humana," *ibid.,* pp. 85, 87.
74. Cf. É. Gilson, *La Philosophie au Moyen Age,* p. 151.
75. *De Anima,* c. 2, PL LXX. 1287; also cc. 8 and 9, cols. 1293-96.
76. Cf. "Virtutes animae naturales quinquepertitas esse voluerunt," *ibid.,* c. 6, col. 1291.
77. *Ibid.,* Text in Appendix II, no. 5.
78. Cf. supra, texts in notes 57 and 58. Compare also the phrase in Claudianus Mamertus, "ratiocinandi oculus," supra, note 71. The doctrine of the various *visiones* of the soul in St. Augustine may also have helped to bring about this extension of *sensus*; cf. supra, note 63. There is finally a possibility in classical Latin itself, since *sententia,* which evidently derives from *sentire,* does refer to an in-

The first power mentioned by Cassiodorus, then, is the sensible. The second is the "imperative." The third is again a very strange power.

The third, the principal, when removed from all activity we are at rest, and with our bodily senses quiet we treat of something very profoundly and firmly.

The "principal" power has a name derived from Stoic doctrine, and a meaning which is somewhat similar to the Augustinian "superior reason"[79] or the Boethian "intelligence." The fourth power is the "vital" or vivifying; the fifth is appetite.

Cassiodorus knows of the medical theory that the soul has its seat in the head;[80] he adds to this the "microcosmic" argument: as God is in Heaven, so the soul is in the head.[81] This argument is repeated by Rabanus Maurus.[82] Gregory the Great re-

tellectual act. Even *sensus* begins at times to be almost "understanding" or "view;" cf. Lewis and Short, *Latin Dictionary*, s. v. *sensus*.

In this connection we may note a somewhat similar use of *sensus* by John Scotus Erigena. "Et ille motus est qui graece διάνοια vel ἐνέργεια latine vero sensus vel operatio vocatur, ipsum dico sensum, qui substantialis est, et interior, qui similiter ab intellectu procedit per rationem," *De Divisione Naturae*, 2.23, PL CXXII. 577D. On the meaning of this phrase, cf. Artur Schneider, *Die Erkenntnislehre des Johannes Eriugena* (Berlin: De Guyter & Co., 1921-1923), pp. 64-65.

79. On this term, cf. Julien Peghaire, C.S.Sp., "Le couple Augustinien 'Ratio superior et ratio inferior' ", *Revue des Sciences Philosophiques et Théologiques* XXII (1934) 221-38.

80. *De Anima*, c. 8, col. 1293.
This passage has striking similarities with that of Galen, *De Hippocratis et Platonis Placitis*, I, c. 6, ed. C. Kuehn, vol. V, p. 185, and II, c. 4, p. 238.

81. Cf. "Quidam sedem animae, quamvis sit in toto corpore diffusa, in corde esse voluerunt. . . . Plurimi autem in capite insidere manifestant (si fas est cum reverentia tamen dicere) ad similitudinem aliquam Divinitatis; quae licet omnia ineffabili substantia sua repleat, Scriptura tamen coelo insidere confirmat," *De Anima*, c. 8, PL LXX. 1293.

82. Rabanus Maurus, *Tractatus de Anima*, c. 5, PL CX. 1114.
On this work, cf. Karl Werner, *Der Entwickelungsgang der mittel-*

tains only the fact of this general localization, which he says is well known.[83]

The third of this group of treatises is the *De Ratione Animae* of Alcuin. Alcuin (735-804) was, by the evidence of his works, not a great thinker or writer. He was an earnest and serious compiler, and a very great force in stimulating the intellectual life of his contemporaries. In general, his treatise on the soul depends on St. Augustine and Claudianus Mamertus.[84] In speaking of the powers of the soul, he mentions two trinities: intelligence, will, and memory;[85] imagination, memory, and the power of dealing with images.[86] These groups are still recognizable, but the clearness of the Augustinian analysis has been obscured.

---

alterlichen Psychologie von Alcuin bis Albertus Magnus (Wien: Gerold, 1876, Separatabdruck aus dem xxv Band der Denkschriften der philosophisch-historischen Classe der kaiserlichen Akademie der Wissenschaften), pp. 9-13, and É. Gilson, *La Philosophie au Moyen Age,* p. 197.

83. "Pene nullum latet quod quinque sensus corporis nostri, videlicet visus auditus gustus odoratus et tactus, in omne quod sentiunt atque discernunt, virtutem discretionis et sensus a cerebro trahunt. Et cum unus sit judex sensus cerebri qui intrinsecus praesidet," St. Gregory the Great, *Libri Moralium,* XI, c. 6, PL LXXV. 957; cf. above note 58.

84. K. Werner, *Der Entwickelungsgang der Mittelalterlichen Psychologie,* pp. 2-9, É. Gilson, *La Philosophie au Moyen Age,* pp. 190-91.

85. "Habet igitur anima in sua natura, ut diximus, imaginem sanctae Trinitatis in eo quod intelligentiam, voluntatem, et memoriam habet," *De Ratione Animae, ad Eulaliam Virginem,* c. 6, PL CI. 641.

86. "Nunc autem consideremus miram velocitatem animae in formandis rebus quae [*sic:* quas?] percipit per carnales sensus, a quibus quasi per quosdam nuntios quidquid rerum sensibilium cognitarum vel incognitarum percipit, mox in seipsa earum ineffabili celeritate format figuras, informatasque in suae thesauro memoriae recondit. . . . Et adhuc mirabilius est, quod incognitarum rerum, si lectae vel auditae erunt in auribus, anima statim format figuram ignotae rei. . . . Quamvis eo puncto quo vult de qualibet una cogitare, cogitet, non quod anima exeat de sede sua ad cognoscendum aliquid, sed in seipsa manet, et in seipsa illam formam recognoscit, quam pridem mira velocitate formavit," *ibid.,* c. 7, col. 642.

Constantinus Africanus and Adelard of Bath

These two twelfth century writers have much in common; they both seem to have traveled much; they were both interested in Arabian science; they both translated scientific works from the Arabic — Constantinus specialized in medical works, Adelard translated Euclid.

Constantinus, in his *Pantegni,* an adaptation of an Arabic work,[87] combines the Aristotelian degrees of soul (vegetative, sensitive, rational) with the three kinds of "spirit" of Galen (natural, spiritual, animal).[88] Obviously there will be difficulties. The combination seems to work out this way: the natural power belongs to merely natural, inanimate things; the spiritual power vivifies; the animal power gives sense and intellect.[89] How this third degree is to be understood cannot be decided here, since the *Pantegni* is not accessible. But the question which seems to be raised here concerning the relation of intellect and the "animal power" will certainly recur later. According to B. Hauréau, Constantinus is also the source of the revived Galenic localization of powers.[90]

---

87. See Lynn Thorndike, *History of Magic and Experimental Science* (New York: Macmillan, 1927: 6 vols.), vol. I, p. 747, where he indicates as the original a *Royal Art of Medicine* by Ali Ibn Abbas.
88. See Hans Willner, *Des Adelard von Bath Traktat De Eodem et Diverso* (Beitraege Baeumker, Muenster: Aschendorff, Band IV, Heft 1, 1903), p. 81. H. Willner states that in this particular, Constantinus was influenced by Isaac Israeli, p. 82; also Charles Homer Haskins, *Studies in the History of Mediaeval Science* (Cambridge: Harvard University Press, 1924), p. 39.
89. Cf. "Virtutes generales sunt tres: una attinens naturae, quae vocatur naturalis; altera solum vivificans est solius animae et vocatur spiritualis; alia dans sensum et voluntarium motum et intellectum similiter est animae et vocatur animata. Actio virtutis naturalis animalibus et arboribus est universalis. . . . Virtus spiritualis animalibus rationalibus vel irrationalibus et non arboribus est communis. Virtus animata partim rationalibus et partim irrationalibus communis est animalibus," *Pantegni,* theor. 4, 1; quoted in Heinrich Flatten, *Die Philosophie des Wilhelm von Conches* (Koblenz: Goerres-Druckerei, 1929), p. 165, note 990.
90. "Tout cela vient de l'Arabie, et Guillaume de Conches en a fait l'emprunt au *Liber oculorum* du moine Constantin," [and in a foot-

Adelard of Bath presents the Galenic localization, with the addition of a nautical metaphor.[91] But his understanding of these powers is not Galenic at all.[92] It seems to be a simplified Augustinian theory (like that in the *De Genesi ad Litteram*) with relations to Cassiodorus. Strangely enough, Adelard thinks that this localization derives from Aristotle.[93] This statement seems to prove that Adelard himself had no knowledge of the physical and psychological writings of Aristotle; the source of his incorrect information is not yet known.

Isaac of Stella and the *De Spiritu et Anima*

In the twelfth century, there arose a movement of speculative mysticism, in which ascetical and mystical doctrines and practices are combined with philosophical theories. The *Epistola de Anima*, of Isaac, Abbot of Stella (l'Etoile) belongs primarily in this movement.[94] It is interesting to us for its remarks on the powers of the soul.

---

note:] "Chap. 2. — Le *Liber oculorum* de Constantin fait partie du manuscript latin de Saint-Victor, inscrit sous le n° 145," B. Hauréau, *Singularités Historiques et Littéraires* (Paris: Calman-Levy, 1894), p. 285.

91. Cf. "Ipsius etiam capitis partes diversas diversis officiis dedicavit — in porta enim imaginatur, in medio ratione utitur, in puppi, id est, occipitio, memoriam abscondit," *De Eodem et Diverso,* ed. Hans Willner, pp. 32-33. Cf. also H. Willner's discussion, p. 81, and É. Gilson, *La Philosophie au Moyen Age,* p. 294.

92. Cf. "In cerebro enim utitur phantastico motu, id est, ingeniali, rationali etiam, id est iudicio, sed et memoriali, id est recordatione. Prius enim intelligit, deinde, quod intellectum est iudicat, tertio ipsum iudicium constantiae commendat," *Quaestiones Naturales,* c. 17, ed. Dr. Martin Mueller, *Die Quaestiones Naturales des Adelardus von Bath* (Beitraege, Baeumker, Muenster: Aschendorff, Band XXXIII, Heft 2, 1934), p. 22.

93. Cf. "Nam et Aristoteles in Physicis et alii in tractatibus aliis sic discernunt, ut phantasiam exerceri dicant in parte cerebri anteriori, rationem in medio, memoriam in occipitio. Inde et tribus illis cellis nomina imposuerunt phantasticam, rationalem et memorialem," *ibid.,* c. 18, pp. 22-23.

94. Cf. É. Gilson, *La Philosophie au Moyen Age,* p. 301; K. Werner,

According to Isaac, there are five powers of the soul: sense, imagination, reason, intellect, and intelligence, which are all really identical, and are called simply *sense*.[95] This five power list seems to be a combination of the four power list of Boethius, with the addition of "intellect" from St. Augustine. The use of the word "sense" seems to derive from Cassiodorus, and the identification of the soul with its powers is here expressed as in Claudianus Mamertus.

These five powers are at the same time five stages on the ascent to contemplation.[96] This doctrine has a Platonic and even a Plotinian cast;[97] the Platonic dualism of soul and body is softened by the introduction of intermediaries.[98]

Der Entwickelungsgang der mittelalterlichen Psychologie, pp. 25-33.
  For example, the physiological theories of localization seem to be almost overlooked; cf. "Capitis humani, quod sedes est animae, et domus quodammodo rationis," *Epistola ad Alcherum de Anima*, PL CXCIV. 1882, and compare this with the full-scale discussions in contemporary writers.

95. Cf. "Sensus qui in ipsa anima est unus, et quod ipsa, et propter ea ad quae cognoscenda exeritur et intendit multiplex dicitur, et multipliciter nuncupatur. Dicitur namque sensus, imaginatio, ratio, intellectus, intelligentia," *Epistola ad Alcherum de Anima*, PL XCXIV. 1879.
  On the identity of the soul with its powers, cf. Wilhelm Meuser, *Die Erkenntnislehre des Isaak von Stella*, (Bottrop: Postberg, 1934), pp. 13-16.
96. Cf. "Animae in mundo sui corporis peregrinanti quinque sunt ad sapientiam progressus: sensus scilicet, imaginatio, ratio, intellectus, et intelligentia," *ibid.*, col. 1880.
97. Cf. É. Gilson, *La Philosophie au Moyen Age*, p. 302.
98. "Itaque quae vere spiritus est et non corpus, et caro, quae vere corpus est, et non spiritus, facile et convenienter in suis extremis uniuntur, id est, in phantastico animae, quod fere corpus est, et sensualitate carnis, quae fere spiritus est," *Epistola ad Alcherum de Anima*, col. 1881.
  This seems to contain an echo of the principle of hierarchy as stated by Dionysius: "Semper fines priorum coadunans initiis secundorum," *De Divinis Nominibus*, c. 7, no. 3, ed. P. G. Théry, O.P., *Etudes Dionysiennes, II. Hilduin, traducteur de Denys* (Paris: Vrin, 1937), p. 254.

The pseudo-Augustinian *De Spiritu et Anima,* now considered to be probably a work of Alcher of Clairvaux,[99] draws on all possible sources. It contains the passages of Isaac referred to above.[100] It has also the selection from St. Augustine's *De Genesi ad Litteram* quoted above, as well as a passage from Hugh of St. Victor's *De Unione* which will be referred to later.

The peculiar syncretism, the multiplication and hierarchization of powers, offer no difficulty; for all these powers are but the Protean manifestations of the pure spirit imprisoned in the body. The basic unity of the soul is underlined by the use of the word "sense" for any and all powers.[101]

FROM WILLIAM OF CONCHES TO ALFRED OF SARESHEL

William of Conches, an energetic twelfth century figure,[102] was a pupil of the school of Chartres. At first he worked in the

---

99. Cf. Dom A. Wilmart, O.S.B., *Auteurs Spirituels et Textes Dévots* (Paris: Bloud et Gay, 1932), pp. 174-75; É. Gilson, *La Philosophie au Moyen Age,* p. 302; K. Werner, *Der Entwickelungsgang der mittelalterlichen Psychologie,* pp. 41-43.

100. In the order of their appearance in notes 95-98 above, the texts in the *De Spiritu et Anima* are, c. 4, PL XL. 782; c. 4, col. 782 and c. 11, col. 786, c. 14, col. 789.

101. Cf. "Duo siquidem in homine sensus sunt, unus interior et unus exterior. . . . Sensus interior reficitur in contemplatione divinitatis, sensus exterior in contemplatione humanitatis," *De Spiritu et Anima,* c. 9, col. 785.

102. On William of Conches, and the identification of his works, see H. Flatten, *Die Philosophie des Wilhelm von Conches,* pp. 9-10; Reginald Lane Poole, *Illustrations of the History of Medieval Thought and Learning,* revised edition (London: Society for Promoting Christian Knowledge, 1920), pp. 293-310; J. M. Parent, O.P., *La Doctrine de la Création dans l'Ecole de Chartres,* (Ottawa: Institut d'Etudes Médiévales, 1938), pp. 115-20. On William's psychology, cf. K. Werner, *Der Entwickelungsgang der mittelalterlichen Psychologie,* pp. 14-21. On his teachings in the field of natural science, cf. K. Werner, *Die Kosmologie und Naturlehre des Scholastischen Mittelalters mit spezieller Beziehung auf Wilhelm von Conches* (Wien: 1873, Sitzungsberichte der kaiserlichen Wiener Akademie der Wissenschaften, philosophische-historische Classe, vol. LXXV).

field of theology; later on he devoted himself to the study of
nature. He begins his discussion of the powers of man by stating that there are three: natural, spiritual, and animal.[103] The
natural is found in the liver, the spiritual in the heart, the animal
powers in the brain.[104] These animal powers are: intelligence,
reason, memory, common sense, voluntary movement.[105] Thus far,
there are recognizable Galenic influences (in the three-fold power
of soul) by way of Constantinus Africanus; and Augustinian and
Boethian (in the list of animal powers). The first two terms seem
to come from Boethius; the next three from the passage in the
De Genesi ad Litteram. The adjective "common" may reflect an
Aristotelian influence; it may also stand for the phrase "all sense"
of the *De Genesi.* That the latter is more likely is indicated by
the fact that "sense" is located in the front part of the brain, and
"movement" in the rear,[106] as in the passage from St. Augustine.
The remaining three powers are localized according to the Galenic
formula.[107]

> In the head there are three cells, in the prow, in the middle,
> in the stern. The first cell is warm and dry, and is called
> "phantastic," that is, visual or imaginative, because in it
> there is the power of seeing and understanding. It is warm
> and dry for this reason, to attract the forms and colors of
> things. The middle cell is called "logistic," that is, rational,
> because in it is the power of discerning. For what the phan-
> tastic cell draws in passes on to this one, and there the soul
> discerns. It is warm and wet so that it can better conform
> itself to the properties of things in discerning. The third is
> called "memorial," because in it is the power of retaining
> something in the memory. For what is discerned in the lo-
> gistic cell passes to the memorial, by a hole, closed by a little

---

103. *Dragmaticon,* 251: quoted in H. Flatten, *Die Philosophie des Wil-
    helm von Conches,* p. 165, note 985. See also William's Commentary
    in Timeum 27D, quoted in Parent, *La Doctrine de la Création dans
    l'Ecole de Chartres,* pp. 144-45.
104. *De Philosophia Mundi* (among the works of Honorius Augusto-
    dunensis), IV, cc. 19, 22, PL CLXXII. 91, 94.
105. *Ibid.,* c. 22, col. 94.
106. *Ibid.,* c. 23, col. 94.
107. Cf. H. Flatten, *Die Philosophie des Wilhelm von Conches,* p. 167.

flap, until it is opened when we want to trust something to memory or bring it back. This cell is cold and dry, that it may retain better. For it is characteristic of the cold and dry to draw together. But someone may say: how could this be proved in any point. We say, by injuries received in those parts.[108]

The terminology seen here reflects that of Constantinus Africanus, as does also the use of the nautical metaphor. The peculiar mechanism of memory: the opening into the rear chamber with its little valve-like appendage, is almost identical with the one contained in the *De Differentia Animae et Spiritus*.[109] The common source (probably only the remote source) for both is Galen. We have already seen his doctrine of the spirit-intermediary. In another work Galen has an involved physiological doctrine of the spirits, complete with opening and trap-door.[110] The temptation to combine these statements must have been very strong. The idea of putting both imagination and intelligence in the front chamber is related to the idea of Cassiodorus that the sensible power gives both of these to man.[111]

John of Salisbury (1120-1180) is one of England's most attractive and versatile personalities. Scholarly student of Latin literature and himself a writer with an excellent Ciceronian style;

---

108. *De Philosophia Mundi,* IV, c. 24, PL CLXXII. 95. The first sentence is corrected according to the reading of Περὶ διδάξεων *sive Elementorum Philosophiae libri quattuor* (Among the works of Bede), PL XC. 1174C. Text in Appendix II, no. 7.
109. This work will be discussed in the next chapter.
110. Cf. Galen, *De Usu Partium Corporis Humani,* VIII, c. 4: «κωνάριον .. φύλακά τινα καὶ οἷον ταμίαν τοῦ ποσοῦ τῆς ἐπιπέμψεως,» ed. C. Kuehn, vol. III, p. 675; «τὸν πόρον ἀνοιγνύναι τε καὶ κλείειν ἠδύνατο,» p. 683, and also pp. 676-77.
111. In a text like: "Ergo merito antiqui dicebant, in capite esse sedem sapientiae. In capite enim habent sedem quae faciunt sapientem, intellectus scilicet, ratio, et memoria," *De Philosophia Mundi,* c. 24, PL CLXXII. 95, the three terms localized in the brain, namely, *intellectus, ratio, memoria,* correspond to the three chambers. This is clear from the long text quoted above, where it is said that in the front chamber "vis videndi est et intelligendi."

wise advisor; able politician; loyal churchman; John reflected
or commented on most of the learning of his time.
He gives a very complex picture of the soul's powers. In one
enumeration, there are seven: *animus, mens,* imagination, opinion,
reason, intellect, memory.[112] This series runs from the principle
of vegetative life (*animus*) all the way up to intellect, which itself turns into an eighth power, intelligence. Fundamentally, what
is the difference between all these powers? In themselves, there is
none; they are but one soul.[113] All the discernible differences
arise from the greater or less refinement of their instrument, which
is a very thin breath.[114] This explanation holds for vegetability
and for the external senses. In explaining the differences of the

---

112. "Septem sunt animae vires in homine: animus, mens, imaginatio,
    opinio, ratio, intellectus, et memoria. Animus est animae virtus
    potestativa, naturae operationibus amica. Mens est vis animi, sen-
    suum officio se excitans et quae sentiendi passio vel actio cuique
    sensui subiecta sit deliberans. Haec vis intellectus exordium pri-
    mum concipit, et sic excessum suum ad rei cognitionem extendit,
    unde alibi: mens est vis animi, intellectum formans et intelligen-
    tiam constituens. Imaginatio est vis animae qua percipimus figuram
    et colorem rei absentis et visae, quae ex sensibus oritur, et ex
    visu praecipue. Sensis quae sunt deprehendit, imaginatio vero quae
    sunt et quae non sunt percipit. Necessaria est imaginatio homini
    ne rem tradat oblivioni. . . . Opinio vero quandoque ex sensu,
    quandoque ex imaginatione oritur. . . . Ratio ex vera opinione
    nascitur hoc modo, cum verum incertum fluctuat, et postea dis-
    cussionibus confirmatur, fit ratio. Et est ratio discretus animi in-
    tuitus, quod verum est et certum a falso discernens. Intellectus
    vero ex ratione oritur. . . . Intelligentia nascitur, quae formam a
    materia abstrahit," John of Salisbury, *De Septem Septenis,* sec-
    tion 4, PL CXCIX. 951 B-D.
113. Cf. "Istae vires ita coeunt in substantiam quod una sunt anima,"
    ibid., col. 952A.
114. Cf. "Anima quandoque per seipsam, quandoque corporeo instru-
    mento res comprehendit. Conformat enim se suis adeo instrumentis,
    ut quale fuerit instrumentum, res ipsa modo consimili comprehen-
    dat, ut si vitro interposito litteras inspexeris: cuiuscumque coloris
    sit vitrum, litteras tibi videre videaris. Anima namque immista
    est spiritui tenuissimo per arterias diffusa, ita scilicet ut spiritus
    ille sit vehiculum animae, et illius spiritus vehiculum sit sanguis,"
    ibid., col. 952C-D.

higher cognitive powers, the place in the brain is also used. For the spirit or breath is progressively refined as it passes from the front to the middle chamber.[115] So, too, the powers of the soul rise in nobility till, in the middle chamber, the soul in its spirituality uses itself as its only instrument, and so becomes pure intelligence.[116]

---

115. "Hermes Mercurius: est autem in prima parte capitis, in cellula quae dicitur phantastica, spiritus quidam subtilior et agilior spiritu per arterios diffuso. Cum autem anima illo spiritu utitur pro instrumento, re absente formam comprehendit in materia. Haec vis animae imaginatio dicitur. Differt a sensu, quia sensus re presente formam comprehendit in materia. Imaginatio vero re absente, et ita confuse, quia non discrete.

In hac eadem cellula quoque spiritus ille fit tenuior et subtilior, et cum eo anima utatur, formas materia mistas comprehendit, nec tamen rerum veritatem comprehendit, sed discernit et inquirit. Materia namque confundit, ne formarum veritas circa eam comprehendi possit. Haec vis animae ratio dicitur, et tunc cellula illa rationalis," *ibid.,* col. 953C-D.

The text of this work in the Patrologia is rather poorly done. If the name "Hermes Mercurius" is supposed to stand at the head of this text, it represents "Hermes Trismegistos," on which see Josef Kroll, *Die Lehre des Hermes Trismegistos* (Beitraege, Baeumker, Muenster, Aschendorff, Band XII, Heft 2-4, 1914), pp. 286-94. However, the doctrine of this text is not found in J. Kroll's discussion, while it is to be found in the sources already studied above. It is true that there are other references to this Hermes in the same section of *De Septem Septenis,* notably the distinction between *animus* and *anima,* which J. Kroll lists as characteristic psychological doctrines. If the text is accurate, we must suppose that John of Salisbury thought of all medical knowledge as somehow going back to this Hermes.

The notion of "imagination" as presented here seems to be in the line of speculation about logical questions. The difference between imagination and reason as expressed by Peter Abelard may well be the source of the expressions used by John and the other writers in this group. On the notion of "image" in Abelard, cf. É. Gilson, *La Philosophie au Moyen Age,* pp. 285-87.

116. The text begun in note 115 continues thus: "In media vero parte capitis, in cellula quae dicitur intellectualis, anima, cum simplex tum immaterialis, ad suam quoque immutabilitatem se recipit, et rerum formas extra materiam in sua immutabilitate considerat.

"Librum Hunc," a commentary on Boethius's *De Trinitate,*
is ascribed to Thierry of Chartres,[117] who was head of the famous
school of Chartres and one of the teachers of John of Salisbury.
Librum Hunc contains a doctrine on the higher powers of the soul,
almost identical with that of John. About the only difference is that
instead of the most refined stage of the subtle breath which John
speaks of, this work introduces the notion of "ethereal light."[118]

Haec vis animae disciplina vocatur, quia per disciplinam et doc-
trinam ad hanc formarum considerationem venitur.

In eadem vero cellula, qua anima formas rerum in sua sim-
plicitate considerat, se ipsa utens pro instrumento, ita scilicet ut
formam circuli non solum a materia abstrahat, verum etiam et
sine omni partium compositione intelligat. Haec vis intelligentia
dicitur, quae solius Dei est, et. . . ." *De Septem Septenis,* section 4,
col. 954A. The Migne text ends with the unintelligible phrase
"praeter hoc." Wilhelm Jansen, *Der Kommentar des Clarenbaldus
von Arras zu Boethius de Trinitate* (Breslau: Mueller und Seiffert,
1926), p. 53, note 5, brilliantly emends: "paucorum hominum." The
phrase then becomes an echo of Plato, *Timeus 51E, interprete
Chalcidio,* ed. J. Wrobel, p. 6: "Quid quod rectae opinionis omnis
vir particeps, intellectus vero Dei proprius et paucorum admodum
hominum?" This conjecture is borne out by the fact that this
same phrase, with a formal reference to Plato, is to be found
Metalogicus, IV, c. 18, PL CXCIX. 927.

On the psychology of *De Septem Septenis,* W. Jansen, *op. cit.,*
has some very helpful discussions, pp. 52-55.

117. Cf. W. Jansen, *Der Kommentar Clarenbaldus von Arras zu Boethius
de Trinitate,* p. 3*.

118. "Quandoque vero subtiliore utitur instrumento, spiritu scilicet quodam tenui, quem in phantastica cellula esse dicunt physici. Utens
igitur illo instrumento, anima aliquanto plus subtiliatur, adeo scilicet
ut formam rei absentato corpore comprehendat, sed confuse. Neque enim album a nigro, ut generaliter loquar, statum a statu discernit vel separat. Haec vero animae vis imaginatio a veteribus
appellatur.

Est autem in media parte capitis, in rationali sciliiet cellula, spiritus
quidam tenuissimus, lux videlicet aetherea. Cum igitur illo spiritu
anima pro instrumento utitur, alleviatur quodammodo pro qualitate
instrumenti subtilior facta, adeo ut statum a statu discernat, ut
hoc ipsum album ab eo statu, quem hoc nomen, scilicet nigrum,
designat. Eodemque modo progredi licet per singula. Formas etiam
rerum, cum hoc utitur instrumento, considerat, non tamen in puri-

This last touch seems to show the influence of the "light-physics and metaphysics."[119]

Clarenbaldus of Arras, associated with the school of Chartres at approximately the same time, has an expanded version of this passage, in which the highest power is called "intellectibility."[120]

tate sua, sed per participatas, admixtas scilicet materiae et coniunctas, ut si ad aures cuiuspiam hoc nomen 'albedo' pervenerit, album statim in animo formet, eo scilicet quod albedinem in puritate sua comprehendere nequeat. Haec ergo vis animae intentio dicitur eique est imaginatio coniunctissima, quemadmodum rationali cellulae affinis valde est et minimo distans spatio a phantastica. Unde et Stoici eandem vim animae illas esse arbitrati sunt. Sed differunt. Imaginatio namque status confundit; ratio vero statum a statu discernit.

Cum igitur tot modis anima instrumentis utatur corporeis, se ipsa quandoque pro instrumento utitur corpori non obnoxia, formasque rerum non admixtas materiae, sed in puritate sua speculatur et considerat. Haec vero comprehendendi vis suo nomine vocatur intelligentia. Quae solius quidem Dei est et admodum paucorum hominum," *ibid.*, p. 7.

119. On earlier references to "lux" especially in connection with intermediaries in the *union* of soul and body, cf. Clemens Baeumker. *Witelo, ein Philosoph und Naturforscher des XII. Jahrhunderts* (Beitraege, Baeumker, Muenster: Aschendorff, Band III, Heft 2, 1908), p. 455. *Lux* has been referred to by St. Augustine, *De Genesi ad Litteram,* VII c. 19, PL XXXIV. 364; IV, c. 28, PL XXXIV. 315; *De Genesi Liber Imperfectus,* V, c. 24, PL XXXV, 228-29; Avicenna, *De Anima,* part 4, c. 5.

120. "Sensus enim, qui est animae prima affectio secundum exteriorem speciem occurrentem, suo utitur instrumento, ut visus oculo, auditus aure, odoratus nare, gustus lingua et palato, tactus manu. Ceterum imaginatio, quae est sensus similitudo per res exteriores oblata, suo quoque utitur instrumento, id est aere multo cum humore exiguuo in phantastica capitis cella incluso; ratio vero spiritu tenuissimo, quem physici lucem aetheream vocant, cum humore sibi sufficienti in logistica cella capitis incluso utitur pro instrumento. At intellectibilitas, ut praedictum est, omni caret instrumento. Unde et Plato solius divini generis eam esse commemorat et admodum paucorum hominum," W. Jansen, *Der Kommentar Clarenbaldus von Arras zu Boethius de Trinitate,* pp. 36*-37*.

"Quia praedicta sensuum instrumenta grossa sunt, obtusam per ea habet cognitionem. At cum per imaginationem anima ipsa rem

Alfred of Sareshel, known also as Alfredus Anglicus,[121] was
a writer of scientific treatises and a translator during the late
twelfth and early thirteenth centuries. He touches on our problem
from a scientific point of view.[122]

In his *De Motu Cordis,* Alfred stresses the idea of the instruments of the soul.[123] These instruments are more or less purified

---

quamlibet secum tractat, tanto subtilius eam considerat, quanto in
eius retractatione subtiliori utitur instrumento.

In parte quippe capitis anteriori, quae phantastica dicitur, multus
aer cum exiguo humore includitur, cui eorum, quae per sensus cognoscuntur, figurae imprimuntur, atque eo aere cum pauca humiditate in imaginando anima utitur pro instrumento, Quanto igitur aeris
substantia compositione manus vel oculi vel nervi subtilior est, tanto
imaginationis cognitio subtilior est sensuali.

Cum vero anima secundum vim rationis rem aliquam comprehendit,
tanto in sua consideratione fit subtilior atque perspicacior, quanto
sui instrumenti essentia imaginationis et sensuum instrumenta prae-
terit subtilitate. Siquidem in media parte capitis, quae logistica dicitur, aer subtilissimus, qui a physicis lux aetherea appellatur, tent-
tur inclusus habetque sibi humorem ideonee comproportionatum.
Unde vis discretionis quaedam inter bonum et malum atque inter
universalia et particularia ipsi animae innascitur. Quanto igitur lux
aetherea est subtilior, tanto anima aethereae lucis adminiculo subtilius rem quam per phantasticam a re discernit.

Cum autem anima ad divinae formae quantulamcumque cognitionem erigitur, nullo prorsus utitur instrumento, quoniam eius cognitionem natura nequaquam dare potuit, qui conditor naturae sub-
sistit et artifex. Sola igitur intellectibilitate adiuta ad divinae formae
cognitionem anima consurgit, estque intellectibilitas solius divini generis et secundum Platonem admodum paucorum hominum," *ibid.,*
pp. 53*-54*.

Anonymus *In Boetium de Trinitate,* Paris: B. N. Lat. 14489,
quoted in Parent, *La Doctrine de la Création dans l'école de Chartres,* p. 193, also uses the term "intellectibilitas."

121. On Alfred's thought, and general background, cf. Clement Baeumker,
*Die Stellung des Alfred von Sareshel (Alfredus Anglicus) und
seiner Schrift de Motu Cordis in der Wissenschaft des beginnenden
13. Jahrhunderts* (Munich: Sitzungsbericht der koeniglichen Bayerischen Akademie der Wissenschaften, philosophisch-philologische und
historische Klasse, 1913, 9. Abhandlung).
122. Cf. É. Gilson, *La Philosophie au Moyen Age,* pp. 550-51.
123. Cf. "Non enim earundem virtutum non eadem sunt instrumenta.

varieties of the "spirit of life,"[124] which is a kind of light[125] shining forth from the heart and being reflected from the mirror of

---

Sensus enim communis universale est organum, per species vero distractus discretis utitur instrumentis. Nervi quoque quidam sensibiles, quidam motivi, cum ex eodem, non secundum eandem partem oriantur principio," *De Motu Cordis,* c. 2, no. 4, ed. Clemens Baeumker, *Des Alfred von Sareshel (Alfredus Anglicus) Schrift De Motu Cordis* (Beitraege, Baeumker, Muenster: Aschendorff, Band XXIII. Heft 1, 1923), p. 11.

It is in virtue of his doctrine of instruments that Alfred can make statements like the following: "Naturales quoque et animales quae dicuntur operationes eiusdem necessitatis lege tenentur, ut memorari, appetere, imaginari, digerere et similia," *ibid.,* c. 7, no. 6, p. 27; "Neque enim anima vel corpus dormit, vel digerit, ratiocinatur vel sentit, sed animal. Non ergo animae vel corporis propria huiusmodi passio vel actus aliquis, sed animalis," *ibid.,* c. 16, no. 11, pp. 91-92; "Quodsi cerebrum contendens anima ratiocinatur, aut id mediis quibusdam efficit, aut sedem permutat," *ibid.,* c. 8, no. 7, p. 27; "Fantasia vero ab actu sensus est motus; ab hac autem aestimatio et mediatio consurgunt; has ratio perscrutatur, omnium vero est memoria," *ibid.,* c. 15, no. 8, p. 81; "Cerebrum vero sensus et motus, fantasiae, aestimationis, rationis, memoriae regimen tenet," *ibid.,* c. 3, no. 2, p. 12.

C. Baeumker, *ibid.,* p. 81, note 4, says that we must not here think of the *vis aestimativa,* but that the word "aestimatio" here means "opinion." However, there seems a very possible influence on the part of Isaac Israeli, who has very definite meaning of *aestimatio*: it means "to consider, hold as." The works of Isaac were known at this time; he uses *aestimatio* and *meditatio* as contrasting terms, and speaks of *perscrutari* in connection with reason. For the texts of Isaac, see the next chapter.

124. In connection with "vital and animal spirits" Alfred himself refers to Galen; *ibid.,* c. 6, no. 8, p. 24.

125. Cf. "Spiritus igitur vitae irradiatione caput ascendit. Pervenit ergo virtus ad cerebrum — sicut color a sole in terrae superficiem, cum tamen media quaedam corpora nullius coloris actionem susceperint, ut sequentia docebunt — et per capillares arteriarum sectiones cerebri cellulis admittitur. Quid cum potentia sit animalis, ibidem digestior purgatiorque, fantasiae rationi memoriaeque ministrans fit actu animalis. Id enim ei tantum deest ad animalitatem, ut organum competens purgatus sortiatur. Eiusdem quoque virtutis irradiatio ad totum corpus a cerebro tamquam a speculi superficie resultat," *ibid.,* c. 10, no. 14, pp. 44-45.

the brain.[126] In every one of its activities, the human soul uses some form of this spirit for its instrument. In this, Alfred has departed from the "pure intelligence" of the preceding writers. He probably knew this doctrine; in fact, he even knew that Aristotle taught that the intellect has no bodily organ at all. This Aristotelian intellect, according to the Englishman, is a separated active intellect, through whose inhabitation in the human soul the latter becomes rational.[127] In a final cryptic phrase, he hints at an immutable principle, which first flows into intelligence, then intellect; finally, it is impressed on human reason on the one hand, and produces the nature of things and their activity on the other.[128] At this point, the influence of Avicenna is dawning, discernible at least to us who know the Arabian doctrine.

From William of St. Thierry to St. Bonaventure

Another line of development, roughly contemporaneous with the preceding, is to be found, not, however, completely out of contact with it. William of St. Thierry (born about 1085, died 1148), was a friend of St. Bernard of Clairvaux and an energetic exponent of the excellence of the monastic way of life. But this did not mean that he had no interest at all in learning or in the activities

---

126. Cf. supra, and *ibid.*, c. 10, no. 15, p. 45.
127. "Constat vero, et ab Aristotele in libro de anima demonstratum est, intellectum corporeo instrumento non uti. Is animam rationalem individua societate necessario inhabitat. Huius domicilium cor esse superius ostensum est. Ipsum ergo mediante anima intellectui sacratum erit domicilium, ut perturbationi affectuum, quae quidem a corde prorumpit rationemque perturbat, impassibile et omni corporea contagione liberrimum remedium assisteret. Ideoque et bruta, quantaecumque sint astutiae, cum intellectus activi non illustrentur acmine, ad rationis apicem non conscendunt," *ibid.*, c. 15, no. 9, pp. 82-83.
128. See "Haec [venerabilis exempli norma] in ipso ab ipso non discrepat; effluens intelligentiam perficit; derivata intellectus fit forma; relata rationi imprimitur, multorum imaginaria resultatione in generis aut speciei essentiam distributa; generata motui ministrat et naturae," *ibid.*, c. 15, no. 1, pp. 75-76. C. Baeumker, *ad locum*, note 4, identifies the phrase "venerabilis exempli norma" as a quotation from Chalcidius's version of the *Timaeus*, 29A.

of his fellow men. In his *De Natura Corporis et Animae,* William reflects his contemporaries like Isaac of Stella and William of Conches, as well as his predecessors like Cassiodorus and St. Augustine.[129]

William holds the theory of the three powers of the soul: natural, spiritual, and animal.[130] In the discussion of the third, or animal, power, he adds to the theory of "spirit-intermediaries" the further complication of "officers" (the organs and nerves), which are the instruments of the spirits.[131] He makes reason, imagination, and memory to be equally mediated by the human brain.[132] Logically he must deny to animals both memory and

---

129. Cf. K. Werner, *Der Entwickelungsgang der mittelalterlichen Psychologie,* pp. 21-25.
130. "Tres quippe sunt virtutes in corporis regimine. Virtus autem est habitus operationis in membro ad id quod efficitur. Quae alia naturalis in epate, alia spiritualis in corde, alia animalis in cerebro," *De Natura Corporis et Animae,* I, PL CLXXX. 700; "Virtus naturalis communis arboribus, bestiis, et hominibus. Virtus spiritualis bestiis et hominibus; virtus animalis animalibus similiter in quibusdam, in quibusdam non. Nam phantasiam et memoriam perfecte non potest habere nisi animal rationale," *ibid.*
131. "Ipse vero [spiritus] transit ad puppis ventriculos per viam mediam prorae et puppis, et memoriam et motum ibi facit; sicut in prora phantasiam et sensum. Est autem prora anterior pars cerebri in anteriori parte capitis locata, puppis vero posterior pars cerebri in posteriore parte capitis posita. Unaquaeque autem quasi proprium domicilium quemdam habet ventriculum, in quo virtus sua continetur, inter quos medius ventriculus rationem continet et intellectum," *ibid., col.* 702.
132. "Et sciendum quia cerebrum per se quaedam facit, quaedam per officiales suos. Rationem in medio positam, sicut reginam et dominam, qua distamus a bestiis, phantasiam in prora, memoria in puppe per se facit; animalem autem virtutem, id est sensum, in prora, motum autem in puppe, alterum per quinque sensus, alterum per nervos a puppe procedentes. Quod autem per se facere dicimus rationem, memoriam, et phantasiam, cum etiam in brutis animalibus esse videantur phantasia et memoria, sicut sensus et motus (alioqui nec canis dominum suum recognosceret, nec avis ad suum nidum rediret), sciendum est nec memoriam eis in esse nec phantasiam, sed inesse eis tanto majorem vim sensuum, aut usum sensualium actionum quanto anima eorum a ratione est aliena, suo

imagination, and in fact he admits only that they have a "greater power of sense."[133] It seems that in this William has not solved, but only restated his problem.

Hugh of St. Victor, who died in 1141, was the prior of the Abbey of St. Victor, and the main reason for the renown of the school. In his power of organizing the matter of which he treats, he could be ranked with the great thirteenth century masters.

At times, Hugh is content to restate the view of his predecessors. For example, he has a lengthy quotation from Boethius on the powers of the soul;[134] he repeats the Platonic tripartite division of soul.[135] In various discussions, Hugh divides the powers of the soul, in general, into cognition and affection;[136] the cognitive powers he further divides into intelligence, imagination, and sense.[137] Sense life has four degrees: external sensation, imagination, memory, and "providence without the discretion of intelli-

---

corpori tota dedita et affixa. . . . Hunc autem spiritualem quidam philosophi animam esse dicebant, qui corpoream animam esse volebant. . . . Sive igitur virtus naturalis, sive animalis, sive spiritualis, non sunt anima, sed animae instrumentum. . . . Diximus quia transiens spiritus spiritualis in posteriorem cerebri puppim, memoriam in eo operatur et motum; memoriam per se, motum per officiales suos, nervi, sicut in anteriori prora phantasiam per se, sensum per officiales suos qui sunt quinque sensus," *ibid.,* col. 702-03.

133. See note 132 *supra.*
134. *Didascalion,* I, c. 1, contains an exact quotation of Boethius, *Commentarium in Porphyrium a se Translatum,* bk. I, PL LXIV. 71, which is quoted above in note 67; in the edition of Brother Charles H. Buttimer, F.S.C., (Washington: Catholic University Press, 1939), pp. 7-9.
    On Hugh's psychological doctrines, see K. Werner, *Der Entwickelungsgang der mittelalterlichen Psychologie,* pp. 33-41; Heinrich Ostler, *Die Psychologie des Hugo von St. Viktor* (Beitraege, Baeumker, Muenster: Aschendorff, Band VI, Heft 1, 1906); John P. Kleinz, *The Theory of Knowledge of Hugh of Saint Victor* (Washington: Catholic University Press, 1944), pp. 20-24, 36-40.
135. Cf. *Didascalion,* II, c. 4, ed. C. Buttimer, p. 28.
136. Cf. *Homiliae* 19. *in Ecclesiasten,* hom. 2; PL CLXXV. 141C.
137. Cf. *Didascalion,* II, c. 5, p. 29.

gence."[138] Just what this fourth degree might be is left unexplained. Above sense,[139] there is rational life, which takes place on three levels or "visions": cogitation, meditation, contemplation.[140] The first term, which has a bearing on the philological side of this investigation, is thus explained:

> Cogitation takes place, when the mind is touched in passing by the notion of things, when the thing itself in its image is suddenly presented to the soul, either entering by the sense, or arising from the memory.

None of the three terms seem to refer to powers; rather, they appear to be three different ways of acting of the one power, reason. The problem of the origin of knowledge, which occurs to a modern reader of the text just quoted immediately and irresistibly, does not seem to have been present to Hugh's mind at all.

Hugh differs from many of the other Augustinians (for example, William of St. Thierry) in making a sharp distinction between reason and imagination. The latter power, which animals also have, is simply a very refined form of that fiery power which is the medium of sensation. On this account, it is "outside the substance of the soul."[141] The difficulties raised by Hugh's posi-

---

138. "Primus enim gradus corporae vitae est sensificatio; secundus per sensum ingrediens imaginatio; tertius per imaginationem conceptorum memoria; quartus secundum possibilem applicationem sensus quaedam sine intelligentiae discretione providentia. In qua quidem quasi rationis imago est, sed ratio nulla est," *Expositio in Hierarchiam Caelestem S. Dionysii,* IX, c. 13, PL CLXXV. 1119A.

139. Hugh frequently uses this term to mean "the power of sensation." Sometimes, however, he uses it in the wide meaning we have become familiar with; cf. for example: "Sic itaque una creatura cujus totus sensus intus erat, et alia creatura erat cujus sensus totus foris erat. Et positus est in medio homo ut intus et foris sensum haberet, intus per sensum rationis, foris per sensum carnis," *De Sacramentis,* I, pars 6, c. 5, PL CLXXVI. 266C-D.

140. See *Homiliae 19 in Ecclesiasten,* hom. 1, PL CLXXV. 116D. This is based on St. Augustine, *De Genesi ad Litteram,* XII. 24. 50.

141. "Ipsa utique vis ignea, quae extrinsicus formata sensus dicitur, eadem forma usque ad intimum traducta imaginatio vocatur. Forma namque rei sensibilis per radios visionis foris concepta . . . per septem oculorum tunicas . . . transiens, novissime purificata et

tion seem to be about as great as those which he has solved.
Richard of St. Victor, who died in 1173, succeeded Hugh as
Prior of the Abbey and head of the school. In his spirit of devo-
tion and his rich Biblical imagery, he follows a path of his own
in the theory and art of contemplation. In matters of doctrine, he
follows Hugh of St. Victor rather closely. Thus, he adverts to the
theory of the instrumentality and localization of "spirits."[142] His
terminology, too, recalls Hugh as well as St. Augustine; thus, he
speaks of the "sense of the flesh" which is wholly exterior, and the
"sense or eye of the heart" which is wholly interior.[143]

According to Richard, the soul has four powers of knowing,
sense, imagination, reason, and intelligence.[144] This is the Boethian

---

collata introrsum ad cerebrum usque traducitur et imaginatio efficitur. Postea eadem imaginatio ab anteriore parte capitis ad mediam transiens, ipsam animae rationalis substantiam contingit, et
excitat discretionem, in tantum jam purificata et subtilis effecta,
ut ipsi spiritui immediate conjungitur, veraciter tamen naturam
corporis retinens et proprietatem. . . . Quod enim imaginatio extra
substantiam animae rationalis sit, argumentum est quod bruta animalia vim imaginandi habere probantur, quae rationem omnino
non habent. . . . Sensus . . . formam . . . intrinsicus reducens . . .
ad cellam phantasticam colligit . . . imaginationem facit. Quae
quidem imaginatio in brutis animalibus phantasticam cellam non
transcendit, in rationalibus autem usque ad rationalem progredi-
tur," De Unione Corporis et Spiritus, PL CLXXVII. 287B-288A.

142. "Nam, ut secundum physicos de his aliquid loquar, sicut sedem
habet in capite spiritus animalis, et in hepate spiritus naturalis,
sic sedem sortitur in corde spiritus vitalis," De Statu Interioris
Hominis, tract. 1, c. 7, PL CXCVI. 1120.
    On the psychology of Richard of St. Victor, cf. J. Ebner, Die
Erkenntnisslehre des Richards von St. Viktor (Beitraege, Baeumker, Muenster: Aschendorff, Band XIX, Heft 4, 1917); and É.
Gilson, La Philosophie au Moyen Age, pp. 306-08.

143. "Visibilia enim solus intuetur sensus carnis, invisibilia vero solus
oculus cordis. Est ergo sensus carnis totus extrinsicus, sensus
vero cordis totus intrinsecus," Benjamin Minor, c. 3, PL CXCVI.
4-5.

144. Cf.: "Absque dubio sensus carnis sensum cordis in cognoscendis
rebus praecedit," Benjamin Major, III, c. 17, col. 96C; "Ecce tria
ista, imaginatio, ratio, intelligentia. Intelligentia obtinet supremum
locum, imaginatio infimum, ratio medium," ibid., I, c. 3, col. 67A.

four power theory. Richard uses this theory in his own way. The imagination is the power[145] of receiving, composing, and even creating images.[146] The "animal" imagination is this power working by itself;[147] it can also be under the disposition and control of both reason and intelligence.[148] Reason is the power of discerning[149] the things pertaining to ourselves (that is, as creatures in a corporeal world).[150] Reason needs the imagination in order to know anything at all.[151] Intelligence, on the contrary,

---

145. "Imaginatio ergo, quando instrumentum significat, est vis illa animae qua cum voluerit quodlibet imaginari valet. Hoc instrumento cum ad aliquid imaginandum mens utitur, actio procul dubio quaedam efficitur, quae similiter imaginatio nominatur," *Benjamin Minor*, c. 17, col. 12B.

146. "Quid his facit phantasmatum corporalium creatrix, moderatrix, et reparatrix imaginatio?", *Benjamin Major*, III, c. 1, col. 109B; "Quidquid a foris animus per auditum haurit, quidquid ab intus ex sola cogitatione concipit, totum imaginatio absque mora et omni difficultate seposita per representationem format," *ibid.*, c. 2, col. 130B.

147. "Bestialis itaque imaginatio est, quando per ea quae paulo ante vidimus vel facimus, sine ulla utilitate, absque omni deliberatione huc illucque vaga mente discurrimus. Haec utique bestialis est, nam et hoc bestia facere potest," *Benjamin Minor*, c. 16, col. 11C.

148. "Sed rationalis imaginatio alia est per rationem disposita, alia intelligentiae permista. Illa utimur quando secundum visibilium rerum cognitam speciem visibile aliud aliquid mente disponimus, nec tamen ex eo invisibile aliquid cogitamus. Ista vero tunc utimur, quando per visibilium rerum speciem ad invisibilium cognitionem ascendere nitimur. In illa est imaginatio non sine ratione, in ista intelligentia non sine imaginatione," *Benjamin Minor*, c. 18, PL CXCVI. 12C.

149. "Non est sensualitatis, nec imaginationis, non denique ipsius affectionis, sed solius est rationis discernere sicut et intelligere," *Benjamin Minor*, c. 67, col. 48D; cf. *De Emmanuele Libri Duo*, II, c. 9, col. 644D; *Adnotationes Mysticae in Psalmos*, Ps. 121, col. 363B-D.

150. "Sensum rationalem dicimus, quo nostra discernimus, intellectualem hoc loco dicimus, quo ad divinorum speculationem sublevamur," *Nonnullae Allegoriae Tabernaculi Foederis*, col. 191D.

151. "Sine imaginatione ratio nihil sciret," *Benjamin Minor*, c. 5, col. 4; "Nisi prius sensibilia per sensum corporeum animus caperet, om-

contemplates Divine things and has no dependence on, nor any admixture with, the imagination.[152] This power is now hindered by sin.[153]

Richard weaves this structure of the soul into a theory of mysticism. In this latter we are interested only to the extent that certain terms pertinent to our subject are used.

In cogitation there is wandering; in meditation, investigation; in contemplation, admiration. Cogitation is from imagination; meditation from reason; contemplation from intelligence. . . . Cogitation always goes from one thing to another in vagrant fashion; meditation perseveringly attends to some one thing; contemplation, under one medium of vision, pours itself out over innumerable things.[154]

According to this, Richard uses the term "cogitation" to express a certain type of activity of the human soul. Cogitation is more than a mere play of images, since such an activity is possible to the brute. It seems to be a kind of knowledge of material things in which the uncontrolled play of the imagination is the chief factor.

---

nino non inveniret quod de eis saltem cogitare potuisset," *Benjamin Major,* III, c. 17, col. 96C.

152. Cf. note 150; "Cogitat per imaginationem, qui necdum videre valet per intelligentiae puritatem," *Benjamin Minor,* c. 14, PL CXCVI. 10; "Comprehensio siquidem rerum invisibilium pertinet ad intelligentiam puram. . . . Intelligentiam puram dicimus, quae est sine admistione imaginationis," *ibid.,* c. 87, col. 62D.

153. "Intellectualis ille sensus invisibilia capit, invisibiliter quidem, sed praesentialiter, sed essentialiter. Sed habet sane oculus hic intellectualis ante se velum magnum expansum ex peccati delectatione fuscatum," *Benjamin Major,* III, c. 9, col. 119A.

154. *Benjamin Minor,* c. 3, col. 67A-C. Text in Appendix II, no. 9. Cf. "Cogitatio autem est improvidus animi respectus ad evagationem pronus," *ibid.,* c. 4, col. 68A; "In prima quidem [speculatione] cogitatio quo eam ducit admiratio solam sequitur imaginationem; in hac autem ipsa imaginatio formatur, disponitur, et moderatur per rationem. . . . Sicut itaque in priori imaginatio post se cogitationem trahit, sic in ista ratio imaginationem circumducit atque disponit. Idcirco autem utraque in imaginatione consistere dicitur, quia circa illam quidem utraque per intentionem vel investigationem occupatur," *Benjamin Major,* II, c. 11, col. 89C-D; the list of degrees mentioned in this text is given in I, c. 6, col. 70.

St. Bonaventure might well seem out of place in this group. His life-span (1221-1274) puts him considerably later than the others, and at this period of history, events in the intellectual world moved rapidly. The world in which this General of the Franciscans and Cardinal of the Church moved was in many ways another world. The Seraphic Doctor knew the whole Avicennan doctrine and even the details of the Avicennan sense psychology. Moreover, his style of writing and the subtlety of his reasoning are peculiarly his own.

In spite of the historical situation and his individual traits, St. Bonaventure is an Augustinian and a contemplative. The lines that bind him to St. Augustine and the Victorines, to Boethius and St. Anselm, are strong, and basic to his whole point of view. If his work is compared with that of Alexander of Hales and Jean de la Rochelle (see Chapter Four), it will be evident that, at least as far as the theory of sensation is concerned, St. Bonaventure belongs, not with his contemporaries, but with men like Hugh and William.

Let us see what he has to say about internal senses. In speaking of the ascent of the mind to God, he says:

> For in the soul there are many apprehending powers: the sensitive, the imaginative, the estimative, the intellective, and all of them we must leave behind.[155]

But a diligent search through the works fails to reveal any other reference to the estimative, or any designation of its function.[156] The other internal senses are spoken of more fully. Common sense follows the special senses[157] and has the special function of sen-

---

155. *Collationes in Hexaemeron,* coll. 2, no. 27 (*Opera Omnia,* Quaracchi: 1882-1902: 10 vols.) vol. V, p. 341. Text in Appendix II, no. 10.

156. The same negative result has been reached by E. Lutz, *Die Psychologie Bonaventuras* (Muenster: 1909), and Bonifaz Anton Luyckx, O.P., *Die Erkenntnislehre Bonaventuras* (Beitraege, Baeumker, Muenster: Aschendorff, 1923, Band XXIII, Heft 3).

The *Compendium Veritatis Theologicae,* a work frequently attributed to St. Albert the Great, (but really written by one of his disciples, Hugo), has also been attributed to St. Bonaventure. In this work, the estimative power is referred to II, ch. 38.

157. *In Hex.,* coll. 22, no. 35, vol. V, p. 442; *in IV Sent.,* d. 12, p. 1, dub. 1, vol. IV, p. 286.

sory consciousness.[158] The imagination retains images;[159] its mode of apprehension is more abstract than that of the exterior senses.[160] Phantasms excite the intellect to knowledge, and, as long as the soul is within the body, the intellect somehow depends on the imagination and the animal spirits.[161] In addition, the imagination has the power of composing images.

> By the sensitive power [the soul] apprehends sensible things; retains what it has apprehended; composes and divides what it has retained. It apprehends by the exterior sensitive power divided into five parts in correspondence with the five principal bodies of the world; it retains by the memory; it composes and divides by the phantasy, which is the first comparative power.[162]

The function of memory is to retain and represent the past.[163]

Thus, by way of scattered phrases, St. Bonaventure shows that he did know the theories about internal sensation. But there seems to be no value in all this for him. He accepts these and kindred doctrines without delaying over them. In a word, they are not the truth that St. Bonaventure is interested in.

CONCLUSIONS

The immediate influence of the Aristotelian analysis seems to have been very short-lived. Though the soul was often a topic of discussion, there was little concern with a philosophical analysis

---

158. *In V Sent.,* d. 50, p. 2, a. 1, q. 1, vol. IV, p. 1045; *in I Sent.,* d. 17, p. 1, q. 2, ad 4, vol. I, p. 297.

159. *In III Sent.,* d. 14, a. 3, q. 2, ad opp. 5, vol. III, p. 321.

160. "Concreta est [species] prout apprehenditur a sensu exteriori, licet sit ibi aliqua abstractio; simpliciter abstracta, prout apprehenditur ab intellectu, medio modo, prout apprehenditur imaginatione," *in III Sent.,* d. 23, dub. 4, vol. III, p. 504; cf. *in II Sent.,* d. 24, p. 1, q. 4, ad 2, vol. II, p. 570.

161. *In II Sent.,* d. 25, p. 2, q. 6, vol. II, pp. 622-23, and ad obj., *ibid.,* p. 624.

162. *Breviloquium,* part 2, c. 9, vol. V, p. 227. Text in Appendix II, no. 11.

163. *In I Sent.,* d. 3, p. 2, a. 1, q. 1 ad 3, vol. I, p. 81; *in II Sent.,* d. 7, p. 2, a. 1, q. 2 ad 3, vol. II, p. 193; *Itinerarium,* c. 3, no. 2, vol. V, p. 303,

of sense-life and its powers. A high point in such analysis was reached by St. Augustine. But this work was based on a Platonic point of view (that sensation is an activity of the soul, not an operation of the composite), and was carried on without any clear notion of a *power*. And for the most part, even this discussion was forgotten by the Augustinians.

What mention there was of internal powers occurred from two points of view. The first was that of the experimental, "medical" localization of powers. The second was that of speculative mysticism, concerned with the grades of ascent to contemplation. In this latter, a discussion of sensory powers was almost incidental. The one important and consistently found element was the notion of "instrument." Here, there is, first, the fundamental notion that a power of knowing can act through an instrument. There is, secondly, the doctrine that differences in type of activity can be explained by the assumption of different instruments.

The first outside influences were those of the Greek and Arabian medical treatises. With them, an interest in brain physiology arose. Powers began to be discussed at much greater length, not from the functional, but from the local point of view. In this later development, there was no properly psychological discussion of internal powers.

CHAPTER 3

JEWISH AND ARABIAN PHILOSOPHERS

Aristotle was the first systematically to describe and analyze human knowledge, its processes and its powers. For twelve centuries after him, no comparable effort was made. Occasionally important doctrines were expressed, but even in these cases, they were rather incidental to the purpose of the work in which they appeared.

From the tenth to the twelfth centuries there was a philosophical resurgence in the Arabic world, and men again became interested in attacking problems for their own sake. These years witnessed careful work that in some instances is of very high quality. Our main concern with this large mass of material is the presentation of sources for St. Thomas's doctrine of the *vis cogitativa*. To complete the picture, it will be necessary to include a few works which were not available to the thirteenth century Latin world.

Isaac Israeli

Isaac was the first of a long and distinguished series of philosophical physicians. During the ninth and tenth centuries, he had a successful career as court physician in North Africa. His medical and philosophical writings were particularly influential in the Arabic world.

In his philosophical writings, Isaac touches on the powers of the soul. Though he continues the Galenic tradition, he has amplified the theory. In the Galenic formula, the Aristotelian "common sense" was not considered. Isaac takes recognition of it by putting common sense as a power between the external and the internal senses.[1] According to his conception, the principal function of

---

1. Harry Austryn Wolfson, "Isaac Israeli on the Internal senses," *Jewish Studies in Memory of George Kohut* (New York, 1935), p. 584.
"Cum sit [sensus communis] inter sensum visibilem scilicet corporeum et informatum qui est in anteriori parte cerebri nominatum

common sense is to convey corporeal characteristics from the sight to the imagination.[2] That this conception is quite different from Aristotle's is evident.

There are three strictly internal powers according to Isaac: imagination, cognition, and memory.[3] The first and third of these powers are of no particular interest here. The word *cognition* as a technical term in this matter has been met before in the Latin translation of Nemesius and St. John Damascene. A brief look at the functions of this power will enable us to determine the genesis of the term, its meaning, and its Greek equivalent. The functions of cognition are:[4] *discernere*,[5] *discretio, interpretatio et discretio, perscrutatio*.[6] It is an intelligible power, one of the powers of the rational soul.[7]

These are the functions of the Galenic διανοητικόν (cogitative) as we find them described in Nemesius-Damascene. It is therefore quite proper to conclude both to the source and the original Greek equivalent of the term.

If *discretio* (judgment, discernment) is a function of reason,

---

phantasia, et propter hoc nominatur sensus communis," *Liber de Elementis,* 2, fol. 9ra, in Harry Austryn Wolfson, "The Internal Senses in Latin, Arabic, and Hebrew Philosophic Texts," *Harvard Theological Review,* XXVIII (1935), p. 95, note 28.

2. H. A. Wolfson, "Isaac Israeli," pp. 584-85.
3. *Ibid.,* p. 587.
4. *Ibid.,* p. 591.
5. "Cogitationis enim est perscrutari et discernere et componere," *Liber de Elementis,* 2, fol. 9ra in H. Wolfson, "The Internal Senses," p. 83, and *idem,* "Isaac Israeli," p. 588.
6. "Intellectualis sensus, qui est interpretatio et discretio et perscrutatio et solutio et ligatio et cognitio rerum secundum veritate," *Ibid.,* 3, fol. 10ra, in H. Wolfson, "The Internal Senses," p. 83, and *idem,* "Isaac Israeli," p. 588.
   Note the expression: "intellectualis sensus."
7. "Definicio cogitacionis: cogitacio est virtus intelligibilis procedens in rebus quoniam cogitacio est una de virtutibus animae racionalis et propter hoc factus est omnis cogitans racionalis," *Isaac Israeli Liber de Definicionibus,* ed. J. T. Muckle, C.S.B., *Archives d'Histoire Doctrinale et Littéraire du Moyen Age,* vol. XI (1937-1938), p. 321, lines 8-11.

how will the actions of animals be accounted for? We have seen
other cases where this function was completely denied to animals.
Isaac's text shows that he encounters similar difficulties in the explanation of animal activity.

> Inferior to the rational soul in the brightness and excellence
> of its order, is the animal soul, for it is born of the rational
> soul, and for this reason is removed from the splendor of in-
> telligence and acquires shadow and darkness. It is deprived
> of the power of examination and discretion; it is made estima-
> tive in reality, and is meditative only metaphorically. For
> it judges about a thing from appearances, not from the side
> of truth. Its properties are sense and movement and local
> change, and for this reason animals are bold in great audacity,
> seeking victory and domination; like the lion which seeks
> domination over other animals without investigation and dis-
> cretion and knowledge of what it is doing. What we see ex-
> emplified in the ass, proves that animals are estimating and
> not discerning beings. . . . They are deprived of investigation
> and discretion and the perception of the truth of things and
> . . . their properties are estimation and meditation.[8]

> The definition of estimation. Estimation is a power pro-
> ceeding in impossibilities. It is said that estimation is a judg-
> ment about a thing from appearance, not from the side where
> truth lies. And for this reason, animals are made estimating
> beings, and not meditating ones, unless this latter be said
> of them by accommodation and metaphor.[9]

A beast has sense and motion, especially local motion. But it has
no investigation, nor discretion, nor knowledge of what it is doing.
Beasts have "reason" or "discernment" only metaphorically. Their
lack of reason is expressed by calling them estimating beings. Isaac
gives a number of illustrations about the donkey, all of which intend to show that this animal acts foolishly and to its own disad-
vantage.

This is confirmed by the definition of "estimation" as a power
"which acts in impossibilities." Still further confirmation is given

---

8. *Ibid.,* "Sermo de Anima," *ed. cit.,* pp. 314-315. Latin text in Appendix II, no. 12.
9. *Ibid., ed. cit.,* p. 324, lines 9-15. Latin text in Appendix II, no. 13.

by what is said about "meditation — *meditari*" which is a standard translation for διανοεῖσθαι.

Apparently then animals have only two internal senses. What seems to be their third power, namely, estimation, really expresses a kind of vacancy in the animal soul. As an explanation of animal activity, this is unsatisfactory. A further difficulty with the list of human powers is the original difficulty of the Galenic division, that of placing reason on a par with two sense powers.

ABRAHAM IBN-DAUD

Of this man we know very little. He is mentioned only because he has a special way of numbering the powers: common sense, imagination, and reason (or phantasy).[10] It is not possible to tell exactly what these various terms mean, but they would seem to derive directly from Aristotle, without any influence from the Galenic tradition.

MOSES MAIMONIDES (1135-1204)

Maimonides was perhaps the most influential Jewish writer in the Arabic world. His main interest lay in helping his compatriots to maintain their faith and culture in an alien and hostile environment. Consequently, he has little space to spare for such parts of philosophy as do not contribute to this purpose. For this reason, his treatment of the powers of the soul is brief and incidental.

Maimonides gives a preliminary general classification of powers into vegetative, sensitive, imaginative, motive, rational.[11] This, in a general sort of way, is equivalently a list of the topics treated by Aristotle in the *De Anima*. In other connections, Moses classifies

10. S. Horovitz, *Die Psychologie bei den juedischen Religionsphilosophen des Mittelalters* (Breslau: Schatzky, 1912), Band IV, Heft 4, pp. 242-50.
11. Simon B. Scheyer, *Das psychologische System des Maimonides* (Frankfurt: Kessler, 1845), p. 10. S. Scheyer does not go into further details. A. Cohen, *The Teachings of Maimonides* (London: Routledge, 1927), has translations of the pertinent passages, pp. 242-44.

the interior faculties as imagination, cogitation, understanding.[12] This is a variation on the so-called Galenic formula.

Maimonides's discussion of the imagination is better than that of Isaac. The imagination is given some of the functions that were later to be assigned to the estimative.[13] In this there is an approach to Aristotle, and consequently a better explanation of animal activity.

DE DIFFERENTIA ANIMAE ET SPIRITUS

In the second quarter of the twelfth century, John of Spain translated the De Differentia Animae ot Spiritus, which is traditionally ascribed to Costa-ben-Luca, a Syrian physician. The Middle Ages more often called him Constabulinus, sometimes Constabulus.

The influence of this work was great, and references were often made to it. It contains a detailed exposition of the theory of "spirit"-intermediaries, after the manner of Galen. Through this theory a classification and a localization of interior powers is developed.

> The brain is divided into its divisions, of which one is in front, and is the larger, and the other is in the rear. In the front division there are two ventricles having an opening to a common space which is in the middle of the brain.[14]
> In the passage and road, that is, in the entrance through which the breath ["spirit"] passes, there is a space and a little particle of the body of the brain, like a worm, which is lifted up and let down in the path. When this particle is lifted up, the hole is opened. . . . When therefore the hole is open, the breath passes from the front of the brain to the rear, and this does not happen except when it is necessary to remember some thing which was given over to forgetfulness at the time when thought is being taken about past things.[15]

---

12. Harry Austryn Wolfson, "Maimonides on the Internal Senses," *Jewish Quarterly Review,* new series, XXV (1935), pp. 441-42.
13. *Ibid.,* pp. 456-59.
14. *Costa-Ben Luca, De Differentia Animae et Spiritus,* tr. a Johanne Hispalensi, ed. by Carl Sigmund Barach (Innsbruck: Wagner, 1878, "Bibliotheca Philosophorum Mediae Aetatis"), ch. 2, p. 124. Latin Text in Appendix II, no. 14.
15. *Ibid.,* ch. 2, p. 125. Latin text in Appendix II, no. 15.

The breath which is in the front ventricles produces the senses, that is, sight, hearing, taste, touch, and smell, and with these produces the *acagum* which the Greeks call phantasy. The breath which is in the middle ventricle produces thought and knowledge and providence. The breath which is in the rear ventricle produces memory and movement.[16]

In the preceding chapter we have seen the Galenic sources for this doctrine.[17] There is nothing particularly original about it, but it is worked out in great detail. For example, the author tells us that when men are puzzled, they shake their heads in order to loosen the little trap door of memory. This mechanical type of "explanation" delights certain temperaments. In addition to this, the *De Differentia* furnished some very convenient definitions, and so was frequently adduced in arguments.

AL-FARABI

Al-Farabi, who was born of Turkish stock in Turkestan, lived from 870 to 950. He studied mathematics, medicine, and philosophy at Bagdad, paying particular attention to the works of Aristotle. The main part of his work was done at Damascus. He was the first of the great Arabian philosophers, and his interpretation of Aristotle gave the impetus to Avicenna's work. His influence on the Latin West was mostly indirect, completely so with respect to the doctrines in which we are interested here.

The work of Al-Farabi marks a great forward step in the doctrine of internal powers of knowledge. He is the first to point out a definite faculty of sensory discernment of good and evil,

---

16. *Ibid.*, ch. 2, p. 130. Latin text in Appendix II, no. 16.

Max Horten, *Die philosophischen Systeme der spekulativen Theologen in Islam* (Bonn: Cohen, 1912), pp. 181-83, interprets the three functions of the middle chamber as: (1) *cogitativa,* similar to the combining imagination; (2) "Unterscheidung," as distinguishing of good and evil, true and false, useful and harmful, and thus as somehow foreshadowing the *vis aestimativa,* and (3) *ratio particularis,* "partikulaeres Erkennen," and so again as a prelude to Al-Farabi.

17. Cf. Chapter 2, notes 41-43 and 110.

and to call it the "estimative sense."[18] It is true that the term
was also used by Isaac Israeli. But the Jewish philosopher had not
used it in a positive technical sense, nor did he mention it when
enumerating the internal powers.

It is frequently said that Al-Farabi's doctrine here was a simple
combination of the Aristotelian powers of common sense, imagination, memory and δόξα with the Galenic imagination, reason, and
memory.[19] This would give the following composite list: (1) common sense, (2) imagination, (3) δόξα (on the sense level), (4)
reason (on the higher level), and (5) memory. The Greek term
would then be represented by *aestimatio* in the Latin version and
wahm in the Arabic.[20] Professor H. A. Wolfson has devoted much
of his attention to the refutation of this derivation.[21] According
to him, δόξα does not appear either in the Galenic tripartite division, nor in that of Al-Farabi-Avicenna. In the former case,
cogitatio translates διάνοια; in the latter, *cogitatio* translates
φαντασία λογιστική (or some equivalent)[22] and "estimation"

---

18. S. Horovitz, *Die Psychologie bei den juedischen Religionsphilo-
    sophen des Mittelalters,* p. 241; Fr. Robert Hanui, O.F.M., *Alfa-
    rabi's Philosophy and its Influence on Scholasticism* (Sydney: Pelle-
    grini, 1928), p. 63; H. Wolfson, "Isaac Israeli," p. 595.
19. For example, S. Horovitz, *Die Psychologie bei den juedischen Re-
    ligionsphilosophen des Mittelalters,* pp. 241-42.
20. For example, Baron Carra de Vaux, *Avicenne* (Paris: Alcan, 1900),
    p. 216; Ludwig Baur, *Dominicus Gundissalinus, De Divisione Philo-
    sophiae* (Beitraege, Baeumker, Band IV, Heft 2-3, Muenster: Aschen-
    dorff, 1903), p. 224; S. Landauer, "Die Psychologie des Ibn Sinâ,"
    Zeitschrift der deutschen Morgenlaendischen Gesellschaft (Leipzig)
    XXIX (1925), pp. 400-02; R. Hanui, *Alfarabi's Philosophy and its
    Influence on Scholasticism,* p. 63; Arthur Schneider, *Die Psycho-
    logie Alberts des Grossen* (Beitraege, Baeumker, Muenster: Aschen-
    dorff, Band IV, Heft 5-6, 1903-1906), p. 155, note 1.
    In a work which appeared after the masterly study of Wolfson,
    the notion that the estimative is opinion is still asserted by G.
    Quadri, *La philosophie Arabe dans l'Europe médiévale,* tr. by Roland
    Huret (Paris: Payot, 1947), p. 111.
21. H. A. Wolfson, "Maimonides on the Internal Senses," p. 454; "The
    Internal Senses," pp. 86-91.
22. H. Wolfson, "Isaac Israeli," p. 587; R. Hanui, *Alfarabi's Philosophy
    and its Influence on Scholasticism,* p. 63, note.

(wahm) translates χρίνειν.[23] It remains to be seen whether the doctrinal study will bear out the conclusion based on the study of terms.

Al-Farabi was not altogether consistent in his classification of the internal powers.[24] There is a list of five powers: imagination, estimation, memory, compositive human imagination, and compositive animal imagination.[25] It is important to note that "memory"

---

23. As can easily be concluded from passages like this: "Das tierische Tun besteht in der Herbeiziehung des Nuetzlichen, wie dies die Begierde verlangt, und in dem Wegstossen des Schaedlichen, so wie dies die Furcht erheischt, und den Zorn ueber ihn waltet. Dies gehoert auch zu den Kraeften des menschlichen Geistes," *Die Petschafte der Weisheitslehre* (Gems of Wisdom), tr. by Friederich Dieterici, *Alfarabi's Philosophische Abhandlungen* (Leiden: Brill, 1892), pp. 119-20.

24. H. Wolfson, "The Internal Senses," pp. 94-95.

25. *Risâlat fusus al Hukmun,* no. 36: "a) Hinter den aeusseren Sinnen liegt es wie Netze und Fallen, um die Bilder, die aeussere Wahrnehmung ergibt, einzufangen. Daraus resultiert erstens eine Kraft, die die "Form-emfangende" [oder activ: Form-bildende] genannt wird und im Vorderteile des Gehirnes ihre Stelle hat. Sie ist es, die die Bilder der Sinnesobjekte festhaelt, nachdem sie ihr nicht mehr gegenuebertreten (Gesichtssinn) noch mit ihr in Verbindung stehen (andere Sinne), und daher entweichen sie aus der aeusseren Wahrnehmung, aber verbleiben in dieser Kraft.

b) Zweitens eine Kraft, die aestimativa (Instinkt, 'Vermutung') genannt wird. Sie erfasst von den objekten das, was durch die aeussere Wahrnehmung nicht ereicht wird. So verhaellt sich die Erkenntniskraft des Schafes. Sie bildet in ihm die Vorstellung der Feindschaft und Bosheit des Wolfes, wenn sein Erkenntnisbild in dem aeusseren Sinne des Schafes erscheint, waehrend der aeussere Sinn allein diese (Vorstellung) nicht erfasst.

c) Drittens eine Kraft, die die Aufbewahrende heisst. Sie ist die Schatzkammer dessen, was die aestimativa erfasst, in gleicher Weise wie die 'Form-emfangende' die Schatzkammer fuer das ist, was der aeussere Sinn wahrnimmt.

d) Viertens eine Kraft, die die 'Nachdenkende' (cogitativa) genannt wird. Sie ist die jenige, die ueber die Residuen beider Schatzkammern, der Formaufnehmenden und des Gedaechtnisses, herrscht und das eine mit dem anderen verbindet oder von ihm trennt. Sie heisst jedoch nur dann nachdenkende, wenn der Geist des Menschen und der Intellekt sie anwendet. Tritt sie aber in die Dienste der

in Al-Farabi and his followers has a very special sense: it is the faculty which retains the knowledge of *estimation*. In all previous uses, memory was the power which retained the forms of either sensation itself or of thought. This function is now designated by the term *imagination*. Estimation, however, is not yet clearly defined. It is said to be the power which grasps in the sensed object something which was not itself sensed. The example given by Al-Farabi is the example of predilection for all his followers: the sheep somehow knows the enmity of the wolf, though it does not sense this.

Again, there is a list of four powers: imagination, estimation, memory, compositive human imagination.[26] At another time, all

aestimativa, so heisst sie (kombinierende) Phantasie (im Gegensatz zu hajâl; bei Avicenna 'vorstellende Phantasie') ;"
No. 42: "Auf der gemeinsamen Grenze der inneren und aeusseren Wahrnehmung befindet sich eine Kraft, die der Sammelort ist fuer die Daten der Sinneswahrnehmung," *Das Buch der Ringsteine Alfarabis*, tr. by Max Horten (Beitraege, Baeumker, Band V, Heft 3, Muenster: Aschendorff, 1906), pp. 24-25, 27. This section is also translated in F. Dieterici, *Alfarabi's Philosophische Abhandlungen*, (and there called "Die Petschafte der Weisheitslehre"), pp. 121-22.
26. "Zu den erfassenden Kraeften der Seele gehoeren ihre hervortretenden Kraefte, sowie die inneren vorstellenden Sinne wie Vermutung, Erinnerung, Nachdenken," *Die Hauptfragen von Abu Nasr Alfarabi* ('Unyn al-Musâi'il) No. 20, F. Dieterici, *Alfarabi's Philosophische Abhandlungen*, p. 105.
Arthur Schneider, *Die Psychologie Alberts des Grossen* (Beitraege, Baeumker, Band IV, Heft 5-6, Muenster: Aschendorff, 1903, 1906), p. 155, note 1, already noticed a discrepancy between this translation of Dieterici and that of F. August Schmoelders, *Documenta Philosophiae Arabum,* (Bonn: Baaden, 1836), p. 55, and thought that one of the internal senses of Alfarabi had inadvertently been omitted by Dieterici's translation. H. Wolfson, "the Internal Senses," p. 94, note 26, explains that the adjective "hervortretenden" should have been a noun, since it translates the Arabic for "formativa."
F. A. Schmoelder's translation reads: "Viribus sensitivis annumerandae sunt vires externae, varii sensus interni modi, imaginatio scilicet, informatio, recordatio, cogitatio," (*Fontes Quaestionum,* c. 20), p. 55. H. Wolfson, *loc. cit.,* notes the inaccuracy of "informatio" here. Schmoelders himself, pp. 116-17, admitted this; having considered "apprehensio" and "opinio" he concludes that the word

the internal activities are combined in the scope of one power, the imagination.[27] There does not seem to be any reasoned explanation of why there should be different faculties, nor any attempt to explain the variations in the lists. For this, as well as for a more detailed notion of the powers themselves, we must wait for Avicenna.

AVICENNA (IBN-SINA)

In his own day (980-1037) in the Eastern Arabic empire, Avicenna was esteemed both as a physician and an author of medical treatises. He also reached eminence as a biologist and a philosopher. In the range of his knowledge and interest, the Greek spirit seemed to live again. His philosophic work is modeled on that of Aristotle, whom he read through the eyes of Al-Farabi.

In its own right, the *De Anima* of Avicenna reveals him to be a clear and very penetrating thinker, a master of psychological analysis. But the Latins were the more impressed since they did not have the psychological doctrines of Al-Farabi as a background.

---

could not be translated. He adds a definition, taken from the *Ta'reefât* (or *Tarifât*) : *"Informatio [Wahm, estimation] vis est corporis humani, pone medium cerebri ventriculum sedens, quae materiales percipit animae rationes* [part of whose function is to perceive outstanding characteristics] rebus sensibilibus adhaerentes, v.g., Zeidi fortitudinem et liberalitatem. Eadem haec vis in ove deprehenditur, utpote quae lupum fugiat, ad parentem vero propensa sit. Illa omnibus corporeis viribus praeest, earumque opera eodem modo, quo intellectus cunctarum intellectualium facultatum ministerio utitur.*" My italics. The first italicized term is misleading; the second unintelligible. The correct translation, which I owe to the kindness of Dr. Emil L. Fackenheim, is given within brackets. The *Tarifât* has been edited by Fluegel, Leipzig: 1845; on it see Ernest Renan, *Averroès et l'Averroïsme* (Paris: Calmann-Lévy, 1869), pp. 106, 137.

27. "The imaginative faculty is that which retains the impressions of the sensible objects after the latter have disappeared from sense-perception, and combines some of these impressions with others and separates some of them from others. . . . Moreover, to this faculty belongs also the apprehension of that which is beneficial or injurious, pleasant or unpleasant," *Sefer ha-Hath alot,* p. 3, in H. Wolfson, "The Internal Senses," p. 95, note 27.

A convenient approach to the doctrine of Avicenna on the
internal senses is through the text in the *Canon*.²⁸ This work does

28. "De Virtutibus animalibus compraehendentibus.
In virtute autem animali duae copulantur virtutes: quarum ipsa
est sicut genus; una est sicut virtus compraehensiva, et alter [*sic;*
altera] virtus motiva.
Et compraehensiva quidem est, sicut duarum virtutum genus. Una
virtus compraehensiva est manifeste, et altera virtus compraehensiva occulte: et virtus quod manifeste compraehensiva est sensibilis quae est genus secundum quosdam quinque virtutum, et octo
secundum alios. . . . Hoc autem certificare est philosophi.
Et virtus quidem compraehensiva occulte, scilicet animalis, est sicut
genus quinque virtutum. Una est virtus quae vocatur sensus communis
et phantasia, et   apud medicos quidem sunt una virtus, sed apud
certificatores qui sunt ex philosophis, duae sunt virtutes. Sensus
enim communis est illa quae omnia sensu percepta recipit, et ab
eorum formis patitur, quae in ipsa coniunguntur. Phantasia vero est
illa quae eas custodit postquam coniunguntur et retinet eas post sensus absentiam. Et quae harum duarum est recipiens alia est a
custodiente. Hoc autem certificare est philosophi. . . .
Et secundus quidem est virtus quam medici vocant cogitativam.
Sed certificatores vocant quandoque imaginativam, quandoque cogitativam. Si enim administraverit eam seu ea usa fuerit virtus existimativa animalis quam postea nominabimus, aut ex se ipsa promo-
verit ad suam operationem vocant eam imaginativam. Et si virtus
rationalis usa fuerit, et reduxerit eam ad illud quod ei prodest, vocatur
virtus cogitativa. Quocumque tamen modo fuerit, inter hanc virtutem
et prima existit differentia, quod prima est recipiens et custodiens
id quod ad eam pervenit de formis sensu perceptis, et ista est illa
quae se exercet in eis, quae in imaginatione recondita sunt, exercitio
componendi et dividendi, et praesentes sibi efficit formas, quemadmodum perveniunt a sensu et alias formas ab eis diversas, sicut
hominem volare, et montem smaragdinum. Sed phantasia non apprae-
sentat nisi quantum recipit a sensu. Et huius quidem virtutis sedes
est ventriculus cerebri medius, et haec quidem virtus est in animali
est occulta compraehensiva.
Et est existimativa, et ipsa quidem est virtus qua animal iudicat
quod lupus est inimicus, et filius est dilectus, et qui annonam praebere
consuevit est amicus a quo non est fugiendum. Et hoc iudicium secundum modum existit non rationale. Amicitia enim et inimicitia non
sensu animalis sunt perceptae, neque sensus eas compraehendit, neque de eis iudicat, nisi virtus alia, et licet non sit compraehensio
rationalis est tamen proculdubio aliqua appraehensio non rationalis.

not seem to have been used by the thirteenth century Latin philosophical writers. Hence, only a summary of the pertinent passage will be given.

In the brief account in the *Canon,* there is a list of five occult comprehensive powers: common sense, phantasy, imagination-cogitation, existimative sense, memory.

Homo etiam plerumque utitur hac virtute in multis suorum iudiciorum, et procedit in hoc, quemadmodum animal non rationale. Et haec quidem virtus dividitur a phantasia, quoniam phantasia sensu percepta retinet, et haec in perceptis sensu discernit intentiones non sensu perceptas.

Et separatur ab ea quam imaginativam vocamus et cogitativam, quoniam illius operationes nullum sequitur iudicium, sed istius operationes non solum iudicium et etiam iudicia sequuntur. Et illius operationes sunt in sensu perceptis compositionem facere, et istius operatio in sensu perceptis iudicare intentiones non sensatas. Et quemadmodum in animali sensus est iudicans de formis sensu perceptis, similiter existimativa est iudicans de intentionibus illarum formarum, quae ad existimativam perveniunt et non ad sensum. Quidam autem hominum sunt qui praesumunt et hanc virtutem imaginativam vocant, sed tamen non curamus, quia de nominibus non disputamus, sed intentiones et differentias intelligere debemus. . . .

Tertia vero illarum, quas nominant medici, est quinta aut quarta, cum certificaverimus quae est virtus conservativa et memorialis, et est thesaurus eius quod pervenit ad existimativam de intentionibus imperceptis sensu extra formas eorum sensu perceptas, sicut phantasia est thesaurus eius quod pervenit ad sensus ex formis sensu perceptis, et eius quidem locus est posterior cerebri ventriculus. Hic vero est locus considerationis philosophicae, utrum virtus conservativa, et memorialis virtus quae reducit illud quod est absens ad memoriam ex eis quae ab existimativa sunt reposita, sit una virtus aut virtutes duae. Medico tamen non est inde curandum quoniam nocumenta quae eis qualitercumque sint [accidunt] sunt homogenea: sunt enim nocumenta quae in ventriculo cerebri posteriori accidunt, vel de genere complexionis vel de genere compositionis.

Reliqua vero virtus, quae est una de virtutibus animae comprehensivis est humana rationalis. Et quia medici virtutem existimativam non consideraverunt propter causam quam diximus, ideo hanc virtutem non consideraverunt," Avicenna, *Liber Canonis* (Venice: Juntas, 1582), bk. 1, Fen 1, Doctrina 6, c. 5, fol. 27v-28r. A much briefer list of the powers, giving only the names and the localization in the brain, is given in bk. 3, Fen 1, tractate 1, c. 2, fol. 181v.

(1) The common sense merely receives the impressions of the external, manifest senses. It is affected by all the objects of the senses, and they are all joined together in it. This much is very similar to the Aristotelian account of common sense. For Avicenna, its place is in the front ventricle.

(2) The phantasy is that power which retains the sensible forms after they are joined in the common sense, even after the sensible things are no longer present. For the philosopher (*certificator*), phantasy is distinct from common sense, though doctors (and Aristotle, too, in a way) identify them. Its place is likewise in the front ventricle.

(3) The third power is called by doctors the cogitative, but by philosophers it is called sometimes the imaginative, sometimes the cogitative. The power is called the imaginative when it acts by itself, or under the influence of the estimative. It is called the cogitative when under the influence of reason. Its place is in the middle ventricle.

(4) The fourth power is called the estimative (existimative). It is the power of sensible judgment. For example, by it the sheep judges that the wolf is hostile. This power perceives and judges "intentions" which are not sensed. It is distinct from the powers already mentioned, and seems to be located in the middle ventricle.

(5) The fifth power is called conservative or memorial power. Its function is to retain the intentions which had come to the estimative. It is a philosophical problem to decide whether the conservative and the memorial power differ. For the memorial is the power of remembering what had been forgotten. The place of this power (or powers) is in the rear ventricle.

This is a list of strictly sensory powers, as is indicated by the fact that the human reason is explicitly excluded from consideration. For a more detailed account which will give some details which are here left unexplained we must turn to the *De Anima* (*Liber Sextus Naturalium*).

In this work, so widely read and quoted in the Latin world of the Middle Ages, Avicenna begins his discussion of the sensitive soul with the motive power,[29] which is here taken in a wide sense so as to include the appetitive. But the discussion is merely preliminary, doing little more than defining terms and giving definitions. After this introduction, the consideration of the apprehensive powers begins.

> But the apprehensive power is two-fold. For there is one power which apprehends from the outside, another from the inside. The external apprehensive powers are the senses, either five or eight.[30]

This introductory distinction is followed by a detailed consideration of the external senses, which is not important for our present purpose.

When Avicenna turns to discuss the inner powers, he sets down some preliminary distinctions. This passage is important, since it seems to be the only explicit statement of what is meant by the "intention" perceived by some of the interior powers.

> Of the interior apprehensive powers, some apprehend sensible forms, but some apprehend the intentions of sensible things. Of apprehensive powers, there are some which both apprehend and operate, some apprehend and do not operate, some apprehend principally and some secondarily.

---

29. "Anima autem sensibilis vel vitalis secundum modum primum habet duas vires, motivam scilicet at apprehendentem. Sed motiva est duobus modis: quod aut est movens ideo quod imperat motui, aut est movens ideo quia est efficiens motum. Motiva autem secundum quod est imperans motui est vis appetitiva et desiderativa; quae vis, cum imaginetur imaginatione de qua postea dicemus forma quae appetitur aut respuitur, imperat alii virtuti moventi ut moveat. Quae habet duas partes, una quae dicitur vis concupiscibilis, quae est vis imperans moveri, ut appropinquatur ad ea quae putantur necessaria aut utilia appetitui delectamenti; aliam quae vocatur irascibilis, quae est vis imperans moveri ad repellendum id quod putatur nocivum aut corrumpens appetitum vincendi," Avicenna, *De Anima,* part I, c. 5, in *Avicenne perhypatetici philosophi ac medicorum facile primi opera in lucem redacta* (Venice: 1508), fol. 4vb. The *De Anima* of this edition has been reedited by George P. Klubertanz, S.J., (St. Louis: School of Philosophy and Science of Saint Louis University, 1949); in this edition the text just quoted is on page 19. All references to the *De Anima* will give both folio and page references.

30. *Ibid.,* p. 20. Latin text in Appendix II, no. 17.

The difference between apprehending forms and apprehending intentions is this. A form is that which the exterior and interior sense apprehend together; but the exterior sense apprehends it first and then gives it to the interior sense, as when a sheep apprehends the form of a wolf, that is, its shape, and its affection and color. But the exterior sense of the sheep first apprehends this, and then the interior sense.

An intention is that which the soul apprehends about a sensible thing, although the exterior sense does not first apprehend it; as the sheep apprehends the intention which it has about the wolf, that is, that it must fear the wolf and run from it, although the exterior sense does not apprehend this in any way. Now that which the external sense first apprehends about the wolf and then the interior, is properly called in this place by the name of form. But that which the hidden powers apprehend without the sense is properly called in this place by the name of intention.

The difference between apprehending by operating and apprehending by not operating is this. It belongs to the actions of one of the interior powers to put together some known forms and intentions with others, and to separate them. Its characteristic therefore is to apprehend and operate even in that which it apprehends. But to apprehend without operating is this: when the form or intention is only designated in the power, so that it cannot act on it in any way. The difference between apprehending principally and secondarily is this: apprehending principally takes place when the form is acquired by some form of acquisition that belongs to the thing by itself; apprehending secondarily, is the acquisition of a thing from another thing which brings the former along with it.[31]

The most important and interesting of the terms and definitions laid down here is the distinction between form and intention. By "form" Avicenna wishes to designate those aspects in sensible things which both external and internal senses grasp, for example, shape and color. An "intention" is that concerning a sensible thing which only the interior sense grasps, while the external senses do not perceive it, for example, the enmity of the wolf. At least a definite terminology has been adopted, and the meaning will become clearer as the discussion proceeds.

---

31. *Ibid.*, fol. 5ra-b, pp. 20-21. Latin text in Appendix II, no. 18.

Avicenna now introduces a summary of his doctrine on all the interior powers.

Of the hidden vital apprehensive powers the first is the phantasy, which is the common sense. It is a power placed in the first concavity of the brain, receiving by itself all the forms which are imprinted on the five senses and given to it.

After this the imagination, or forming power, which is a power placed in the rear portion of the front concavity of the brain, retaining what the common sense receives from the five senses. This remains in it after the sensible things are removed. Now, you know that to receive belongs to a power which is different from that to which it belongs to retain; consider this in the case of water, which has the power of receiving carved figures and images, or, in general, shape, and does not have the power of retaining. We will give the proof of this later.

After this is the power which is called the imaginative with reference to the sensitive soul, and the cogitative with reference to the human soul. This is a power placed in the middle concavity of the brain where the nerve is, and its work is to put together one thing in the imagination with another, and then separate one from another, as it pleases.

Next in the series is the power of estimation, which is a power placed in the rear of the middle concavity of the brain, apprehending the not-sensed intentions which are in singular sensibles, like the power which is in the sheep, judging that it should flee from this wolf, and take pity on this lamb. It seems also that this power produces in the imagination composition and division.

Then there is the memorial and reminiscing power, which is a power placed in the rear concavity of the brain, retaining what the power of estimation apprehends concerning the not-sensed intentions of singular sensible things. The relation of the memorial power to the power of estimation is like the relation of the imagination to common sense. The relation of this [memorial] power to the intentions is like the relation of the other power [imagination] to sensible forms.

These are the powers of the living or sensible soul. But the powers of the human rational soul are divided into the power of knowing and the power of acting, and each of these powers is called "intellect" equivocally or by similitude.[32]

---

32. *Ibid.*, fol. 5rb, pp. 21-22. Latin text in Appendix II, no. 19.

Avicenna is careful both at the beginning and the end of this out-
line to indicate that he is discussing strictly sensory powers. In
most points this summary agrees with the position in the *Canon*.
We will therefore restrict the discussion to points of difference.

(1) Common sense is here called "phantasy." This is an
unusual expression, and will enable us easily to identify dependencies on this text. Here, too, common sense receives the further
function of perceiving motion.

(2) The second power is called the imagination, or forming
power.

(3) The third power is called the imaginative with respect
to the sensitive soul, and cogitative with respect to the human soul.

(4) The estimative is now explicitly located in the rear of the
middle ventricle.[33] It is said to effect composition and division in
the imagination.

(5) The fifth power is this time called "the memorial and
reminiscing power." This form of expression reflects the usage of
Aristotle.

After this tentative summary, Avicenna proceeds to prove
(*certificare*) the different kinds of powers. He tells us that all
knowledge involves some kind of abstraction. Yet the external
senses do not have a true abstraction, for the thing must exist in
matter if it is to be sensed. The imagination abstracts from matter,
but not from the appendages or accidents of matter. The estimation transcends this order of abstraction, for its object is only
accidentally material. For goodness and evil, suitability and un-
suitability, are in themselves not material. The proof of this is
that they are understood without matter. Nevertheless, though
such intentions are not material, the estimation apprehends them

---

33. H. Wolfson, "The Internal Senses," p. 105, note 52, points out that
"summo" is used in the sense of "extremo." Cf. Martin Winter,
*Ueber Avicennas Opus Egregium De Anima, Liber Sextus Natu-
ralium* (Munich: Wolf, 1903), p. 31, who translates "summo" as
"oberst (hinterest)."

only when they happen to be in matter. Therefore, the estimation apprehends material things, and abstracts them from matter, just as it apprehends non-sensible intentions, which are material. But, though it abstracts its intentions from matter, it does not abstract them from the accidents of matter. For it knows its object as particular, and as related to its proper matter; as joined to a sensible form, and surrounded with material accidents. Hence, there is still a similarity between estimation and imagination.[34]

This proof seems' to show that there are three levels of sensitive knowledge: the external senses and common sense; the imagination and the imaginative and cogitative powers; and finally, the estimation and memorial-reminiscing powers. Beyond these powers is the wholly immaterial power of intellect.

After these general considerations, the *De Anima* launches into a detailed study of each of the external senses. Finally, in part four, the topic of the internal senses recurs. This more detailed discussion adds certain items of information to the doctrine as it has been explained so far.

---

34. "Sed estimatio parum transcendit hunc ordinem abstractionis, eo quod apprehendit intentiones immateriales, quae non sunt in suis materiis, quamvis accidat illis esse in materia; quia figura et color et situs et his similia sunt res quas non est possibile haberi nisi a materiis corporalibus. Bonitas vero et malitia et conveniens et inconveniens et his similia sunt in se res non materiales, quibus tamen accidit esse materiales. Ratio autem quod hae non sunt materiales haec est, scilicet quod si hae essent materiales ex se ipsis non intelligerentur bonitas vel malitia vel conveniens vel inconveniens nisi accidens corpori. Intelligitur autem sine corpore. Constat ergo quod hae in se non sunt materiales, sed accidit eis esse in rebus materialibus. Extimatio autem non apprehendit neque assequitur nisi similia horum. Ergo extimatio apprehendit res materiales et abstrahit eas a materia, sicut apprehendit etiam intentiones non sensibiles, quamvis sint materiales. Ergo haec abstractio purior et vicinior est simplicitati quam duae primae. Sed cum hoc tamen non expoliat formam hanc ab accidentibus materiae, eo quod particulariter apprehendit eam secundum propriam materiam, et secundum comparationem eius ad illam et ligatam cum forma sensibili, et stipatam accidentibus materiae; et est convenientia imaginationis cum illa," Avicenna, *De Anima,* part II, c. 1, fol. 7ra, p. 29.

The sense which is common is different from the one held
by those who thought that the common sensibles had a common sense. For the common sense is the power which receives all the sensed objects.[35]

This is the power which is called common sense; it is the
center of all the senses; from it are derived the nerves; to
it the senses report; and it is the power which truly senses.
But to retain the things which this power apprehends belongs
to that power which is called the imagination and the formal
power, and phantasy. Perhaps men distinguish between the
imagination and the phantasy as they please, and we are of
the number of those who do so. Now, the forms which are in
common sense, and the common sense and the imagination
and the phantasy are as it were one power, and as it were
are not distinguished in their substance, but in their form;
that is, that which receives is not that which retains. For
the power which is called formal and phantasy and imagination retains the sensible form, and does not discern it in any
way, except in the sense that it retains it. For common sense
and the exterior senses discern in some way and judge; for
they say that this moving thing is black, and this red thing
happens to be. By this retaining power, however, nothing is
discerned about anything which is, except about that which
is in it, namely, that it has this or that form. Now, we also
know that it most truly belongs to our nature that we put
together sensibles among themselves, and divide them, according to the form which we see outside, although we do not
believe them to be or not to be. It is therefore necessary that
there be in us a power which does this, and this is the power
which when ruled by intellect is called cogitating, and when
ruled by the animal power is called imaginative.

Then sometimes we judge about sensible things by means
of intentions which we do not sense, either because by their
nature they are not sensible in any way, or because they are
sensible, but we do not sense them in the moment of judgment. But those which are not sensible of their very nature,
are like enmity and malice and mutual repugnance. This is
what the sheep apprehends concerning the form of the wolf,
and in general the intention which makes it flee from the latter.
Such is also the concord which it apprehends concerning its
mate, and in general the intention which makes it pleasing

35. *De Anima,* part IV, c. 1, fol. 17 rb, p. 81. Latin text in Appendix
II, no. 20.

to it. Such are the things which the sensible soul apprehends, although the external sense has not given it any such information. Therefore the power by which these things are apprehended is a different power, and is called the estimative.

Or the intentions are sensible in this way. For example, when we see something [yellow], we judge it to be honey and sweet. This is not something the sense brings us at the moment, though it is of the genus of sensible things; although its judgment is not sensed in any way, and although its parts are of the genus of sensible things, it is not apprehended at present; but it is a judgment which judges what perhaps is in it, and is made by some other power.

Estimation produces in man its own judgments. Among them is the following: when the soul stubbornly denies that there are things which are not imagined nor known by that power, and in general does not want to believe that they are. Without doubt, there is in us that power which is the judging power in the animal. This type of judgment is not a defining judgment like the intellectual judgment, but an imaginable judgment, conjoined with singularity and sensible form. From it there arise most of the actions of animals. Now, the usage is that what the sense apprehends be called form and that what the estimation apprehends be called intention.

Each one of these powers has its treasury. The treasury of that which the sense apprehends is the imaginative power, whose location is the front part of the brain. Consequently, when some infirmity affects that part, this formal mode [of knowledge] is also affected; either through the imagination of non-existent forms, or because it is difficult for it to stabilize what is in it. The treasury of the power which apprehends intentions is the conserving power, whose location is the rear part of the brain; consequently, when some infirmity occurs there, that whose property is to conserve these intentions is affected. This [conserving] power is called memorial and also retaining. It is called retaining because that which is in it adheres firmly. It is called memorial on account of the quickness of its aptitude to recall when the form which is being remembered has fallen into oblivion. This happens when the estimation is turned to its estimative power, and the latter presents each of the forms which are in the imagination, so that, as it were, it sees that these are its forms. But when the form appears which apprehends the intention which had been destroyed, then the intention appears as it had appeared outside, and the memorial power stabilizes it in itself, as it had done before, and memory occurs.[36]

The discussion begins by cautioning the reader against a mistake that is quite easy to make. "Common sense" is not the sense of the common sensibles, as some have thought, but is the center of all the senses, and the power which truly senses.

An interesting note is made on the use of terms. The power which retains the forms received from common sense is called imagination, and also formal power. Now, says Avicenna, some distinguish between the imagination and the phantasy as they please. For common sense and the imagination and the forms which are in the common sense are as it were one power; they are not distinguished in their substance, but in their form, that is, in their function.

It is obvious that there is in us a power of composing and dividing images. When this power is ruled by intellect, it is called "cogitating" (— the cogitative mentioned before); when it is ruled by the sensitive power, it is called the imaginative.

The treatment of the estimative is considerably longer here. We judge, remarks Avicenna, about sensible things through intentions which are not sensed. We learn, further, that intentions are of two kinds: not sensible of themselves, and not sensible here and now. Examples of the first kind are the enmity of the wolf for the sheep, and the friendship of its mate. In man, too, the estimative performs its own judgments. An example of this occurs when a man stubbornly denies the existence of things which cannot be imagined. Perhaps Avicenna himself met such men, who did not believe in the intelligences or the world of essences which are so important in his philosophy, and yet were unable to give any rational account of their refusal to accept the theories. At any rate, the example is intriguing.

A very important statement is made about the judgment of the estimative. It is not a defining judgment. In other words, the estimative judgment does not employ concepts. It is an imagined judgment, always joined to singularity and sensible form.[37]

---

36. *Ibid.*, fol. 17 va-b, pp. 82-84.
37. Cf. Carra de Vaux, *Avicenne*, p. 215.

In a kind of way, the estimative also seems to operate judgments which are like the compositions and divisions of the cogitative. In saying this, Avicenna gives a puzzling function to the estimative, although his statement may be much clearer in the Arabic. This remark is made, because the passage ends by explaining that all the other interior sensory powers act as instruments of the estimative.[38]

Chapter two deals with the operations of the imagination and the imaginative-cogitative sense. On it, Avicenna makes a characteristic remark, which we will just note in passing.

We will first deal with the formal power. This formal power is the imagination, and it is the last in which sensible forms reside, and the face which it has turned to sensible things is the common sense.[39]

Chapter three of this part deals with the estimative and the memory.

After we have finished the section on the disposition of the imaginative and formal power, we must now speak of the disposition of the memorial, and the difference between it and the cogitative in the moment of estimation. We will say therefore that estimation is the highest judge in animals, which judges after the manner of an image invented when it is not

---

38. "Si autem implicitum fuerit tibi hoc ex hac parte, ut non facile intelligatur, et sensus reddiderit formam rei, revocabitur et residebit in imaginatione, et redibit comparatio tui ad illud, et residebit in memoria. Et haec virtus quae componit inter formam et formam, et inter formam et intentionem est quasi virtus estimativa. Et hoc propter locum, non propter hoc quod iudicat, immo quia facit pervenire ad iudicium. Iam autem posuerunt locum eius in medietate cerebri, ideo ut habeat continuitatem cum intentione et cum forma.

Videtur autem quod virtus estimativa sit virtus cogitativa et imaginativa et memorialis, et quod ipsa est diiudicans. Sed per seipsam est diiudicans; per motus vero suos et actiones suas est imaginativa et memorialis; sed est imaginativa per id quod operatur in formis, et memorialis per id quod eius ultima actio. Sed retentiva est virtus sui thesauri. Et videtur quod formalis et cogitativa huius sit memoria, quae pervenit ex intentione ipsa quae intelligitur hominis," Avicenna, *De Anima*, part IV, c. 1, fol. 17 vb, p. 84.

39. *Ibid.*, c. 2, fol. 18ra-b, p. 85. Latin text in Appendix II, no. 22.

certain. This is something like that which happens to a man when he thinks that honey is filthy because it is like dung. For estimation judges it to be so, and the soul follows the estimation though the power of intellect holds back. But animals, and men who are like them, follow in their actions only this judgment of estimation. This has no rational understanding connected with it, but is like the manner of a fiction which is in the soul alone.

The powers of man because of the presence of reason have something which makes his interior powers different from the powers of an animal. Consequently, from the uses he makes of composite sounds and colors and odors and tastes, he has some acts of hope and desire which other animals do not have. Likewise, his interior imaginative power is such that it is useful for the sciences; particularly, the power of his memory is of great help to knowledge, because it gives us experiences which the memory retains, and considerations of singulars, and other like benefits.

Let us now return to the discussion of estimation. We say that it is necessary to look for the reasons of the consideration of estimation in points in which the intellect makes no conjecture in the moment of estimation.

The question is: how does estimation apprehend the intentions which are in sensible things as soon as the sense apprehends the forms, under the condition that nothing of these intentions is sensed, and under the further condition that many of them are of no future nor present use. We will say therefore that estimation itself takes place in many ways.

One of these is precaution, which comes to be from the divine clemency, like the disposition of an infant which shortly after it is born sucks the breast, and the disposition of an infant, which, being placed erect and beginning to fall, immediately runs to someone, or to something, to hold to it, or to protect itself. And when someone wishes to cleanse the eye of an infant, it closes it, before it can understand the situation, and what it should do, as if this were the nature of its soul, and as if it did not do this by choice. In a similar way also, animals have natural precautions. The cause of this are the relations which exist between these souls and their principles which are their unceasing guides; relations which sometimes are, and sometimes are not, for example, [which causes us] to consider with our intellect, and bring something suddenly to the mind; for all such things come from there. And by means of these precautions estimation apprehends intentions which are mixed with sensations about things which are harmful or helpful. And so the sheep fears the wolf even if the sheep had never seen it before nor suffered any evil from it. So, too, many animals are afraid of the lion. Likewise, other birds fear hawks and associate with other birds, without understanding. This is one way.

Another way is like that which happens by experience. For when the animal has had pain or pleasure, or there has come to it either sensible advantage or sensible harm together with some sensible form, and the form of that thing has been impressed in the formal power, as well as the form of that which was a help to it; and there has likewise been impressed on the memory the intention of the operation which joins them, and the judgment about them (that is, that the memory by itself naturally apprehends this); and then, when later the form appears outside the imaginative power, then it is moved by that form, and there is moved together with it that which was helpful among the intentions of the useful and harmful; and then there will be a process in the memory like the motion and investigation which is in the nature of the imaginative power. But estimation senses this whole together at once, and will see the intention by means of the form. And this is the way which comes about by experience. For this reason, dogs are terrified of stones and clubs and the like.

Sometimes judgments arise from the estimation by the mode of similitude. For when a thing has had some form joined with an intention of estimation in some particular case — an intention which is joined in all such cases, then, when the form is seen the intention will be seen.

Sometimes animals are different in this judging power, which requires, in its actions, that the other powers obey it. That which it requires most is memory and sense. The formal image is needed because of recollection and memory. Now, even animals have memory. But recollection, which is the skill in recollecting that which was forgotten, is not to be found, I think, except in man alone. For to know that something had been possessed which afterwards was rubbed out of knowledge belongs only to the rational power; if it can pertain to any other power besides the rational it could be an act of estimation, but only of such as is joined with reason. For the other animals, if they remember, only remember. But if they do not remember, they do not desire to remember, nor do they think about it.[40]

---

40. *Ibid.*, c. 3, fol. 19rb-va, p. 91. Latin text in Appendix II, no. 23.

In this rather lengthy discussion several further points are made. It is said here that the estimative is the highest judge in the animal.[41] Its judgment is something like a compositive imagination. It is also something like the judgment of a man who thinks that honey is unpleasant because it is dung-colored. Now, animals must follow their estimative sense, but men have a higher power, intellect. Nevertheless many men follow only their sensory judgment, which is somewhat different from that of animals in so far as the interior powers of man are more perfect because of the co-presence of reason.

The estimative judgment is of several kinds. One is the natural judgment which concerns the natural helps and hindrances of the being. The infant's sucking of milk, his running for support when falling, the blinking of the eye, are adduced as examples of actions taking place through natural judgment. Avicenna's first statement about this type of judgment comes close to implying that intentions of this sort are innate. Within a few sentences, it begins to appear that such intentions are infused, just as concepts are infused in the Avicennan system.

The second type takes place through experience. The animal can remember that a certain sensory object caused pleasure or pain. It likewise retains the intention of the action joining them. In this way, when the sensible form is presented through the senses

---

41. Compare: "Intellectus autem efficiens est rector illius colligationis animae cum corpore. Intellectui autem efficienti deservit extimatio. Extimationi autem deserviunt duae virtutes: virtus posterior ea, et virtus prior ea. Virtus autem posterior est virtus quae retinet quod reddit extimatio memoriali. Virtus autem prior est super omnes virtutes vitales. Deinde virtuti imaginativae deserviunt duae virtutes diversam actionum: virtus autem appetitiva deservit ei cum obedientia, quia extimativa imperat ei moveri aliquo modo perceptionis; virtus autem imaginativa servit extimativae, per hoc quod ostendit ei formas retentas in ea, quae sunt aptae ad recipiendum compositionem et divisionem. Deinde haec dominantur aliis. Virtuti autem imaginativae servit fantasia. Fantasiae vero serviunt quinque sensus. Virtuti autem appetitivae serviunt concupiscibilis et irascibilis. Sed concupiscibili et irascibili servit virtus movens quae est in lacertis. Et hic terminantur virtutes vitales vel sensibiles," ibid., part I, c. 5, fol. 6ra, p. 24.

or the imagination, the estimation at once senses the combination of sensible form, of pleasure (or pain), and the operation concerned. Quite like this is the estimative judgment through similarity. If a certain form has had an intention joined to it often, then, when the form is perceived, even in a different instance, the estimative will make its judgment.

There is another interesting text on the judgment of the estimative, which apparently was not available to the thinkers of the Middle Ages.

There is further in the living thing a power which definitely judges about an object that it is so or otherwise. Through this power the animal avoids what it has to fear, and strives after the desirable. Now it is clear, that this power cannot be identical with the common sense, since the latter presents the sun in the way that the senses reported in its apparent size, while the former arrives at an altogether different result. Just so, the lion sees the object of its chase from a distance as if it were the size of a little bird, but it has no doubt about the form and size of the object, and immediately darts after it. It is not less clear, that this power is not identical with the phantasy, for the latter works in such a way that we do not believe that the things which it represents are truly thus. This power is called the estimating or judging power.[42]

According to this, the estimative keeps the animal from being deceived by illusions of perspective, and so forth. There is also a vaguely disquieting analogy between this text and what Aristotle has to say about the difference between opinion and imagination. Unfortunately, the text is too brief to enable us to judge the full meaning of the suggestion. However, as far as the Avicenna known to the thirteenth century is concerned, we can simply disregard the passage.

A few remarks remain to be made. Avicenna seems to be the first explicitly to put common sense among the internal senses.[43] He is apparently not altogether certain about the relations of common sense, imagination, and the imaginative-cogitative power.

---

42. S. Landauer, "Die Psychologie des Ibn Sînâ," pp. 400-02. German text of Landauer in Appendix II, no. 24.
43. Wolfson, "Isaac Israeli," p. 585.

The term "cogitative" designates a sensory power, as we have seen.[44] It is really the same as the imaginative, except that it is under the control of reason, and so is to be found only in men.[45] Now, a sensory power, concerned with the images of sensible forms, seems certainly to be equivalent, at least in part, to Aristotle's φαντασία. As being under the control of reason, it should be designated by some adjective indicating this relation. Such an adjective might well be διανοητική, or something similar.[46] What about "estimative" and «δόξα»? It is true that an opinion can intervene between a mere representation and appetite. So does an intellectual judgment. An image may affect us like a picture; if we are to act upon it, we must be persuaded, believe, opine that things are indeed so. And to this extent the estimative is like opinion. However, the estimative was not thought of in relation to this problem. The particular problem concerned actually sensed objects ("the sheep sees the wolf and flees"). In such a situation there is no need for an opinion about reality, but only a judgment about utility (or harmfulness).[47] The faculty of making this kind of judgment, once discovered, could then later on be seen to have other functions, like to those of opinion, practical intellect, and the like.

ALGAZEL

Algazel, who lived from 1059 to 1111, was an Arabian thinker

---

44. Compare above, and also *De Anima,* part IV, c. 3.
45. Carra de Vaux, *Avicenne,* p. 216, says that the animal has the cogitative power. This must have been a slip of the pen.
46. Cf. e.g., Aristotle, *De Anima,* III, c. 10, 433b29; c. 11, 434a8-10.
47. Cf. A. M. Goichon, *Lexique de la Langue Philosophique d'Ibn Sînâ* (Paris: Desclée, 1938), no. 787, pp. 442-43, no. 405, p. 209, no. 610.28, p. 337; *Vocabulaires Comparés d'Aristote et d'Ibn Sînâ* (Paris: Desclée, 1939), p. 40, s. v. *"wahm"*: "Wahm: faculté estimative . . . se rapproche de τὸ κριτικόν, commun à l'homme et aux animaux, à des degrés diverse . . . bien que le wahm offere un sens beaucoup plus précis et occupe une place important dans la psychologie avicennienne, on peut le tenir pour esquissé chez Aristote"; *Introduction à Avicenne, Son Epître des Définitions* (Paris: Desclée, 1933), p. 43, note 43.

who was primarily a theologian. His main interest was to combat what he thought to be the rationalism of the philosophers. A peculiar historical accident made him appear to the Latin thinkers as a philosopher of the school of Avicenna.[48] For Algazel intended to summarize accurately and correctly the philosophical positions, particularly those of Avicenna. This he did in a work called the *Intentions of the Philosophers.* This little work was followed by another, called the *Destruction of the Philosophers.* In the twelfth century, the former of these works was translated, and was called variously the *Physics* or *Metaphysics* of Algazel. Under this title, and without any reference to a consequent refutation, this work naturally made Algazel look like an Avicennan. Consequently, this is the way in which he served as a source for the thirteenth century.

In psychology, Algazel holds five internal senses: (1) common sense or (recipient) imagination; (2) conservation; or retentive imagination; (3) estimation; (4) memory; (5) compositive imagination, or cogitation.[49] In this summary of Avicenna, Algazel succeeds in sharpening a bit the former's argument. Thus, the necessity for admitting estimation is grounded on the fact that relations like harmfulness can neither be sensed nor imagined.[50] He expresses the traditional examples more briefly, and adds a few

---

48. Étienne Gilson, *La Philosophie au Moyen Age,* 2nd ed. (Paris: Payot, 1944), p. 356; Auguste Schmoelders, *Essai sur les Ecoles Philosophiques chez les Arabes* (Paris: Didot, 1842), p. 245; Friederich Ueberweg, *Grundriss der Geschichte der Philosophie,* vol. II, herausgegeben von Dr. Bernhard Geyer (Berlin: Mittler, 1928), p. 311.

49. H. Wolfson, "The Internal Senses," p. 102.

50. "Virtus vero apprehendens dividitur in exteriorem, ut est sensus, et in interiorem, ut est fantasia et estimacio, et memorialis, et cogitacio, de quarum certitudine postea loquemur. Si enim bruta animalia non haberent virtutem interiorem preter sensus, tunc contingeret aliquem cibum nocere sibi, et statim abhorreret illum; postea iterum non abhorreret comedere illum, nisi gustaret prius . . . . Nisi autem esset virtus interior, contingeret quod omnis [sic; nonne ovis?] non apprehenderet inimicicias lupi numquam visi ut fugiat ab eo. Inimicicie enim non videntur," *Algazel's Metaphysics,* ed. by J. T. Muckle, C.S.B. (Toronto: St. Michael's College, 1933), pars 2, tractate 4, "Diccio de anima animali," p. 164.

more of his own.[51] In some ways, he is more careful about terminology. Thus, he knows that the term "cogitative" properly belongs to reason, and is applied to the imagination only in so far
as the latter is the instrument of reason.[52] At other times, he seems
to use words more loosely; thus, he applies the term "phantasy"
to both the imagination itself and the image.

There is another text in which the doctrine of Algazel is presented, namely, in Averroes's *Destructio Destructionum*. Accord-

---

51. "Estimativa est virtus qua apprehenditur intencio de sensibilibus sicut
inimicicie gatti adversus murem, et lupi adversus ovem, et amor
ovis circa agnum filium suum; hoc igitur eciam pendet ex materia
eo quod si ponantur non esse apprehensio forme lupi sensibilis, non
intelligetur esse apprehensio huiusmodi," *ibid.*, "Diccio de anima
humana," pp. 173-74.

52. "Scias quod sensus interiores quinque sunt eciam scilicet sensus communis et virtus imaginativa, et cogitativa, et virtus estimativa, et
virtus memorialis. Sensus vero communis est sensus a quo omnes
isti quinque derivantur . . . . Imaginativa est virtus retentiva eius
quod impressum fuit sensui communi. Retinere autem aliud est
quam recipere; unde aqua recipit formam et figuram, sed non retinet . . . . Si autem contingeret impediri anteriorem partem cerebri
destruetur retencio fantasiarum . . . . Estimativa est virtus apprehendens de sensato quod non est sensatum, sicut ovis apprehendit
inimicicias lupi; hoc autem non fit per oculum, sed par aliam
virtutem, que hoc est brutis animalibus, quod est intellectus homini.
Memorialis vero est conservatrix harum intencionum, quas apprehendit estimativa, et ideo est archa intencionum sicut imaginativa,
conservatrix formarum est archa formarum, et hec due scilicet
estimativa et memorialis sunt in posteriore parte cerebri. Communis vero et imaginativa sunt in anteriore parte cerebri. Cogitacio
vero est virtus in medio cerebri, cuius est movere, non apprehendere; perquirit enim nunc de his que sunt in archa formarum, nunc
de his que sunt in archa intencionum, quoniam fixa (sita) est inter
eas, et operatur in his duabus componendo et dividendo tantum . . . .
Hec autem in homine solet vocari cogitativa. Cogitativa autem secundum veritatem est racio, sed fantasia instrumentum est cogitacionis, non quod ipsa sit cogitativa," *Ibid.*, "Diccio de Sensibus
Interioribus," pp. 169-71. H. Wolfson, "The Internal Senses," p.
104, note 58, says that "cogitativa" above, line 2, (and "cogitacio,"
in a section here omitted), is an error for "fantasia." Fr. Muckle
gives the reading "fantasia" as that of Ms. B. N. 6552 in his Appendix B.

ing to Professor Wolfson, this work was not translated into Latin until 1328.[53] Several propositions from this text need some comment.

> The internal powers are three: of which the first is the imaginative power. . . .
> The second is the cogitative power, and it is the one which apprehends intentions; but the first apprehended forms. . . .
> The third power is the power which is called in animals the imaginative, and in man the estimative, and its nature is to compose sensible forms with each other, and to compose intentions with forms. . . . Averroes says: this entire discussion is nothing more than the recitation of the opinion of the Philosophers about these powers and their attributes, except that in this he follows Avicenna.[54]

We are likely to be startled by one point: the reversed use of the terms "cogitative" and "estimative." Professor Wolfson[55] explains this inversion by the fact that in the Hebrew, from which this translation was made, the same term is used for both. This does explain the possibility of the change. But why then should two different words have been used, and used so unusually? There is no evident solution for this difficulty, at least at this stage.

AVERROES (IBN-ROUSCHD)

Averroes, a Spanish Arab, lived from 1126 to 1198. Like the rest of this group of philosophers, he was a physician; in addition to this, he was a man of affairs, rising to the position of Cadi of Seville. But above all, he was a philosopher; so eminent a student of Aristotle was he, that he was referred to simply as the Commentator.

With regard to the problem of internal sensation, Averroes can be located in a preliminary way by the position he takes with

---

53. H. Wolfson, "The Internal Senses," p. 122, and note 38.
54. Averroes, *Destructio Destructionum*, in physicis, disputatio secunda (a principio locutionis Algezelis) (Venice: Juntas, 1574), vol. IX, fol. 135 I - 136C. Latin text in Appendix II, no. 25.
  (The Venice edition of 1550, in which this passage is in vol. IX, fol. 59a line 58 to b line 46, has exactly the same text.)
55. H. Wolfson, "The Internal Senses," p. 104, note 57.

respect to Avicenna-Algazel. After having quoted Algazel, and having said that he merely summarizes Avicenna, Averroes continues thus:

> But he differs from the philosophers in this, that he posits in the animal a power in addition to the imaginative power, which he calls "cogitative" [= estimative] in place of the cogitative [= reason] in man. He says that the Ancients prefer the name of "imaginative" for this power. When they say this, the imaginative in the animal will be in place of the cogitative [= reason], and it will be in the middle ventricle of the brain. When the term "imaginative" will be used for that power which includes [the knowledge of] figure, it is used of the power which is situated in the front part of the brain. There is no difficulty in this that the conservative and memorative powers are in the rear part of the brain, for conservation and remembrance are two in act, but one in subject.
>
> But what is clear from the opinion of the Ancients is that the imaginative is the power in the animal which judges that the wolf is hostile to the lamb and that the sheep is friendly. For the imaginative is a power of apprehension and necessarily judges, without needing the intervention of another power besides the imaginative power. What Avicenna says would be possible, if the imaginative power were not apprehensive. Hence, to add a power besides the imaginative power in an animal comes to nothing; this is particularly true in an animal which has many arts naturally. For images in such animals are not apprehended by sense; the apprehensions are as it were midway between intelligible and imagined forms. The disposition of this kind of form has been explained in the *De Sensu et Sensato*, and so we will pass it by here.[56]

Averroes explicitly rejects the Avicennan scheme of internal senses. The main reason for this, as he himself says, is that the Ancients, that is, Aristotle, assigned the power of discerning to the imagination.

Though this text is sufficient to show that Averroes is not an

---

56. Averroes, *Destructio Destructionum*, in physicis, disputatio secunda, vol. IX, fol. 136L-137B. Text in Appendix II, no. 26.

(The present state of knowledge on the Latin translations of Averroes's works is summarized by Harry Austryn Wolfson, *Speculum* (1931), pp. 412-21).

Avicennan, it raises further problems about his own positive position. How does he understand localization? How many powers are there, and what is their relation to each other? What is the explanation of animal activity, and what are the "innate arts?"[57] What is the cogitative power?

Localization, after all, is not an Aristotelian, but a Galenic doctrine. How does Averroes handle it?

> The powers of the brain, that is, the imaginative and the cogitative, and the reminiscing and conserving powers, although they do not have members or instruments, nevertheless have proper places in the brain, in which their operations are manifested, and so we must speak of them. We say that the imaginative power stands in the prow of the brain, and it is the power which retains the shape of a thing after it has been separated from common sense. But the cogitative is more manifest in the middle chamber, and by this power man cogitates in those matters to which cogitation and choice belong until he apprehends what is more convenient. Therefore this power is not found except in man, and to the brute animal there was given the estimative in place of it. The place of the reminiscing and conserving power is the stern or rear part of the head. Between the conservative and reminiscing powers there is no difference except that the conservative is a continuous conservation, and the reminiscing is an interrupted one. . . . In the place where the imaginative is, there necessarily is the cogitative, because cogitation is nothing but the composition of imagined things and their separation. . . . The place and root of the habitation of common sense is the heart.[58]

Localization for Averroes is not a question of organ or instrument. The parts of the brain are only places where the powers show themselves, and perhaps only show themselves more plainly. In this way, imaginative power is in the front ventricle, memory in the rear. The cogitative is more manifest in the middle chamber,

---

57. Cf. also, Averroes, *Aristotelis . . . Posteriorum Resolutorium* (Post. Analytic.), libri duo, cum Averrois Cordubensis magnis commentariis, comm. on bk. 2, c. 11, textus commentum no. 103 [t. c. 103] (Venice: Juntas, 1574), vol. I, part 2, fol. 562C.
58. *Collegit*, bk. 2, c. 20, vol. X, fol. 30FG, K. L. Latin text in Appendix II, no. 27.

but is really in the same place as the imaginative. On the other hand, common sense has no place in the brain at all, but is in the heart.

What is the relation of the powers to their places in the brain?

Concerning these powers, it is clear that their operations are not completed except in the brain. Hence, because the brain is easily affected, being cold and wet, for this reason the greater part of the infirmities of these powers comes from the disposition of the brain; either because the disposition is the direct cause, or because of the communication of the members [of the brain] with each other. If the cause is in the whole brain, all the powers will be affected. If the causes are in some proper place, then the power of that proper place will be affected. When the cause is in the prow of the brain, the imagination will be injured. When it is in the middle part, then reason and cogitation will be injured; and when in the rear part, then memory and conservation.[59]

This seems to be as far as Averroes has gone; we can say only that the operations of imagination, cogitation, and memory are somehow completed in certain places in the brain.[60]

The second question was one about the number and relations of the powers. In speaking of the states of knowledge, Averroes tells us that there are five orders of form.

The first is corporal, of the great cortex [of the brain?], and it is the sensible form outside the soul.
The second is the being of this form in the common sense, and is the first of the spiritual orders.
The third is its being in the imaginative power, and is more spiritual.
The fourth is in the "distinguishing" power.
The fifth is its being in the memorative power.[61]

---

59. *Ibid.*, bk. 3, c. 40, fol. 56BC. Latin text in Appendix II, no. 28.
60. *Ibid.*, bk. 2, c. 30, fol. 30H-M; cf. bk. 2, cc. 11, 18.
61. *Averrois Paraphrasis de Memoria et Reminiscentia,* vol. VI, part 2, fol. 22B. Latin text in Appendix II, no. 29.
   Cf. "Per illam [humorem vitreum in oculo] aspicit sensus communis formam. Et cum sensus communis recipit formam, reddit eam informans receptione magis spirituali, et tunc illa forma erit in tertio ordine. Formae igitur habent tres ordines; quorum unus

This well-known passage from Averroes's *Paraphrase of the De Memoria et Reminiscentia* (referred to in the *Destructio* as *De Sensu et Sensato*[62]) raises further problems. The first concerns the "sensible form outside the soul." If we relate this doctrine to the one just mentioned, of localization by way of "completion," we may conclude to a kind of modified Platonism. External sensation (not including common sense) seems to be an operation of the composite (body + soul). But imagination, cogitation, and memory are separated ("spiritual"), are really only in the soul alone, and are only *completed* in the body. This notion of "spirituality" or abstractness is a second problem. The third is the identification of the "distinguishing power" (*virtus distinctiva*).

There are three more short texts in this same work which deal with the relations of the powers among themselves.

> There are therefore three actions of the three powers, of which two are fixed by two simple things, from which there is put together a form composed of them. Of these things one is the image of a thing, the second is the intention of the image of the thing, and the third is the power putting these two intentions together.[63]

This text seems to be speaking of imagination, memory, and compositive power. The act of imagination is the image; the act of memory is the knowledge that the image is an image [= the intention of the image]; and the compositive power associates these two knowledges. But now note these texts:

> It is the work of the memorative power to make present the intention of an imagined thing after its absence, and to judge that it is the intention which it formerly sensed and imagined.[64]
> To judge that this intention is of this imagined thing in man is the work of intellect, because the judgment in him

---

est corporalis, et secundus est in sensu communi, et est spiritualis, tertius autem est in virtute imaginativa, et est magis spiritualis," *Ibid.*, 16 I. For a similar treatment, compare St. Thomas Aquinas, *De Veritate* XIX. 1.

62. Cf. H. Wolfson, "The Internal Senses," p. 108.
63. *Averrois Paraphrasis de Memoria et Reminiscentia,* vol. VI, part 2, fol. 21H. Latin text in Appendix II, no. 30.
64. *Ibid.*, fol. 21EF. Latin text in Appendix II, no. 31.

is according to affirmation and negation, and in animals which can remember there is a similar action. For this power is in man by knowledge, and so he investigates by reminiscence. In other animals it is by nature, and so animals remember, but do not investigate by remembering. And this power in animals has no name; and it is this which Avicenna calls estimation; and by this power the animal avoids the things that would naturally harm it, although it may never have sensed them.[65]

This is indeed a puzzling account of memory. The compositive power joins imagination and memory, while both memory and intellect recognize the memory to be of this image. Now, if the act of the compositive power follows the recognition, it seems to be superfluous; if it precedes, it would seem to be some kind of automatic process by which images are successively paraded before the memory till one is recognized. We will leave this "parade of images" as a problem for later.

In man, recognition of the past as past is a function of memory and intellect. Because intellect is unlimited in its scope, man has both memory and reminiscence. This is not the Aristotelian position. But stranger still is the situation in animals. Here remembering is a function of both memory and nature. Of course, in a kind of way, everything animals do they do by nature. But to say that they remember by nature seems a bit forced.

Averroes then procedes to involve himself in an interpretation of Avicenna. The Avicennan estimative, he says, is a name for the "nature" by which animals remember. By this power animals avoid the harmful things they have never seen. Are they remembering? It does seem that they remember intentions, that is, knowledge. Now, in a previous text, we have seen that Averroes

---

65. *Ibid.*, fol. 21GH. Latin text in Appendix II, no. 32. H. Wolfson, "The Internal Senses," p. 75, note 35, corrects the phrase, "per cognitionem" to "per cogitationem et deliberationem"; this emendation of the Latin text on the basis of the original is justified for Averroes himself, though it cannot be used to represent the Averroes whom St. Thomas knew. For this reason the text is given in the mediaeval version. Moreover, the correction does not essentially modify the thought.

believes animals to have innate arts. By the logic of his position, he interprets Avicenna as holding innate knowledge also. It seems much more likely that Avicenna believed the intentions to be infused from the higher intelligences.

How many powers are there for Averroes? Basically, there seem to be three: imagination, cogitative, and memory. At times, he speaks of an estimative, but by it he seems to mean the imagination in so far as it discerns the useful and the harmful, or in so far as it has innate arts.

In this discussion, we have seen Averroes's explanation of animal activity. This does not constitute a grave problem for him. Sense and imagination are judging powers, as Aristotle had said, and Avicenna failed to make him recognize that there are different kinds of judgment involved. So he can say, echoing Aristotle:

> It belongs to the disposition of an animal that it have a power by which to discern the useful from the harmful, and this power is called the sensitive power.[66]

The last and most difficult point is the meaning of "cogitative" in Averroes. From the texts which we have already seen, this is a problem. Several texts seemed to equate cogitative power and reason. On the other hand, it was said that "cogitation is nothing but the composition of imagined things and their separation."[67] There are several fairly explicit texts on the meaning of this word.

> We can understand by the term "cogitative part" the speculative intellect, and by the part which is called "intellect" the operative intellect.[68]

There is no problem here at all: the term "cogitative" can be used for the speculative intellect, but this is a rare usage, and does not

---

66. *Aristotelis . . . Posteriorum Resolutorium* (Post. Analyt.), comm. on bk. 2, c. 11, t. c. 103, vol. I, part 2, fol. 562C. Latin text in Appendix II, no. 33.
67. *Collegit,* bk. 2, c. 20, fol. 30L; complete English version quoted above, Latin text in Appendix II, no. 27.
68. *In Librum Tertium de Anima,* t. c. 46, vol. VI. i. 2, fol. 192B. Latin text in Appendix II, no. 34.

concern us. The same is to be said of the passage in which "cogitative part" means the rational soul.[69]

Slightly more common, and more in harmony with the normal
Latin usage is this.

> The apprehension which properly is of things whose prin-
> ciples are not in our power is called speculative science; and
> the apprehension which properly is of beings whose causes
> are in our power is called operative knowledge, and I mean
> such knowledge in which there is cogitation for the sake of
> operation. For we do not meditate nor cogitate about opera-
> tion concerning things whose operation cannot be in our power,
> but is in the power of nature. Man makes use of operative
> cogitation in those things, which can come from the will.
> Since this is so, the cogitative is one of the parts of the ra-
> tional soul which receives reason, and the other is the specu-
> lative part.[70]

The use of the term "cogitative" for practical reason is frequent
in the *Commentary on the Ethics*.[71]

There is a fourth and quite original meaning of "cogitative."

> And so we must not object to this argument [about the
> separation of the intellect] that there is a change in the in-
> tellect on account of the change in the imaginative and cogi-
> tative power particularly; for this latter is the way in which
> we think that weariness is found in intellect. It is there only
> accidentally. For the cogitative power is of the genus of
> sensible powers. Now, the imaginative and the cogitative
> and the memorative powers are only in the place of sensa-
> tion, and so they are necessary only in the absence of the
> sensible object, and they all help each other to represent the
> image of a sensible thing, so that the separated rational
> power may look at it, and extract from it the universal in-
> tention, and then receive it, that is, comprehend it.[72]

---

69. Cf. "in habente rationem . . . in anima [*variant*: animali] rationali
    et hoc intendebat cum dixit 'in parte cogitativa,'" *In III de Anima*,
    t. c. 42, fol. 190D.
70. *Aristotelis Stagiritae libri moralem totam philosophiam complec-
    tentes cum Averrois Cordubensis commentariis*, comm. on bk. VI,
    c. 1, vol. III, fol. 81M-82A. Latin text in Appendix II, no. 35.
71. For example: "Ergo operatio quae est partis cogitativae, quae est a
    bono et a malo est veritas et falsitas," *ibid.*, c. 2, fol. 82H.
72. *In III De Anima*, t. c. 7, fol. 155B. Latin text in Appendix II, no. 36.

This text again is clear and indisputable: the cogitative is a sense power. What is it and what does it do?

It is said that the imaginative power is in the front of the brain, and the cogitative in the middle, and the memorative in the rear. And this was not only said by the physicians, but also in the *De Sensu et Sensato*. But Galen and the other physicians reason about it, that these powers are in these places, by means of the argument from concomitance, and this argument produces only opinion and is not true. But it has been declared in the *De Sensu et Sensato* that this is the order of those powers in the brain, by an argument that gives their being and cause. But that does not contradict what was said here. For the cogitative power in Aristotle is the individual "distinguishing" power, that is, which discerns only individually, not universally. For it was declared there that the cogitative power is only the power which discerns the intention of a sensible thing from its image in the imagination. And this is the power whose proportion to these two intentions (that is, to the image of the thing, and the intention of the image of it) is like the proportion of the common sense to the intentions of the five senses. For the cogitative power is of the genus of powers existing in the body. And Aristotle openly said this in that book, when he posited the individual "distinct" powers in four orders. In the first place the common sense, then the imaginative power, then the cogitative, and then the memorative. . . . Although therefore man properly has a cogitative power, that does not make this power to be the rational distinctive power. . . . Galenus thought that the cogitative power is the material rational power.[73]

The word "distinct" in the seventh last line, according to H. A. Wolfson,[74] is a mistranslation by the Latin translator; it should read "separable" or "separate." The latter seems preferable, both because Averroes's theory of localization, and because he himself calls them "spiritual" in the *Paraphrase of the De Memoria et Reminiscentia* (referred to here as the *De Sensu et Sensato*).

The "distinguishing power" [*virtus distinctiva*] was met before. According to Professor Wolfson,[75] it reflects the Aristotelian κριτική, which was one of the functions of διάνοια that is to say,

---

73. *Ibid.*, t. c. 6, fol. 154AC. Latin text in Appendix II, no. 37.
74. H. Wolfson, "The Internal Senses," p. 109, note 76.
75. *Ibid.*, pp. 108, 78, 81.

the distinguishing of truth and falsity. Hence, he concludes that
"cogitative" (*fikr*) in this passage (and in the *Paraphrase of the
De Memoria*) means "human thinking" and not "compositive human
imagination."

In the first place, "cogitative" in one of its uses, means a
sense power, which cannot do human thinking. In this text itself,
a clue is given. Galen, as Professor Wolfson himself admits,[76]
was speaking of the human reason and "human thinking." Averroes
sharply criticises Galen, and points out the source of his error.
The physician failed to distinguish between the "individual distinguishing power" (= cogitative) and the "universal distinguishing power" (= material rational power).

What precisely does the sensory cogitative do? It distinguishes
between the sensation (= intention of a sensible thing = image)
and the image precisely as image (= the intention of the image).
In another text the cogitative has a slightly different function.

> There are three powers in man, whose being was declared
> in the *De Sensu et Sensato*, that is, the imaginative and the
> cogitative and the memorative. For these three powers are
> in man to present the form of an imagined thing, when
> sensation is lacking. And so it was said there, that when
> these three powers help each other, they will perhaps represent
> an individual thing, even though we do not sense it.
>
> And Aristotle means here by the term "passible intellect"
> the forms of imagination in so far as the cogitative power
> proper to man acts on them. For this power is a kind of
> reason, and its action is nothing more than to put the inten-
> tion of a form of imagination together with its individual
> which is in the memorative power, or to distinguish the one
> from the other present in the formative power. And it is
> evident that the intellect which is called "material" receives
> the imagined intentions after such distinction.[77]

The cogitative is a kind of reason, whose function is to combine the imagined with the remembered form, or to distinguish
them. In this way it serves to present to intellect a sensible individual, even when it is not being sensed.

---

76. *Ibid.*, pp. 70-74, 78-81.
77. *In III De Anima*, t. c. 20, vol. VI, i. 2, fol. 164C. Latin text in
    Appendix II, no. 38.

An explanation of one of the ways in which this sensory composition or judgment takes place is quite revealing.

Aristotle says that "imagination is in other animals, but cogitation in rational ones." For to choose to perform this imagined thing and not that, belongs to the action of cogitation and not to the action of imagination. For that which judges that this imagined object is more lovable than that must necessarily be the same power which numbers ["individualizes"] the images and in the case of some judges they are more pleasing. . . . Likewise, cogitation numbers images, and puts them together, until it can be affected by the imagination of one of them. And this is the reason why the rational animal has opinion; for opinion is a consent which rises from cogitation.[78]

Suppose a man is in a situation where he must act or wants to act. He is not naturally determined to any particular act. So his cogitative makes to pass before its sight a series of images, till one of them stirs an emotion. The quasi-discursive process of the parade of images leads to "election" or "choice" which for Averroes is certainly not free, and looks like a merely mechanical process.[79]

There are thus two different situations in which the cogitative employs the technique of the lineup. One is remembering (as we saw before), where the cogitative has as it were one eye fixed on the intention of memory, and the other fixed on the images parading through the imagination. The process goes on till recognition occurs. The second situation is that of deliberation. Here the cogitative starts the parade, and it goes on till one or the other image sets the imagination in motion, so that appetite and action follow.

So, when Averroes says that the cogitative in man replaces the estimative (or the imaginative[80]) in animals, he means the

78. *Ibid.,* t. c. 57, fol. 198BC. Latin text in Appendix II, no. 39.

79. In the first place, there is only one appetitive power in man, and that is the concupiscible soul; cf. *in III de Anima,* t. c. 29, fol. 170E. The apparent difference between will and sense appetite, in the second place, is this, that the former is preceded by cogitation and the latter is not; *ibid.,* t. c. 50, fol. 194.

80. See "Alia enim animalia non habent cogitationem, sed in loco cogitationis habent imaginationem," *ibid.,* t. c. 48, fol. 193B.

following. In animals a definite image for action, either innate or
from sense experience, is always at hand. There is neither hesita-
tion nor deliberation nor flexibility in animals. In man, a review
of images must be held before action; sometimes, perhaps most
frequently, a composite or divided image must be produced before the imagination and appetite are affected.

This process of parading and composition can even lead to
the representation of a sensible object that was never experienced
before.

> It is possible that a man cogitate about some thing, so that
> from this he discovers an individual which he has not sensed
> before; but he did sense a similar one, yet not this one.[81]

In all these instances, the cogitative helps to pick out an
individual. At times, Averroes uses precisely this function as the
characteristic of the cogitative.

> Aristotle did not intend that the senses comprehend the es-
> sence of things, as some have thought, for this is the work
> of another power which is called intellect. He intended to
> say that the senses, together with the comprehension of their
> proper sensibles, comprehend the individual intentions divided
> into genera and species. They comprehend therefore the in-
> tention of this individual man, and universally the intention
> of each of the ten individual predicaments, and this seems
> to be proper to the senses of man. For this reason Aristotle
> says, in the *De Sensu et Senato,* that the senses of other
> animals are not like the senses of man — or words to that
> effect. This individual intention is the one which the cogi-
> tative power distinguishes from the imagined form, and strips
> it of all the common and proper sensibles which are joined
> to it, and places it in the memorative. And this is the same
> form that the imaginative comprehends, but the imagina-
> tive comprehends it joined to the sensibles, though its com-
> prehension is more spiritual.[82]

> The cogitative power is not the material intellect . . . but
> it is a particular material power. . . . One must not say that

81. *Ibid.,* t. c. 33, fol. 173B. Latin text in Appendix II, no. 40.
      Cf. "Possumus etiam per hanc virtutem [conservativam, imagina-
tivam] fingere formas imaginabiles quarum individua numquam sensimus," *in II De Anima,* t. c. 153, fol. 130E.
82. *In II De Anima,* t. c. 63, fol. 82EF. Latin text in Appendix II, no. 41.

it composes singular intelligibles. . . . For there is no cogitation, except in distinguishing the individual of those intelligibles, and presenting it in act, as if it were present to sense. And so, when such individuals are present to sense, then cogitation ceases, and the action of intellect remains. And from this it is clear that the action of intellect is different from that of the cogitative power which Aristotle calls the "possible intellect," and which he said was generable and corruptible . . . since it has a limited instrument, that is, the middle ventricle of the brain; and man is not generable and corruptable except through this power.[83]

The term "intellect" has many meanings. Averroes points out that in the *De Anima* it has four. "It is said of the material intellect, and of the intellect in habit, and of the agent intellect, and of the imaginative power."[84] The imagination is an intellect in a loose sense.[85] The "agent" and the "recipient intellect" are eternal substances.[86] The "material intellect," designates the "contact" of the agent intellect with the sense powers of man and the actually understood intention.[87] The "passive intellect" is either "the forms of the imagination in so far as they are acted on by the cogitative,"[88] or the imagination itself.[89] And the text last quoted above says that the "possible intellect" is the cogitative power. Hence, it is quite clear that the term "intellect" in Averroes is an equivocal term, and that no valid argument can be drawn from the consideration that the cogitative is called an intellect.

To summarize the Averroistic doctrine on the cogitative power, it is necessary to begin by saying that it, too, is an equivocal term. It can mean the intellect in general, or the speculative or practical intellect, or, finally, a strictly sense power. It is this last sense that is noteworthy. The sensory cogitative is a power peculiar to man, which distinguishes between the image of the imagination and the memory-image, and composes or divides them. In

---

83. *In III De Anima,* t. c. 33, fol. 173C. Latin text in Appendix II, no. 42.
84. *In III De Anima,* t. c. 20, fol. 165A.
85. *Ibid.,* t. c. 5, fol. 139A.
86. *Ibid.,* t. c. 18, fol. 161E.
87. *Ibid.,* fol. 161, and t. c. 5, fol. 138D-152F.
88. *In III De Anima,* t. c. 20, fol. 164C.
89. *Ibid.,* t. c. 5, fol. 151B.

this way, it succeeds in attaining the individual, either as experienced, or, more rarely, even before experience. This same activity of composition and division results in preparing the image for abstraction by the agent intellect. This same activity also, under different circumstances, results in "choice," the selection of an image to be made.

What about the provenance of the term "cogitative"? It may well originally represent διάνοια; in some of its uses it still means "thought, planning, reasoning," and the like. But when it is used to designate a sense power, it loses contact with its Aristotelian sources; it is purely an Averroistic term.

SUMMARY

The composite picture of man's internal powers drawn from these philosophers is remarkably confused. Taken singly, Al-Farabi, Avicenna-Algazel, and Averroes have different classifications and different uses of terms. Taken as a group, the doctrines are unmanageable. It is, however, possible to make some progress by putting the teachings under several heads.

How *many* internal senses are there? The answers vary all the way from one (Al-Farabi on occasion) to seven (in Avicenna). And in Avicenna there are apparently various ways of combining these seven to be five, four, or three.

What is *common sense?* According to Isaac Israeli, it is a power intermediate between the external and internal senses. In Al-Farabi-Avicenna-Algazel, it is an internal power, comparable to the other internal senses, whose function is unification of the external senses, sensory awareness, and apprehension of the common sensibles. In Averroes it is not a distinct power in the genus of accident, but rather the root of sensation, which is differentiated into the special senses. At times it seems to be almost the same as the sensitive soul.

What is the *cogitative?* In Avicenna it is the compositive imagination, formally distinct from the merely retentive imagination, having a distinct organ in the brain. In Averroes, it is more rarely reason in general, or either speculative or practical intellect; most often it is the sensory power of distinguishing image from memory, of initiating the parade of images, of knowing the material singular, and the like. It is very difficult to discover just how the three internal sensory powers are distinct for Averroes.

What is the *estimative*? It is a distinct power of perceiving the intentions of the useful and harmful in Al-Farabi, Avicenna, and Algazel. It is the absence of reason for Isaac Israeli. In Averroes, when it is mentioned, it is a special name for a special function of the imagination, or for the innate arts of the imagination, or for nature itself.

Which is the *supreme sensory power*? By the "supreme sensory power" is meant the power which is the ultimate guide of sensory activity on the level of sense. In Al-Farabi and his group, it is the estimative; in Averroes it is either the imagination or the memory.

Localization. The only way this picture can be presented is by a diagram.[90]

	Front Ventricle	Middle Ventricle	Rear Ventricle
Alfarabi	Inner sense?	(no clear statement)	
Costa-Ben-Luca	1. Sense 2. Imagination	Intellect-Reason Cogitation	1. Memory 2. Motion
Avicenna (De Anima)	1. Common Sense 2. Imagination	1. Cogitative 2. Estimative	Memory
(Psychology) [Landauer]	Imagination	Cogitative Estimative	Memory
Algazel	1. Common Sense 2. Imagination	Cogitative	1. Estimative 2. Memory
Averroes (Destructio)	Imagination	Estimative Cogitative	Memory
(Otherwise)	Imagination	Cogitative	Memory

In addition to this divergence, it is necessary to recall that the very idea of localization is different in these authors.

90. Cf. A. Schneider, *Die Psychologie Alberts des Grossen,* p. 182, note 2, and Max Horten, *Das Buch der Ringsteine Farabi's,* pp. 221-25.

CHAPTER 4

FROM GUNDISSALINUS TO ST. ALBERT THE GREAT

We have seen that the first traces of Arabian influence in the field of psychology are to be found in the earliest translators and their immediate contemporaries. But this influence was rather uncertain, and was directed rather toward the medical and biological backgrounds of psychology than to strictly psychological doctrines. This is explained by the character of the works which were first translated.

The distinctive psychological doctrines of the Arabians, especially of Avicenna, were as yet not very well known. With Gundissalinus the situation changes.

Gundissalinus

In the twelfth century, Archbishop Raymond of Toledo gathered a group of translators. His purpose was to make the Arabian scientific and philosophical writings available to the Christian world by having them translated into Latin.

Gundissalinus (Gundisalvi) was a member of this group. When he came to write works of his own, it was quite natural for him to borrow some of the ideas he had gleaned through his work of translation.[1] In his *De Divisione Philosophiae* he presents a theory of the degrees of abstraction, in the course of which he mentions estimation. Both the setting and the notion of this function are interesting.

Abstraction is any apprehension of the form of a thing. Sense apprehends this form in one way, the imagination in another, estimation in another, intellect in still another. . . .
    Estimation transcends this order [i.e., of the imagination] of abstraction, because it apprehends material intentions which

---

1. Cf. Étienne Gilson, *La Philosophie au Moyen Age*, 2nd ed. (Paris: Payot, 1944), p. 379.

are not in their proper matters, although it happens to them to be in matter.[2]

The second sentence of this passage is an echo of the famous Boethian sentence, except that the last two terms of the latter's enumeration (reason, intelligence) are here replaced by "estimation" and "intellect." The remark about the abstraction of estimation is taken from Avicenna. But because not enough of the passage is quoted, the remark can seem to have a relation to Algazel's definition of mathematics.[3] However, the examples which illus-

---

2. "Abstraccio est forme rei qualiscumque apprehensio. Hanc autem formam aliter apprehendit sensus, aliter ymaginacio, aliter estimacio, aliter intellectus. Ex hiis enim alia abstrahunt formam rei perfecte, alia imperfecte . . . visus imperfecte formam rei abstrahit, quoniam eam nonnisi in praesente materia et cum multis accidentibus apprehendit: ymaginacio vero plus aliquantulum formam a materia abstrahit quia ad hoc ut forma in se subsistat presenciam materie non requirit, sed tamen formam ab omnibus accidentibus materie non secernit. . . .

Estimacio vero transcendit hunc ordinem abstraccionis quoniam apprehendit intenciones materiales que non sunt in suis materiis quamvis accidat eis esse in materia. Figura enim et color et situs et hiis similia sunt res que non possunt esse nisi in materiis corporalibus: bonum vero et malum, licitum et illicitum, honestum et hiis similia in se quidem sunt res non materiales quamvis accidat eis esse materiales. Si enim in se essent materiales, numquam intelligerentur nisi in corpore. Materia enim hic accipitur substancia corporea. Estimacio ergo cum apprehendit res materiales abstrahit eas a materia et apprehendit intenciones non materiales quamvis sint materiales et hec abstraccio purior est et vicinior simplicitati quam due priores. Sed non omnino exspoliat formas ab accidentibus materie, eo quod particulariter apprehendit eam secundum quamquamque materiam et secundum comparacionem eis ad illam ligatam cum forma sensibili et stipatam accidentibus materie et cum conveniencia ymaginacionis in illa," *De Divisione Philosophiae,* ed. Ludwig Baur (Beitraege, Baeumker, Muenster: Aschendorff, 1903, Band IV, Heft 2-3), pp. 28-29.

Compare Michael Scotus, in Vencentii Bellovacensis *Speculum Doctrinale* (XVIII [XVI], 1), "Similiter abstrahit aestimatio formam non materialem quamvis ei accidit esse in materia, sicut amicitiam et inimicitiam, quae est in cane et lupo," Baur, p. 399.

3. Cf. "Tractat de his quae possunt aestimari absque materia, sed non

trate this object of estimation, as the "good, the evil, the licit," and so forth, seem to be taken from Algazel's treatment of estimation (seen in the previous chapter).

In another work, the *De Immortalitate Animae,* which is more closely dependent on Avicenna and Algazel,[4] the estimative sense is explained much more accurately.[5] In this closer contact with Avicenna, Gundissalinus comes to grips with the Galenic localization used by many of the twelfth-century Latin writers. Avicenna, as we have seen, did not consider the intellect to be localized. Gundissalinus follows him in this.[6] Against the quasi-experimental proof of localization from bodily injuries, he answers in quite an Augustinian fashion:

> its operation is only hindered or destroyed on the part of that which is from below, that is, on the part of sensibles. For the stable impression of sensible forms is like a second book for it, which book is offered or shown to it by the imaginative power.[7]

The doctrine of the "two faces of the soul" is quite clearly hinted at here. The lower function ("face") of knowledge, concerned with reading the book of sensible things, depends on the bodily organ which contains that book. The function of the middle cell of the

---

habent esse nisi in materia," *Algazel's Metaphysics,* ed. J. T. Muckle, C.S.B. (Toronto: St. Michael's College, 1933), tr. 1, 1; p. 3.

4. Cf. É. Gilson, *La Philosophie au Moyen Age,* p. 379.

5. "Aestimativa enim virtus, quae procul dubio in huiusmodi [bruti] anima est, forte proprie nullam [formam] nisi sensibilem recipit. 'Proprie' diximus, quia nullum proprium videtur aestimabile brutis nisi sensibile nocumentum aut commodum, circa quae duo virtus aestimativa brutorum maxime versatur," *De Immortalitate Animae,* ed. Georg Buelow, *Des Dominicus Gundissalinus Schrift von der Unsterblichkeit der Seele,* (Beitraege, Baeumker, Muenster: Aschendorff, 1897, Band II, Heft 3), p. 10.

6. "Manifestum est virtutem istam [intellectualem] non habere instrumentum operationis suae in corpore," *De Immortalitate Animae,* ed. G. Buelow, p. 20.

7. *Ibid.,* pp. 20-21. Text in Appendix II, no. 44. The text continues: "Has igitur cum abstrahere et spoliare a condicionibus particularibus non potuerit propter perturbationem aut laesionem mediae cellulae, in quam transeant a virtute imaginativa."

brain seems consequently to be this presentation of the book of the imagination to the intellect.

There is also a treatise *De Anima* commonly attributed to Gundissalinus.[8] In this treatise, chapter nine deals with *De Viribus Animae*, and its third section treats particularly of *De Interioribus Virtutibus Animalium*. In the latest edition of this work,[9] the editor shows that this entire section is a mosaic of Avicenna's *De Anima* put together in the following order: part 1, chapter 5; part 4, chapters 1, 2, 4, and 5.[10] In the matter of the interior senses, Gundissalinus here presents Avicenna's text itself.

WILLIAM OF AUVERGNE

William of Auvergne (William of Paris) was born at Aurillac at the end of the twelfth century. In 1228 he was made bishop of Paris, and held this position till his death in 1249. During his long stay in Paris, he was active both in teaching and in writing. Though he opposed certain points of the Avicennan philosophy, he did accept others, following to some extent the lead of Gundissalinus.

Thus, in his *De Immortalitate Animae*, he incorporated the passage of Gundissalinus's work of the same name which was referred to above.[11] In his *De Anima*, the Bishop of Paris again adverts to the Galenic localization.[12] After an objective presenta-

---

8. Recently this treatise has been attributed to John of Spain (Avendeath, etc.), by Gabriel Théry, *Tolede* (Oran: Heintz Frères, 1944).
9. By J. T. Muckle, C.S.B., "The Treatise *De Anima* of Dominicus Gundissalinus," *Mediaeval Studies* II (1940), pp. 23-103.
10. In the edition just cited, the section is on pages 71-83, where the passages of Avicenna are identified.
11. Cf. G. Buelow, *Des Dominicus Gundissalinus Schrift von der Unsterblichkeit der Seele,* pp. 45, 57.
12. "Quemadmodum igitur est in oculo idoneitas fieri aptitudo recipiendi formas sensibiles, sic in corpore humano ex contemperantia saepe nominata in praecedentibus est idoneitas recipiendi formas intelligibiles; existimo quoniam idoneitas ista non potest dici in toto corpore esse, sive sparsa per totum illud, quemadmodum ponunt in media cellula capitis, in qua opinantur huiusmodi idoneitatem esse, quoniam et medici ipsi communiter cellulam illam nominant cellulam

tion of the doctrine, he begins his discussion of it with a strong condemnation: "May that opinion perish together with its followers."[13] His argumentation against the theory that reason is an organic power is like that of Avicenna.

In spite of this position, William continues to mention reason among the inner powers.[14] These powers: common sense, the imagination, estimative, reasoning, and memorative powers, are quite obviously related to the powers mentioned by Avicenna,[15] though the correspondence is not exact. It is hard to determine the differ-

---

rationis, quemadmodum et posteriorem partem capitis cellulam memorativam, et anteriorem et imaginativam usualiter vocant," *De Anima*, in *Guilielmi Alverni Opera Omnia* (Orleans: 1674), c. 5, pars 5; vol. II, supplement, fol. 119a.

13. *Ibid.*, fol. 119, 120.

14. "Amplius si pluralitas atque diversitas operationum sufficerent facere debere esse pluralitatem animarum, esset numerus animarum tam in homine quam in aliis animalibus juxta numerum virium et operationum quae in illis sive ex illis. Quare juxta numerum quinque sensuum essent quinque animae in homine, et alia quinque juxta numerum virium aliarum, videlicet sensum communem, imaginativam, aestimativam, ratiocinativam, rememorativam," *De Anima*, c. 4, pars. 3, fol. 108a.

15. "Neben der fuenf auessern Sinnen kennt Wilhelm auch innere Sinne. Hier scheint er, wie auch Alexander von Hales und Thomas von Aquin, dem Avicenna zu folgen. Aristoteles naemlich hatte nur einen einzigen innern Sinn angenommen, den Centralsinn und den Sitz desselben in das Herz verlegt. Dieses war das Subject aller hierher gehoerige Thaetigkeiten, der Phantasie- und Gedaechtnissvorstellungen. Abweichend hiervon unterschied dagegen Avicenna neben den auessern empfindende Vormoegen noch fuenf innere Sinne, welche er sich an einzelnen Teilen des Gehirns lokalisiert dachte. In aehnliche Weise zaehlt Wilhelm vier innere Sinne auf, welche die Vorder-, Mittel- und Hinterzelle des Kopfes zu ihren Organen haben, naemlich der Gemeinsinn, die Einbildungskraft oder Phantasie, dann das sinnliche Gedaechtniss und endlich die sinnliche Urteilskraft," Matthias Baumgartner, *Die Erkenntnisslehre des Wilhelm von Auvergne*, (Beitraege, Baeumker, Muenster: Aschendorff, 1893, Band II, Heft 1), p. 26. However, it is difficult to see that this is precisely the teaching of Wilhelm on localization; rather, the function of the central cell is vague, as in Gundissalinus.

ences, since William has very little more to say about them.[16] There are occasional passing remarks about one or the other internal sense.[17] Common sense, imagination, and memory are said to be storehouses or libraries of external things.[18] The various external senses act upon each other;[19] they have a relation to intellect[20] and to desire.[21] A significant doctrine is that of the double memory of singulars: one in the soul itself,[22] one outside the soul (*extra animam*), namely, the phantasms in the brain cells.[23] This last remark seems to indicate a Platonic conception of the relation of soul to body.

16. Cf. *ibid.,* p. 26.
17. E. g., "Idem est videre de apprehensivis ab intus, sicut in sensu communi, imaginatione, et memoria : nihil enim potest sensus communis non impeditus ut diximus, nisi prout recepit a particularibus, et imaginatio simpliciter, nisi prout recepit a sensu communi ac si diceretur prout ei traditum est," *De Virtutibus,* c. 9, vol. I, fol. 120bF. "Non distinguimus a sensu ea quae in sensu relinquuntur, videlicet imaginationem et memoriam : ista enim videntur esse sensus repositi et thesaurisati," *De Legibus,* c. 27, vol. I, fol. 88a; cf. also *De Universo,* 2, pars 3, c. 21, vol. I, fol. 1057a, and *De Virtutibus,* c. 9, vol. I, fol. 120b, 122a.
18. "Sensus vero communis et imaginatio et etiam memoria sunt sicut armaria vel libraria continentes omnium quae foris sunt vel fiunt vel facta sunt descriptiones, quemadmodum apud Reges fieri consuevit," *De Virtutibus,* c. 9, vol. I, fol. 122bF.
19. "Vis enim memorativa in vi imaginativa interdum generat apprehensionem imaginativam et vis sensitiva agit in memorativam, thesaurizans in ea formas sensibiles et quod amplius est, secundum eandem vim agit et patitur in se ipsa," "*De Virtutibus,* c. 1, vol. I, fol. 107bD; *ibid.,* c. 9, fol. 120bG.
20. "Sic creatio animarum humanarum [extra corpora] in parte otiosa esset, et inutilis prorsus, videlicet, quantum ad vires . . . . Haec autem sunt vires sensibiles, necnon virtus imaginativa ac memorativa corporalis," *De Anima,* c. 5, pars 9, vol. II, supp., fol. 124b.
21. Cf. *De Legibus,* c. 13, vol. I, fol. 44aG.
22. *De Anima,* c. 7, pars 15, vol. II, supp., fol. 222a.
23. "Phantasmata igitur quae extra animam sunt videlicet in quacumque ex tribus cellulis humani capitis non est mirum si sublato capite toto vel vulnerato aliquae illorum in toto vel in parte amittuntur ; ea vero quae in ipsa animae essentia jam collocata et fixa sunt non est necesse," *Ibid.,* fol. 221b; cf. Hugh of St. Victor, text cited above, chapter II, note 141.

ALEXANDER OF HALES

Alexander of Hales was a native of Gloucestershire. He became a Master at the University of Paris, entered the Franciscan
order in 1236, and died in 1245. In the *Summa Theologica* ascribed to him there is a rather full discussion of the interior
senses.[24]

The first question concerns St. John Damascene's three powers,
here called the "imaginative, the excogitative, and the memorative." What is the "excogitative"?

To this we must say that, as Avicenna says, this power receives two names, so as to be called sometimes the "imaginative" sometimes the "cogitative." There is this difference,
that when the animal estimative governs it, then it is called
"imaginative;" but if the rational power governs it, and leads
it to that which is profitable to it, it is called "cogitative."
Therefore, whether the estimative govern it or the rational
power, it is always counted among the sensitive parts, as
he says.[25]

This is good Avicennan doctrine, even to the choice of words. But,
as we have seen, the localization, which St. John took from Nemesius and ultimately from Galen, really has as its second power
human reason or intellect.

In the discussion of the estimative, Alexander follows Avicenna
in placing it in the back part of the middle cell of the brain.[26]
But he has some difficulty with the doctrine. After objecting to
himself that the "intentions" of the estimative are innate, and
that therefore that power has no organ, he concedes that the intentions really are innate, and that in a way the estimative has
no organ of its own. But because it deals with material things,
it is bound up some way or other with the imagination.[27] Alex-

---

24. *Summa Theologica,* Prima Pars secundi Libri, (Ed. Quaracchi,
    1928: 3 vols.), nos. 357-362, vol. II, pp. 434-39.
25. *Ibid.,* (Inq. 4, tract. 1, sect. 2, q. 2, titl. 1), membr. 2, c. 1, no. 357,
    p. 435. Text in Appendix II, no. 45.
26. *Ibid.,* c. 3, no. 359, p. 436.
27. "Obj. 1. . . . intentiones quae licet inveniantur in rebus sensibilibus
    inveniuntur tamen extra res sensibiles nec ex sensu extrahuntur

ander adds that there are two estimatives: the sensible, dealing with intentions bound up with sensible forms; and the rational, dealing with abstract intentions.[28]

Though there are certain modifications of Avicenna's doctrine to be discovered,[29] they do not prevent Alexander from thinking that Avicenna is the recognized master with respect to the internal senses.[30]

JEAN DE LA ROCHELLE

Jean de la Rochelle (John of Rupella), who lived from 1200 to 1245, studied under Alexander of Hales. But his interests seem to have gone beyond those of his master, for his *Summa de Anima* is a meeting place for many doctrines. For this reason, and per-

---

apud aestimativam; ergo apud aestimativam secundum se sunt innatae; si ergo iudicat de eis non iudicat mediante aliquo organo.

Ad 1. . . . licet intentiones quas apprehendit aestimativa possunt esse secundum se extra materiam corporalem, tamen ut apprehendit aestimativa sensibilis sunt in materia corporali et ideo indiget quadam colligatione cum corpore; unde dicitur quod apprehendit intentionem ligatam cum forma sensibili et est aliqua convenientia imaginationis cum illa, non tamen utitur organo in se, sed in quantum est in re imaginata." *Ibid.*, obj. 1 and ad 1, p. 436; cf. "Ab intus habet," *Ibid.*, c. 4, a. 2.II, no. 360, p. 438.

28. "Aestimativa rationalis apprehendit etiam intentiones abstractas a materia; aestimatio autem sensibilis apprehendit eas cum colligatione formae sensibilis," *Ibid.*, c. 3, ad 2, no. 359, p. 436.

29. In addition to those already noted, we may add this distinction on how to reconcile Aristotle and the doctors: "medici ad causam propinquam, . . . philosophus vero ad causam primam," of localization, *ibid.*, c. 4, a. 1.II, no. 360, p. 438.

30. In addition to the indications already given, note that Alexander's summary at the close of his treatment again invokes Avicenna, *ibid.*, c. 4, a. 2.I, no. 360, p. 438.

Another work that follows Avicenna rather closely is the *Summa Philosophiae* formerly attributed to Grosseteste; chapter 8 of this work gives a short account of the internal powers which is very like that of Avicenna; see the edition by Ludwig Baur (Beitraege, Baeumker, Muenster: Aschendorff, 1912, Band IX), pp. 306, 549, 463, 478-79.

haps still more because of his fundamental loyalty to the principles of St. Augustine, this work was at one time extremely popular.

In his discussion of the interior senses, John names Avicenna as his guide.[31] But this does not exclude doctrines of quite different origin. He has a discussion of the order of abstraction which is strongly reminiscent of Avicenna as summarized by Gundissalinus.[32] In answering the question about the functions of the various parts of the brain, John gives two answers. The first is that of St. Augustine's *De Genesi ad Litteram*;[33] in the development of this, light is introduced as the medium of sensation.[34] The second answer is of the Galenic type, apparently as given by St. John Damascene.[35]

---

31. Cf. G. M. Manser, O.P., "Johann von Rupella," *Jahrbuch fuer Philosophie und spekulative Theologie* XXVI (1912), pp. 299-300.
32. "Aestimatio vero parum transcendit illum ordinem abstractionis [*sc.* imaginationis]. Apprehendit enim formas quae sunt intentiones sensibilium, non secundum se similitudinem habentes cum formis materialibus, ut bonitas, malitia, conveniens et inconveniens; sed tamen aestimatio non apprehendit hanc formam expoliatam ab omnibus accidentibus materialibus, eo quod particulariter apprehendit eam et secundum propriam materiam et per comparationem ad formam corporalem, sicut patet ex praedictis," *Summa de Anima,* part 2, no. 35, in G. Manser, "Johann von Rupella," p. 306. Compare with the text from Gundissalinus, quoted above, note 2, second paragraph, and Avicenna, chapter 3, note 34.
    For a somewhat different interpretation of this passage, see É. Gilson, *La Philosophie au Moyen Age,* pp. 437-38.
33. The remaining texts of the *Summa de Anima* have been transcribed from a microfilm of the fourteenth century manuscript, Bruges, 515. In the *Summa de Anima,* this text is on fol. 19 r b, lines 36-40. The text of St. Augustine is from *De Genesi ad Litteram,* bk. 7, c. 18, PL XXXIV. 364, and is quoted above in chapter 2.
34. *Summa de Anima,* fol. 19 r b, lines 43-50.
35. "In prima parte cerebri vis animalis vocatur phantastica, id est ymaginativa quia in ea rerum imagines in similitudines imprimuntur. Unde et phantasticum dicitur. In media parte vocatur rationalis sive excogitativa, quia ibi examinat et iudicat quod per ymaginationem representatum. In ultima parte vocatur memorialis," *ibid.,* fol. 19va, lines 1 ff. Cf. *ibid.,* fol. 20 r b, where St. John is explicitly referred to, and compare Alexander of Hales, first text quoted above.

John next turns to the problem of the powers of the soul. Here we find the "three kinds of sight (vision) according to St. Augustine,"[36] but also the Boethian levels of knowledge as modified by Isaac of Stella and the *De Spiritu et Anima.*[37] The next step is the treatment of strictly internal powers. Here there are two ways of dividing: the first, into three powers according to St. Augustine and St. John Damascene; the second, into five powers according to Avicenna.[38] In this second list, the phrase: "the phantasy which is common sense," identifies the source as Avicenna's *De Anima,* part 1, chapter 5.

The treatment of the Avicennan powers follows the development given in the *De Anima* quite literally up to the discussion of the estimative. Here there is a sudden departure. The basis for this modification is not clear; it may be the doctrine of Alexander of Hales.[39]

> Now, [the estimative] is a transcendent power, because its apprehension is not only of the forms of sensible and material things, but also of immaterial things; for goodness and evil, the suitable and the unsuitable, the useful and the harmful, in themselves are forms . . . not material, not subject to the exterior senses.[40]

This summary of what Avicenna has to say about the degree of abstraction of the estimative seems to make this power almost

---

36. *Summa de Anima,* fol. 19 v a-b.
37. "sensus, imaginatio, ratio, intellectus, intelligentia . . . secundum sanctum Augustinum," *ibid.,* fol. 20 r b. The texts from Isaac of Stella and the *De Spiritu et Anima,* which John must have considered an authentic work of St. Augustine, are to be found in chapter II.
38. "Secundum Augustinum et Joannem, imaginativa sive phantastica, excogitativa sive rationalis, memorialis . . . alio modo per quinque differentias secundum Avicennam, phantasia, quae est sensus communis, ymaginatio, ymaginativa, estimativa, memorialis," *ibid.,* fol. 25 r a, lines 41-49.
39. This, however, cannot be decided until critical editions of both works have been made. On the other hand, the relationship may work in the other direction.
40. *Summa de Anima,* fol. 26 r a-b. Text in Appendix II, no. 46.

a spiritual power. But John does not quite say this, nor does he draw the conclusions which might be drawn.

It seems more correct to say that John attempts a synthesis of the various doctrines known to him under the guidance of Avicenna. His attitude is that in sense psychology Avicenna is the master, whose doctrine is best in itself, and provides also the means of absorbing other points of view.

St. Albert the Great

St. Albert was born in Suabia in 1193. In 1223, he entered the Dominican order, and completed his studies at Padua and Bologna. His teaching years were spent at Cologne and Paris. This career was interrupted for a short time, when he was made bishop of Ratisbon. But he resigned his see, and went back to teaching and writing. He died in 1280.

Albert received his appellation of "the Great" from the literally astounding range of his interests and the range of his knowledge. When he began teaching, the most alert of his contemporaries were reaching out to absorb and sometimes to criticise Avicenna and Algazel. St. Albert also made use of Avicenna, and to an even greater extent, particularly in scientific (and especially biological) matters. And, for the first time in the Middle Ages, Albert made use of Averroes and of Aristotle directly.[41]

---

41. Cf. É. Gilson, La Philosophie au Moyen Age, pp. 504-05; Karl Werner, Der Entwickelungsgang der mittelalterlichen Psychologie von Alcuin bis Albertus Magnus (Wien: 1876, Gerold). Separatabdruck aus dem XXV Bande der Denkschriften der philosophisch-historischen Classe der kaiserlichen Akademie der Wissenschaften), pp. 45-82. Lest there be any doubt of St. Albert's knowledge of Averroes, there is a discussion of the various "peripatetic" positions on internal sensation in his Commentary on Aristotle's De Memoria et Reminiscentia: "Non enim distincte cognoscitur res ex ipsa ejus figura, quia si hoc esset verum, tunc distincte quamlibet cognosceremus rem cujus figuram apud nos habemus . . . sed distinctam rei cognitionem operatur in anima, quando cognoscitur quod haec figura hujus rei et non alterius intentio est. Oportet igitur quod ante memoriam quaedam virtus operetur quae ex ipsa figura elicit earum intentiones singulares: et hanc quidem Avicenna bene et proprie vocavit aesti-

St. Albert wrote commentaries, after the Avicennan manner of paraphrase, on most of the Aristotelian works. Of this group of works, we are especially interested in the *Libri Tres De Anima*, a presentation, apparently in his own name, of all the "Peripatetic" doctrines.

mationem. Averroes autem improprie vocat cogitativam animalium brutorum, per quam fugiunt nociva et persequuntur convenientia. . . . Propter quod dicit Averroes elegantur in hujus libri commento quinque loca apprehensivorum organorum esse in capite, quorum unus est exteriorum organorum, quem vocat calde corporalem duri corticis, quia in cortice praesentiae rei accipit, et complementum hujus loci est in organo sensus communis in prima parte, capitis medullosa et humida. Secundus autem locus est sensus communis, qui primus est locorum spiritualium, sicut diximus alibi, qua sensus communis formalis est ad sensus proprios comparatus. Ideo iste locus est complementum ut diximus loci primi. Tertius autem qui ut complementum se habet ad secundum organum est imaginationis locus. Imaginatio enim est spiritualior quam sensus communis, et accipit imaginatio pro eodem cum phantasia. Qualiter autem se habet veritas de hoc, in libro De Anima determinatum est. Quartus locus est in organo virtutis distinctae, quam vocat Averroes cogitativam brutorum, quae distinguit intentiones a figuris rerum. Quintus est in organo virtutis memorativae. . . .

Receptio sensus communis et imaginatio sunt in anteriori, cognitio sive distinctio in medio, conservatio et memoria in posteriori. . . . Ex his igitur patet quod conservativa secundum Averroem non differt a memoriali, nisi secundum esse, quia conservatio conservat tam imagines quam intentiones. . . ." *In De Memoria et Reminiscentia,* tract 1, c. 1, ed. August Borgnet (Paris: Vives, 1890), vol. IX, pp. 98-99.

This is quite an accurate summary. There is a peculiarity in the term "cogitativa brutorum" ascribed to Averroes; on this see Harry Austryn Wolfson, "The Internal Senses in Latin, Arabic, and Hebrew Philosophic Texts," *Harvard Theological Review* XXVIII (1935), p. 119. It can perhaps be explained by a faulty manuscript, which contained an error similar to the strange translation found in the Latin version of Averroes's *Destructio Destructionum,* which we saw in the preceding chapter. As technical terms, these various designations of Avicenna and Averroes were not all universally known before the work of St. Albert, since he tells us that he intends to make known to his contemporaries the doctrines of the Greeks and Arabians.

In this work, the doctrine on common sense is taken partly
from Avicenna, partly from Aristotle himself.[42] The doctrine on
imagination is, as in Aristotle, developed from the experience we
have of images that are different from sensations.[43] The remaining three powers, not named at first, are developed from the fact
that we know and retain "intentions," and compose and divide
both forms and intentions.[44] In this treatment, there are traces
of Avicenna, Algazel, and Averroes.

---

42. "Oportet esse unam partem ex quo omnis sensus oritur, et ad quem
   omnis motus sensibilium referatur sicut ad ultimum finem, et hic
   fons vocatur sensus communis. . . . In quantum autem communis
   est, habet duo sine quibus sensibilis cognitio non perficitur, quorum
   unum est judicium sensibilis operationis, sicut nos apprehendimus
   videre quando videmus, et audire quando audimus, et sic de aliis.
   Si enim hoc judicium non esset in animalibus, non esset satis utile
   videre et audire, secundum alios sensus apprehendere.
      Secundum autem est comparare sensata diversorum sensuum per
   per hoc quod invenit ea in uno communi sensato conjuncta vel distincta. Hoc enim non potest facere aliquis sensus propriorum, quia
   comparatio inter plura est, et oportet comparantem plura simul apud
   se habere. Et ideo sensus communis comparat sensata, dicendo cit-
   rinum esse dulce, et unum dulcius alio, per hoc quod ad ipsum referuntur omnium propriorum sensuum sensata. Haec igitur cogunt ponere
   sensum communem," *Libri Tres de Anima*, in *Opera Omnia*, ed.
   Borgnet, lib. 2, tract. 4, c. 7, vol. V., pp. 302-03.
43. "Nos autem percipimus in nobis esse cognitionem sensibilium formarum etiam quando res non est praesens," *Ibid.*, p. 303.
44. "Nos autem in nobis circa sensibiles formas triplicem experimur in
   genere cognitionem, quarum una est quae est circa formas acceptas
   per sensum hoc modo quo sensatae sunt: alia autem quae est circa
   intentiones quae numquam in sensu fuerunt, sed tamen a sensibilibus
   conditionibus non sunt separatae, sicut esse conveniens vel inconveniens,
   et amicum vel inimicum, et esse filium et non filium, matrem et non
   matrem, sicut ovis noscit filium et illi et non alii porrigit ubera lac-
   tando, et fugit lupum ut inimicum, et canem sequitur ut custodem: et
   utraque istarum cognitionum est de his quae sunt apud nos re non
   praesente. Est autem et quaedam tertia quae agit tam in formis
   sensatis quam in intentionibus componendo et dividendo quae est
   quasi communis virtus ad quam referuntur tam formae sensatae
   intentiones elicitae sicut sensata particularia ad sensum communem,"
   Ibid., p. 303.

There are then five inner senses: (1) common sense; (2) *imago, imaginatio, virtus formalis;* (3) estimative power; (4) memory; (5) phantasy, called also in men cogitative.[45] According to H. A. Wolfson, this account follows Algazel's as given in his *Metaphysics*.[46] This is true, except that the term *virtus formalis* is not found in that passage, and must have been taken directly from Avicenna.

In the localization of these powers, the general source again seems to be Algazel,[47] except for the place of the estimative. In Algazel, this power is in the posterior part; in Avicenna, in the middle chamber; in St. Albert, in the middle chamber, too; however, later on, he seems to place it in the front chamber.[48] This may indicate an advertance to the teaching of Averroes that the estimative is really the same as the imagination. This difficulty is never resolved.

---

45. "Formarum sensatarum vocaverunt Peripateci imaginem, alias imaginationem: et quibusdam placuit quod vocitetur virtus formalis . . . . Activum autem et elicitivum intentionum vocarunt aestimationem . . . . Coati sunt invenire virtutem animae quae tenet intentiones elicitas ab aestimativa virtute: et hanc vocarunt memoriam. . . . Opertet quod . . . sit aliquid commune ad quod tam formae quam intentiones referuntur, sicut ad quoddam commune. Et hoc vocarunt phantasiam," *Ibid.,* p. 303.

"Phantasia autem ab apparitione dicta est: quoniam illa est major cognitio quam habeat anima sensibilis, et est ultimum virtutis ejus, et haec a vulgo in hominibus vocatur cogitativa; cum tamen proprie cogitare rationis sit proprium," *Ibid.,* p. 304.

46. "The Internal Senses," pp. 117-18.

47. Cf. "Sensum communem in anteriore parte cerebri posuerunt in loco ubi concurrunt nervi sensitivi quinque sensuum . . . post quem locum dixerunt thesaurum formarum in quo retinentur formae et immobilitantur, qui thesaurus imaginativa vel formalis dicitur. In prima autem parte mediae cellae cerebri vel cellulae . . . ipsam posuerunt aestimativam. . . . Thesaurum autem ejus in posteriori parte cerebri posuerunt . . . phantasiam autem . . . posuerunt in media mediae cellae tamquam centrum inter imaginativam et memoriam," *De Anima,* bk. 3, tract, 1, c. 2, vol. V, p. 317.

48. Cf. "Organum ejus etiam aut idem est cum organo imaginationis aut propinquum est unum alteri, substantialiter idem existens, et secundum esse dispositionis differens," *ibid.,* p. 318.

The function of the estimative is to be not wholly an apprehending power, but also a motive power.[49] This suggestion seems to be derived from Algazel.

The compositive imagination (phantasy) is very important in St. Albert. Avicenna had hesitated about admitting the presence of compositive imagination in brutes. If it had to be admitted, he would consider that its operations were under the control of the estimative sense. Thus, in either case, the estimative is the supreme sensory power. Algazel easily admitted compositive imagination in brutes; but for him, too, the estimative is the supreme sensory power. Averroes on the contrary insisted that the imagination is the supreme sense power, on the ground that, as Aristotle said, it is the highest power of sense apprehension. St. Albert submits to Aristotle-Averroes that the phantasy is supreme. But having identified retentive imagination with estimation, and having defined phantasy as compositive imagination, St. Albert arrived at a position all his own. This kind of imagination, he says, is found only in such animals as practise something similar to human art and prudence. In the purposive actions of such higher animals, there is the working of a power which combines and separates the images of sensory experience, and sets them together with the intentions of estimation. Clearly then, the compositive imagina-

---

49. "Ea autem potentia quae aestimativa dicitur ab imaginatione differt. Quod enim non sit imaginativa patet quoniam ad imaginem rei solam non sequitur motus vel affectus vel laetitiae vel tristitiae vel fuga vel insecutio : ad aestimationem autem mox sequitur istorum quoddam, vel quodlibet. . . . Oportet igitur quod sicut intellectus practicus se habet ad speculativam, ita se habeat aestimativa ad imaginationem : et ideo haec virtus non penitus apprehensiva est, sed et motiva est, per hoc quod determinat ad quid movere debet animal et quo fugere. Propter quod quidam philosophorum hanc opinionem esse dicebant, quod tamen non congruit, quia opinio rationalis quidem habitus est, aestimatio autem omnium est quorum est sensus. . . . Tres ergo istos inferiores sensus, sensum communem scilicet et imaginationem et aestimativam habet omne animal . . . omne habens desiderium habet imaginationem et aestimationem quae non substantia sed secundum esse differt ab imaginatione," *ibid.*, p. 317.

tion is the highest sensory power.[50] Thus, where Avicenna had stressed finality and tendency, St. Albert stresses association and cognition, so profoundly modifying the Avicennan framework and terminology.

The *Summa de Homine* presents an at least apparently different arrangement. In the first place, common sense is put with the external senses.[51] In this point, H. A. Wolfson sees a probable influence of Isaac Israeli.[52] As he remarks, against A. Schneider,[53] this should not be called an un-Aristotelian stand, since Aristotle did not speak of outer and inner senses.

In this *Summa*, St. Albert goes systematically through the account of common sense and the interior senses. It may be of some interest to follow his presentation.

Common sense has three functions: the comparison of different sensibles, sense awareness, and the apprehension of the common sensibles. There can be three functions, because only the third is the fundamental act of the common sense, from which the other two are derived.[54] This position, as we have seen, had been formally rejected by Avicenna.

---

50. Cf. texts quoted above in notes 45 and 49; also: "Aliquid simile electioni quod expresse videtur quibusdam in brutis . . . nos autem videmus ea per modum artis facere casas, et providere cibum in longum tempus: cujusmodi operum oportet esse principium animae sensibilis potentiam aliquam: hoc autem esse non potest nisi illa virtus quae componit et dividit imagines et intentiones modo supra dicto: haec etiam opera non in omnibus videmus in quibus est imaginatio et aestimatio, sed in quibusdam quae perfectiora sunt. Oportet igitur phantasiam secundum aliquid esse differentem ab imaginatione et aestimativa . . . videtur tota formalitas sensibilis virtutis esse phantasia," *ibid.,* c. 3, p. 318; cf. *ibid.,* tract 5, c. 4.
51. Cf. "Sed quia iterum apprehendere deforis duplex est, scilicet sensus duplex est, scilicet sensus proprius et sensus communis," *Summa De Homine,* (Part 2), title of question 18, vol. XXXV, p. 164; later on, he lists the "apprehensivae deintus" as "imaginatio, phantasia, aestimatio, memoria, reminiscentia," *ibid.,* q. 37, title, p. 323.
52. "The Internal Senses," p. 118.
53. Arthur Schneider, *Die Psychologie Alberts des Grossen* (Beitraege, Baeumker, Muenster: Aschendorff, 1903, 1906, Band IV, Heft 5-6), p. 132.
54. *Summa de Homine,* q. 36, a. 1, sol., vol. XXXV, p. 320.

The work of the imagination is very simply expressed: it simply retains the forms received through sensation.[55]

Phantasy has two meanings. In the wide sense, it includes the imagination, and the phantasy strictly so called, and estimation.[56] This had already been said by Averroes. In the strict sense, it is the power which composes and divides images[57] (or, in another place) images and intentions.[58] St. Albert says that the definition in terms of composition and division of images is derived from Algazel, though the latter adds the division and composition of intentions as well. He also insists, with Algazel, that the phantasy should be called cogitative only in men.

The next power, the estimative, determines the approach or flight of the animal.[59] It apprehends intentions as joined with sensible things, and as ordered to appetite.[60] In fact, it is nothing more than a certain extension of the phantasy to practice, just as the speculative intellect is extended to become practical.[61] There

---

55. *Ibid.,* q. 37, a. 1, sol., p. 323.
56. *Ibid.,* q. 38, a. 1, p. 331; cf. a. 4, p. 334.
57. Cf. "Stricte accipitur pro potentia collativa imaginum per compositionem et divisionem, et sic definitur ab Algazele: et ideo dicit Algazel, quod quidam appellant eam potentiam cogitativam, sicut eam appellat Avicenna; sed tamen cogitativa non est proprie nisi in hominibus," *ibid.,* q. 38, a. 1, p. 331. Cf. *Algazel's Metaphysics,* part 2, tract. 4, "Diccio de Sensibus Interioribus," ed. J. T. Muckle, C.S.B., p. 170; text quoted in chapter three above.
58. *Summa de Homine,* q. 42, a. 2, sol., vol. XXXV, pp. 360-61.
59. *Ibid.,* q. 39, a. 1, p. 337; cf. *Summa Theologiae,* p. 2, tr. 12, q. 70, m. 1, sol.
60. Cf. "Dicendum cum Avicenna, quod intentiones acceptae a sensibus non apprehensae per sensum, apprehenduntur per duos modos, scilicet per rationem universalis: et sic elicere eas a sensibus est experientiae et virtutis intellectivae. Alio modo accipiuntur per intentiones numquam separatas a sensibus, quae sunt hic et nunc: et sic accipiuntur duobus modis: scilicet prout sunt principium veri et falsi in partibus, et sic sunt phantasiae; vel prout determinant nocivum vel conveniens in appetibilibus, et sic sunt aestimativae," *Ibid.,* a. 2, p. 338.
61. Cf. "Aestimativa enim nihil aliud est quam extensio phantasiae in praxim, sicut etiam intellectus speculativus extendendo se sit [*sic:* fit?] practicus," *ibid.,* a. 3, p. 339.

is no explanation here of how the estimative determines the appropriate and the harmful, nor of what is meant by this "extension" of the phantasy.

Memory turns back upon a thing previously experienced, by means of an image retained in the soul, with a consideration of past time.[62] Reminiscence is really identical with memory, but differs in this, that it proceeds from a determined starting-point according to the discourse of reason.[63]

According to this account, there are four internal senses.[64] A point of interest lies in the principle of division, according to which the number four is arrived at. St. Albert says that the final reason for asserting a real distinction of these powers is to be found in the kind (or perhaps, degree) of animal spirit required for the particular operation.[65]

There is a kind of circulation of these animal spirits through the chambers of the brain.[66] In the front chamber, called "phan-

---

62. "Memoria reflectitur in rem in praeterito acceptam a sensibus per imaginationem rei permanentis apud animam cum consideratione temporis praeteriti," *ibid.*, q. 40, a. 1, p. 344.

63. "Reminiscentia est virtus sensibilis animae, et est in subjecto eodem cum memoria, sed differunt in ratione," *ibid.*, q. 41, a. 2, p. 354; cf. q. 42, a. 2, pp. 360-61.

64. Namely, imagination, estimative, *phantasia,* and memory-reminiscence. I do not see how one can speak of these as "five" interior senses; St. Albert states explicitly, and several times, that memory and reminiscence differ only by a distinction of reason — "in ratione." Hence, I must differ from H. A. Wolfson, "The Internal Senses," p. 117, who speaks of the interior senses in the *Summa de Homine,* "assuming that they were meant to be five;" I must differ also from George C. Reilly, O.P., *The Psychology of St. Albert the Great* (Washington: Catholic University Press, 1934), pp. 28-29. Fr. Reilly is aware that in the *De Anima* St. Albert had identified memory and reminiscence; he explains what seems to him to be a difference, thus: in the *De Anima,* St. Albert repeats Aristotle, while in the *Summa de Homine* he gives his own doctrine.

65. Cf. *Summa de Homine,* q. 38, a. 4, p. 334.

66. Cf. "Dicendum, quod tres sunt cellulae capitis, scilicet anterior, posterior, et media. Prima dicitur phantastica ab antiquioribus, secunda syllogistica, tertia memorialis. Spiritus autem animalis a priori transit in mediam, et a media in postremam. Et in prima operatur

tastica" by the Ancients, the spirit produces the external sensation and common sense; in the middle of the front part it produces imagination; and in the rear of the front part it produces
phantasy and estimation. In the rear chamber it produces memory.[67]
St. Albert has departed from the localization used by Avicenna;
he himself refers to the *De Differentia Animae et Spiritus* of Constabulinus; the actual terminology recalls rather William of Conches.

With this summary notion of the internal senses as presented
in the *Summa de Homine,* we can compare the treatment of St.
Albert's *De Anima,* bk. 2, tract. 4, c. 7.   H. A. Wolfson points out
that the order of treatment in the former follows Avicenna's *De
Anima,* the latter follows Algazel's *Metaphysics.*[68] However, in
matters of doctrine, there is very little difference.[69]

In relation to its sources, the Albertinian doctrine on the
interior senses shows that the greatest dependence was perhaps
on Algazel, though not without a direct knowledge and borrow-
ing from Avicenna. From Averroes is taken the notion that the
compositive imagination is the supreme sensory power, although,
unlike the Averroistic cogitative, the Albertinian phantasy is found
in both men and beasts.

As for the relations of the main texts of St. Albert among

---

sensum proprium in organis sensuum, sensum communem in prima
concavitate cerebri, et imaginationem in media anterioris partis
cerebri, et phantasiam et aestimationem in posteriori parte anterioribus partis, ut supra dictum est, ut dicit Constabulinus," *ibid.,* q. 38,
a. 3, sol., p. 333. St. Albert has a long discussion of the anatomy
of the brain, in the course of which he speaks of the "meatus"
and the oval-shaped body, "uvalia"; cf. *De Animalibus,* bk. 1, tract.
3, c. 1, ed. Dr. Hermann Stadler (Beitraege, Baeumker, Muenster:
Aschendorff, 1916, 1921, Band 15-16), Band XV, pp. 189-190. Thus
it is clear that St. Albert knew the sources of, and even admitted
many of the individual elements of, the doctrine of the physico-
biological mechanics of cognition held by Costa-ben-Luca and William
of Conches. Yet there is no trace of this doctrine in St. Albert;
surely a triumph of his critical sense.

67. Cf. note 66, and q. 42, a. 2, p. 360-61.
68. "The Internal Senses," pp. 117-18.
69. As against G. Reilly, *The Psychology of St. Albert the Great,* pp.
    28-29.

themselves, we have already seen that the differences between them are minor. The reason that some authors have found such inconsistency in St. Albert lies mainly in this, that they have tried to combine the doctrine already seen with that contained in several dubious works.[70]

Clearly spurious works, like the *Compendium Theologicae Veritatis,*[71] or the *De Potentiis Animae,*[72] need not be considered here. There is also a *Tractatus de Sensu Communi et de Quinque Potentiis Animae Interioribus* (sometimes found as two treatises), which is variously ascribed to St. Albert, or St. Thomas, or at times has no designation of authorship.[73] This treatise (or treatises) seems to agree with parts of the text of the *Summa de Creaturis.*[74] If this is the case, nothing new would be added from a consideration of it.

There are two larger works, the *Liber de Apprehensione* and

---

70. Thus, H. A. Wolfson, "The Internal Senses," pp. 116-20, uses the *Isagoge* without any reservations; A. Schneider, *Die Psychologie Alberts des Grossen,* pp. 2-3, lists the same work in his discussion of the sources, without any reference at all to its possible non-Albertinian origin.

71. Cf. P. G. Meersseman, O.P., *Introductio in Opera Omnia B. Alberti Magni, O.P.,* (Bruges: Beyaert, 1931), p. 142.

72. *Incipit*: "Sicut dicit Damascenus impossibile est." Cf. D. O. Lottin, "L'authenticité du de Potentiis Animae d'Albert le Grand," *Revue néo-scholastique de philosophie,* XXXII (1930), pp. 321-38. This work may belong to Albert of Orlamunde.

73. P. Meersseman, *Introductio,* p. 138.
    The *De sensu communi* is thus identified: *inc.*: "Quaeritur de sensu communi et primo quaeritur quae sit necessitas ponendi sensum communem," *des.*: "communis dicitur quia per posterius sentit omnia sensata propria"; the *De Quinque Potentiis Animae Interioribus, inc.*: "Sunt autem secundum quosdam philosophos partes animae sensibilis," *des.*: "est enim in subiecto eodem vel eadem cum memoria."

74. Cf. Pearl Kibre, "A Fourteenth Century Scholastic Miscellany," *New Scholasticism,* XV (1941), pp. 261-71, esp. pp. 267-68.
    Dr. Martin Grabmann, *Die Werke des hl. Thomas von Aquin,* 3rd ed. (Beitraege, Baeumker, Muenster: Aschendorff, 1949, Band XXII, Heft 1-2), pp. 400-02, says that the work contains the same doctrine as the *Summa de Homine.*

the *Isagoge* or *Philosophia Pauperum*. The authorship of these two works is still doubtful.[75] Hence, doctrines drawn from them should not be added to others which are certainly those of St. Albert. On the other hand, the picture of the interior senses presented in these two works differs at least to some extent from the Albertinian type as it appears from the *De Anima* and the *Summa de Homine*. For these reasons it will be necessary to consider the *De Apprehensione* and the *Isagoge* separately and briefly.

LIBER DE APPREHENSIONE

This is a treatise in dialogue form dealing with knowledge. We will glance at the section on the interior senses, noting phrases and indicating sources and similarities with the certainly authentic Albertinian doctrine.

The order of treatment in this work is practically the same as that found in St. Albert's *De Anima*, bk. 3, tract. 1, chapter 9. We have seen that this order follows the one given by Avicenna in his *De Anima*.

1. The first of the interior senses is common sense, the source of all the proper senses.[76] The object of this power is the common sensibles.[77] This doctrine resembles St. Albert's discussion in the *De Anima* quite closely.

2. The imaginative power conserves forms; it is also called "formalis," "species," and "thesaurus formarum."[78] The term "species" seems to replace the Albertinian "imago."

---

75. Cf. P. Meerssman, *Introductio,* pp. 130-32.
76. "Scire debes unum esse principium seu fontem ex quo oritur sensibilis cognitio communicata sensibus quinque. Ex uno enim fonte omnes sensus oriuntur, et ad eumdem omnes motus sensibilium ut ad finem ultimum referuntur, et pars ista sensus communis vocatur," *Liber De Apprehensione* (among the works of St. Albert, vol. V), part 3, no. 1, p. 577.
77. "Objecta principalia per se sunt motus, quies, figura, magnitudo, numerus," *ibid.,* no. 5, p. 579.
78. "Imaginativa . . . dicitur etiam formalis . . . et species . . . et etiam thesaurus formarum dicitur, quia formas conservat sine materiae praesentia, nec tamen discernit eas," *ibid.,* no. 6, p. 581.

3. The estimative elicits intentions from the forms retained in the imaginative power.[79] It is for brutes what intellect is for man.[80] There is in this section an explicit reference to Algazel, and the doctrine is similar to that of St. Albert.

4. The phantasy combines and divides images and intentions among themselves.[81] It is the highest sensible power,[82] and indeed contains the whole formality of sensibility.[83] The imaginative, the estimative, and the phantasy do not differ in their common essence.[84] This last remark seems to go a bit beyond St. Albert's doctrine,[85] but the other statements are clearly recognizable as Albertinian.

5. The memory conserves the intentions of the estimative;[86] it is really identical with reminiscence, though the latter has a mode of operation influenced by reason.[87] The doctrine on memory

---

79. "Virtus tertia sequens imaginativam aestimativa vocatur. Haec a formis in imaginativa retentis elicit intentiones quae numquam in sensu fuerunt, sed a sensibilibus conditionibus non sunt separatae, sicut esse conveniens," *ibid.,* no. 10, p. 581.

80. "Adverto ex his quod aestimativa est hoc brutis quod intellectus est homini, secundum quamdam similitudinem, ut dixit Algazel," *ibid.*

81. "Virtus quarta phantasia est, quae componit imaginationes cum imaginibus et imaginationes cum intentionibus, et intentiones cum imaginibus, et intentiones cum intentionibus, aut etiam dividit," *ibid.,* pars 4, no. 1, p. 583.

82. It is "cognitio particularium major quam in sensibili anima haberi potest. Unde et phantasia dicta est ab apparitione, et in homine rationi juncta a vulgo excogitativa nominatur," *ibid.,* no. 2, p. 583.

83. "Sicut omnis sensus in sensu communi tota est formalitas, sic omnis virtutis sensibilis ultimum et tota formalitas in phantasia esse videtur," *ibid.,* no. 3, p. 584.

84. "Imaginativa et aestimativa et phantasia in communi essentialitate non differunt, ideo saepe una ponitur pro alia, et 'phantasia' omnes comprehendit," *ibid.,* no. 4, p. 584.

85. Cf. *supra,* notes 49 and 61.

86. "Memoria est conservatrix harum intentionum quas apprehendit aestimativa, et ideo est arca intentionum," *Liber de Apprehensione,* pars 4, no. 7, vol. V, p. 585.

87. "Scias memoriam et reminiscentiam esse unam virtutem subjecto, sed duas secundum modum et rationem; quia reminiscentia licet

here seems to be closer to Avicenna than to St. Albert.

Finally, the localization of all these powers is given in terms which are quite like the picture drawn in the *Summa de Homine*.[88] In summary, the *Liber de Apprehensione* seems, from a cursory inspection of the internal evidence, to be either a work of St. Albert or at least definitely in the Albertinian tradition. If we include this work in the general picture, very little would have to be changed or added.

ISAGOGE OR PHILOSOPHIA PAUPERUM

The section of this work dealing with the interior senses begins with a reference to Avicenna.

1. The first interior sense is common sense, which is the phantasy.[89] This is the terminology of Avicenna's *De Anima*, part 1, chapter 5; it is also used in Jean de la Rochelle's *Summa de Anima;* and as far as I know by no other Latin author.

2. The imagination is in the front ventricle of the brain, retaining what common sense received. There is only a formal difference between these two powers.[90]

---

sit corporea virtus, sicut ipsa memoria, tamen habet sibi conjunctum actum rationis," *ibid.,* no. 9, p. 586.
88. "Tres scis cellulas capitis fore, scilicet anteriorem, mediam, et posteriorem: et spiritus quidem animalis a primo transit in mediam et ab hoc in ultimam. . . . Nam in hac prima . . . constituitur sensus communis, . . . et post hunc, locum . . . damus imaginativae; . . . tertium autem locum primae cellulae . . . aestimativae concedimus. Memoriam vero reservantem intentiones posteriori parti totius cerebri assignamus. . . . Phantasiam . . . in medio totius cerebri," *ibid.,* no. 15, p. 589.
89. "Sequitur de potentiis animae sensibilis apprehensivis deintus, quae sunt quinque secundum Avicennam: quarum prima est phantasia quae est sensus communis, secunda est imaginatio, tertia imaginativa seu cogitativa, sive formativa, quarta aestimativa, quinta memorativa sive memorialis," *Isagoge in Libros de Anima (Philosophia Pauperum)* (among the works of St. Albert, vol. V), c. 14, p. 517.
90. "[Imaginatio] est autem, sicut dicit Avicenna, vis ordinata in extremo concavitatis anterioris partis cerebri, retinens quod recipit sensus communis. . . . Et sunt [sensus communis et imaginatio] quasi

3. The third power is the imaginative or formative. It is the power of combining or separating what is found in the imagination. Under the control of intellect it is called "cogitative," under that of the "animal power" it is called "imaginative;" in so far as it composes and divides it is called "formative."[91] Some even call it phantasy.[92] The triple designation of this power seems to be peculiar to this author.

4. The estimative apprehends the intentions of sensible things. It is a transcendent power, because it can apprehend immaterial forms.[93] This doctrine is like that of Jean de la Rochelle, even to the phrasing.

5. The memory retains the intentions of the estimative.[94] The name of Avicenna recurs all through this discussion. Characteristic Albertinian phrases like "tota formalitas" are altogether lacking. The peculiar Albertinian notion of phantasy is not to be found. Contrarywise, there are two rather striking similarities

---

una virtus, et non diversificantur in subjecto sed in forma," *ibid.*, c. 15, p. 518.

91. "Tertia virtus est quae vocatur imaginativa sive formativa, quae secundum Avicennam est vis ordinata in media concavitate cerebri potens componere aliquid de eo quod est in imaginatione cum alio, et dividere cum vult. . . . Et haec virtus in quantum imperat ei intellectus vocatur cogitativa; inquantum vero illi imperat virtus animalis, vocatur imaginativa; inquantum autem operatur componendo et dividendo formativa vocatur. Haec enim virtus facit castra in Hispania," *ibid.*, c. 16, p. 518.

92. "Et nota quod quidem hanc virtutem . . . appellant phantasiam," *ibid.*, p. 519.

93. "Est autem aestimativa sicut dicit Avicenna vis ordinata in summo concavitatis mediae cerebri, apprehendens intentiones sensibilium . . . . Est autem virtus transcendens, quia apprehensio sua non est formarum sensibilium et materialium, sed immaterialium," *ibid.*, c. 18, p. 521.

94. "Memorativa est vis ordinata in posteriori concavitate cerebri, retinens quod apprehendit vis aestimativa de intentiones sensibilium. . . . Differentia ergo memoriae et reminiscentiae est quia memoria est retentio specierum sive intentionum sensibilium, sed reminiscentia est representatio formarum a memoria deletarum per oblivionem et per similia," *ibid.*, c. 19, p. 522.

to Jean de la Rochelle's *Summa de Anima*.[95] If this work were St. Albert's, we would be forced to say that his doctrine is inconsistent and even internally contradictory.

---

95. After completing this analysis, I discovered that Dom Odo Lottin, O.S.B., *Psychologie et morale aux XIIe et XIIIe siècles* (Louvain: Gembloux (1942), tome I, pp. 497-99, has concluded that the *De Potentiis Animae (inc.:* "Sicut dicit Damascenus"; not identical with the work previously spoken of) at least in some doctrines is related to the Franciscan school by way of Odo Rigaud. Furthermore, this *De Potentiis* either is an extract from the *Philosophia pauperum* (B. Geyer), or has been inserted into the latter (O. Lottin). It is therefore becoming more evident that the *Philosophia pauperum* cannot be a work of St. Albert.

PART II

CHAPTER 5

INTRODUCTION TO THOMISTIC TEXTS

The text situation in St. Thomas is quite different from that which we have met in preceding writers. In them, the internal senses are referred to but a comparatively few times in their works, and at least in the case of some, the discussions are very full. In St. Thomas, the "key" texts are very brief, but there is a very large number of shorter references to the same problem.

Almost all the modern authors who have touched on this problem in St. Thomas agree that the main texts are five: *Commentary on the Sentences*, bk. 3, d. 26, q. 1, a. 2; *Contra Gentiles*, bk. 2, 60, 73, 76; *Commentary on the De Anima*, bk. 2, lect. 13; *Summa Theologiae* I. 78.4, 81.3; *Quaestio Disputata de Anima*, a. 13. These five texts are very brief; almost astonishingly so in comparison with the discussions of St. Albert. The one extended discussion, that in the *Contra Gentiles*, really contains very little positive doctrine, as we shall see; it is almost entirely concerned with the refutation of a particular aspect of Averroes's theory.

Additional direct references to the *vis cogitativa* occur in the *Commentary on the Sentences*,[1] *De Veritate*,[2] *Contra Gentiles*,[3] *Commentary on the Ethics*,[4] *Summa Theologiae*,[5] *Quaestio Disputata de Anima*,[6] and in the doubtful work *De Principio Individuationis*.[7]

---

1. Loci in the *Commentary on the Sentences*: III d. 23, q. 2, a. 2, q. 1 ad 3; IV d. 7, q. 3, a. 3, q. 2, obj. 1 and ad 1; III d. 26, q. 1, a. 2; IV d. 23, q. 2, a. 2, q. 1 ad 3; d. 49, q. 22, a. 2, sol.; d. 50, q. 1, a. 1 ad 3; a. 3 ad 3 in contrar.
2. *De Veritate* I. 11, X. 5, XV. 1 ad 9, XV. 1, XVIII. 7 ad 5.
3. *Contra Gentiles,* II. 60, 73, 76, 80, 81; III. 84.
4. *Commentary on the Ethics,* VI, lect. 1, 7, 9.
5. *Summa Theologiae* I. 85.7, 111.2 ad 2, 115.4, 79.2 ad 2; I-II. 50.3 ad 3, 51.3, 30.3 ad 3, 74.3 ad 1; II-II. 2.1 ad 2; III. 72. 11, arg. 3 and ad 3.
6. *Quaestio Disputata de Anima,* XX ad 1 in contrar.
7. *De Principio Individuationis,* a medio (see Appendix I).

149

Ratio particularis is spoken of in *Commentary on the Sentences,*[8] *De Veritate,*[9] *Contra Gentiles,*[10] *Commentary on the Ethics,*[11] *Commentary on the De Anima,*[12] *De Principio Individuationis,* and *Summa Theologiae.*[13]

Vis aestimativa is discussed in *Commentary on the Sentences,*[14] *De Veritate,*[15] *Contra Gentiles,*[16] *Commentary on the Ethics,*[17] *Commentary on De Sensu et Sensato*[18] and *De Memoria et Reminiscentia,*[19] and in *Summa Theologiae.*[20]

Instinctus is mentioned with reference to the actions of animals in *Commentary on the Sentences,*[21] *Contra Gentiles,*[22] *Commentary on the Metaphysics,*[23] *Commentary on De Memoria et Reminiscentia,*[24] *Summa Theologiae,*[25] and *Quaestio disputata de Anima.*[26]

It is obvious that some of these references will overlap, since these terms naturally combine and contrast among themselves.

8. *Commentary on the Sentences,* II d. 24, q. 2, a. 1 ad 3; IV d. 50, q. 1, a. 1 ad 3; a. 3 ad 3 in contrar.
9. *De Veritate* II. 6, X. 5, XIV. 1 ad 9, XV. 1.
10. *Contra Gentiles,* II. 60.
11. *Commentary on Aristotle's Ethics,* VI, lect. 1, 7, 9.
12. *Commentary on Aristotle's De Anima,* II, lect. 16.
13. *Summa Theologiae* I. 20, 1 ad 1, 79. 2 ad 2; 80. 2 ad 3; I-II. 51. 3, 30. 3 ad 3.
14. *Commentary on the Sentences,* II d. 20, q. 2, a. 2 ad 5; II d. 24, q. 2, a. 1 and ad 2; d. 25, q. 1, a. 1 ad 7; III d. 17, q. 1, a. 1, q. 3 ad 2; d. 15, q. 2, a. 2, q. 3 ad 3; d. 35, q. 1, a. 2, q. 2 ad 1; IV d. 49, q. 2, a. 2.
15. *De Veritate,* I. 11, XV. 1, XVIII. 7 and ad 7; XXIV. 2; XXV. 2.
16. *Contra Gentiles,* II. 47, 48, 60.
17. *Commentary on Aristotle's Ethics,* VI, lect. 7, 9.
18. *Commentary on Aristotle's De Sensu et Sensato,* lect. 1.
19. *Commentary on Aristotle's De Memoria et Reminiscentia,* lect. 2.
20. *Summa Theologiae* I. 81.2 ad 2; I-II. 6.2, 77.1.
21. *Commentary on the Sentences,* II d. 20, q. 2, a. 2 ad 5.
22. *Contra Gentiles,* II. 47; III. 131.
23. *Commentary on Aristotle's Metaphysics,* I, lect. 1.
24. *Commentary on Aristotle's De Memoria et Reminiscentia,* lect. 1, 8,
25. *Summa Theologiae* I.18.3, 83.1; I-II.3.6, 9.1 ad 2, 11.2, 12.5 and ad 3, 15.2, 17.2 ad 3, 40.3 and ad 1, 46.4 ad 2, 50.3 and ad 2.
26. *Quaestio Disputata de Anima,* XIII.

It should also be stated that this list does not pretend to be exhaustive, except in the sense that all the important passages are considered.

Another point to be noted is that some very important texts do not explicitly refer to any of these terms. For example, the long and very important discussion on prudence in *Summa Theologiae* II-II, qq. 47 and 49, is shown to concern our problem only by means of St. Thomas's own reference to the sixth book of Aristotle's *Ethics,* and by means of St. Thomas's own development of the Aristotelian doctrine.

The chapter divisions of this part follow almost naturally from the chronology of the works. A glance at the "key" texts shows a division into three groups: the first comprising the *Commentary on the Sentences,* the *De Veritate,* and the *Contra Gentiles,* which precede most if not all of the commentaries on Aristotle; the second group will take in the passages occurring in commentaries on Aristotelian works; the third including the *Summa Theologiae* and the *Quaestio Disputata de Anima.* More accurate dating, for example, of the relative position of the Aristotelian *Commentaries* with relation to each other, is not always certain, and, as we shall see, has almost nothing to offer us. These chapters of textual study will be followed by a general conclusion.

Standard translations of the works of St. Thomas, where they exist, will not be made use of. One reason is that a textual study requires a certain literalness of translation that would otherwise be out of place. Another reason is to ensure the same translation for the same terms. A third is to show, by textual analysis, that the term *"vis cogitativa"* is capable of translation and not merely of transliteration.

CHAPTER 6

THE *VIS COGITATIVA* IN THE EARLIER WORKS

A convenient division of the Thomistic *corpus* is based on the Aristotelian *Commentaries*. There will still be some overlapping, particularly because of the uncertainty concerning the date of the beginning of the *Summa Theologiae*. However, an absolute and certain dating is not essential for this study; if the investigation does not base itself more on chronology than the present status of our knowledge will allow, it may even furnish data for some other investigator to advance our knowledge of chronological relations.

SCRIPTUM SUPER LIBROS SENTENTIARUM

With this word of caution, a beginning will be made with the main texts from the *Commentary on the Sentences*. It is to be noted that these texts deal explicitly, not with sensory cognition, but with sensory appetite. It may perhaps seem strange that there is no full-scale consideration of the sensory cognitive powers in themselves. This difficulty will disappear if it is remembered that this work of St. Thomas's is a commentary, which will necessarily be guided, at least in the disposition of the matter discussed, by the order and arrangement of the original. The first text deals with the number and the specification of the sense appetites; the second with the meaning of the word *"sensualitas."*

I answer. It must be said that passive powers vary, according as they are made to be moved by different active powers, speaking *per se*. Now, the proper moving principle of the appetitive power is the apprehended good. Hence, it is necessary that according to the different apprehending powers there be also different appetites: that is, the appetite of reason, which concerns a good apprehended by reason or intellect, and so concerns a good apprehended simply and universally; and the sensitive appetite, which concerns a good apprehended by the sensitive powers, and so concerns a particular good and as it is now. But because a passive power

152

is not extended to more objects than the power of its active
principle (as the Commentator says in the Ninth book of the
Metaphysics, that there is no passive power in nature to which
a natural active power does not correspond), therefore, the
sense appetite extends itself only to those goods, to which
the sensitive apprehension is extended.

Now because, as Dionysius says in the seventh chapter of
De Divinis Nominibus, the divine Wisdom joins the ends
of the first things with the beginnings of the second, because
every inferior nature in its highest element touches the lowest
element of the superior nature, according as it participates
something of the superior nature, although deficiently; therefore, as well in apprehension as in sensitive appetite there is
to be found something in which the sensitive part touches
reason.

For, that an animal imagine the forms apprehended by
sense, this is according to the nature of sensitive apprehension taken in itself; but that it apprehend those intentions
which do not fall under sense, like friendship, hatred, and
the like, this belongs to the sensitive part according as it
touches reason. And so that part in men, in whom it is more
perfect on account of its being joined to the rational soul,
is called "particular reason," because it compares particular
intentions; but in other animals, because it does not compare,
but has the power of apprehending such intentions from a
natural instinct, it is not called "reason," but "estimation."

Likewise also on the part of appetite, that the animal seek
those things which are suitable to sense, pleasing it, is according to sensitive nature, and belongs to the concupiscible power.
But that it tend to some good which does not please the
sense . . . this is in the sensitive appetite according as sense
nature touches the intellective; and this belongs to the irascible power. And so, just as estimation is a different power
than imagination, so the irascible is a different power than
the concupiscible. For the object of the concupiscible is a
good which is made to please the sense; of the irascible,
however, a good which has difficulty. And because that which
is difficult is not appetible as such, but is, in relation to some
other pleasing good, or by reason of some good mixed with
the difficulty — but to compare one thing with another, and
to discern the intentions of difficulty and goodness in one and
the same thing, belongs to reason — therefore, properly, to
seek such a good belongs to the rational appetite. But it
pertains to the sensitive, according as it touches the rational

by an imperfect participation, not indeed by comparing or
discerning, but by being moved to it with a natural instinct,
as we said of estimation.[1]

I answer. It must be said that "sensuality" and "sensibility" differ. For "sensibility" comprehends all the powers
of the sensitive part, as well the exterior apprehensive as the
interior, and also the appetitive. But "sensuality" more properly is the name of that part alone by which the animal is moved
to seek or avoid something. Just as it is in intelligible matters, that that which is apprehended does not move the will
unless it be apprehended under the aspect of good or evil,
because the speculative intellect says nothing of imitating or
avoiding, as is said in the third book of the *De Anima*; so
also is it in the sensitive part, that the sensible apprehension
does not cause any movement unless the "suitable" or "unsuitable" is apprehended. And so it is said in the second book
of the *De Anima*, that as regards those things which are in
the imagination we are as if we were considering some terrible
things in paintings, which would not excite any passion of
fear or anything similar.

Now, the power which apprehends such aspects of the suitable seems to be the estimative power, by which the lamb
avoids the wolf and follows its mother. This power has the same
relation to the appetite of the sensible part, that the practical
intellect does to the appetite of the will. Hence, properly speaking, "sensuality" begins from the boundary of the estimative
and the consequent appetite, so that "sensuality" has the relation to the sensitive part that will and free choice have to
the intellective part.

Now, this suitable which moves sensuality, or the aspect
of its suitability, either is apprehended by the sense, as are
the things pleasant to the single senses which animals seek
after; or it is not apprehended by the sense, as the sheep

---

1. *Scriptum super Tertium Librum Sententiarum, (In III Sent.),* d.
26. q. 1, a. 2, sol., ed. Mandonnet-Moos, vol. III, pp. 816-17. Text in
Appendix II, no. 47. (The first three books of the *Commentary on
the Sentences* will be quoted according to the edition of Pierre Mandonnet, O.P., and M. F. Moos, O.P., Paris: Lethielleux, 1929-1933).

The reference to the *De Divinis Nominibus* is to ch. 7, no. 4.
St. Thomas apparently used the translation of Sarrazin; cf. *Dionysiaca* (Paris: Desclée de Brouwer, 1937), p. 407, "et semper fines
priorum conjungens principiis secundorum."

perceives the enmity of the wolf neither by seeing nor by hearing but only by estimating. And so the movement of sensuality tends to two ends: that is, to those things which are pleasing to the exterior senses, and this is what is said, that from sensuality rises the movement to the senses of the body; or to those things which are known to be harmful or suitable by the estimation alone, and so from sensuality is said to rise the appetite of things pertaining to the body.[2]

These texts will repay careful study. In the former, St. Thomas begins by showing that passive powers, such as appetites, have their primary and intrinsic distinctions rooted in the corresponding active principles. Or, in another way, no passive power extends the field of its operations beyond the limits of the corresponding active power. Now, the proper moving cause of appetite is the known good. Consequently, sensory appetite, being moved by the good apprehended by sense, stays within the latter's limits.

Sense and intellect are different. This proposition is to be understood in an Aristotelian sense, as is well known and as will appear abundantly in the course of this study. There is a complementary point of view, which St. Thomas also stresses. This is the neo-Platonic, specifically Dionysian feeling for hierarchy. In St. Thomas's world, there are real differences between things which are never blurred over; but there are no gaps. The non-living thing in its most developed compounds acts something *like* the simplest plant. Some high grade plants can hardly be distinguished in their external activities from simple animals. The highest species of animal approaches close to man in some of its activities. And man himself, the highest type of corporeal being, has some activities that are like those of separate substances.[3]

---

2. *In II Sent.*, d. 24, q. 2, a. 1, sol., vol. II, pp. 601-02. Text in Appendix II, no. 48. Cf. *ibid.*, q. 3, a. 1, vol. II, p. 617.

3. "Cum enim, ut Dionysius dicit, natura inferior in sui supremo attingit infimum superioris naturae, natura sensitiva in aliquo sui quodammodo rationi coniungitur; unde et quaedam pars sensitiva, scilicet cogitativa, alio nomine ratio dicitur, propter confinum eius ad rationem," *In II Sent.*, d. 24, q. 2, a. 1, ad 3, vol. II, p. 603, text corrected according to the Roman edition, vol. VI, fol. 77; "animalia continuantur hominibus in vi aestimativa quae est supremum in eis,

In this context the study of animal life is approached. Sense power, as being the heart and innermost principle of a certain kind of life, includes even the imagination. But the power of an animal to apprehend intentions which do not fall under sense is in it the analogue of reason.

In man, such a power *is present*, but it is not the same. Sensibility is a genus, and is found differently in different species.

> To the fourth argument the answer is that, although man and horse agree in being capable of sense, it does not yet follow that the sensible souls have the same character in man and in the horse, because man and horse are not one animal according to their species. And so in man, the sensible soul is much nobler than in the other animals with respect to its principal acts, as is clear in the acts of the interior senses, and in the operation of touch, which is the principal sense. For, in every "potestative" whole, the lower power joined to the higher is found to be more perfect, as the power of a superior is much more excellent in a king. For the sensible soul in man is by its essence joined to the rational soul, and so the whole is by creation.[4]

In other words, essentially the same power of apprehending "intentions" is present in man and in *other* animals, but the mode of operation in the two cases is very different. Because the human estimative is the power of a spiritual soul, its mode of operation is a kind of comparison of particular "intentions." Because of this type of activity, the human estimative is called *ratio particularis,* "the particular reason." In brutes, on the other hand, the capacity for apprehending such intentions is inborn.

Thus, the two key texts give an extremely brief summary of St. Thomas's doctrine on the estimative power and *vis cogitativa*. To understand it at all, we must examine it point by point in the light of other remarks in the *Commentary*.

---

secundum quam aliquid simile operibus rationis operantur," *In III Sent.,* d. 35, q. 1, a. 2, q. 2 ad 1, vol. III, p. 1179.

4. *In II Sent.,* d. 18, q. 2, a. 3 ad 4, vol. II, p. 471. Text in Appendix II, no. 49.

REASONS FOR THE ESTIMATIVE POWER.

Why do we speak of an estimative power at all? There is a strong argument, drawn from a consideration of both the intellect and the imagination. Not every intellectual cognition arouses appetite; it is necessary that the object be not only known, but be known *as good*.

> To the second argument the answer is that, as the appetite of reason does not follow every apprehension of reason, but when something is apprehended as good, so, too, the act of the sensible appetite does not take place except when something is apprehended as suitable. Now, this does not happen by the exterior sense which apprehends sensible forms, but by the estimation, which apprehends the aspects of the suitable and the harmful which the exterior sense does not. And so in the sensitive part there is only one appetite in genus, which is divided, as into species, into the irascible and concupiscible, both of which are counted under "sensuality."[5]

In relation to action, the senses are like the speculative intellect, and the estimative is like the practical.

Again, in the case of the imagination, it is possible to have a mere image, which of itself is as little calculated to action as is a picture regarded simply as a picture. In this case, imagination also is comparable to the speculative intellect.

> The estimative properly has the same proportion to it [sensuality] as the practical reason to the free choice, which also is a moving cause. But the simple imagination and the preceding powers are rather remote, like the speculative reason to the will.[6]

Merely speculative knowledge does not lead to action, except remotely. Appetite and action follow only upon *practical* knowledge

---

5. *In III Sent.*, d. 17, q. 1, a. 1, q. 2 ad 2, vol. III, p. 531. Text in Appendix II, no. 50.

6. *In II Sent.*, d. 24, q. 2, a. 1 ad 2, vol. II, p. 603. Text in Appendix II, no. 51. Cf. "Praeterea, intellectus speculativus proportionaliter respondet imaginationi, sicut intellectus practicus aestimationi, quae est in parte sensitiva," *ibid.*, d. 23, q. 2, a. 3, q. 2, obj. 2, vol. III, p. 730. Cf. *Contra Gentiles*, II. 60, "Praeterea. Forma."

— that is, knowledge of a thing as good, and the like. Neither the external senses, nor common sense, nor imagination, seem to give us knowledge of this kind.

But it is necessary to make a distinction. Pleasant colors, soft music, tasty foods, and so forth, are agreeable to the senses as such. Consequently, their apprehension through common sense is of itself accompanied by an emotion of pleasure, while their opposites cause pain and so dislike. There are other sensory goods which do not cause pleasure in the external sense, at least at the present moment, while there are other sensory evils which are not causing pain as apprehended by the external sense. It is this second class of sensory objects which is designated by the term "suitable" and "unsuitable."

From this consideration it is clear that the suitable as such does not give an immediate sensory pleasure. In fact it may involve pain; it seems always to involve effort. From this point of view, the suitable will be a *bonum arduum* — a difficult good. Here there is a problem. It is easy to see how an intellect would act when confronted with such a situation: it could consider the two aspects separately, and weigh one against the other, and thus finally could choose the difficult in so far as it was good, or reject the good in so far as it was difficult. But such comparison obviously involves an understanding of what it means that a thing is good. What about the animal? Since such a process is impossible for it,[7] it shall have to be innately determined to desire what is good for it, even when such good involves pain.

---

7. Cf. "Inclinatio appetitus sensitivi partim est ab appetente, inquantum sequitur apprehensionem appetibilis, unde dicit Augustinus quod animalia moventur visis; partim ab obiecto, inquantum deest cognitio ordinis in finem," *In II Sent.,* d. 27, q. 1, a. 2, sol., vol. III, p. 861; "Inter hos duos appetitus [naturalem et voluntarium] est unus medius qui procedit ex cognitione finis sine hoc quod cognoscatur ratio finis et proportio eius quod est ad finem in finem ipsum; et iste est appetitus sensitivus," *ibid.,* p. 859.

Compare: "Quia homo inter cetera animalia rationem finis cognoscit et proportionem operis ad finem, ideo naturalis conceptio ei indita, qua dirigitur ad operandum convenienter lex naturalis vel ius naturale dicitur; in ceteris autem aestimatio naturalis vocatur," *In IV Sent.,* d. 33, q. 1, a. 1, ed. Parma, vol. VII, p. 967.

St. Thomas: Early Works

Are animals in fact confronted with such difficult goods? The answer is evidently in the affirmative. For example:

> Now [hope] is found, not only in men, but also in other animals; and this is clear, because animals are found to work for the sake of some future good estimated to be possible, as birds make a nest for the bringing up of their young.[8]

Other examples are adduced by St. Thomas: the young animal following its mother, the spider spinning its web, and the like. Examples of the unsuitable are also easy to find: the traditional example of the sheep and the wolf is frequently mentioned.

But St. Thomas's main interest is obviously in the *human* estimative. It may be questioned whether this expression is legitimate. Most writers on St. Thomas avoid it; and at least once it has been condemned as falsifying St. Thomas's own scheme of human internal senses.[9] It is therefore necessary to show that there is an estimative in man.

> To the fifth argument the answer is that other animals do not seek the suitable and avoid the harmful by the deliberation of reason, but by the natural instinct of the estimative power, and such natural instinct is also in children; and so they take the breast, and take other suitable things, without anyone teaching them.[10]

There are other, briefer texts, in which the estimative power is explicitly attributed to men.[11]

Furthermore, in dealing with the human estimative, the greater number of texts speak of the difference between it and the animal estimative.

---

8. *In III. Sent.,* d. 26, q. 1, a. 1, sol., vol. III, p. 814. Text in Appendix II, no. 52.
9. See for example, Max Horten, *Das Buch der Ringsteine Farabi's* (Beitraege, Baeumker, Muenster: Aschendorff, 1906, Band V, Heft 3), p. 231.
10. *In II Sent.,* d. 20, q. 2, a. 2 ad 5, vol. II, p. 515. Text in Appendix II, no. 53. Compare the solution of the same article.
11. *In III Sent.,* d. 15, q. 2, a. 2, q. 3 ad 3, vol. III, p. 492; *In IV Sent.,* d. 50, q. 1, a. 3 ad 3 in contrarium, ed. Parma, vol. VII, part 2, p. 1251.

To the seventh argument the answer is that animals do not apprehend the character of the suitable by comparison, but by a certain natural instinct. So, animals have estimation, but not knowledge; as they also have memory, but not reminiscence; although all these pertain to the sensitive part. Consequently, they perform their actions through a determination of nature, not from their own determination. Hence, all of the same species perform similar actions, as every spider makes a similar web. This would not be if they disposed their works from themselves, as if by an operative art; and for this reason there is no free choice in them.[12]

THE INSTINCT OF NATURE.

If we re-examine all the texts so far considered, it will be seen that the animal estimative is said to work through or by "a determination of nature" or "a natural instinct." It is necessary to consider carefully what is meant by "instinct."

In modern usage, the word "instinct" usually means "a natural aptitude which guides animals in the unreflecting performance of complex acts useful for the preservation of the individual or the species."[13] In this sense, it is readily admissible that to say "the sheep flees the wolf by instinct" is to distinguish and classify this act, but not to explain it.[14]

In St. Thomas the term *instinctus* is more general and has a wider application; it is opposed to a (violent) motion from the outside. Hence it could be translated as "determinate (intrinsic) impulse."[15] In speaking of animals, the adjective "natural," or the genitive "of nature," is usually added, to indicate the innate char-

---

12. *In II Sent.*, d. 25, q. 1, a. 1 ad 7, vol. II, p. 647. Text in Appendix II, no. 54.

13. This definition is taken from Michael Maher, S.J. *Psychology*, 9th ed. (London: Longmans, 1925), p. 587; Fr. Maher indicates that it is a commonly accepted one.

14. *Ibid.*

15. The term "instinctus" is used of the necessary impulse of animal nature; the texts are listed below, note 16; but conscience is said to be "spiritus nostri instinctus," *De Veritate*, XVII. 1 ad 8; divine inspiration which guided the actions of the Apostles is called "instinctus Spiritus Sancti," In *Ep. ad Galatas*, c. 2, lect. 1, principio; *Expositio in Psalmos Davidis*, prooemium.

acter of this determination.[16] The normal function of this term
is to be the counterfoil to such terms as "free, deliberate, reasonable."

Moderns speak of "instinctive activity" or "unlearned drives;"
St. Thomas, at least in the fuller passages, combines the terms "instinct" and "estimation." For him, the activity designated as instinctive or unlearned is explained in terms of appetite (or sensory
impulse); the appetite in terms of a "judgment" of suitability
(and the like); and this "judgment" in terms of an innate determination.

Vis Cogitativa — MEANING AND DERIVATION OF THE TERM.

We have already seen that the human estimative is sometimes
called by St. Thomas the "ratio particularis." There are also other
terms.

> To the third argument the answer is that the passive in-
> tellect, about which the Philosopher speaks, is not the possible
> intellect, but the particular reason, which is called *vis cogi-
> tativa,* having a definite organ in the body, that is, the middle
> cell of the head, as the Commentator says in the same place;
> and without this the soul knows nothing now. But it will know
> in the future, when it does not need to abstract from phan-
> tasms.[17]

This text requires discussion on several points. Let us begin with
localization. St. Thomas mentions it here and in several places,[18]
usually with a reference to Averroes or to "doctors." His general

---

16. For example, *In II Sent.,* d. 20, q. 2, a. 2 ad 5; d. 25, q. 1, a. 1
ad 7; *In III Sent.,* d. 26, q. 1, a. 2; *Summa Contra Gentiles* II.
47; III. 131; *In De Memoria et Reminiscentia,* lect. 1, 8; *In Metaphysica,* I, lect. 1; *Summa Theologiae,* I. 18. 3; 83. 1; I-II. 15.
5 ad 3; 17. 2 ad 3; 40. 3 ad 1; 50. 3 ad 4; II-II. 60. 1 ad 1;
Q. D. De Anima, a. 13. All these texts are quoted in the course of
this investigation.

17. *In IV Sent.,* d. 50, q. 1, a. 1 ad 3, ed Parma, vol. VII, pt. 2, p. 1248.
Text in Appendix II, no. 55.

18. E. g., *In IV Sent.,* d. 7, q. 3, a. 3, q. 2, obj. 1. ed. Parma, vol.
VII, pt. 2, p. 579, and see also later sections.

attitude toward the localization is hesitant.[19] He seems to imply
that it is really a question of natural science. At any rate, his own
analysis is not based on localization at all, and consequently can
stand independently of the fate of the biology.

A second point is the use of the term "passive intellect." There
is here merely a statement that the passive intellect, on which
Averroes reared such an imposing structure, is simply the *vis cogitativa*. For the explanation of this stand, we shall have to wait for
the *Summa Contra Gentiles*. We shall see later that in the *Commentary* on this passage of the *De Anima* St. Thomas interprets the
term differently. It will then be necessary to determine whether
the change in terminology involves a change in doctrine. On the
doctrine contained in this text, one statement, with its reason, is
important. Without the *vis cogitativa*, we read, the soul cannot
understand in this life. The reason given is that here the intellect
depends on the phantasm. We conclude that the necessity for the
vis cogitativa is based on the need for the phantasm. In other
words, the *cogitativa* is necessary for any and all understanding
in this life, at least to the extent that it is necessary to have a phantasm. The relation between the act of having a phantasm and the
act of the *cogitativa*, to the best of my knowledge, is not explained
in the early works, and explained only indirectly later. Hence this
will have to be transmitted to Chapter Nine.

The meaning and use of the term *"vis cogitativa"* is the third
point to be noted in our text. It is very important in any textual
study to make sure that a word does or does not have several
meanings. And if it should turn out to have more than one meaning, it is also important to see whether they constitute a simple
equivocation or form a related series.

A text that will be very helpful in this matter is one in which
St. Thomas explains the meaning and application of *cogitatio*.

> To the third argument the answer is that that power, which
> is called *"cogitativa"* by the philosophers, is on the boundary
> of the sensitive and intellective parts, where the sensitive part
> touches the intellective. For it has something from the sensi-

---

19. "Er hielt sie wohl nicht fuer hinreichend sichergestellt," M. Horten,
Das Buch der Ringsteine Farabi's, p. 232.

tive part, namely, that it considers particular forms; and it
has something from the intellective, namely, that it compares;
and so it is in men alone. And because the sensitive part is
better known than the intellective, for this reason, just as
the determination of the intellective part is denominated from
the sense, as was said, so every comparison of the intellect
is named from *"cogitatio."*[20]

Because of the very great importance of this usage, I will restate
the content. There is a sense power, just at the point of juncture
of sense and intellect, which is called *"vis cogitativa."* This power
considers particular forms, and so is a sense power, but it does
this by "comparison" or "discursus," which is from the intellect.
The formal object of this power is not stated in this definition;
all that is stated is its mode of operation. As far as identifying
this power is concerned, in this passage St. Thomas says nothing.
From the terms of the definition it could even be an exterior sense.
However, it is implied that it is an interior sense, in so far as it
is said to be on the border between sense and intellect.

What does this notion enable St. Thomas to do? It makes
it possible for him to adapt statements of Averroes to an Avicennan
framework without falling into the pitfall of eclecticism.[21] It also
enables him to undertake the searching critique of the Averroistic
cogitativa in the *Summa Contra Gentiles.* If by *cogitativa* St.
Thomas always and primarily meant the "collative estimative," this
critique would be at least partly irrelevant.

Cogitativa is a power in whose *operation intellect* is concerned.
For this reason, when St. Thomas speaks of sensibility as such, or
of the infant, and so forth, he will not speak of the *cogitativa*, be-

---

20. *In III Sent.,* d. 23, q. 2, a. 2, q. 1 ad 3, vol. III, p. 727. Text in
    Appendix II, no. 56.
21. A charge that St. Thomas is merely an eclectic on this matter is
    apparently implied by the following statement: "What Thomas
    really does here is this: He takes *cogitativa* in the Averroian sense
    of reason in man and correlates it with the Avicennian *aestimativa*
    in animals. Thomas evidently was not aware of the difference in
    the use of *cogitativa* by Avicenna and Averroes," Harry Austryn
    Wolfson, "The Internal Senses in Latin, Arabic, and Hebrew Philo-
    sophic Texts," *Harvard Theological Review,* XXVIII (1935), p. 121.

cause then intellect is absent by definition, or is not operative by virtue of the concrete case. We shall return to this notion of the *cogitativa* as instrumentally reasonable later.

A second meaning of *cogitativa* is "the discursive (collative) estimative power, as it is found in man, under the control of reason." It seems that this is the more common use in St. Thomas. This usage is derived from the first, in so far as the power whose mode of operation is discursive is said to be the equivalent in man of the animal estimative.

A third meaning seems to be "reason."

> The pleasure which follows the operation of the appetitive power is of a different nature than the pleasure which follows the operation of the *cogitativa*. For as a *cogitatio* about murder or lust without any appetite is not reduced to the genus of lust or murder unless it be inordinate, but to another genus, which is curiosity or vanity, so also the pleasure following upon such *cogitatio* does not pertain to the genus of murder. . . .[22]

The position of the distinction here made makes *cogitativa virtus* stand for "reason." In the text we have been analyzing for the past several pages, it is said that "every comparison of the intellect is named from '*cogitatio*'." For these two reasons, it seems quite probable that we should translate the phrase "operatio cogitativae" of the present text as "the operation of discursive thought."

In summary, St. Thomas's use of the term *vis* (more rarely, *virtus*) *cogitativa* is manifold. Basically, the term means "a power characterized by a special way of acting, that is, by comparison, composition, or discursus." Its more common application is to the estimative power of man, to indicate that this human estimative is under the control of reason. Much more rarely, the term can be applied to reason itself.

PRACTICAL REASON AND THE DISCURSIVE POWER.

A further function of the *vis cogitativa* is brought out in connection with the relation between practical intellect and action.

---

22. *In II Sent.*, d. 24, q. 3, a. 4 ad 5, vol. II, p. 627. Text in Appendix II, no. 57.

To the third argument the answer is that the practical intellect, in order that it may deal with singulars, as it is said in the third book of the *De Anima*, needs the particular reason, by means of which the universal opinion which is in the intellect is applied to a particular work. There is thus a syllogism, whose major is universal (which is the opinion of the practical intellect); and the minor singular (which is the estimation of the particular reason, which is also called the discursive power); and the conclusion consists in the choice of the work.[23]

To discuss the use of, and the variations in, the term "practical syllogism" would lead into a long and unnecessary digression. It is sufficient to point out that the "syllogism" here spoken of is not the same kind of thing as the demonstrative syllogism. The term does serve to bring out one important fact: the passage from universal to singular in the practical order (more specifically, the passage from universal knowledge to election of the singular, or even to singular action) is a discursive process.

St. Thomas states that if the intellect is to deal with the singular, it has need of the discursive power. By means of this power the universal proposition is applied to the particular thing. What is the way in which this is done? In general, the process is the following.

To the second argument the answer is that our intellect in the state of this life uses singulars, composing propositions and forming syllogisms, in so far as it reflects back to the powers of the sensitive part, as was said, and is somehow in

23. *In IV Sent.*, d. 50, q. 1, a. 3 ad 3 in contrarium, ed. Parma, vol. VII, pt. 2, p. 1251. Text in Appendix II, no. 58.

Cf. "Ideo cum ratio in operandis quodammodo syllogizet, invenitur iudicium rationis in maiori propositione quae universalis est; in minori autem propositione quae particularis est admiscetur passio, quae circa particularia viget; unde sequitur corruptio rationis in conclusione electionis," *In II Sent.*, d. 24, q. 3, a. 3, sol., vol. II, pp. 623-24; "Conclusio autem . . . ad conscientiam pertinet . . . quia conscentia et factis remurmurat, et faciendis contradicit; et inde dicitur conscientia, quasi cum alio scientia, quia scientia universalis ad actum particularem applicatur," [with a reference to *Nich. Ethic.*, VI, c. 8], *In II Sent.*, d. 24, q. 2, a. 4, sol., vol. II, p. 613; *De Malo*, III. 9.

contact with them, according as their movements and operations are terminated in the intellect, as the intellect receives
from them.[24]

It is interesting to note that knowledge of the particular is treated
in a way that seems to indicate that it is an affair of the judgment
and not of the apprehension of the *quod quid est*.[25]

Continuatio — THE PROBLEM AND ITS SOLUTION

The intellect, as it makes use of particulars, reflects upon
and is "in contact with" (*continuatur*) the sensory powers. It has
been said that this *continuatio* is an obscure, difficult, and almost
meaningless expression.[26] In one or two texts this expression de-

---

24. *In IV Sent.*, d. 50, q. 1, a. 3 ad 2 in contrarium, ed. Parma, vol. VII,
     part 2, p. 1251. Text in Appendix II, no. 59.
25. Cf. "Cum ergo omnis actio sit per formam, forma autem quantum
     est de se sit universalis; per talem modum non potest deveniri in
     cognitionem rerum singularium. . . . Per potentiam illam cognos-
     citivam in qua formae a rebus omnino immaterialiter recipiuntur,
     directe singularia non cognoscit, sed solum per potentias organis
     affixas; sed indirecte, et per quandam reflexionem, etiam per in-
     tellectum qui organo non utitur cognoscit singulare, prout scilicet ex
     obiecto proprio redit ad cognoscendum suum actum, ex quo actu
     redit in speciem, quae est intelligendi principium, et ex ea procedit
     ad considerandum phantasma," *In IV Sent.*, d. 50, q. 1, a. 3, sol.,
     ed. Parma, vol. VII, part 2, p. 1250; *ibid.*, ad 1; "Et quia intelli-
     gentia est proprie universalium, quae sub tempore non cadunt, et
     ita quodammodo praesentis formam retinent; ideo intelligentia di-
     citur praesentium non solum universalium, quibus indiget prudens
     ad recte ratiocinandum de agendis, sed etiam singularium quae nunc
     sunt," *In III Sent.*, d. 33, q. 2, a. 1, q. 1 ad 1, vol. III, p. 1074; "Ad
     quartum dicendum quod intellectiva apprehensio est secundum mo-
     tum a rebus ad animam. Et quia in anima intellectiva recipitur ali-
     quid abstractum ab omnibus conditionibus materialibus individuan-
     tibus, ideo nulla apprehensio intellectiva concernit aliquod tempus
     determinate, quamvis possit esse de quolibet tempore; unde in com-
     ponendo et dividendo implicat tempus," *In III Sent.*, d. 26, q. 1, a.
     5 ad 4, vol. III, pp. 829-30; *In II Sent.*, d. 24, q. 2, a. 3 ad 4, vol.
     II, p. 611; *Contra Gentiles*, II, 96.
26. Rudolf Allers, "The Intellectual Cognition of Particulars," *The
     Thomist*, III (1941), pp. 106-07.

notes hierarchical participation of the kind that was noticed before.[27] But in the majority of cases it is a technical term borrowed from the Arabian philosophers. At times St. Thomas explicitly points this out.[28] The term is used in the Latin translations of Avempace,[29] Avicenna,[30] and especially Averroes.[31] In all these instances, *continuatio* (or *coniunctio*) means union between the separated intellect and man, in and through an operation.[32] Obviously, when St. Thomas uses the term, he does not imply a separated intellect, but he is speaking of a dynamic union — a union through operation or causality. Such a union can be of two kinds: the union between agent and patient, or that between principal and instrumental cause. Both of these may occur, but the former type does not seem to be in question here.

---

27. Cf. "In intellectus simplici visione continuatur homo superioribus substantiis, quae intelligentiae vel angeli dicuntur, sicut animalia continuantur hominibus in vi aestimativa, quae est supremum in eis, secundum quam aliquid simile operibus rationis operantur," *In III Sent.*, d. 35, q. 1, a. 2, q. 2 ad 1, vol. III, p. 1179; *ibid.*, d. 27, q. 1, a. 4 ad 3, vol. III, p. 870; *Contra Gentiles*, III. 61.
28. See "Secundum philosophos . . . continuatio intellectus possibilis ad intelligentiam agentem," *In II Sent.*, d. 18, q. 2, a. 2, sol., vol. II, p. 464; a long discussion of *coniunctio et continuatio*, with reference to Averroes, contains the remark "coniunctio intellectus cum specie intellecta est per operationem," *ibid.*, d. 17, q. 2, a. 1, vol. II, pp. 426-27; *continuatio* and *copulatio* are spoken of in *De Unitate Intellectus*, c. 3; ed. Leo W. Keeler, S.J., (Rome: Gregorian Univ. Press, 1936), nos. 63-65.
29. Compare "Avempace in epistola sua, quam appellavit Continuationem intellectus cum homine," Averroes, *in III De Anima*, t. c. 5 (Venice: Juntas, 1574), vol. VI. i. 2, fol. 148C.
30. See e.g., *De Anima*, part 4, c. 4 .
   On this term cf. A. M. Goichon, *Lexique de la Langue Philosophique d'Ibn Sînâ* (Paris: Desclée, 1938): "Ittisal — 2. Continuité par contact . . . le rapport de l'intellect actif et de l'âme humaine dans l'act d'intellection," mo. 775, pp. 434-35.
31. *In De Anima*, III, t. c. 5 (Venice: Juntas, 1574), vol. VI. i.2, fol. 147D, 148C; t. c. 20, fol. 163-165; t. c. 26, fol. 165E. Other texts could be found without difficulty.
32. See St. Thomas's explicit statement quoted in note 28; add also *Summa Theologiae* I.88.1.

This is a very important notion, and a side of St. Thomas's psychology that is neglected only on pain of distorting it. In the kind of analysis he borrowed from Avicenna, we arrive at a multiplicity of powers. There are ten distinct cognoscitive powers in man — and we seem to have arrived at an atomistic breakdown of the given unity of human operation.

In Chapter Two, we noted a tendency to deny the real value of such analysis. Both the Stoics and the Augustinians seem to have had a strong feeling for the experimentally perceived unity of man. Their solution was to blur all distinctions of the powers among themselves, and even to assert the real identity of the substance of the soul with its powers.[33] This solution sacrifices all philosophical precision, and makes unintelligible the real diversity in human activity, which after all is just as much a datum as its unity.

Because of the importance of the notion of the unity of human operations, and also because of the way in which St. Thomas grounds it, it is expedient here to discuss it at some length.

In the Augustinian view of man, there is a tendency, which only rarely is fully yielded to, to translate the experimentally perceived unity of man's operation into one internally simple operation. This one operation flows from a power whose multiplicity is rather from the side of its relation to many objects. This unique power, in turn, tends to be identified more or less closely with the soul.[34] Finally, these theses are frequently connected with a doctrine that tends in the direction of identifying man with his

---

33. Cf. E. Portalié, "Augustinisme," *Dictionnaire de Théologie Catholique,* ed. A. Vacant and E. Mangenot, tome I, col. 2504; and D. Odo Lottin, "L'Identité de l'âme et de ses facultés pendant la première moité du XIIIe siècle," *Revue Neo-Scholastique,* XXXVI (1934), pp. 191-210. Dom Lottin mentions several authors who held an essential identity, and then goes on to show that this view displeased many Augustinians, who gave as their reason that only God was essentially simple. The solution rather commonly adopted was that the soul was not essentially identical with its powers, but was substantially identical with them.

34. *Ibid.,* cf. É. Gilson, *La Philosophie au Moyen Age,* pp. 306-421, 437, 444-45; 454, 461.

soul.[35] There seems to be here a tendency to favor unity at the cost of multiplicity, and simplicity at the cost of composition. Certain it is that man's operations of sensing and knowing are not considered to be composite, but are regarded as activities of the soul alone.

In St. Thomas the movement of thought is quite other, and consciously so. Man is a composite of body and soul in order to know.[36] More fully: the human intellect comes into being as a mere potency. It is therefore necessary that man have not only an intellect but also senses. The act of sensation involves the body. Hence, the kind of intellect (and soul) that a man has requires him to be a composite being, with a body as well as a soul.[37]

Though composite, man is in and by himself one being.[38] The real unity of man means that his body and soul are related to each other as matter and form. For this is the only way that

35. Cf. É. Gilson, *Introduction à l'Etude de Saint Augustin,* 2nd ed. (Paris: Vrin, 1943), pp. 56-72, 321-22; *La Philosophie au Moyen Age,* p. 323.
36. There are a number of texts to this effect; for example: *Summa Theologiae,* I.75.3 ad 7; 84.7; *In II Sent.,* d. 1, q. 2, a. 5; *Quaestio Disputata de Anima,* a. 1 ad 1, a. 8; *Contra Gentiles,* II.90 "Adhuc"; 91 "Item, substantia"; cf. É. Gilson, *Le Thomisme,* 5th ed. (Paris: Vrin, 1944), pp. 266, 269-70; 278-80; *La Philosophie au Moyen Age,* p. 537.
37. *Summa Theologiae* I.76.5.
   How fully aware St. Thomas was of the implications of this stand may be seen in this remarkable text, so thoroughly opposed to Platonic and Augustinian dualism: "Nec tamen est verum quod aliquis actus sit hominis in vita praesenti in quo corpus non communicet; quia, quamvis in actibus intellectivae partis non communicet corpus sicut instrumentum actus, communicat tamen sicut repraesentans obiectum; quia obiectum intellectus est phantasma, sicut color visus, ut dicitur in III *De Anima.* Phantasma autem non est sine organo corporali; et sic patet quod etiam intelligendo, et in aliis actibus animae, utimur aliquo modo corpore," *Quodlibetum* VII, a. 11 ad. 3, ed. Parma, vol. IX, p. 561.
38. *Summa Theologiae* I.76.1; *Contra Gentiles,* II.56, 57, 59, 68-70; *Commentary on Aristotle's De Anima,* II, lect. 4; III, lect. 7; *De Spiritualibus Creaturis,* a. 2; *Q. D. De Anima,* a. 1, 2.

composition in the order of essence can at the same time constitute one being.

It is precisely this same potential nature of intellect which makes it necessary that man have many powers.[39] Note here the close relation between diversity inside essence and multiplicity on the level of operation.

There is not only diversity in the order of essence, there is also unity of composition. Corresponding to this unity, which is due to the soul as form, there is an order among the many potencies.[40]

By this very fact, the problem of *continuatio* ("contact") of man's powers with each other is solved in principle.[41] This is not the place to prove or even discuss that St. Thomas was right in maintaining the matter-form composition of man. But it is necessary to insist that, once granted this composition which gives a real and intelligible unity, a real *unum per se,* one is logically bound to follow St. Thomas on to holding a number of powers and a contact or composition between them. If the body is really a part of man's being, then it likewise has an intelligible work to do, even in relation to man's proper and specific work, which is understanding. Again, if one admits that the human intellect is itself in potency, and receives its objects from sense through imagination, then the dependence of intellect in all its operations is decided in principle. To admit "imageless thought," in the sense that intellect in some operation does not need an image, is tacitly to deny one of these principles.

With this brief reference to the metaphysical backgrounds of *continuatio* in St. Thomas, the parenthesis can be closed, and we

---

39. *Summa Theologiae* I.77.2; *In De Anima* II. lect. 6; *Q. D. De Anima,* a. 13.

40. *Summa Theologiae* I.77.4; *Q. D. De Anima,* a. 13 ad 10.

41. There is a striking text on the function of order with respect to dynamic contact in the immaterial sphere: "Quod autem est in corporalibus situs, est in spiritualibus ordo; nam situs est quidam ordo partium corporalium secundum locum; et ideo ipse ordo substantiarum spiritualium ad invicem sufficit ad hoc quod una influat in alteram," *Quodlibet.* III, a. 7, ed. Parma, vol. IX, p. 489.

can return to the discussion from the historical point of view, and on the level of operation itself.

As we have seen, there was a tendency among philosophers to deny the real diversity and distinction of powers, and to insist on the unity of human operation. St. Thomas was quite ready to grant that the act of perception presents itself as one — as a concrete unit.[42] Nevertheless, he also maintained the analysis. There is, therefore, an analytically discovered multiplicity of powers, and an experimentally given unity of operation. Such a situation calls for a synthesis that will unify without obliterating all distinctions.

What is the key to the unification of a multitude of the type in question here? It is precisely the notion of *order*.[43] In the multiplicity of cognitive powers there is a manifold order. We have seen that St. Thomas, in the first passage quoted in this chapter, prefaces his discussion with a statement of the Dionysian principle of hierarchy. This is nothing more or less than an order of participation — an order of extrinsic formal causality. Consequently, even from the static point of view of formal analysis, we never have a mere unrelated multiplicity of powers. Even from this limited point of view, there is a unity in cognition, inasmuch as cognition is an analogous term.

There is secondly an order of final causality. In man, sense is not for its own sake alone, but also, and even primarily, for the

---

42. In an Aristotelian framework, this doctrine comes clearly to the fore in the discussion of the "sensible per accidens"; cf. *In IV Sent.,* d. 49, q. 2, a. 2, text discussed below; *in De Anima,* II, lect. 13; text discussed in the next chapter; also *Summa Theologiae* I.12.3 ad 2.

In the Augustinian frame of reference, St. Thomas interprets the Augustinian trinity-in-unity as precisely operational; cf. *Summa Theologiae,* I.77.1 ad 1, "Augustinus loquitur de mente secundum quod noscit se et amat se," ed. Leon, vol. V. p. 237; 93.6 ad 4, vol. V, p. 408. The same doctrine is to be found in the *Scriptum Super Libros Sententiarum,* II, d. 3, q. 3; q. 4, a. 1, 2; q. 5, but it is not quite so clearly and sharply expressed.

43. See *Summa Theologiae* III.2.1; I.21.3; 42.3; II-II.26.1; *De Potentia* VII.11, X.3; *in III Sent.,* d. 1, q. 1, a. 1; *Contra Gentiles,* IV.35 "Amplius, nomen."

sake of intellect.[44] This unity in finality is very frequently referred to, particularly in the arguments against a "plurality of forms" in man.

A third, and in some ways the most fundamental, order, is that of the origin or "emanation" of the potencies from the substance.[45] It is because the potencies flow from the soul, not with equal immediacy, but according to a definite order, that there can be an order in their operations. This order seems to be, reductively, an order of efficient causality.

Finally, based on these orders, there is the dynamic order designated as *continuatio*. The activities of analogically similar beings form a kind of unity; in a sense it is true to say that they are understood as one.[46] But two causes, no matter how otherwise related, do not produce one action or operation — one, that is, without any qualification — unless they stand in the relation of instrumentality.[47] This kind of dynamic relationship, and it alone, explains both the experientially given concrete unity of operation, and the real differences therein. For example, when a man writes with a pen, there is only one writing, and yet this one activity has within it the virtuality of both causes concerned.

To prevent misunderstandings, a remark on "instrumentality" is in place. The designations "principal" and "instrumental" apply to efficient causes, that is, to things acting as efficient causes by

---

44. See *Contra Gentiles,* III.33; *Summa Theologiae* I.76.5, 84.5, 84.8 obj. 1 and ad 1; *De Veritate* X.6, XI.1.

45. See *In I Sent.,* d. 3, q. 4, a. 3; *in II Sent.,* d. 24, q. 1, a. 2; *Summa Theologiae* I.77.6.

46. Thus, this universe is one world, though composed of many distinct things, and tends toward one end, though there are distinct tendencies in each thing.

It is correct, from St. Thomas's own point of view, to consider *operation* as being in the order of activity, which is in modern terms frequently designated the "dynamic order." Cf. St .Thomas's very valuable discussion of finality, activity, and operation in *Summa Contra Gentiles,* II.56; III.22.

47. See *Summa Theologiae* I.45.5; 105.6; III.62.1 ad 7; 4 ad 4; 72.3 ad 2; 82.1 ad 1; *Contra Gentiles,* III.109; IV.56; *In IV Sent.,* d. 1, q. 1, a. 4, q. 3; d. 8, q. 2, a. 3, q. 9; *In V Metaphysic.,* lect 3, medio.

means of distinct substantial instruments and by way of transient action. The distinctions, applied to several powers of one subject whose actions are immanent, will be analogous.

Continuatio AND THE KNOWLEDGE OF THE SINGULAR.

In this way, the indirect intellectual knowledge of the singular is one act, involving the use of two powers. This is the way in which the intellect forms propositions about singulars. The intellect reflects back upon its operation and then to the phantasm, following back the order in which knowledge came to it, and using the phantasm as its instrument, knows the singular of which the phantasm is the representation.

For the sake of completeness, it may help to ask two questions of St. Thomas, and give the outlines of the answers. How can the intellect know singulars at all? It must be kept in mind that "universal" and "singular" are not precisely essential designations.[48] Nevertheless they are convenient designations of the difference between sense and the human intellect.[49] Now, intellect does not know particulars the way sense does;[50] such an assertion would blur the distinction between the powers. Singulars are not necessarily unintelligible by virtue of their singularity,[51] but only material singulars known by abstraction. And since there is a complex way of knowing, indirectly, there is a possibility of knowing the material singular intellectually.

---

48. "Universale et particulare non diversificant essentiam neque habitum," *In III Sent.*, d. 26, q. 2, a. 4 ,sol., vol. III, p. 842.
49. " 'Universale est dum intelligitur, particulare dum sentitur,' referendum est ad cognitionem nostram quae in sensu est per formam materialem, et in intellectu per formam universalem, et ideo particularia non cognoscimus nisi per virtutem in qua est aliquid particulariter," *In I Sent.*, d. 36, q. 1, a. 1 ad 1, vol. I, p. 832.
50. "Ad tertium dicendum quod intellectus qui singulare cognoscit alio modo cognoscit quam sensus . . . et sic adhuc remanet differentia inter intellectum et sensum," *In IV Sent.*, d. 50, q. 1, a. 3 ad 3, ed. Parma, v. VII, pt. 2, p. 1250.
51. "Nec oportet omne singulare esse intelligibile tantum in potentia," *In II Sent.*, d. 17, q. 2, a. 1 ad 3, vol. II, p. 429.

Why are not material singulars directly intelligible? Material singulars are such through designate matter.[52] Human knowledge takes place by way of "reception" from things. In other words, we are determined to know through the action of sensible things upon us. Now, all action takes place through form.[53] Form of itself is universal, and so by the direct process the singular thing will not be known.

The singular *essence* is never known by man at all. For the senses in no wise know the essence of things, and so know neither the universal nor the singular essence. The senses grasp the external accidents of a thing as it is here and now. The intellect, knowing the (universal) essence, and rejoining (*reflectendo*) the origin of its knowledge in the sense powers, will be able to know the essence as realized here and now. In fact, abstracting from this somewhat deductive approach, and turning to the data of actual experience, we find that the only intellectual knowledge we have of singulars is this: we know that they are of a certain kind (have a certain essence), with certain sensible qualities at a given time and place.

THE DISCURSIVE MODE OF OPERATION.

Once the relation between reason and the discursive power has been clearly understood, it will be easy to form a clear notion of the *collatio* exercised by the latter power. The animal judges the useful or harmful according as it is naturally determined. Man, on the contrary, after he has attained the use of reason, makes his sensory judgments concerning sensory goods through a comparison. What does he compare? Directly, he compares the sensible object under the aspect of being useful or harmful with that same object under other aspects of being pleasant, and so forth. It seems clear that this comparison involves another, namely, of

52. Texts and discussion can be found in M. D. Roland-Gosselin, O.P., *Le 'De Ente et essentia' de S. Thomas d'Aquin* (Kain: Le Saulchoir, 1926).
53. Cf. *In IV Sent.,* d. 50, q. 1, a. 3, sol.; the text is quoted above in note 25.

different objects among themselves. To make such a comparison it is not necessary that the discursive power apprehend usefulness as such; it is sufficient that reason, the principal cause of the comparison, understand this. Because reason has a knowledge of this abstract notion as such, it can direct the operation of the discursive power in such a way that a kind of abstraction takes place in the sense.

This may seem a violent statement. But after all, the imagination, for example, is also capable of performing certain abstractions, and that prior to the exercise of intellect or will.[54] And, as far as the discursive power is concerned, there is the function of rationally directed attention to single out aspects of the object.

THE DISCURSIVE POWER AND SPECULATIVE KNOWLEDGE.

All these considerations of the discursive power have centered around purely practical knowledge. There is a single text in the *Scriptum Super Sententias* which seems to go beyond this.

> *Per accidens* that is sensed which does not affect the sense inasmuch as it is a sense, nor as it is this sense, but as joined to those things which of themselves affect the sense, as "Socrates," and "the son of Diares," and "friend," and other like things. These things are known in the universal by the intellect; in the particular, they are known by the discursive power in men, and by the estimative in other animals. Such things the exterior sense is said to sense, even though only *per accidens,* when from that which is sensed in itself, the apprehensive power, whose task it is to know them in themselves, immediately, without hesitation or reasoning knows them; as we see that someone lives from the fact that he speaks.[55]

---

54. For example, a common image abstracts in a way from some individual traits or particularisations. Again, the image of space arises in the imagination, though no space exists as an object for the external senses. It seems to be legitimate to understand this "abstraction" somewhat after the manner in which a composite photograph can be produced.

55. *In IV Sent.,* d. 49, q. 2, a. 2, ed. Parma, vol. VII, pt. 2, pp. 1201-02. Text in Appendix II, no. 60.

St. Thomas is here working on a problem of immediate perception. The technical apparatus of the discussion, the order of development, and the very examples used show that he has in mind a passage of Aristotle's *De Anima*. There is an obvious difficulty in that he mentions the estimative and discursive powers. Secondly, the comment made here is too brief to enable us to be certain of its full implications. And, since he has commented on this precise passage of the *De Anima*, it will be wiser to defer the explanation of this text till the next chapter.

QUAESTIO DISPUTATA DE VERITATE

Although there are no explicit and systematic discussions of the internal senses in the *De Veritate*, there are several important passages dealing with one or the other of them. The cognition of material singulars is discussed from several points of view.

> Just as every form, as far as it is in itself, is universal, so the relation to form does not make it possible to know matter except with a universal knowledge. . . .
>
> And so it is clear that our intellect cannot directly know singulars. The singular is directly known by us through the sensitive powers, which receive forms from things in a corporeal organ, and thus receive them under definite dimensions, and in a way that they lead to a knowledge of singular matter. For as universal form leads to a knowledge of universal matter, so an individual form leads to a knowledge of designate matter, which is the principle of individuation.
>
> Nevertheless, our intellect concerns itself with singulars accidentally, in so far as it is in contact with the sensitive powers, which deal with particulars. This contact is of two kinds. One is the way according to which the movement of the sensitive part ends in the intellect, as happens in the movement from things to the soul. Thus the intellect knows the singular by a kind of reflection, that is, in so far as the intellect, knowing its object which is a universal nature, returns to the knowledge of its act, and further to the species which is the principle of its act, and further still to the phantasm from which the species was abstracted. In this way it acquires some knowledge of the singular.
>
> A second way is the one according to the movement which is from the soul to things; which begins in the intellect, and pro-

ceeds to the sensitive part, in so far as the intellect rules the lower powers. In this way the intellect concerns itself with singulars by means of the particular reason, which is a power of the sensitive part composing and dividing individual intentions. This power is also called the discursive, and it has a definite organ in the body, that is, the middle cell of the head. Now it is not possible to apply the universal judgment, which the intellect has about things which can be done, to a particular act, except through some intermediate power which apprehends the singular. Thus, there results a syllogism, whose major is universal, namely, the judgment of the intellect; whose minor is singular, which is the application of the particular reason; whose conclusion is the election of a singular work, as is clear by what is said in the third book of the *De Anima*.[56]

As the *Scriptum super Sententias* had already pointed out, the intellect makes use of the discursive power in practical knowledge of the singular. For the human intellect is actively joined with the singular (*continuatur*) in two ways. One is the way of speculative knowledge (*secundum motum ad animam*), and in this way the mind knows the singular by the process of reflection already seen.[57] The second is the way of practical knowledge (*ab anima*

---

56. *De Veritate,* X. 5, Parma, vol. IX, p. 162. (This edition will be used for references to the *Quaestiones Disputatae*.) Text in Appendix II, no. 61.

  Cf. "Ad secundum dicendum quod dispositio sapientis de singularibus non fit per mentem nisi mediante vi cogitativa, cuius est intentiones singulares cognoscere, ut ex dictis in corpore articuli patet," *ibid.,* ad 2; "Ad quartum dicendum quod intellectus sive ratio cognoscit in universali finem ad quem ordinat actum concupiscibilis et actum irascibilis imperando eos. Hanc autem cognitionem universalem mediante vi cogitativa ad singularia applicat, ut dictum est," *ibid.,* ad 4; "Ad particularia applicatur [providentia] mediante ratione particulari, quam oportet mediam intercedere inter rationem universalem moventem et motum qui in particularibus consequitur," *De Veritate* X.2 ad 4, Parma, vol. IX, p. 158; cf. also *ibid.,* X. 4.

57. This is again explained in *De Veritate* II.6 and ad 3, Parma IX, p. 37. Cf. "Praeterea. Nullus cognoscit compositionem nisi cognoscat compositionis extrema. Sed hanc compositionem 'Socrates est homo' format mens; non enim posset eam formare aliqua sensitiva potentia, quae hominem in universali non apprehendit. Ergo mens singularia cognoscit. — Ad tertium dicendum, quod secundum hoc intellectus

ad res). In this order, the discursive power is explicitly mentioned
as a necessary link. Though the intellect can be a moving cause
of our actions, it is always a remote (or principal) cause, while
the proximate (and therefore instrumental) cause is the discursive power and the phantasm.[58] Note that St. Thomas has not
excluded this power from the first active union; he simply has
not mentioned it.

Why should there be this difference? Let us look again at
sensibility on the irrational level. Sensibility as a power of cognition has as its highest form imagination. As a form of life, its
highest power is the estimative.[59] This power in animals is a kind
of natural prudence, that is to say, practical knowledge.[60] It has

---

potest de singulari et universali propositionem componere, quod singulare per reflexionem quamdam cognoscit, ut dictum est." *ibid.*, X.5
ad 3, p. 162; "Ad quartum dicendum quod scientia est de aliquo
dupliciter: uno modo primo et principaliter, et sic scientia est de
rationibus universalibus, super quas fundatur; alio modo est de
aliquibus secundario et quasi per reflexionem quamdam, et sic de
illis rebus, quarum sunt illae rationes, in quantum illas rationes
applicat ad res etiam particulares, quarum sunt, adminiculo inferiorum virium. Ratione enim universali utitur sciens et ut re scita
et ut medio sciendi. Per universalem enim hominis rationem possum
iudicare de hoc vel de illo," *In Librum Boethii de Trinitate,* q. V,
a. 2 ad 4, ed. Paul Wyser, O.P., (Fribourg: Société Philosophique,
1948), p. 35.

58. *De Veritate,* II.6 ad 2, Parma, vol. IX, p. 37.

59. "Vis imaginativa competit animae sensibili secundum propriam rationem, quia in ea reservantur formae per sensum acceptae; sed vis
aestimativa, per quam animal apprehendit intentiones non acceptas
per sensum, ut amicitiam vel inimicitiam, inest animae sensitivae
secundum quod participat aliquid rationis; unde ratione huius aestimationis dicuntur animalia quamdam prudentiam habere, ut patet
in principio *Metaphysicorum*; sicut quod ovis fugit lupum, cuius
inimicitiam numquam sensit. . . . Aestimativa [est superior] inter
ceteras virtutes sensitivae partis." *ibid.*, XXV.2, Parma, vol. IX,
p. 381.

60. "Illud quod est superioris naturae, non potest esse in inferiori natura
perfecte, sed per quamdam tenuem participationem; sicut in natura
sensitiva non est ratio, sed aliqua participatio rationis, inquantum
bruta habent quamdam prudentiam naturalem, ut patet in principio
Metaphysicorum. . . . Bruta non dicuntur habere rationem aliquam,

a direct connection with appetite.⁶¹ This natural estimation must
be inborn, for animals must act, and yet have no power of specu-
lating about their actions.⁶² Further, this power is naturally determined, for experience tells us that the same kinds of animals
act in the same ways,⁶³ and this must be so, for they have no
judgment about themselves and their judgments, but only the act
of judging about the appropriate and the harmful.⁶⁴ This deter-

quamvis aliquid prudentiae participent: sed hoc inest secundum quamdam aestimationem naturalem," *ibid.*, XV.1, Parma, vol. IX, p. 250.

61. "Appetitus vero interior sensitivae partis, qui sensualitas dicitur,
tendit in ipsam rem appetibilem prout invenitur in ea id quod est
ratio appetibilitatis: non enim tendit in ipsam rationem appetibilitatis
. . . tendit in omne id quod est sibi utile vel delectabile . . . et propter
hoc indiget apprehensione. . . . Apprehenso quod est delectabile, de
necessitate fertur in illud. Unde datur intelligi, quod obiectum . . .
appetitus vero sensibilis [est] haec res inquantum est conveniens vel
delectabilis. . . . Et sic differt apprehensio sensus et intellectus, nam
sensus est apprehendere hoc coloratum, intellectus autem ipsam naturam coloris," *ibid.*, XXV.1, Parma, vol. IX, p. 238.

62. "Ad septimum dicendum quod animalia bruta in sui principio accipiunt naturalem aestimationem ad cognoscendum nocivum et conveniens, quia ad hoc ex propria inquisitione pervenire non possunt.
Homo autem ad haec et multa alia potest per rationis inquisitionem
pervenire," *ibid.*, XVIII.7 ad 7, Parma, vol. IX, p. 287.

63. "Ex iudicio naturali agunt et moventur omnia bruta. Quod quidem
patet tum ex hoc quod omnia quae sunt eiusdem speciei, similiter
operantur, sicut omnes hirundines similiter faciunt nidum: tum ex
hoc quod habent iudicium ad aliquod opus determinatum, et non ad
omnia; sicut apes non habent industriam ad faciendum aliquod aliud
opus nisi favos mellis; et similiter est de aliis animalibus. Unde
recte consideranti apparet per quem modum attribuitur motus et
actio corporibus naturalibus inanimatis, per eumdem modum attribuitur brutis animalibus iudicium de agendis. Sicut enim gravia et
levia non movent se ipsa, ut per hoc sint causa sui motus, ita nec
bruta iudicant de suo iudicio, sed sequuntur iudicium sibi a Deo
inditum, et sic non sunt causa sui arbitrii, nec libertatem arbitrii
habent," *Ibid.*, XXIV.1, Parma, vol. IX, p. 351; cf. *ibid.*, I.11.

64. "Unde secundum quod aliquid se habet ad rationem, sic se habet ad
liberum arbitrium. . . . Bruta autem habent aliquam similitudinem
rationis, inquantum participant quamdam prudentiam naturalem, secundum quod natura inferior attingit aliqualiter ad id quod est
naturae superioris. Quae quidem similitudo est secundum quod

mination, however, is not such as to exclude the possibility of passive learning through memory and association.[65]

Let us turn now to human sensibility. The human being has the same four internal senses as the animal.[66] But because human sensibility is the sensibility due to a rational soul,[67] there will be a difference between the acts of these powers in man and in animals. Moreover, the difference will be found to be greater in the higher

---

habent iudicium ordinatum de aliquibus. Sed hoc iudicium est eis ex naturali aestimatione, non ex aliqua collatione, cum rationem sui iudicii ignorent. Propter quod huiusmodi iudicium non se extendit ad omnia, sicut iudicium rationis, sed ad quaedam determinata. . . . Ovis viso lupo necesse habet timere et fugere; et canis insurgente passione irae, necesse habet latrare," ibid., XXIV.2, Parma, vol. IX, p. 354; cf. ibid., ad 1, 2, 3, 5; and ibid., XXII.7, Parma, IX, p. 324.

65. "In brutis est iudicium naturale determinatum ad hoc quod id quod uno modo proponitur vel occurrit, eodem modo accipiatur vel fugiatur. Contingit autem ex memoria praeteritorum beneficiorum vel flagellorum ut bruta aliquid apprehendant quasi amicum, et prosequendum . . . inducuntur ad obediendum nutui instructoris," Ibid., XXIV.2 ad 7, Parma, vol. IX, p. 354.

66. "Unde, cum necessarium sit humiditatem praecipue in cerebro abundare in pueris, in quo vis imaginativa, et aestimativa, et memorativa et sensus communis organa sua habent; harum virtutum actus necesse erat impediri, et per consequens intellectum qui immediate ab huiusmodi potentiis accipit, et ad eas convertit se quandocumque est in actu," Ibid., XVIII.8, Parma, vol. IX, p. 288; "Ad quintum dicendum quod imaginativae virtutis organum, et memorativae et cogitativae, est in ipso cerebro, quod est locus summae humiditatis in corpore humano; et ideo propter abundantiam humiditatis quae est in pueris, magis impediuntur actus harum virium quam sensuum exteriorum. Intellectus autem accipit immediate non a sensibus exterioribus, sed interioribus," Ibid., ad 5.

67. "Actio quae debetur naturae animalis fit in homine secundum quod competit principiis speciei humanae; unde et homo perfectius habet actum virtutis imaginativae quam alia animalia, secundum quod competit eius rationalitati," De Potentia II.2, Parma, vol. VIII, p. 17; "Ad primum ergo dicendum, quod licet anima sensibilis in hominibus et brutis sit eiusdem rationis secundum genus, non tamen est eiusdem rationis secundum speciem, sicut nec idem animal specie est homo et brutum; unde et operationes animae sensibilis sunt multo nobiliores in homine quam in brutis, ut patet in tactu et in apprehensivis interioribus," Ibid., III.11 ad 1, Parma, vol. VIII, p. 54.

than in the lower powers.[68] As we have seen, the highest purely
sensory power is the estimative. Consequently, it will be this
power which is most different in man and beast. Again, according
to the principle of hierarchy, the highest power of the lower order
is close to, and similar to, the lowest power of the higher.[69] The
estimative is similar to reason, and particularly to practical reason
for it is "a certain sharing in reason, in as much as brutes have a
certain natural prudence."[70] If then sense life and intellect are in
"contact" through the highest power of the former, it seems obvious that their first point of juncture will be as principles of appetite and action. At this stage of the investigation, however, it
is not possible to follow out this line indicated by the texts themselves. Nevertheless, this discussion will serve as a preliminary
and tentative answer to the question raised above: why is the discursive power mentioned in the discussion of practical knowledge
of the singular, while it is omitted in the corresponding discussion of speculative knowledge.

We have noted above that the term *"vis cogitativa"* designates
immediately a mode of operation, and only through that a definite
potency. This same development is to be found in the *De Veritate*.
In a discussion of the definition of faith as "cogitare cum assensu,"
St. Thomas objects that this is not a good definition, since the
potentia cogitativa is a sense power, while faith belongs to the soul
(*mens*). To this objection he answers:

> To the ninth argument the answer is that the discursive power
> is that which is highest in the sensitive part, where the latter
> somehow touches the intellective part so as to participate that
> which is lowest in the intellective, namely, the discourse of
> reason, according to the rule of Dionysius, *De Divinis No-
> minibus*, c. 7 that "the beginnings of the second things are
> joined to the ends of the first." And so the very discursive
> power is called "particular reason," as is clear from the Com-
> mentator in the third book of the *De Anima,* and is to be found
> only in man. In place of it there is in other brutes the natural

68. Cf. the texts quoted in note 67, and compare *Summa Theologiae*
I.78.4.
69. *De Veritate* XXV.2, quoted in note 59.
70. *Ibid.,* XV.1, quoted in note 60.

estimation. And so also the universal reason which is in the intellective part, on account of the similarity of its operation, is also designated by *cogitatio*.[71]

In view of the importance of what I considered the direct meaning of *cogitativa* as gathered from the texts quoted from the *Scriptum super Sententias*, I should like to offer an expanded translation of a part of this text. "That is the 'discursive' power which is the highest in the sensitive part [that is, the generically highest power in its highest species], where [sensibility] in a way touches the intellectual so as to have a share in that which is lowest in the latter, namely, the discourse of reason. . . . And so also the universal reason, which is in the intellectual part, is designated by terms derived from '*cogitatio*' on account of the likeness of their operations."

SUMMA CONTRA GENTILES

The preceding discussions, long or short, touching the internal senses directly or indirectly (by way of illustration, or reason for what is said and so forth), have this in common, that they are positive presentations of what is said. Here the majority of texts have an altogether different orientation. Several long texts are summaries, almost centos, of Averroistic doctrine. Other texts concern a refutation of this. Only a very few and quite brief references give St. Thomas's own notion of the discursive power.

The remote context of pertinent passages is the nature of man. The preliminary chapter (book 2, ch. 56) establishes the possibility of a union between intellectual substance and body. But there are a number of theories concerning the nature of this union. The second one is that of Averroes. This commentator has tried to maintain a union between man and the separated

---

71. *De Veritate*, XIV.1 ad 9, Parma, vol. IX, p. 228. Text in Appendix II, no. 62. Cf. "Interdum .ipsa vis cogitativa, quae est potentia animae sensitivae, ratio dicitur, quia confert inter formas individuales, sicut ratio proprie dicta inter formas universales, ut dicit Commentator in III *De Anima* [t. c. 58] ; et haec habet organum determinatum, scilicet mediam cellulam cerebri, et haec ratio absque dubio alia potentia est ab intellectu," *Ibid.*, XV.1, p. 250.

intellect through operation (*continuatio*). St. Thomas's weightiest objection is that then man is basically a brute, a theory which flies in the face of facts (ch. 59). But St. Thomas realizes that Averroes had, as it were, foreseen this objection, and had tried to establish that man has a specific intrinsic power which distinguishes him from other animals.

To these reasons an answer is made according to the position mentioned. For the aforesaid Averroes says that man differs in species by the intellect which Aristotle calls the "passive," which is the discursive power that is proper to man, in place of which other animals have a natural estimative. The work of this discursive power is to distinguish individual intentions, and to compare them among themselves, just as the intellect which is separate and not mixed [with matter] compares and distinguishes universal intentions. Because through this power, together with the imaginative and the memorative, phantasms are prepared to receive the action of the agent intellect by which they become actually intelligible (just as there are some arts which prepare the matter for the principal artisan), so this power is called by the name of intellect and reason, and of it the physicians say that it has its seat in the middle cell of the head. According to the disposition of this power one man differs from another in talent and in other things which belong to understanding. By its use and exercise man acquires the habit of science. Consequently, the habits of the sciences are in this passive intellect as in their subject. This passive intellect is present in a child from the beginning; and from it it acquires the specification of being human, before it actually understands.

That all these things are false, and are an abuse of language, is evident.[72]

This is a summary of the Averroistic position, and it must be admitted that it is an accurate reproduction. With Averroes, St. Thomas fails to assign the formal object of the discursive power, and defines it in terms of the manner of its operation: that which distinguishes and composes individual "intentions" or particulars.[73]

---

72. *Contra Gentiles,* II.60, ed. Leon, vol. XIII, pp. 419-20. (This edition will be used for all references to this work.)

73. Cf. "Nec potest dici quod solus intellectus passivus sit movens; quia intellectus passivus est solum particularium; in movendo autem acci-

In addition to this, the word "intention" is not defined here.

These obscurities make no difference to St. Thomas's critique. For he does not concern himself with the existence or non-existence of this power, nor does he discuss the adequacy of Averroes's sense-psychology. The criticism bears on one point alone, the only reason for mentioning the doctrine at all. For Averroes has admitted that man is man by the discursive power and that this is a strictly sense power.

A second discussion arises concerning the unicity of intellect. St. Thomas mentions several reasons for holding that every man has his own intellectual soul. Then he considers the attempts of Averroes to evade similar arguments.

> But if it be said that this individual man does not acquire his species from the phantasms themselves, but from the powers in which the phantasms reside, that is, the imaginative, memorative, and discursive which is proper to man and which Aristotle calls the passive intellect, still the same difficulties follow. For, since the discursive power has an operation only concerning particulars whose intentions it composes and divides, and since it has a bodily organ by which it acts, it does not transcend the genus of the sensitive soul. But from his sensitive soul man does not have the perfection of being man, but that of being an animal. And so it still follows that the soul is multiplied in us only in what concerns man as animal.
> Again. The discursive power, since it works through an organ, is not that by which we understand, since understanding is not the work of any organ. Now, that by which we understand is that by which man is man, since understanding is the proper work of man following upon his species. Consequently, this individual is not a man through the discursive power: neither is this power that by which man substantially differs from the brutes, as the aforesaid Commentator pretends.
> And again. The discursive power has no relation to the possible intellect by which man understands, except by its act by which the phantasms are prepared so that they can become actually intelligible through the agent intellect and

pitur et universalis opinio, quae est intellectus possibilis, et particularis, quae potest esse intellectus passivi," *ibid.*, p. 420.

perfect the possible intellect. Now, this operation does not always remain the same in us. It is therefore impossible that man through it be in contact with the principle of the human species, or through it have his specific perfection.[74]

They say that the subject of the habit of science is not the possible intellect, but the passive intellect and the discursive power. . . .
But the passive intellect does not know universal, it knows particular intentions. Consequently it is not the subject of the habit of science. . . .
The mistake of placing the habit of science in the passive intellect seems to have arisen from this, that men are found to be more or less ready for the considering of the sciences according to the different disposition of the discursive and imaginative power.
But this readiness depends on those powers as on remote dispositions. This is something like the dependence it has on the delicacy of touch and the bodily complexion; as Aristotle says in the second book of the *De Anima* [c. 9, 421a], that "men of delicate touch and soft flesh have an apt mind." Now, from the habit of science there arises a facility of consideration as from the proximate principle of the act. For it is necessary that the habit of science perfect the power by which we understand, so that it may act easily as it pleases, as other habits do the powers in which they are present.
Again. The dispositions of the aforesaid powers are on the side of the object, namely, the phantasm, which on account of the excellence of these powers is prepared easily to become actually intelligible through the agent intellect. Now, the dispositions which are on the side of the objects are not habits, but those dispositions which are on the side of the powers. For it is not the dispositions by which terrible things become tolerable that are the habit of courage; courage is the disposition by which a part of the soul, namely, the irascible power, is disposed to bear terrible things. And so it is clear that the habit of science is not in the passive intellect, as the aforesaid Commentator says, but rather in the possible intellect.[75]

---

74. *Ibid.*, 73, p. 460.
75. *Ibid.*, p. 461.

Besides, when the aforesaid Commentator places the habits of science in the passive intellect as in their subject, then the unity of the possible intellect does not bring it about that there is numerically one science in the teacher and the student. For it is clear that the passive intellect is not numerically identical in different individuals, since it is a material power.[76]

But it can be said that the agent intellect always acts in so far as in it lies, but that the phantasms do not always become actually intelligible, but only when they are disposed for this. They are thus disposed by the act of the discursive power, whose use lies in us. Through this it happens that not all men understand those things of which they have phantasms, because not all have an appropriate act of the discursive power, but only those who are instructed and accustomed to it.

But this answer does not seem to be entirely satisfactory. For the disposition to understanding which comes from the discursive power, must either be a disposition of the possible intellect to receive the intelligible forms which flow from the agent intellect, as Avicenna says; or it must be that the phantasms are disposed to become actually intelligible, as Averroes and Alexander say. . . .

In the same way, it does not seem satisfactory that the phantasms are disposed by the discursive power to become actually intelligible and move the possible intellect, if the agent intellect is posited as a separate substance.[77]

In all the texts so far quoted from the *Summa Contra Gentiles,* there are only two admissions by St. Thomas. First, there *is* a sensory power of composition and division (a sensory discursive power), irrespective of what its formal object may be. Secondly, the phantasms are prepared for abstraction by the agent intellect by imagination, the discursive power, and memory. There is no attempt in these passages to explain what this preparation consists in. St. Thomas merely correlates the facts adduced by Averroes with two statements of Aristotle: (a) that the excellence of understanding is in proportion to the excellence of the entire

76. *Ibid.,* 75, p. 476.
77. *Ibid.,* 76, p. 481.

sensory equipment;[78] (b) that memory and experience are needed for the first principles of science and art.[79] Thus it is clear that these texts cannot be used to identify and expound St. Thomas's own teaching beyond the limits indicated. St. Thomas's procedure in criticising the Averroistic position is instructive in this regard. The critique bears mainly on the separation of the agent intellect, and on the unicity of the rational soul which Averroes should logically hold. There are, however, a few texts which contain positive statements. Thus, there are several texts on the estimative power and the lack of freedom in animals.

Even in brute animals the forms which are sensed or imagined are not constructed by these brute animals themselves, but are received in them from exterior sensible things which act upon the sense, and are judged by the natural estimative power (*aestimatorium*). . . . For in so far as their appetite moves their members, they are said to move themselves; a perfection they have beyond that of inanimate things and plants. But in so far as the very appetition necessarily follows in them from the forms received through sense and the judgment of their natural estimation, they are not their own causes of movement.[80]

That which moves itself is divided into that which moves and that which is moved. That which moves is the appetite, moved by intellect or phantasy or sense, whose characteristic

78. Cf. Aristotle, *De Anima*, II, c. 9, 421a.
79. Cf. *Idem, Metaphysics* A, c. 1, 980b; *Posterior Analytics* II, c. 15, 100a.
   Cf. also: "Ex sensibus fiunt in nobis memoriae, ex quibus experimenta de rebus accipimus, per quae ad comprehendum universalia scientiarum et artium principia pervenimus," *Contra Gentiles,* II.83, p. 522.
80. *Contra Gentiles,* II.47, vol. XIII, p. 377.
   Cf. "Naturalis enim appetitus requirit ut unumquodque animal sibi provideat in necessariis suae vitae; unde animalia quae non quolibet tempore anni necessaria vitae invenire possunt, quodam naturali instinctu, ea quae sunt vitae suae necessaria congregant illo tempore quo inveniri possunt, et ea conservant; sicut patet de apibus et formicis," (in an objection against voluntary poverty), *ibid.,* III.131, vol. XIV, p. 398.

is to judge. Therefore only these things judge freely which move themselves in judging. Now, no judging power moves itself to judge unless it reflects on its act; for it is necessary that, if it makes itself judge, it knows its judgment. . . .

Besides. Some things lack freedom of judgment, either because they have no judgment at all, as those which lack knowledge like stones and plants; or because they have a judgment which is determined by nature to a single act, like irrational animals. For by a natural estimation the sheep judges that the wolf is its enemy, and from this judgment it avoids the wolf; similarly in other cases.[81]

The judgment of the estimative is not a reflective one. In other words, the animal "estimates" something to be harmful, but it does not know its own estimation. Not knowing its own judgment, it has no means of judging except as it is determined. This determination comes partly from the object — the wolf is of a certain color, odor, etc., — and from the nature of the sheep.

One of the concessions made to Averroes, as was pointed out above, was that the phantasms are prepared for abstraction by the interior senses. It is important to note that this is more than a momentary granting of an argument. In an objection against the immortality of the soul, based on the impossibility of its doing anything after death, St. Thomas says:

The soul also needs, for understanding, the powers which prepare the phantasms to become actually intelligible, namely, the discursive and memorative powers. Of these powers it is certain that, since they are the acts of certain organs of the body by which they operate, they cannot remain after the death of the body. And so Aristotle also says . . . that [the soul] "understands nothing without the passive intellect" which he calls the discursive power, which is corruptible [De Anima, bk. 3, c. 5, 430A].[82]

In answering this objection, he remarks:

As long as the soul is in the body, it cannot understand without the phantasm, nor, likewise, can it remember except through the discursive and memorative powers, by which the

81. *Ibid.*, II.48, vol. XIII, p. 379.
82. *Ibid.*, 80, p. 505.

phantasms are prepared, as is clear from what was said above. And for this reason, understanding, as far as this way is concerned, and likewise remembering, is destroyed when the body is destroyed.[83]

In this text, a distinction seems to be drawn: the discursive power is necessary for remembering, but is not specifically mentioned as required for understanding as such. No further explanation is offered. In another passage St. Thomas speaks of the operation of the three interior powers without making this distinction. He says: "the operation of the intellect cannot be completed without the operation of the bodily powers, which are the imagination and the memorative and discursive powers."[84]

There are two interesting remarks on reflection and the knowledge of the particular.

Although we said that the intelligible species received in the possible intellect is not that which is understood but that by which something is understood, this does not deny that the intellect by a kind of reflection understands itself, and its act of understanding, and the species by which it understands. Its act of understanding it understands in a two-fold way: the first, in particular, for it understands that it is now understanding; the second, in the universal, according as it reasons about the nature of its act. Consequently it understands the intellect and the intelligible species in the same two ways: on the one hand perceiving itself to be and to have an intelligible species, which is to know them in particular; and on the other considering its own nature and that of the intelligible species, which is to know them in the universal.[85]

For it is not being an individual which is repugnant to being actually intelligible. For it is necessary to say that the possible and agent intellects themselves, if they are posited to be separate substances subsisting by themselves not united to a body, are certain individuals, and yet they are intelligible. But that which is repugnant to intelligibility is materiality. The sign of this is that in order that the forms of material things be actually intelligible, they must necessarily be abstracted from matter.

---

83. *Ibid.,* 81, p. 506.
84. *Ibid.,* III.84, vol. XIV, p. 249.
85. *Ibid.,* II.76, vol. XIII, p. 475.

And thus, in those things in which individuation takes place
through this designate matter, the individuals are not actually
intelligible. But if individuation takes place not through matter, there is no reason why the individuals should not be
actually intelligible. Now, the intelligible species are individu-
ated by their subject, which is the possible intellect; just as
all other forms are. Consequently, since the possible intellect
is not material, the intelligible species are not prevented by
it from being actually intelligible.[86]

This is a crucial point in St. Thomas's explanation. The two
kinds of reflection are quite different acts. We are not here concerned with the second kind, by which the intellect reasons to the
nature of its act, of itself, and of its intelligible species. But the
first kind of reflection, which is a direct perception *that* it understands, that it is, and that it has an intelligible species, is an important step in attaining the knowledge of the material singular.
For this kind of knowledge, which is of an actually intelligible
singular, is intermediate between the knowledge of intelligible universals, and that of material singulars. This same doctrine is explained more briefly, but perhaps more clearly, in the *Summa
Theologiae,* and will be treated in connection with the relevant
texts from the later work.

One thing only must be pointed out. When St. Thomas says
that the imagination, the discursive power, and memory prepare
phantasms for intellection, he is not saying anything at all about
the way this takes place, nor about the reasons for it. The reasons
for insisting on the limitations of these texts will become clear later.

---

86. *Ibid.,* Cf. also, I.63-65.

CHAPTER 7

THE ARISTOTELIAN COMMENTARIES

In the first chapter, the works of Aristotle were investigated to see whether he said anything about the *vis cogitativa*. The evidence shows that this power was not so much as mentioned by him. In the sixth chapter, St. Thomas seemed to be saying that Aristotle did hold this power, for we find him interpreting certain passages of Aristotle in this sense. Moreover, the *vis cogitativa* and related doctrines are to be found in his commentaries on Aristotle's *Ethics, De Anima* (books two and three), *Posterior Analytics, De Memoria et Reminiscentia,* and *Metaphysics.*

The chronological sequence of these various commentaries is approximately represented in this list. The *Metaphysics* might be placed before the *De Anima* (books two and three); but since the *Commentary on the Metaphysics* may have been composed, and was certainly at least retouched around 1271 or 1272, the order as given may well stand.

It has been decided not to follow this chronological order in the discussion of pertinent passages. The reason for this, as will appear in the following, is that in no single work is there a complete discussion from all points of view, while the same points may be treated in several works. The procedure will therefore be a more analytical one, that of gathering texts under various heads. If in any instance chronological relations should be significant, they will be mentioned.

One more preliminary question must be asked. Can the doctrines expressed in the Aristotelian *Commentaries* be considered, without any qualification at all, to be St. Thomas's own deliberately held teaching?[1] In some sense, this is a real problem. How-

---

1. Cf. Martin Grabmann, *Mittelalterliches Geistesleben* (Munich: Hueber, 1926), pp. 296-306.

This problem is of particular relevance in the study of the internal senses. In a detailed study of the *sensus communis,* the Reverend Edmund J. Ryan, C.PP.S., has proved that St. Thomas's personal

ever, we need not delay in attempting to answer the question put
thus universally. For, in practice, and from the limited point of
view of the precise doctrine we are here concerned with, the answer can be quite simple.

Passages in these *Commentaries* can conceivably stand in one
of three relations to the doctrine explained in the other works. The
Commentaries can (a) treat some point which is not treated at
all anywhere else; (b) run parallel with some other passage, from
which they may in addition differ in the greater or less explicitness
of discussion; (c) contradict some explicit teaching. In any of
these three cases, the procedure would be quite clear. The matter,
however, cannot be decided until the *Summa Theologiae* has been
studied.

The mere possibility of divergence does, however, impose one
caution. If interpretation of one passage by another has to be
made, it would seem to be unsafe to let the *Commentaries* be the
rule and standard according to which everything else is to be understood. With this word of caution, we can now consider the doctrines concerning the discursive power in the *Commentaries*.

ST. THOMAS ON ARISTOTLE AND THE INTERNAL SENSES.

In the first chapter, reference was made to a comment of St.
Thomas on Aristotle's psychology of the interior senses. This passage merits a little more attention.

> It remains that phantasy be a movement originating from
> the sense which has been put in act. But further, that this
> movement requires a power different from the sensitive, this
> Aristotle does not decide. But it seems that, since powers are
> distinguished according to the differences of their acts, and
> since differences of movement require different things which
> are moved, because that which is moved does not move it-

---

doctrine on sensory awareness and on the apprehension of the common sensibles is different from the doctrine expounded in his *Commentary on the De Anima;* see *The Role of the "Sensus Communis"
in the Psychology of St. Thomas Aquinas* (Carthagena, Ohio: Messenger Press, 1951), pp. 125-28.

self, but something else — it seems necessary that the "phantastic" or imaginative power be different from the sense.[2]

From this passage it is quite clear that St. Thomas understood that there was not even a doctrine of distinct internal powers in the work of Aristotle himself. But he makes it clear that he considers this doctrine to be a perfectly legitimate development, since it is based on principles formally found in this and other works.

How does St. Thomas look on this development? In the *Commentary on the De Memoria et Reminiscentia,* he says:

> It might seem to someone from the statements made here, that phantasy and memory are not powers distinct from common sense, but are affections thereof. But Avicenna reasonably shows that they are different powers.[3]

---

2. *Commentarium in Aristotelis Libros de Anima,* III, lect. 6, ed. Angelo Pirotta, O.P., (Turin: Marietti, 1924), no. 667.

3. *Commentarium in De Memoria et Reminiscentia,* lect. 2, ed. Parma, vol. XX, p. 201. Cf. "[In hoc libro] non facit de aliis mentionem, scilicet de imaginatione et aestimatione, quia haec non distinguuntur a sensu ex parte rei cognitae, sunt enim praesentium vel quasi praesentium," *Commentarium in De Sensu et Sensata,* lect. 1, ed. Parma, vol. XX, p. 147a.

The text from the *De Memoria* continues thus: "Cum enim potentiae sensitivae sint actus corporalium organorum, necesse est ad diversas potentias pertinere receptionem formarum sensibilium quae pertinent ad sensum, et conservationem earum, quae pertinet ad phantasiam sive imaginationem. . . .

Similiter ad aliud principium pertinet recipere formam, et conservare receptam per sensum, et intentionem aliquam per sensum non apprehensam; quamvis aestimativa percipit etiam in aliis animalibus, vis autem memorativa retinet, cuius est memorari rem non absolute sed prout est in praeterito apprehensa a sensu vel intellectu.

Contingit tamen quod diversarum potentiarum est una quasi radix et origo aliarum potentiarum, quarum actus actum ipsius primae potentiae praesupponunt, sicut nutritiva est quasi radix augmentativae et generativae potentiae, quarum utraque utitur nutrimento. Similiter autem sensus communis est radix phantasiae et memoriae, quae praesupponunt actum sensus communis," *ibid.*

St. Thomas uses the Aristotelian phrase commented on here in *Summa Theologiae,* I.78.4, obj. 3. Fundamentally, his answer is the same, with a reference to a previous article on the origin of potencies.

The doctrine of distinct internal potencies (and *a fortiori* of *vis aestimativa* and *cogitativa*) is a "reasonable" (or perhaps better, "reasoned") development of Aristotle first made by Avicenna.

It is well, I believe, to remember that this is the attitude of St. Thomas. We shall see later that it is borne out in other ways.

THE MEANING OF *"Intellectus Passivus."*

In the *Commentary on the Sentences,* the *De Veritate,* the *Summa Contra Gentiles,* and the *Commentary on the Ethics,*[4] St. Thomas interpreted the *intellectus passivus* of the *De Anima* as the *vis cogitativa.* In this interpretation, he suggests that he is following the lead of Averroes. In the *Commentary on the De Anima* he enters into a longer discussion of the meaning of this term.

> But the passive intellect is corruptible, that is, that part of the soul which is not without the aforesaid passions is corruptible; for they pertain to the sensitive part. And yet this part of the soul is called an "intellect," as it is also called "rational," in so far as it shares in reason to an extent, obeying reason and following its movement, as is said in the first book of the *Ethics.* Now, without this part of the bodily soul, the intellect understands nothing. For it does not understand anything without the phantasm, as will be said below. And so when the body is destroyed, the knowledge of things does not remain in the separated soul according to the same way in which it now understands. But how it will then understand it is not the present purpose to explain.[5]

In this analysis, two points are to be noted. The first is that *vis cogitativa* and *ratio particularis* are *not* given as synonyms of this "passive intellect." The second point is that the part of the soul called the "passive intellect" is connected with certain passions, such as "love and hate, reminiscence and the like;"[6] and is also sometimes called "rational by participation." From these two

---

4. *Commentarium in Libros Ethicorum,* VI, lect. 9, ed. Angelo Pirotta, O.P., (Turin: Marietti, 1934), no. 1249. Text quoted and discussed below.

5. *In III De Anima,* lect. 10, Pirotta mo. 745.

6. *Ibid.,* just above the text quoted.

items, we can conclude that the "passive intellect" is here understood as a comprehensive term, including that part of the sensitive soul which contains the sensory powers from imagination to
sense appetite. This is very similar to the interpretation of Themistius,[7] which St. Thomas could have found in Averroes's *Commentary*.[8] Let us note that, whereas the early works rather frequently
use this term, after the *De Anima* it is to be found very rarely.[9]

A different version appears in the *Commentary on the Metaphysics*. Faced with the term *"intelligibilia singularia"* St. Thomas
offers this explanation.

> "Singular intelligibiles" are like mathematical circles. That
> in mathematics some singulars are considered is clear from
> this, that there are in that science several individuals of one
> species, like several equal lines, and several similar figures.
> And this kind of singulars is called "intelligible" according
> as they are comprehended by the phantasy alone without
> sense. The phantasy is sometimes called "intellect," accord-
> ing to the phrase in the third book of the *De Anima*, "The
> passive intellect is corruptible."[10]

The "passive intellect" is a power which is neither intellect in the
strict meaning of that word, nor an external sense or senses. Posi-
tively, it would seem to be mainly the imagination.

Generally speaking, we may say that before the *Commentary
on the De Anima* was written, St. Thomas thought that the term
"passive intellect" designated the discursive power; in this commentary, and occasionally later, he gives it a wider meaning, approximately equivalent to "the complex of sense powers associated
with the phantasm." As such, it is a vague and general term, for
which St. Thomas no longer has much use.

What are the implications of this change of meaning? It in-

---

7. Cf. supra, chapter 1, note 89; also, Themistius, *In De Anima* III,
   c. 5 (*Commentaria in Aristotelem Graeca*, Berlin: 1899), ed. R.
   Heinze, vol. V, part 3, p. 101, line 5.
8. Averroes, *In De Anima*, III, t. c. 20.
9. See the next chapter, note 62. These would seem to be the only
   occurences of this term in the *Summa Theologiae*.
10. *Commentarium in Metaphysicam Aristotelis*, VII, lect. 10, ed. M.
    R. Cathala, O.P. (Turin: Marietti, second edition, 1926), no. 1494.

dicates obviously that St. Thomas gained a better knowledge of
the Aristotelian text precisely through commenting on the *De Anima.*
On the score of his personal doctrine, no change can be discovered
which arises from this change in terminology.

Vis Cogitativa AND THE *Sensibile per Accidens.*

A second point of Aristotelian interpretation was likewise
raised in the *Commentary on the Sentences.* The Aristotelian *sensibile per accidens* is apparently the intelligibile in that which is
sensed.[11] To this, St. Thomas added the object of the estimative
and discursive powers.[12] What is the source of this addition?

As we shall see, it is apparently the *Commentary* of Averroes. To establish this point, we shall first enter into some preliminary discussions, and then look at the passages of St. Thomas
and Averroes on *sensibile per accidens* side by side.

As a first preliminary statement, we shall recall that the method
St. Thomas used was inspired by Averroes. This dependence is
now universally admitted. By this we do not mean that there are
no differences. For example, Averroes seems quite sincerely con-
vinced that what he is saying is the purest Aristotelianism. As
we have seen, St. Thomas evinces a comparatively sophisticated
awareness of the exact bearing of the text.

Another dependence of St. Thomas on Averroes is to be found
in doctrine. Again, everyone realizes that St. Thomas accepted
certain statements of Averroes as accurate formulations of Aristotelian doctrine.[13] Strangely, or perhaps significantly, this kind
of reference is almost lacking in the second and third book of the

---

11. See Aristotle, *De Anima,* II, c. 6, 418 a 20-25; and compare the
    usages of St. Thomas in *Summa Theologiae* I. 17. 2; 78. 3 ad 2.
12. See the preceding chapter, note 55.
13. Thus, for example, there are several implied references to Averroes,
    or summaries of his arguments, especially against the Platonic po-
    sition, to be found in *Summa Theologiae,* I, qq. 75-90. Such refer-
    ences are more numerous and explicit in a different subject matter,
    for example, in the *Physics.*

De Anima.[14] There is another kind of dependence in subject matter, which consists in this, that St. Thomas derives from Averroes the points which he comments, but not what he says about these points.[15]

In thus providing a kind of framework of commentary Averroes's influence pervades the *Commentary on the De Anima.* It has been traced with reference to the utilization of Themistius in the second and third books.[16] It is to be found in many historical references. At times, it is the only reason why a certain subject is mentioned at all in a given place.[17]

It is this kind of influence of Averroes that explains why the internal senses are mentioned in St. Thomas's *Commentary.* The Aristotelian text to be commented concerns itself with the *sensible*

---

14. There is neither explicit mention of Averroes's name, nor implicit reference under the rubric of *quidam* to be found. Averroes is mentioned only by name, in II, lect. 23. no. 534, as holding a false explanation of touch. There are several veiled allusions to "quidam" who hold false theories about the agent or possible intellect.

15. To begin with, there are the references to the separated intellect in III, lect. 8, no. 719, and lect. 10, no. 734-37, the latter of which is introduced with the words "occasione autem horum." Other points may be instanced:
    a) Averroes, II, t. c. 23, fol. 60C, mentions animals which lack one or more senses, as the mole or sponge; St. Thomas, II, lect. 3, nos. 255, 260, mentions the mole and the oyster.
    b) Averroes, II, t. c. 41, fol. 71D, says that fire is an instrumental cause of nutrition; so St. Thomas, II, lect. 8, nos. 331-32.
    c) Averroes, II, t. c. 64, fol. 83A cites Themistius as holding that all the senses perceive all the common sensibles; St. Thomas refers to this theory as that of "quidam" in II, lect. 13, no. 386.
    d) Averroes, II, t. c. 80, fol. 92, uses the analogy of the stone cast into the water and the ripple to explain the propagation of sound; so too St. Thomas, II, lect. 16, no. 447.
    This is not an exhaustive list, but one gathered at haphazard. On this matter, cf. M. Grabmann, *Mittelalterliches Geistesleben,* "Die Aristoteleskommentare des h. Thomas von Aquin," vol. I, p. 282.

16. See Marcel DeCorte, "Themistius et St. Thomas d'Aquin. Contribution à l'étude des sources et la chronologie du Commentaire de S. Thomas sur le *De Anima,*" *Archives* (Gilson and Thery, 1932), pp. 47-84.

17. See note 15, and also St. Thomas, bk. II, lect. 13, Pirotta nos. 395-98.

per accidens. Averroes asserts that the *sensible per accidens* is apprehended by "common sense" and "distinguished" (that is, thought about; *distinguit* =διανοεῖται) by the discursive power. It is therefore by reference to Averroes, not to Aristotle, that St. Thomas here speaks of his own theory of the discursive power. For this reason the corresponding commentaries of Averroes and St. Thomas are presented side by side.

AVERROES	ST. THOMAS
He did not mean that the sense comprehends the essences of things, as some thought; for this belongs to another power which is called intellect. But he meant that the senses, together with the comprehension of their proper sensibles, comprehend individual intentions distinct in genera and species. Therefore they comprehend the intention of this individual man, and the intention of this individual horse, and generally the intention of the ten individual predicaments, and this seems to be proper to the senses of man. . . . And this individual intention is that which the cogitative power distinguishes from the imagined form and strips it from the common and proper sensibles which are joined to it, and places it in the memorative power. And this is the same which the imaginative power comprehends, but the imaginative comprehends it joined with these sensibles.[18]	Therefore, now that we have seen how *per se* sensibles are spoken of, both common and proper, it remains to be seen 5 how something is said to be sensible *per accidens.* We must therefore know that, in order that something be sensible *per accidens,* it is first necessary 10 that it happen to that which is sensible in itself, as it happens to a white thing to be a man, and it happens to it to be sweet. Secondly, it is necessary, that 15 it be apprehended by the one sensing; for if something happened to a sensible that remained hidden to the one sensing, it would not be said to be sensed 20 *per accidens.* It is therefore necessary that it be known in itself by some other cognoscitive power of the one sensing. And this is either another sense 25 or the intellect, or the discursive power, or the estimative power. . . .

What therefore is not known by 30 the proper sense, if it be something universal, is known |

18. Averroes, *In II De Anima,* t. c. 63 (Venice: Juntas, 1574: 12 vols.), vol. VI, i. 2, fol. 82E-F. Text in Appendix II, no. 41.

And the comprehension of the individual intention, though it is the action of the common sense, and so,very often, it will be necessary in the comprehension of an individual intention to use more than one sense (as doctors do in recognizing with more than one sense life in a man who is thought to have full veins), yet it seems that this action belongs to common sense, not as it is common sense, but as it is the sense of some animal, for example, an intelligent animal. This therefore is one of the ways *per accidens*, namely, that it happens to the senses to comprehend the differences of individuals in so far as they are individuals, not in so far as they are simple senses, but in so far as they are human; this is especially true of substantial differences. For it seems that the comprehension of the intentions of individual substances about which the intellect considers is proper to the senses of man. And you ought to know that the comprehension of an individual intention is of the senses; and the comprehension of an universal intention is of the intellect. And universality and individuality are comprehended by the intellect, namely, the definition of the universal and the individual. Then he says, "and so they

by the intellect; yet not everything that can be known by the intellect can be called sensible 35 *per accidens*, but only that which is immediately apprehended by the intellect on the appearance of the sensed thing. Thus, as soon as I see someone 40 speaking or moving himself, I apprehend by my intellect his life, and so I am able to say that I see him live. But if it is apprehended in the singular, for example, 45 when I see this colored thing, I perceive this man or this animal, this kind of apprehension takes place in man by the discursive power, which 50 is also called particular reason, because it compares particular intentions, as the universal reason compares universal ones.

55 Nevertheless this power is in the sensitive part, because the sensitive power in its highest element shares in something of the intellective power in man, 60 in whom the sense is joined to intellect. But in an irrational animal, the apprehension of an individual intention takes place by the natural estimative, as 65 the sheep by hearing or sight knows its offspring, or something similar.

But with regard to this there 70 is a difference between the discursive and estimative powers. For the discursive apprehends an individual, as standing under [*existens sub*] a common nature. 75 This happens to it, in so far as it

are not affected, etc.," that
is, sight is not affected by
the intention of the sensible
per accidens, for, if it were
affected by some individual
in so far as it is that individual, it ought not to be
affected by another individual.[19]

is united to the intellective in the
same subject. And so it knows this
man   as this man, and this wood as
this wood. But the estimative does
80 not apprehend any individual as it
is under a common nature, but only according as it is the term or
principle of some action or passion; as the sheep knows this lamb,
85 not as this lamb, but as something
to be suckled, and this herb, as its
food. And so, other individuals
to which its action or passion is
not extended are not known by its
90 natural estimative in any way. For
the natural estimative is given
to animals, that by it they may be
directed to proper actions or
passions which are to be sought
95 or avoided.[20]

It is not intended at this juncture to analyze the relation between Averroes and St. Thomas, nor to point out differences between their theories. We are interested in similarities. Thus, common expressions are: "individual intentions" (A. [—Averroes],
line 10; T. [—St. Thomas], line 52); "in recognizing . . . life" —
"I apprehend . . . life" (A. lines 41 - 42, T. lines 40 - 41); "proper
to the senses of man," and a series of allied phrases (A. lines 18 - 19,
56, 63, 56 - 57; T. lines 48 - 49, 60, 75 - 77)..

As has been remarked before, the term "intention" in this
connection is not found to be defined where we would expect it
to be. In Averroes, it usually means "*ratio,* thing known, knowl-

19. *Ibid.,* t. c. 65, fol. 83D-F. Text in Appendix II, no. 63.
20. St. Thomas, *in De Anima,* II, lect. 13, ed. Pirotta, nos. 395-98. Latin
    text in Appendix II, no. 64. Because of the close and almost verbal
    reasoning that will be used, it has been thought advisable to have
    at least some manuscript authority. For this purpose, the edition
    of Fr. Pirotta has been compared with a microfilm of Vat. Latin
    762, fol. 79. Variants are given together with the Latin text in the
    appendix.

edge (in an univocal sense)."[21] In St. Thomas, "intention" as referring to cognition, means "cognition, knowledge (as object, i.e., *species*), under the aspect of its having a direction toward an object," and is clearly used in an analogous sense.[22]

With this as a background, the statements of St. Thomas can now be considered in detail. He says that if the *sensible per accidens* is a universal, like "life," it is perceived by the intellect (T. lines 30 - 43; compare A. lines 1 - 6). But if it is apprehended in the singular (for example, seeing this colored object, I perceive this man), it is so apprehended by the discursive power. This statement corresponds to Averroes's expression: "they comprehend individual intentions distinct in genera and species. Therefore they comprehend the intention of this individual man" (lines 9 - 13). Averroes had just warned us that this is not a question of the essences of things, nor of a quasi-intellectual knowledge. For Averroes it seems that this knowledge of the "intention of the individual" takes place by way of such a combination of images that the composite image will be of one individual exclusively.

The discursive power is called "a particular reason," because it compares particular intentions, as the intellect compares universal ones (lines 50 - 53). By a discursive process reason arrives at the essence and *ratio* (in this passage, — definition) of a determinate thing. By a similarly discursive process, the discursive power arrives at an individual intention, or at a knowledge orientated to a definite individual as such.

In spite of having a discursive activity, the discursive power is still a *sensory* power (lines 55 - 59; compare Averroes, lines 1 - 5, 63 - 70). A sense power can share in such an activity, because it is the highest sensory power, and so shares something of the intellectual power — that is, in man, in whom sense is joined to intellect in a unity of operation[23] (lines 60 - 61, compare Averroes, lines 48 - 49).

---

21. See *supra,* chapter III, section on Averroes.
22. See next chapter, section on *intentio*.
23. Cf. preceding chapter, discussion of "continuatio." Also the very clear text in *Summa Theologiae* I. 85.1 ad 4, "Illuminantur quidem [phantasmata] quia sicut pars sensitiva ex coniunctione ad intellectum

The estimative power likewise apprehends an individual in-
intention. An example of this is the knowledge the sheep has of
its own (particular) offspring through sight or hearing (lines
62 - 67). But the limit of estimative knowledge is action and being acted on. For the sheep knows its offspring in the particular
as something to be suckled, or grass as edible. Objects with respect to which there is no action or being acted on for the animal,
are not known by it as individuals (lines 87 - 90). To illustrate
this statement of St. Thomas, it might be said that the sheep
knows a rock in the field as brown — precisely in terms of the
formal object of sight, and that alone. In other words, the animal's
world is a universe of sensory experiences, integrated at intervals
into a knowledge of individuals which are reference points of the
practical order; and this latter, for the animal, is a realm of purely
physical action and being acted on.

But the discursive power is different from the animal estimative in three ways. First, its mode of action is by way of comparison of individual intentions (lines 52 - 53), and this mode is
possible to a sense power because of the dynamic unity between
it and intellect in man (lines 60 - 61).

Secondly, the animal knows the individual only with reference to physical action and passion, while the discursive power
knows the individual "as standing under (*existens sub*) a common
nature" (lines 72 - 74, 79 - 90). In what way is the individual
under a common nature?

No one can doubt that one of the ways in which a particular
stands under a universal is precisely the way in which a particular
practical proposition stands under its universal.[24] This relationship in the practical order is often expressed by St. Thomas in

efficitur virtuosior, ita phantasmata ex virtute intellectus agentis
redduntur habilia ut ab eis intentiones intelligibiles abstrahantur,"
ed. Leon, vol. V, p. 332; also, *S. T.* I.88.1, and *in De Anima,* II, lect.
15, "Oportet autem quod color moveat diaphanum in actu, puta
aerem vel aliquid huiusmodi; et ab hoc movetur sensitivum, id est
organum visus, sicut a corpore sibi continuato," ed. Pirotta, no. 432.
24. Cf. the illuminating expression concerning a similar relationship:
"finis particularis sub illo universali comprehensus," *Summa Theologiae* I-II.9.1, ed. Leon, vol. VI, p. 74.

terms of the "practical syllogism,"[25] which expression is also to be found in his *Commentary on the De Anima*.[26] Taken in this sense, the discursive power knows the individual, not only with reference to merely physical action and passion, but precisely as standing under the intelligible light and direction of intellect.

Can we interpret this passage to mean that the discursive power apprehends any material singular (irrespective of the order of knowledge) as standing under a universal nature? If we answer in the affirmative with almost all the interpreters, then we must answer three questions. *First*, why in the explanation of the indirect intellectual knowledge of the singular, when both contexxt and examples prove conclusively that there is question of speculative knowledge, neither the *Commentary on the De Anima*[27] nor

---

25. Cf. *In Libros Ethicorum*, VI, lect. 4 ,Pirotta no. 1174; lect. 7, Pirotta no. 1214-15; also the texts quoted below, texts to notes 50 and 51; *In IV Sent.*, d. 50, q. 1, a. 3, ad 3 in contrar.; *in II Sent.*, d. 24, q. 2, a. 4, q. 3, a. 3, texts quoted in the preceding chapter, as well as others referred to in the following.

26. "Et primo sciendum est quod ratio speculativa, quam appellat scientificum, non movet, sed in quiete est, quia nihil de imitando vel fugiendo dicit, ut supra dictum est. Ratio autem practica, quaedam est universalis, et quaedam particularis. Universalis quidem, sicut quae dicit, quod oportet talem tale agere, sicut filium honorare parentes. Ratio autem particularis dicit quod hoc quidem est tale et ego talis, puta quod ego filius, et hunc honorem debeo nunc exhibere parenti.

Haec autem iam opinio movet, sed non autem illa quae est universalis. Aut si utraque movet, illa quae est universalis movet ut causa prima et quiescens, particularis vero ut causa proxima et quodammodo motui applicata. Nam operationes et motus in particularibus sunt; unde oportet ad hoc quod motus sequatur, quod opino universalis ad particularia applicetur," *In III De Anima*, lect. 16, Pirotta no. 845-46.

27. Cf. "Sed oportet quod alia potentia 'discernat esse carni,' id est, quod quid est carnis. Sed hoc contingit dupliciter. . . .

Cognoscit enim naturam speciei, sive quod quid est, directe extendendo seipsum; ipsum autem singulare per quamdam reflexionem, inquantum redit super phantasmata, a quibus species intelligibiles abstrahuntur," *In III De Anima*, lect. 8, Pirotta nos. 712-13; cf. nos. 714-16. The reading has been corrected according to the text of the Roman edition, vol. III, 45.

other certainly authentic works[28] mention the discursive power,
whereas the passages dealing with practical knowledge do?[29] *Secondly,* how are we to explain the text in which the particular
which the discursive power apprehends is said to be the operable?
(This text, from the *Commentary on the Ethics,* will be considered
below). *Thirdly,* how is it possible to extend the "apprehension
of the sensibly suitable or unsuitable" to include the speculatively
considered singular?

To avoid misinterpretations to which these questions may quite
possibly leave me open, some explicit statements of the problem
as it appears to me are necessary. There is no doubt that in all
knowledge, the imagination, the discursive power, and the memory
are somehow concerned. This is true even when the intellect is
framing some universal speculative proposition. There is, in other
words, a minimal activity of the internal senses without which
knowledge is impossible. In addition to this, the discursive power
probably has a special bearing on the *verb* in any judgment.[30]

---

28. See *In IV Sent.,* d. 20, q. 1, a. 2 ad 2 in contrarium; *ibid.,* sol.,
in III Sent., d. 26, q. 1, a. 5 ad 4; *De Veritate,* II.6 and ad 3; *Contra Gentiles,* II, c. 76; *Commentary on the Posterior Analytics* II,
lect. 20; *Summa Theologiae* I.86.1, and a series of minor passages
referred to in the next chapter, note 86.
    The one exception that I have found is the *De Principio Individua-
tionis,* a doubtful work, on which see the Appendix I.
29. See *In III Sent.,* d. 17, q. 1, a. 1, q. 2 ad 2; *in IV Sent.,* d. 30, q.
1, a. 3 ad 3 in contrarium; *De Veritate* X.5; *Commentary on the
Ethics,* VI, lect. 1, lect. 9; *Commentary on the Metaphysics,* I, lect.
1; *Summa Theologiae,* I.86.1 ad 2.
30. The verb, according to St. Thomas, properly signifies action (*In
Perihermeneias,* I, lect. 5, no. 5, ed. Leon., vol. I, p. 24), and the
actions we know immediately are always in space and time (*ibid.,*
no. 7. p. 24). Now, it is obvious that the knowledge of time involves memory, and, as will be shown in the next chapter, memory
involves a preceding operation of the discursive or estimative power.
The same doctrine is arrived at from another point of view. The
first operation of the mind has of itself nothing to do with space and
time, but in the second operation — judgment — these come in
(*Summa Theologiae* I. 85. 5 ad 2; 86. 1; 58. 4; 16. 2; *De Veritate*
X. 11, sed contra, 3; *in III Sent.,* d. 14, q. 2, a. 3, q. 2; *De Potentia,*
X. 1; *Contra Gentiles,* II. 96). St. Thomas seems to have drawn

The question now concerns the intellectual knowledge of the singular (as signified by a noun, either by itself or as subject-term of a proposition but prescinded from its verb). In such knowledge, which involves a "turning" of the intellect to the sense powers, does the intellect turn to these three powers the same way in every case? Put in terms of the power we are concerned with here, the question is: does the intellect turn to the discursive power, in the knowledge of every material singular? Conversely, is the discursive power used in a special way in apprehending a singular (object) which stands under a universal in all orders of knowledge?

These questions can be answered only in a preliminary and tentative fashion at this stage. Both on the basis of the texts and for the reasons advanced above, we propose the hypothesis that the discursive power has a special function in the knowledge of the material singular in the practical order. Further verification will be made later.

To resume after this digression. According to the text from the *Commentary on the De Anima*, the discursive power differs from the simple estimative in three ways. First, in its mode of operation, which is by way of comparison of individual intentions. Secondly, the estimative knows the individual only with reference to physical action and passion, while the discursive power knows the operable as standing under the intelligible light and direction of intellect. These two points have been studied. The third point of difference is a kind of consequence of the other two. Because of its purpose (physical action and passion) and the mode of activity (innately determined), the estimative is very restricted in its scope. It knows only a very few intentions, and these in a very concrete and therefore limited fashion. The discursive power, on the contrary, because it is ordered to intellect, and because it participates in the rational discursus, has a much greater scope.

---

this doctrine, or at least its particular formulation, from Aristotle, *De Memoria et Reminiscentia*, 430a8-10; cf. *In De Memoria et Reminiscentia*, lect. 2.

The *"Experimentum"*

There are two famous passages in Aristotle dealing with the *experimentum*: one in the beginning of the *Metaphysics*, the other at the end of the *Posterior Analytics*. On both of these, St. Thomas has a commentary; in the former, the discursive power is mentioned, in the latter it is not. Is there any reason for this difference?

In his *Commentary*, St. Thomas amplifies the steps or degrees of knowledge which Aristotle speaks of. Let us follow St. Thomas through the steps mentioned in the *Metaphysics*.

There are three degrees in which sense cognition may be found. The first degree is that of sensation without a distinct imagination and so without memory. The second degree is that of sensation and memory.[31] Out of this there grows an animal "prudence."

> But those animals, which have memory, can have something of prudence. But prudence is spoken of differently in brute animals and in men. In men, there is prudence, in so far as they deliberate by reason what they ought to do. Hence, it is said in the sixth book of the *Ethics*, that prudence is the correct reason of things to be done. But the judgment about things to be done, not made from the deliberation of reason, but from some instinct of nature, is called prudence in other

---

31. Here and in the *Commentary on the De Sensu et Sensato,* there seems at first sight to be a slight conflict between the doctrine found in other works and that expressed here. In other places, St. Thomas explicitly puts the estimative as the highest sense power. In the *Commentary on the Metaphysics* the estimative is omitted from the list of degrees, and seems merely to be involved in memory. In commenting on the *De Sensu et Sensato,* he says: "Memoria . . . est . . . supremum quoddam in cognitione sensitiva," lect. 1, ed. Parma, vol. XX, p. 147. Is there really a conflict?

The solution seems to lie along the following lines. Memory, in a way, includes the estimative, in so far as it is the power of retaining the intentions thereof, as well as to the extent that remembering involves estimation. The involvement of memory with estimation is spoken of more fully by St. Thomas in the *Summa Theologiae*. In this sense, St. Thomas is here saying that that part of sensory functions which includes imagination, estimation, and memory is higher than the part including the common sense and the external senses.

animals. And so prudence in other animals is the natural estimation about suitable things to be sought and harmful things to be avoided, as the lamb follows its mother and avoids the wolf.[32]

This is a very brief, yet very accurate account of the internal senses on the animal level, as we have seen it in other works. Let us note the explicit placing of the estimative in the practical order, as the correlate to prudence. This is put in other words thus:

> But in this, that he determines the knowledge of animals by comparison with the government of life, he gives us to understand that knowledge is in animals, not on account of the knowing itself, but on account of the necessity for action.[33]

There is, however, a still higher degree of sense cognition: that of sense with memory and hearing. For those animals which have hearing can be taught by way of habit.

Above this degree of knowledge, there is the *experimentum*, which animals do not have, though they share in it to some extent.

An "experiment" arises from the comparison of many singulars received in the memory. This kind of comparison is proper to man, and pertains to the discursive power, which is called particular reason, because it compares individual in-

---

32. *Commentary on the Metaphysics*, I, lect. 1, ed. Cathala, no. 11.

33. *Ibid.*, no. 14.

Add also these very brief references to animal nature: "Cetera animalia non ex deliberatione, sed ex quadam naturali instinctu operantur," *In De Memoria et Reminicentia*, lect. 8, Parma, vol. XX, p. 213; cf. *ibid.*, lect, 1, pp. 197-98, and *In De Sensu et Sensato*, lect. 1, Parma, vol. XX, p. 120.

There is also a remark in the commentary on the *Physics*, which connects with many of the other explanations, though it is not very explicit. Commenting on finality in animal nature, St. Thomas says, "Manifestum est in operationibus eorum, quod propter aliquid operantur. . . . Sed tamen ex hoc fit manifestum, quod non operentur ex intellectu, sed per naturam, quia semper eodem modo operantur: omnis enim hirundo similiter facit nidum, et omnis araneus similiter facit telam. . . . Unde, quia hoc est a natura et non ab arte . . . manifestum est, quod causa finalis invenitur in iis quae fiunt et sunt a natura," *In Physic.*, II, lect, 13, ed. Leon., vol. II, no. 5, p. 93.

tentions, as the universal reason, universal ones. And, because, from many sensations and memory animals become accustomed to seek or avoid something, hence it is that they seem to share in something of the "experiment," even though but little. But men have, above the "experiment," which pertains to the discursive power, a universal reason, by which they live, as by that which is chief in them.

Now, as "experiment" is to the particular reason, and custom to memory in animals, so art is related to the universal reason.[34]

So far, several points have been brought out. The "experiment" takes place through a comparison of many singulars retained in the memory. This comparison is able to be effected by man alone, not by animals, except in a kind of analogous fashion. St. Thomas has more to say about the way in which "experiment" comes about.

From memory in men, the "experiment" is caused. Now, the way of causing is this: from many memories of one thing, man obtains an "experiment" about something, by means of which "experiment" he is able to act easily and correctly.[35]

Further refinements in this notion are made by comparing the "experiment" with art.

The way in which art arises from "experiment" is the same as the aforesaid, in which "experiment" arises from memory. For, as from many memories there arises one "experimental" knowledge, so from many "experiments" apprehended there arises an universal taking of all similar cases. And so art has this over "experiment": that "experiment" deals only with singulars, but art with universals.[36]

The first difference, then, between art and "experiment" lies in the former's greater universality. Is this an advance, and in what sense?

And therefore he says that, as regards acts, "experience" seems in no way to differ from art. For when we come to action, the difference of universal and singular found between "experiment" and art disappears, because, as "experiment" works with singulars, so, too, art. And so the aforesaid dif-

34. *Commentary on the Metaphysics,* I, lect. 1, Cathala nos. 15-16.
35. *Ibid.,* no. 17.
36. *Ibid.,* no. 18.

ference lay in knowing alone. But, although in their way of operating, art and "experiment" do not differ, because both deal with singulars, they still differ in the effectiveness of operation. For the "experienced" do better in action than those who have the universal knowledge of art without "experiment."

And the reason for this is, that actions are about singulars, and of singulars alone is all becoming.[37]

In respect to operation, the man who has "experience" alone without art is in a better way than the one who has art alone. For that knowledge is most efficacious for operation which more nearly deals with singulars.

It has, however, been suggested that as *knowledge* art is higher than "experiment." In this respect, art has a threefold superiority. First, it is knowledge in a truer sense.[38] Secondly, he who has art can explain and defend his knowledge.[39] Thirdly, art comes closer to wisdom, for wisdom is rather a matter of knowing than of doing.[40] For, says St. Thomas:

Prudence and art are concerned with the practical part of the soul, which is of a kind as to reason about contingent things that can be done by us.[41]

What conclusions can be drawn from this discussion? First, "experiment" is a practical "know-how," a technique of operation, a skill in dealing with particulars.[42] Secondly, this kind of skill or "practical wisdom" pertains to the discursive-estimative in man,

---

37. *Ibid.*, nos. 20-21.
38. Cf. "Nullum sensum dicimus sapientiam, scilicet propter hoc quod licet aliquis sensus cognoscat quia, tamen non propter quid cognoscit. . . . Ergo experti qui habent singularium cognitionem causam ignorantes sapientes dici non possunt," *ibid.*, no. 30.
39. Cf. "Artifices autem docere possunt, quia cum causas cognoscunt, ex eis possunt demonstrare. . . . Experti autem non possunt docere, quia non possunt ad scientiam perducere cum causam ignorent. Et si ea quae experimento cognoscunt aliis tradant, non recipientur per modum scientiae, sed per modum opinionis vel credualitatis," *ibid.*, no. 29.
40. *Ibid.*, no. 23.
41. *Ibid.*, no. 34.
42. Cf. *ibid.*, no. 35.

and has its faint image in the "prudence" of the animal, which is due to the animal's estimative sense.

On the other hand, the discussion in the *Posterior Analytics* deals with a different matter. The question there concerns the origin of first principles of demonstration. St. Thomas, following Aristotle closely in this, had pointed out that the sense does not and cannot know the universal.[43] Yet the universal arises from sense. The process, in summary, consists in memory, "experiment," and the abstraction by the agent intellect.[44] Nowhere, however,

---

43. "Manifestum est enim quod sensus cognoscit aliquid tale et non hoc. Non enim obiectum per se sensus est substantia et quod quid est; sed aliqua sensibilis qualitas, puta calidum, frigidum, album, nigrum et alia huismodi. Huismodi autem qualitates afficiunt singulares quasdam substantias in determinato loco et tempore existentes; unde necesse est quod hoc quod sentitur, sit hoc aliquid, scilicet singularis substantia, et sit alicubi et nunc, id est in determinato loco et tempore. Ex quo patet quod id quod est universale non potest cadere sub sensu. Non enim quod est universale determinatur ad hic et nunc, quia iam non esset universale. Illud enim universale dicimus, quod est semper et ubique. . . . Sensus est singularium, scienta autem consistit in hoc quod universale cognoscimus," *Commentarium in primum librum Posteriorum Analyticorum,* lect. 42, ed. Leonine, vol. I, pp. 311-12; "Intellectus vel ratio est universalium, quae sunt ubique et semper; sensus autem est singularium quae sunt hic et nunc. Et ideo sensus secundum suam propriam rationem non est cognoscitivus nisi praesentium," *In De Sensu et Sensato,* lect. 1, Parma, vol. XX, p. 147.
44. Cf. "Ostendit quid sit illud principium cognoscitivum praeexistens. Et quantum ad hoc ponit tres gradus in animalibus, quorum primus est quod videtur inesse communiter omnibus animalibus quae omnia habent quamdam connaturalem potentiam ad iudicandum de sensibilibus, quae vocatur sensus, quae non acquiritur de novo, sed ipsam naturam consequitur.

Secundum gradum ponit ibi. . . . Et forte contingit quod circa aliqua animalia remanet aliqua impressio quantum ad aliqua sensibilia, quae sunt vehementiora. . . . Sed animali in quibus inest huiusmodi remansio impressionis contingit adhuc habere quandam cognitionem in anima praeter sensum, et ista sunt, quae habent memoriam.

Tertium gradum ponit . . . et dicit quod cum multa sint animalia habentia memoriam, inter ea ulterius est quaedam differentia. Nam

in quibusdam fit ratiocinatio de his quae remanent in memoria, sicut in hominibus, in quibusdam autem non, sicut in brutis. . . . Ex sensu fit memoria, in illis animalibus in quibus remanet impressio sensibilis. . . . Ex memoria autem multoties facta circa eandem rem in diversis tamen singularibus fit experimentum, quia experimentum nihil aliud esse videtur quam accipere aliquid ex multis in memoria retentis. Sed tamen experimentum indiget aliqua ratiocinatione circa particularia, per quam confertur unum ad aliud, quod est proprium rationis. . . .

Hoc est ergo quod dicit, quod sicut ex memoria fit experimentum, ita etiam ex experimento, aut etiam ulterius ex universali quiescente in anima, quod scilicet accipitur ac si in omnibus ita sit, sicut est experimentum in quibusdam. . . .

Posset autem aliquis credere quod solus sensus vel memoria singularium sufficiat ad causandum intelligibilem cognitionem principiorum . . . et ideo ad hoc excludendum Philosophus subdit, quod cum sensu oportet praesupponere talem naturam animae, quae posset pati hoc, id est sit susceptiva cognitionis universalis, quod quidem fit per intellectum possibilem, et iterum quod possit agere hoc per intellectum agentem, qui facit intelligibilia in actu per abstractionem universalium a singularibus . . . .

Si enim accipiantur multa singularia, quae sunt indifferentia quantum ad aliquid unum in eis existens, illud unum secundum quod non differunt, in anima acceptum, est primum universale, quidquid sit illud, sive scilicet pertineat ad essentiam singularium, sive non. . . . Qualiter autem hoc unum accipi possit, manifestat consequenter. Manifestum est enim, quod singulare sentitur proprie et per se, sed tamen sensus est quodammodo et ipsius universalis. Cognoscit enim Calliam non solum in quantum est Callias, sed etiam in quantum est hic homo, et similiter Socratem in quantum est hic homo. Et exinde est, quod, tali acceptione sensus praeexistente, anima intellectiva potest considerare hominem in utroque. Si autem ita esset quod sensus apprehenderet id quod est particularitatis, et nullo modo cum hoc apprehenderet universalem naturam in particulari, non esset possibile quod ex apprehensione sensus causaretur in nobis cognitio universalis.

Quia igitur universalium cognitionem accipimus ex singularibus, concludit manifestum esse quod necesse est prima universalia principia cognoscere per inductionem. Sic enim, scilicet per viam inductionis, sensus facit universale intus in anima, in quantum considerantur omnia singularia," *In secundum librum Posteriorum Analyticorum,* lect, 20, ed. Leon., vol. I, pp. 399-402.

is the discursive power mentioned, even though the discussion is quite full. The reason for its omission here is readily intelligible on the hypothesis that the discursive power apprehends the individual as standing under a common nature specifically in the practical order.

There remains the detailed discussion of the discursive power in relation to action and prudence, one of the lengthiest discussions of this power in the Thomistic *corpus*.

Scientificum-Ratiocinativum

A preliminary point concerns the use of this couplet. An historical discussion is in place, for St. Thomas's use of these terms in various works shows a very definite change.[45] In the *Commentary on the Sentences* it is stated, on the authority of Aristotle, that the *scientificum* pertains to the universal, the *ratiocinativum* to the contingent and practicable; it is implied that these are two really distinct potencies.[46] In the *De Veritate*, the terms are discussed at greater length; it is clearly stated that they are two potencies, and in fact it seems that they are two species of intellect.[47] In

---

45. Cf. Bernard Lonergan, S.J., "The Concept of *Verbum* in the Writings of St. Thomas Aquinas," *Theological Studies*, VII (1946), p. 382.

46. Cf. *In II Sent.*, d. 24, q. 2, a. 2, obj. 2 and ad 2, ed. Pierre Mandonnet, O.P., (Paris: Lethielleux, 1929-1933), vol. II, pp. 604, 606-07.

47. "Scientificum autem et ratiocinativum diversae quidem potentiae sunt, quia quantum ad ipsam rationem intelligibilis distinguuntur. . . . Obiectum autem intellectus est quod quid est, ut dicitur in III *De Anima*, et propter hoc actio intellectus extenditur quantum potest extendi virtus eius ad quod quid est: per hanc autem primo ipsa principia cognita sunt ex quibus cognitis ulterius ratiocinando pervenitur in conclusionum notitiam; et hanc potentiam quae ipsas conclusiones in quod quid est nata est resolvere Philosophus scientificum appellat. Sunt autem quaedam in quibus non est possibile talem resolutionem facere ut perveniatur usque ad quod quid est, et hoc propter incertitudinem sui esse; sicut est in contingentibus inquantum contingentia sunt. Unde talia non cognoscuntur per quod quid est, quod erat proprium obiectum intellectus; sed per alium modum, scilicet per quamdam coniecturam de rebus illis de quibus plena certitudo haberi non potest. Unde ad hoc alia potentia requiritur," *De Veritate*, XV.2 ad 3, ed. Parma, vol. IX, pp. 253-54.

the *Commentary on the Ethics* these two terms are discussed again, and their status is definitely settled once for all.

> Contingent things can be known in two ways. One way is according to universal characteristics (*secundum rationes universales*); the other, in the particular. . . . For the science of nature is not only about necessary and incorruptible things, but also about corruptible and contingent things. And so it is clear that contingent things thus considered belong to the same part of the intellective soul as the necessary. This part the Philosopher here calls the "scientific"; to this conclusion the reasons here laid down lead. In the second way, contingent things can be considered as they are in the particular. In this way they are variable; and the intellect does not touch on them except through the mediation of the sensitive potencies. Hence, among the sensitive parts of the soul there is placed one potency which is called the particular reason, or the discursive power, which confers about particular intentions. In this passage, the Philosopher understands "contingent things" in the second way, for this is the way that they fall under counsel and operation. For this reason he says that necessary and contingent things belong to different parts of the rational soul, since they are universal things to be speculated about, and particular things to be done.[48]

> It must therefore be said that the practical intellect has its beginning in a universal consideration, and thus is identical as to its subject with the speculative intellect; but its consideration terminates in a particular thing to be done. Hence, the Philosopher says in the third book of the *De Anima* that the universal reason does not move without the particular. And in this way the *ratiocinativum* is placed as a distinct part from the "scientific."[49]

In this analysis, St. Thomas asserts that there is a two-fold knowledge of the contingent. One is an intellectual knowledge of the contingent which works out of universal knowledge. The other is a knowledge of the contingent in its particularity. Taken in this latter way, the contingent is variable, and so a possible object con-

---

48. *In Libros Ethicorum*, VI, lect. 1, Pirotta no. 1123.
49. *Ibid.*, lect. 2, Pirotta no. 1132.
    Cf. Aristotle, *De Anima* III, c. 11, 434 a 18-20, and St. Thomas, *in III De Anima*, lect. 16, Pirotta nos. 845-46.

cerning which man can act. This second kind of knowledge the
intellect has through the mediation of the sense powers, especially
of the discursive power. In other words, knowledge of the particular
and contingent, when it is a practical knowledge, implies a distinct
power. Note that this kind of knowledge is essentially a sort of
of reasoning process — St. Thomas frequently calls it "the practical
syllogism." At the beginning of the process only the practical intellect is involved, which is identical with the speculative or "scientific." In its term, which is the consideration of the particular
operable, practical knowledge needs a distinct power, for the practical intellect reaches this term by the mediation of the discursive
power.

It will be worthwhile to compare this analysis with that of
the *Summa Theologiae*. There these two terms are said to denote
the same power with two different relations to two different habits.
The habits concerned are science and opinion, which differ as perfect and imperfect.[50] The discussion in the *Summa* seems to be
concerned with speculative knowledge alone, for the contingent
and the necessary are compared solely with respect to their being
and truth. If this is a correct interpretation, then the following
analysis of St. Thomas's various positions can be made. In the
beginning the arguments of Aristotle were considered as pertaining
to knowledge in general. In the *Commentary on the Ethics* St.
Thomas saw that the Aristotelian argument for two distinct potencies is valid only in the order of practical knowledge, and at
that only in its final considerations about the particular operable.
He was therefore free later on to maintain, in consequence of his
principles, that the two Aristotelian terms denote only one power
(when they are used to designate varieties of speculative knowledge).

Prudence and the Discursive Power.

Having made the distinction of the scientific and the *ratiocinativum,* St. Thomas with Aristotle assigns to the latter the virtue
of prudence.

---

50. See *Summa Theologiae,* I. 9. 9 ad 3 and ad 2.

He shows what is the subject of prudence, and he says that since there are two parts of the rational soul, of which one is called the scientific and the other *ratiocinativum* or opiniona-tive, it is clear that prudence is the virtue of the second of them, namely, of the opinionative. For opinion is about such things which can be otherwise, just as prudence is. And yet, although prudence is in this part of reason as in its subject, by reason of which it is called an intellectual virtue; it is not with reason alone, like art or science, but it requires the uprightness of the appetite. And a sign of this is, that that which is in reason alone can be forgotten, like art and science, unless it be a natural habit like understanding; but prudence is not forgotten by lack of use. It is abolished when the ap-petite ceases to be upright; as long as this appetite remains, it is continuously exercised about the things which belong to prudence, so that forgetfulness cannot creep up.[51]

The relation of prudence to the powers of the soul requires further investigation.

Therefore, he says first that both science and prudence are susceptible to, or attainable by (according to another ver-sion) "intellect," that is, they have some relation to that "in-tellect" which is the habit of principles. For it was said above that intellect is of certain terms or extremes, that is, of in-demonstrable principles, of which there is no reasoning, be-cause they cannot be proved by reason, but are immediately known by themselves.

"Now this," that is, prudence, "is of an extreme," that is, of a singular operable, which it is necessary to take as a principle in things to be done. Of this extreme there is no science, for it is not proved; but there is of it a sense, for it is perceived by some sense — not indeed that sense by which we sense the kinds of proper sensibles like color, sound, and the like, which is the proper sense; but by an interior sense, by which we perceive imaginables. As in mathematics we know an extreme triangle, that is a singular imagined triangle, be-cause also there, that is, in mathematics, a stand is taken

---

51. *In Lib. Ethicorum*, VI, lect. 4, Pirotta no. 1174.
   Cf. "Prudentia, quae est in ratione praedicta [i.e., practica] sicut et ars, quia per prudentiam proprie dirigitur electio," *ibid.*, I, lect. 1, no. 8.

at a singular imaginable; so also in natural science a stand is taken at a singular sensible thing. And to this sense, that is, the interior one, prudence rather belongs. By prudence the particular reason is perfected to have a right estimation about singular operable intentions. So too, brute animals which have a good natural estimative power are called prudent.[52]

This looks like a rather difficult passage, and the extreme compactness of the thought needs careful analysis. The discussion begins by asserting a similarity between the intellectual habit called *intellectus,* and prudence. *Intellectus* is an absolute starting point, and is prior to all processes of reasoning. So, too, prudence has an absolute starting point, namely, the singular operable. The singular sensible is a starting point in that it is not proved, but perceived.

How can the operable be said to be sensed? It does not yet exist. Consequently, it is not sensed by any external sense. But then, neither is the singular of mathematics, which yet is sensed. Now, in mathematics, the sense in question is an internal sense, namely, the imagination.

In the imagination, there are images of sensible things, and with such images natural science works; these images, as well as actually sensed objects, can be called *singular sensibles.* In the same power, there are abstract images, such as those which mathematics deals, the *singular imaginables.* In a third case, there are in the imagination the images of things to be done, *singular operables.* Such images are indeed produced in and by the imagination, but they are not ascribed to the imagination. For, operability is neither a sensible quality, nor an imaginable abstraction like extension, but a cognition of the order of utility, suitability, and so forth. Hence, the operable is ascribed to that power to which such inten-

---

52. *Ibid.,* VI, lect. 7, Pirotta nos. 1214-15.
     On the last remark of the text, cf. "Per quamdam similitudinem homines quasdam bestias dicunt esse prudentes, quaecumque scilicet videntur habere quamdam potentiam provisivam circa propriam vitam, non quidem ex ratione, quod proprie ad prudentiam pertinet," *ibid.,* lect. 1, no. 1187.

tions belong, namely, the estimative or discursive power.[53] For this reason prudence, which brings about an habitually correct estimation of the singular operable, perfects the *ratio particularis*,[54] and not the imagination.

---

53. "Sed intellectus qui est in practicis, est alterius modi extremi, scilicet singularis, et est alterius propositionis, id est non universalis, quae est quasi maior, sed singularis, quae est minor in syllogismo operativo. Quare autem huiusmodi extremi dicatur intellectus, patet per hoc, quod intellectus est principiorum.

Huiusmodi autem singularia, quorum dicimus esse intellectum, principia sunt eius, quod est gratia cuius, id est sunt principia ad modum causae finalis. Et quod singularia habeant rationem principiorum, patet, quia ex singularibus accipitur universale. Ex hoc enim, quod haec herba fecit huic sanitatem, acceptum est, quod haec species herbae valet ad sanandum. Et quia singularia proprie cognoscuntur per sensum, oportet quod homo horum singularium, quae dicimus esse principia et extrema, habeat sensum non solum exteriorem, sed etiam interiorem, cuius supra dixit esse prudentiam, scilicet vim cogitativam sive aestimativam, quae dicitur ratio particularis. Unde hic sensus vocatur intellectus, qui est circa sensibilia vel singularia. Et hunc vocat Philosophus in tertio *de Anima* intellectum passivum, qui est corruptibilis," *In Lib. Ethicorum,* VI, lect. 9, Pirotta nos. 1247-49. Cf. "Et propter hoc eorum [operabilium] iudicium consistit in sensu, etsi non in exteriori, saltem in interiori, per quem aliquis bene aestimat de singularibus ad quem pertinet iudicium prudentiae, ut infra dicetur," *ibid.,* II, lect. 11, no. 381.

St. Thomas's interpretation differs considerably from that of Averroes in the same place. The latter says: "Intellectus invenietur ex ultimis, id est ex particularibus secundum species duas: una quarum est apprehensor terminorum primorum, qui sunt rebus necessariis, et sunt principia demonstrationum speculativarum; et altera est apprehensor terminorum primorum, qui sunt rebus prioribus, et sunt principia conclusionum operativarum, et sunt quidem termini universales, eo quod universale quidem invenitur particularibus, et intellectus non est aliquid nisi apprehensio universalis," *Aristotelis . . . moralem totam philosophiam . . . cum Averrois Cordubensis commentariis* (Venice: Juntas, 1574), VI, c. 11, vol. III, fol. 90EG.

54. Up to this point the development had been quite like that of Averroes, see above, chapter III, text to reference no. 67. The introduction of *ratio particularis* seems to be St. Thomas's own development.

St. Thomas returns to this discussion a little later.

> For because it was said above that the "intellect" which
> is [a knowledge] of operable principles is reached by experi-
> ence and age, and made perfect by prudence, hence it is that
> it is necessary to attend to the opinions and statements of
> experienced men about things to be done. . . . It is to be con-
> sidered in relation to the things said in this passage, that,
> as it belongs to intellect in the realm of universals to have
> an absolute judgment about principles, and to reason it be-
> longs to proceed from principles to conclusions, so too with
> regard to singulars the discursive power is called "intellect"
> according as it has an absolute judgment about singulars. . . .
> It is called "particular reason," according as it proceeds from
> one to another.[55]

The discursive power is called either an "intellect" or a "reason,"
but from different points of view. It is called "reason," when the
discursive process used by it is the main element in view. When,
however, there is a non-discursive apprehension of a sensory good
as presented by the imagination, it is called "intellect." This is
all that is meant by the phrase "an absolute judgment about
singulars."

An interesting and valuable remark is made on the knowledge of the singular and practical syllogism.

> And he says, that because there are two kinds of propo-
> sitions which the practical reason uses, namely, the universal
> proposition and the singular, nothing would seem to prevent
> one from acting without regard to the science he has, when
> such an one habitually knows both propositions, but actually
> considers only the universal and not the singular. And this
> is so, because actions are about singulars. . . .

---

55. *In Libr. Ethicorum,* VI, lect. 9, Pirotta nos. 1254-55. On "eubulia,"
see *ibid.,* lect. 8; on "synesis" and "gnome," lect. 9.
    Cf. "Dicit ergo primo quod signum eius quod supra dictum est,
scilicet quod prudentia non sit solum circa universalia, sed etiam
circa particularia, est quia iuvenes fiunt geometrici et disciplinati,
id est in scientiis disciplinalibus sive mathematicis docti, et fiunt
sapientes in talibus, id est ad perfectionem istarum scientiarum per-
tingentes; non autem videtur quod iuvenis fiat prudens. Cuius causa
est, quia prudentia est circa singularia quae fiunt nobis cognita per
experientiam," *ibid.,* lect. 7, Pirotta no. 1208.

It is necessary to know that a "universal" can be taken in two ways. One way, as it is in itself, for example, if we say that dry foods are good for every man. Another way, according as it is in the singular, for example if we say that this man or this food is dry. It can therefore happen that a man know both habitually and actually the universal considered in itself; but the universal considered in this singular thing he either does not have, that is, does not know habitually, or does not do, that is, does not know actually.[56]

A new way of stating the "intellectual knowledge of the singular" is here expressed, namely, the "knowledge of the universal in the singular." It may be that for some this would be one of the best ways to explain St. Thomas's conception of this difficult point.

Conclusions.

St. Thomas seems to be fully aware that the doctrine of internal sense powers is not to be found as such in Aristotle. Occasionally he mentions Avicenna as the "inventor" of this doctrine. But though the doctrine as such is not in Aristotle, it is for St. Thomas fully in harmony with Aristotelian principles. Moreover, it is not merely a harmonious addition, it is a necessary completion, and this in several ways. First, the distinction of potencies not only may, but must be made. To assume only one potency would be self-contradictory, since a potency is defined in terms of its object.

Secondly, animal activity is not sufficiently explained in terms of imagination, for animals manifest a kind of "prudence," a similarity to reason, which imagination as such is not suited to explain.

Thirdly, the discursive power is necessary in the explanation of practical knowledge. To say that prudence involves sense, is true enough, but too vague. To add that it involves internal sense is still too vague. To pick out the common sense is impossible, because prudence is obviously not an affair of sensory consciousness. To choose the imagination is better, but insufficient, be-

---

56. *Ibid.*, VII, lect. 3, Pirotta nos. 1339-40.

cause the imagination as such is presentative of past experience. But prudence implies practical knowledge, knowledge ordered to action. In the sensory sphere such ordering to action is done by the estimative-discursive power.

For all these reasons, Aristotle's sense psychology must be completed by that of Avicenna. Whether Avicenna himself is adopted without modification we have not as yet determined.

CHAPTER 8

THE *SUMMA THEOLOGIAE*

This great work of St. Thomas was in process of writing for at least five years, possibly for as many as eight. Yet in many respects it can be considered as his last work. The Latin (Augustinian) tradition had been dealt with at least once before, in the *Commentary on the Sentences,* and sometimes oftener with respect to certain special points. The doctrines of Avicenna were met and discussed at various points throughout the works, as we have seen. Further, many of the commentaries on Aristotle were written before or during the period of composition of the *Summa.* It is therefore natural to expect to find here the mature position of St. Thomas on the internal senses. It is, of course, wrong to conclude at once that there has been either change or development; this is rather a question to be answered by this chapter. It is also to be hoped that certain questions, raised and not answered in the preceding two chapters, will be answered here.

There is an embarrassing wealth of texts on the *vis cogitativa* and related doctrines in the *Summa.* The method followed will be this: the detailed analysis of the entire system of interior sensory powers as given in Prima Pars, question 78, article 4, will be quoted in full. The argument of this text will then be studied in detail, in connection with texts mentioning the same point. These shorter texts will be quoted only when they add something to the doctrine already presented. The main effort of this chapter will be to find answers to the questions already raised, as well as to note any further clarifications. Finally, developments not brought out in the key text will have to be considered.

> I answer. It must be said that since nature does not fail in cases of necessity, there must be so many actions of the sensitive soul as are sufficient for the life of a perfect animal. As many of these actions as cannot be reduced to one principle require different powers, since a power of the soul is nothing but the proximate principle of the operation of the soul.
> Now it is to be considered that for the life of a perfect

221

animal it is necessary, that it apprehend a thing, not only in the presence of the sensible object, but also in its absence. Otherwise, since the movement and action of an animal follow apprehension, the animal would not be moved to seek for something absent. The contrary is apparent, especially in perfect animals, which move with a progressive motion, for they are moved when something absent is known. It is therefore necessary that the animal by its sensitive soul not only receive the species of sensible things, but also retain and conserve them. Now to receive and to retain are reduced in the corporeal world to different principles; for moist things receive well and retain poorly, and the contrary is true of dry. Consequently, since a sensitive power is the act of a bodily organ, it is necessary that the power which receives the species of sensible things be different from that which conserves them.

Again, it must be considered that if an animal were moved only because of the pleasurable and painful according to sense, it would not be necessary to place in the animal anything more than the apprehension of forms which the sense perceives, in which it is pleased or from which it recoils. But it is necessary for an animal to seek or avoid some things, not only because they are suitable or not suitable to sensation, but also because of some other advantages and benefits or ills. So, a sheep, seeing a wolf approaching, flees, not because of the inappropriateness of its color or shape, but as if it were hostile to its nature; and in the same way a bird collects straws, not because they please the sense, but because they are useful for nest building. It is therefore necessary for an animal that it perceive such intentions which the external sense does not perceive. And of this perception there must be some distinct principle; since the perception of sensible forms takes place through the change wrought by the sensible thing, but not the perception of the aforesaid intentions.

Therefore, for the reception of sensible forms there is established the proper and common sense, about whose distinction something will be said later. — For the retention or conservation of these forms there is established the phantasy or imagination, as it were a treasury of forms received through the sense. — For the apprehension of intentions which are not received through sense, there is established the estimative power. — For their conservation, the memorative power, which is a treasury of such intentions. A sign of this is, that the beginning of remembering in animals arises from some such intention, for example, because something is harmful or suitable.

And the very note of "pastness," which the memory attends
to, is counted among such intentions.

Now, it is to be considered that as far as sensible forms are
concerned, there is no difference between men and other animals;
for they are changed in the same way by external sensibles.
But as far as the aforesaid intentions are concerned, there is
a difference; for other animals perceive such intentions only
by a certain natural instinct, but man perceives them also
by a comparison. And so the power which in other animals
is called the natural estimative, in man is called discursive,
because it discovers such intentions by a kind of comparison.
Hence it is also called the particular reason, to which physicians assign a definite organ, namely, the middle part of the
brain; for it collates particular intentions, as the intellectual
reason collates universal intentions. On the part of the memorative power, man not only has memory, like other animals,
consisting in the sudden recollection of past things, but also
reminiscence, as it were syllogistically seeking the memory of
past things according to individual intentions.

But Avicenna posits a fifth power intermediate between the
estimative and the imaginative, which composes and divides
imagined forms; as is seen when from the imagined form of
gold and the imagined form of mountain we compose one form
of gold mountain, which we have never seen. But this operation is not evident in other animals besides man, in whom
the imaginative power is sufficient for this. To it also Averroes attributes this activity, in a book which he wrote, *De
Sensu et Sensibili*.

And so it is necessary to posit only four interior powers of
the sensitive part: that is, common sense and imagination,
the estimative and the memorative.[1]

---

1. *Summa Theologiae,* pars prima, quaestio 78, art. 4 (I.78.4), ed. Leon.,
vol. V, pp. 255-56. (This edition will be used for all references to
the Summa.)

Compare the somewhat shorter text in the *Quaestio Disputata
de Anima,* art. 13, "Ad perfectam autem sensus cognitionem, quae
sufficiat animali, quinque requiruntur. . . . Quarto autem requiruntur intentiones aliquae quas sensus non apprehendit, sicut nocivum
et utile et alia huiusmodi. Et ad haec quidem cognoscenda pervenit
homo inquirendo et conferendo; alia vero animalia quodam naturali
instinctu, sicut ovis naturaliter fugit lupum tamquam nocivum; unde
ad hoc in aliis animalibus ordinatur aestimativa naturalis, in homine

Briefly, the argument of this text has seven steps. (1) What
is to be explained at this point is the sensitive life of the higher
animals. As a background of this discussion, St. Thomas recalls
that there is a stable nature which is the source of the specific
activities of things.   (2) If these various activities cannot be reduced to one proximate principle, then we shall have to conclude
to distinct potencies, for a potency is precisely a proximate principle of operation. These two steps constitute the foundation of
the proof. St. Thomas then turns to consider the problem in particular.

(3) We find that higher animals are capable of knowing objects not present to their senses, for they go out in search of such
objects. They must therefore be capable of retaining sensible forms.
The power of retention must be distinct from the power of reception (found in external sense and common sense), for we see
throughout the realm of material things that objects which are
easily modified do not retain that modification long, while those
which retain a modification are more resistant to receiving it. This
difference is due to a different combination of the elements which
compose these objects. Therefore, the imagination will be distinct
from the external sense and the common sense.

(4) We see that animals respond to sensible gratification and
its opposite. This activity is explained by sense cognition quite
simply. But animals need more than such sensory guidance; they
must react to some situations which contain no element of sense
gratification or its opposite. In fact, animals avoid their natural
enemies; they plan somehow for the care of their offspring, and
the like. There must be some principle (or potency) for such activity. This potency must be one which somehow perceives the intentions of suitability, and the like. Obviously, external sense does

---

autem vis cogitativa, quae est collativa intentionum particularium;
unde et ratio particularis dicitur, et intellectus passivus," ed. Parma,
vol. VIII, p. 503. This text, more or less contemporary with that
of the *Summa,* differs from the latter almost solely in that it is a
bit shorter.

not perceive them, and consequently neither does imagination. A distinct power is therefore required.

(5) The argument is summarized thus: (a) For the reception of sensible forms there are external sense and common sense; (b) for their retention, imagination. (c) For the apprehension of "intentions" there is estimative power. (d) Finally, the intentions once apprehended must be themselves retained by memory. In fact, we see that the principle of remembering for animals is some past experience of utility and the like. Moreover, "pastness" itself is an intention, not a sensible form.

(6) Man is not different from other animals in the basic type of his awareness of sensible qualities. There is, however, a difference in his apprehension of the intentions. Animals perceive their intentions by a natural instinct, man perceives them also by a comparative process. Hence the natural estimative of animals is replaced in man by the discursive-estimative, also called "particular reason," and according to medical men to be found in the center of the brain. In memory, likewise, man differs from animals; the latter have only a sudden recall of past events, but man can also, as it were, reason in order to recall. This power is called reminiscence.

(7) Avicenna would have a fifth sense power, to compose and divide imagined forms. There is no evidence that animals carry on such activity, while in man the imagination alone is sufficient to account for it. And on this point, Averroes has already settled the question.

As a summary, this article of the *Summa* is a brilliant piece of work. It is not, however, a monograph, nor a complete excursus; it is precisely an article in an organic whole, so that what is said here in a brief phrase may be a whole paragraph in some other location. Indeed, a modern reader, attacking the problem of the *cogitativa*, desires certain clarifications. There are four areas on which further development may be looked for, namely: the principle of distinction of powers; the estimative sense; the discursive estimative and its relation to intellect; memory.

THE DISTINCTION OF POTENCIES

The principle of distinction of potencies stated in question 78, article 4, is a brief recapitulation of the preceding question. There it was determined that potencies can be spoken of proximately in terms of their acts, ultimately in terms of their objects. Now, a potency, as such, is ordered to act. Therefore, the nature of the potency is discoverable from the nature of the act, consequently, potencies are multiplied as the kind of act is multiplied. The kind of act, in its turn, is determined by the kind of object (*ratio obiecti*) with which it is concerned.[2]

An interesting light on St. Thomas's argument is thrown by his discussion of the external senses. He notes that some have tried to explain the distinction and number of the external senses by the organs, or the medium, or the natures of the sensible qualities. He rejects the last way as proceeding on the level of intellect rather than of sense. The first two ways, by organ or by medium, are not proper ways to determine the number and nature of the senses, because the organ is for the sense, and not the sense for the organ.[3] This does not mean that St. Thomas's psychology ignores the body; far from it. But the relation between potency and organ is that of form to matter.[4] Hence, the primary and decisive consideration concerns the potency as such. This formal point of view is simply incomplete as psychology without the complementary consideration of the organ. However, in the *Summa*, St. Thomas limits his consideration to such matters as have a theological bearing.[5] Specifically, he deals with potencies which are the subject of virtue and vice, and only indirectly with other

---

2. *Summa Theologiae,* I.77.3, vol. V, p. 241; cf. II-II. 58.4; *Quaestio Disputata de Anima,* a. 13; *Contra Gentiles,* III, c. 56, ed. Leon., vol. XIV, p. 155.

   For the Aristotelian basis of this, cf. *S. T.* I-II.54.1 ad 1, where St. Thomas refers to *Metaphysics V* (1024b9) and *Ethics VI* (1139a8).
3. *S. T.* I.78.3, vol. V, pp. 253-55.
4. *S. T.* I.77.5, 6, 8, vol. V, pp. 244-46, 248-49.
5. *S. T.* I.75, preliminary remark on the division of the articles, vol. V, p. 194.

powers, in so far as a knowledge of the latter is useful and necessary.[6]

These considerations may explain the purely formal discussion of the internal senses. St. Thomas knows the doctrine of
localization, for he refers to it as a medical teaching. He was also
aware of the complex physiological mechanisms so ingeniously
constructed by his contemporaries.[7] Unlike St. Albert, who ultimately based the distinction of internal powers on physiological
and even physical doctrines, St. Thomas knows where the primary
consideration lies (in the idea of potency as such), and can afford
to ignore complementary points of view almost entirely.

THE ESTIMATIVE SENSE

WHY AN ESTIMATIVE POWER?

Animals obviously act because of the pleasures of the senses.
For the explanation of this evident fact there are necessary only
sense and appetite.[8] In addition to such sensibly pleasant objects,
animals also act with respect to objects that apparently cause
neither immediate sensory pleasure or displeasure. For example,
they perform many actions where pleasure comes only in the final
stage. Thus, it seems that they can foresee the future results of
their actions.[9] At times, we are tempted to say that they ex-

---

6. *S. T.* I.78, preliminary remark, vol. V, p. 250.
7. Cf. *S. T.* I.76.7, vol. V, p. 231.
8. See *S. T.* I-II.30.1 ad 3, vol. VI, p. 209.
9. Cf. "Ad primum ergo dicendum, quod quamvis bruta animali non
cognoscant futurum, tamen ex instinctu naturali movetur animal ad
aliquid in futurum, ac si futurum praevideret. Huiusmodi enim
instinctus est eis inditus ab intellectu divino praevidente futura,"
S. T. I-II.40.3 ad 1, vol. VI, p. 267; "Respondeo dicendum quod interiores passiones animalium ex exterioribus motibus deprehendi
possunt. Ex quibus apparet quod in animalibus brutis est spes. Si
enim canis videat leporem, aut accipiter avem, nimis distantem, non
movetur ad ipsam, quasi non sperans se eam posse adipisci; si autem
sit in propinquo, movetur, quasi sub spe adipiscendi. . . . Unde in
operibus brutorum animalium, et aliarum rerum naturalium, apparet
similis processus sicut et in artis operibus," *ibid., corp.;* also, *ibid.,*
ad 3; I.79.11 obj. 3 and ad 3, vol. V, pp. 278, 279; I.103.1 ad 1, p. 453.

ercise prudence.[10] The facts thus referred to need some kind of explanation.

At the level of imagination there is a further problem. We know from our own experience that images in our imagination do not necessarily arouse sensory appetite nor lead to action, as Aristotle had already pointed out.[11] On the other hand, some images do arouse the sense appetite.[12] The difference between these two situations needs to be made clear, and a reason for it assigned.

It is possible to treat these problems on different levels of explanation. Usually in the *Summa* they occur in the context of other problems, and receive a treatment in harmony with that context. Perhaps the most general context is that of tendency. St. Thomas tells us that tendency operates in three different ways. It can be an immediate consequence of the substantial (specific) form; it can follow necessarily from a sensitively apprehended form; thirdly, it can establish its own end consequent upon an intellectually apprehended form.[13] The second class will be grouped with the third if our point of view is that of cognition.[14] With

10. Cf. "Sicut perfecta prudentia invenitur in homine, apud quem est ratio rerum agibilium; imperfecta autem prudentia est in quibusdam animalibus brutis, in quibus sunt quidam particulares instinctus ad quaedam opera similia operibus prudentiae," *S. T.* I-II. 3. 6, vol. VI, p. 33; II-II. 172. 1 ad 2 and ad 3, vol. X. p. 378.
11. Aristotle, *De Anima,* III, c. 3, 427 b 20-25.
12. *S. T.* I.81.3 ad 2, vol. V. p. 291.
13. Cf. "Sed quamvis huiusmodi animalia formam quae est principium motus per sensum accipiant, non tamen per seipsa praestituunt sibi finem suae operationis vel sui motus, sed est eis inditus a natura, cuius instinctu ad aliquid agendum moventur per formam sensu apprehensam," *S. T.* I.18.3, vol. IV, p. 228; I.80.1 and ad obj., vol. V, p. 282; 103. 8, p. 461; I. 6. 1 ad 2, vol. IV, p. 66; I-II. 26. 1, vol. VI, p. 188; I. 59. 1, vol. V, p. 92.
14. Cf. "Ad tertium dicendum quod appetitus naturalis est inclinatio cuiuslibet rei in aliquid ex natura sua; unde naturali appetitu quaelibet potentia desiderat sibi conveniens. — Sed appetitus animalis consequitur formam apprehensam. Et ad huiusmodi appetitus requiritur specialis animae potentia, et non sufficit sola apprehensio," *S. T.* I. 78. 1 ad 3, vol. V, p. 251; and I-II. 58. 1, vol. VI, p. 372.

respect to the apprehension of the end as end, relation of means to end, freedom, and the like, the second class will be grouped with the first.[15]

Tendency which flows from a sensitively apprehended form is animal appetite. Why does the animal appetite respond to one form and not another? In general terms, because the animal appetite is naturally determined.[16] But all appetite is consequent upon apprehension. It follows therefore that the determination of animal appetite is more ultimately based on the necessary, natural determination of the sensitive powers.[17] This determination, or *instinctus naturae*,[18] consists in this, that there is in the animal a power, the estimative, which by its very structure as a potency, apprehends some objects as suitable and so desirable.[19] The

15. "Dicendum quod bruta animalia moventur ad finem, non quasi considerantia quod per motum suum possint consequi finem, quod est proprie intendentis; sed quasi concupiscentia naturali instinctu, moventur ad finem quasi ab alio mota, sicut et cetera quae moventur naturaliter," *S. T.* I-II. 12. 5 ad 3, vol. VI, p. 97; cf. 1. 2, p. 9; 11. 2, p. 91; 12. 5, p. 97; 13. 2 ad obj., p. 99; 15.2, p. 111; 16. 2 ad 2, p. 115; 46. 4 ad 2, p. 295; I. 81. 2, vol. V, p. 289; 83. I, p. 291.
16. "Ad secundum dicendum quod brutum animal accipit unum prae alio, quia appetitus eius est naturaliter determinatus ad ipsum. Unde statim quando per sensum vel per imaginationem representatur sibi aliquid ad quod naturaliter inclinatur eius appetitus, absque electione movetur ad ipsum. Sicut etiam absque electione ignis movetur sursum, et non deorsum," *S. T.* I-II. 13. 2 ad 2, vol. VI, p. 99; cf. *ibid.*, 15. 2, p. 111, and ad 1 and 2; I-II. 13. 2 ad 3, p. 100.
17. Cf. "Dicendum quod vis sensitiva non est vis collativa diversorum, sicut ratio, sed simpliciter aliquid unum apprehendit. Et ideo secundum illud unum determinate movet appetitum sensitivum. Sed ratio est collativa plurium, et ideo ex pluribus potest moveri appetitus intellectivus, scilicet voluntas, et non ex uno ex necessitate," *S. T.* I. 82. 2 ad 3, vol. V, p. 297.
18. On the meaning of this word, see chapter VI.
19. Cf. "In brutis autem fit impetus ad opus per instinctum naturae, quia scilicet appetitus eorum, statim apprehenso convenienti vel inconvenienti, naturaliter movetur ad prosecutionem vel fugam. Unde ordinantur ab alio ad agendum, non autem ipsa seipsa ordinant ad actionem. Et ideo in eis est impetus, sed non imperium," *S. T.* I-II. 17. 2 ad 3, vol. VI, p. 119.

operation of this same power explains why some images move the appetite and others do not.[20]

One further detail can be added. Though the sense appetite is generically one, it is divided into two species, irascibility and concupiscibility.[21] Is it possible to specify the relation of the estimative to each?

The passions most commonly referred to when there is question of the estimative are fear and hope. These, together with their opposites, as well as anger, are passions of the irascible appetite.[22] It seems, therefore, that the irascible appetite is moved by the estimative power alone.[23]

The concupiscible appetite is certainly moved by the apprehensions of the special senses, as is clearly stated in question 78, article 4. On the other hand, it seems that the estimative can also move this appetite, since the affection of the mother sheep for its offspring is said to be based on a judgment of the estimative. Another indication may be found in this, that the passions of the irascible appetite take their rise in those of the concupiscible.[24]

The facts of animal activity (the so-called "instinctive activities") demand that the animal have a power of apprehension which goes beyond the special senses, and consequently beyond the retention of the knowledge thus acquired. This power, in the animal, is innately limited and determined to certain specific apprehensions. Let us now examine what it is that the estimative apprehends.

---

20. *S. T.* I-II. 9. 1 ad 2, vol. VI, pp. 74-75; cf. I. 81. 3 ad 2, vol. V, p. 291.
21. *S. T.* I. 81. 2, vol. V, p. 289.
22. *S. T.* I-II, pp. 40-48, contains a detailed discussion of these passions.
23. Cf. "Dicendum quod, sicut in apprehensivis virtutibus in parte sensitiva est aliqua vis aestimativa, scilicet quae est perceptiva eorum quae sensum non immutant, ut supra dictum est, ita etiam in appetitu sensitivo est aliqua vis appetens aliquid quod non est conveniens secundum delectationem sensus, sed secundum quod est utile animali ad suam defensionem. Et haec est vis irascibilis," *S. T.* I. 81. 2 ad 2, vol. V, p. 289.
24. See *S. T.* I. 81. 2, vol. V, p. 289.

THE OBJECT OF THE ESTIMATIVE

St. Thomas, following Avicenna, calls that which the estimative power perceives an *"intentio."* This term in the Thomistic
writings is used to designate seven or eight different things.[25]
Although an attempt has been made to find a common (analogical) signification,[26] it still seems better to admit with St. Thomas
that it is an equivocal term with at least two irreducible meanings[27]
— for St. Thomas says in a particular instance that "it is taken
equivocally in the two cases."[28]

If we adopt the position that it is an equivocal term, it will
be necessary to consider only the series of uses of it in the cognitive order. In this order, there are three groups of *intentiones*:
of the intellect, of the discursive and estimative powers, and of the
senses.[29] Fr. Simonin says that the common notion here is that
of "la possession spirituelle de l'objet connu par la faculté."[30]

Can this definition be used in all three instances? In question 78, article 4, it is said that "it is necessary, therefore for the
animal that it perceive such intentions," and again, that "for the
apprehension of the intentions which are not received from the
senses the estimative power is made." According to Fr. Simonin's
definition, the first phrase would read: "it is therefore necessary

---

25. Thus: "motio instrumentalis, intendere (as act of the will), intentio rei, intentio rationis (or virtutis ᵕcognoscitivae), intentio intellecta, intentio individualis, sensibilis, intentio generis, intentio prima,
etc.," cf. H. D. Simonin, O.P., "La notion d' 'intentio' dans l'oeuvre
de S. Thomas d'Aquin," *Revue des Sciences philosophiques et
théologiques,* XIX (1930), pp. 445-63.

Or in another listing: "effort, intention, attention, design or purpose, meaning (of an author), *species cognoscitiva, virtus instrumentalis,"* cf. André Hayen, S.J., *L'Intentionnel dans la philosophie
de Saint Thomas,* (Bruxelles: L'Edition Universelle — Paris: Desclée, 1942), pp. 46-7; cf. also G. Rabeau, *Species. Verbum* (Paris:
Vrin, 1938), pp. 62-77.

26. See A. Hayen, *L'Intentionnel,* who concludes that it always is "une
relation allant de l'esprit à l'objet," p. 217.

27. Cf. H. Simonin, "La notion d' 'intentio,'" pp. 446-47, 451.

28. *De Veritate,* XXI. 3 ad 5, ed. Parma, vol. IX, p. 307.

29. H. Simonin, "La notion d' 'intentio,'" p. 457.

30. *Ibid.*

that the animal perceive the spiritual possession of the object known." As far as I can see, this definition would result in making the estimative indistinguishable from the common sense. Furthermore, the utility (and the like) which is apprehended by the estimative is not within the cognition of the external sense. St. Thomas says that the intentions are "not sensed."

From these considerations it seems more reasonable to think that *intentio* means "cognition" (or "object known.")[31] In this case, we would translate, "it is necessary that the animal perceive this sort of knowledge" (cognate accusative). Advantages of this translation are: it makes an intelligible sentence, while some translations do not; secondly, it is sufficiently vague so as not to prejudice any consequent interpretation.[32] One advantage is that it misses the full flavor of *intentio*; it fails to reproduce the connotations of relation and finality suggested by the Latin term.[33] A final suggestion would be that *intentio* be paraphrased as "cognition, under the aspect of its having a direction (finality, or tendency) toward an object."[34]

---

31. This meaning corresponds to that of the original Arabic word which *intentio* was used to translate; cf. *"Ma'na* — idée, ou mieux en latin *intentio*. Ma'na désigne presque toujours l'intelligible, cependant cette traduction convient plutôt à ma'qul, d'autant que ma'na est employé quelquefois pour un degré d'abstraction inférieur à l'abstraction intellectuelle . . . au plus bas degré, ma'na se rapporte à l'idée particulière, à la saisie par l'estimative," A. M. Goichon, *Lexique de la Langue Philosophique d'Ibn Sînâ* (Paris: Desclée, 1938), no. 469, pp. 253-54.

32. See A. Hayen, *L'Intentionnel,* definition quoted above in note 26; also his making equivalent *intentio non sensata* and *intentio intelligibilis,* p. 53.

33. Alberto Gomez Izquierdo, O.P., "Valor cognoscitivo de la 'Intentio,'" *Ciencia Tomista,* XXIX (1924), pp. 169-88, especially "la *forma* [*cognoscitiva*] es el fundamento de aquella *relación activa* de la potencia al objecto conocido, la cual constituye, segun Santo Tomas, la essencia de la intencion en su aspecto cognoscitivo," p. 178.

34. Furthermore, this paraphrase will also be usable for such phrases as *intentio sensus, intentio intellecta,* and *intentio prima.* This is a further argument for its validity. Cf. Ulrich Daehnert, *Die Erkenntnislehre des Albertus Magnus* (Leipzig: Gerhardt, 1933), pp. 28-29.

In concrete terms, the estimative perceives the sensibly useful, suitable, harmful, and the like. Generalizing from this, we
might say that the knowledge which the estimative gathers is of
certain definite and concrete relations. It does not seem possible
to find more than this in St. Thomas.

How Does the Estimative Work?

In the key text, St. Thomas says simply that the estimative
has a certain kind of knowledge. On other occasions, he says that
"the animal judges with a natural judgment."[35] It is very easy

---

35. *S. T.* I.83.1, vol. V, p. 307; cf. "Respondeo dicendum quod inter virtutes naturales et rationales haec differentia assignatur, quod naturalis virtus est determinata ad unum, virtus autem rationalis ad
multa se habet. Oportet autem ut appetitus animalis vel rationalis
inclinetur in suum appetibile ex aliqua apprehensione praeexistente;
inclinatio enim in finem absque praeexistente cognitione ad appetitum pertinet naturalem, sicut grave inclinatur ad medium. Sed
quia aliquod bonum apprehensum oportet esse obiectum appetitus
animalis et rationalis; ubi ergo istud bonum uniformiter se habet,
potest esse inclinatio naturalis in appetitu, et iudicium naturale in
vi cognitiva, sicut accidit in brutis. Cum enim sint paucarum operationum propter debilitatem principii activi quod ad pauca se extendit, est in omnibus unius speciei bonum uniformiter se habens.
Unde per appetitum naturalem inclinationem habent in id, et per
vim cognitivam naturale iudicium habent de illo proprio bono uniformiter se habente; et ex hoc naturali iudicio et naturali appetitu
provenit quod omnis hirundo uniformiter facit nidum, et omnis
aranea uniformiter facit telam, et sic est in omnibus aliis brutis
considerare. Homo autem est multarum operationum et diversarum;
et hoc propter nobilitatem sui principii activi, scilicet animae, cuius
virtus ad infinita quodammodo se extendit. Et ideo non sufficeret
homini naturalis appetitus boni, nec naturale iudicium ad recte agendum, nisi amplius determinetur et perficiatur. Per naturalem siquidem appetitum homo inclinatur ad appetendum proprium bonum;
sed cum hoc multipliciter varietur, et in multis bonum hominis con-
sistat, non potuit homini inesse naturalis appetitus huius boni deter-
minati, secundum conditiones omnes quae requiruntur ad hoc quod
sit ei bonum; cum hoc multipliciter varietur secundum diversas conditiones personarum et temporum et locorum, et huiusmodi. Et eadem
ratione naturale iudicium, quod est uniforme, et ad huiusmodi bonum
quaerendum non sufficit; unde oportuit in homine per rationem,

to suspect that he has fallen victim to the fallacy of "humanizing the brute." It is therefore necessary to see precisely what "judgment" means.

1. For the Philosopher says in the first book of the *Ethics* [1094b27] that "everyone judges well that which he knows"; and so judgment seems to pertain to the cognoscitive power. But the cognoscitive power is perfected by prudence. Therefore judgment pertains more to prudence than it does to justice, which is in the will, as was said.

To the first argument the answer is that the name "judgment" according to its original imposition means "the correct determination of what is just". It has been extended to signify "a correct determination" in any matter, as well speculative as practical. But in all cases, two things are necessary for a correct judgment. One of these is the power enunciating the judgment. In this case, judgment is an act of reason, for to say or to define something belongs to reason. The second is the disposition of the one judging, from which he has the suitability for a correct judgment. And in this case, in those matters which pertain to justice, judgment arises from justice, as also in those which pertain to courage, they arise from courage. Thus, therefore, judgment is an act of justice, as of something inclining to correct judgment, and an act of prudence, as of something enunciating the judgment. Thus also, "synesis," pertaining to judgment, is said to "have a good judgment," as was said above.[36]

Two important points are made here. First, the word *"iudi-*

<hr>

cuius est inter diversa conferre, invenire et diiudicare proprium, secundum omnes conditiones determinatum, prout est nunc et hic quaerendum. . . . Oportuit quod ratio practica perficiatur aliquo habitu ad hoc quod recte diiudicet de bono humano secundum singula agenda. Et haec virtus dicitur prudentia, cuius subiectum est ratio practica," *De Virtutibus in Communi,* q. I, a. 6, ed. Parma, vol. VIII, p. 557.

Compare: "Ad quartum. Dicendum quod anima intellectiva . . . habet virtutem ad infinita. Et ideo non potuerunt sibi determinari a natura vel determinatae existimationes naturales, vel etiam determinata auxilia vel defensionum vel tegumentorum. . . . Sed loco horum omnium homo habet naturaliter rationem et manus," *S. T.* I. 75. 5 ad 4, vol. V, p. 228.

36. *S. T.* II-II. 60. 1 obj. 1 and ad 1, vol. IX, p. 25.

cium" is originally a legal term, and in its original usage meant "a correct determination of what is just." Second, in its wider usage, the term signifies a "correct (right, accurate — *recta*) determination in any field." In the application of this to his problem, a further distinction is made. "Determination" can be taken actively and elicitively, and in this sense it belongs to reason or intellect alone. "Determination" can also mean the disposition according to which the one making the judgment is apt to judge correctly.

Remembering then that judgment can mean "a right determination by way of a disposition which is apt for the correctness thereof," let us look at a typical text.

> Some things act without judgment, as the stone is moved down; and in like manner all things lacking knowledge.
> Some things act with judgment, but not a free one, as the brute animals. For the sheep, seeing a wolf, judges it ought to be avoided, with a natural judgment, and not a free one, because it judges this, not from a comparison, but from natural instinct.
> But man acts with judgment, because by his knowing power he judges something to be avoided or sought. But because this judgment does not arise from a natural instinct in the case of a particular operable, but from a comparison of reason, for this reason he acts with a free judgment, which can be decided in various ways.[37]

The division here is related to the three-fold division of tendency or appetite. Some things lack judgment altogether; that is, they have no right determination of what is to be done, for they lack knowledge. A second group of things does have a judgment, but not a free judgment. A sheep, for example, judges, (that is, knows distinctly and accurately), that a wolf is its enemy. This is a natural judgment, for it proceeds from an inborn disposition or determinate impulse (*instinctus*). On the contrary, man's judgment is free, for it does not proceed from an inborn disposition, but from a kind of comparison instituted by reason.

This interpretation of "judgment" is confirmed by what St. Thomas has to say about the *iudicium sensus*. The proper sense

---

37. *S. T.* I. 83. 1, vol. V, p. 307.

judges its proper sensible, in that it accurately knows and can discern one of its proper sensibles from another.[38] This does not mean that the eye, for example, institutes a formal comparison between its various objects, nor that it knows what color is. It means only that the eye determinately and accurately knows a particular sensible appearance.[39]

Similarily, the estimative does not know what usefulness and the like are, but it does determinately and accurately apprehend a particular concrete useful thing.

But does not the estimative depend on the external senses? How then can its knowledge go beyond theirs? St. Thomas answers this question by a comparison. Somewhat as the cognition of sense bears within itself the intelligible in potency, yet without grasping it, so too the cognition of the external senses bears within itself what may be called the "estimable," again without knowing it.[40] How this works out may be thus understood. The external senses apprehend a given object according to certain proper sensible qualities and according to certain common ones. In addition to this, the sense of touch may give certain obscure but very important information concerning the state of the animal's body, its functioning well or ill, and so forth. All the sensations about the animal's own body may be called "propriosensation." The data of the external senses, if they are gathered by more than one, are united to each other and to propriosensation by the common sense.

---

38. Cf. "Ad secundum dicendum quod sensus proprius iudicat de sensibili proprio, discernendo ipsum ab aliis quae cadunt sub eodem sensu, sicut discernendo album a nigro vel a viridi. Sed discernere album a dulce non potest neque visus neque gustus; quia oportet quod qui inter aliqua discernit, utrumque cognoscat. Unde oportet ad sensum communem pertinere discretionis iudicium, ad quem referantur sicut ad communem terminum, omnes apprehensiones sensuum; a quo etiam percipiantur intentiones sensuum, sicut cum aliquis videt se videre," *S. T.* I. 78. 4 ad 2, vol. V. p. 256.
39. Cf. *S. T.* I. 78. 3, vol. V, pp. 253-55.
40. Cf. "Ad quartum dicendum quod licet intellectus operatio oriatur a sensu, tamen in re apprehensa per sensum intellectus multa cognoscit quae sensus percipere non potest. Et similiter aestimativa, licet inferiori modo," *S. T.* I. 78. 4 ad 4, vol. V, p. 257.

But whether the common sense carries on such a unifying process or not, it always perceives the *intentio sensus*. In other words, in the awareness of the common sense, there is always a complex object: the external thing sensed and the animal itself as actually sensing, and, at least sometimes, the content of propriosensation. This complex object is then presented to the estimative. Just as the eye, without knowing or being able to know what color is, apprehends color when it is presented, so the estimative, without being able to know what usefulness is, apprehends the useful when it is concretely presented.[41]

This is still not altogether satisfactory. But we are in the difficult position that we are men, not animals. Our estimative, in adult life, works precisely as discursive. Properly to understand the operation of the estimative, we would have to remember why and how, as little children, our sense appetites were aroused. If we were able to remember this, it would be most probably impossible to give any intelligible account of it. It seems therefore inevitable that we must rest content with a merely analogical knowledge of how the estimative works.

THE PRACTICAL DIRECTION OF ANIMAL SENSIBILITY

St. Thomas has compared the estimative to the intellect. This comparison was made on the basis of the relation of both these powers to external sense. Another comparison can be made on the basis of their respective ends. From this point of view, the estimative corresponds, not to reason in general, but specifically to *practical* reason, while to speculative reason there corresponds the imagination.[42] This conclusion can readily be reached from a consideration of the various objects of the estimative: the useful, and

---

41. Cf. *S.T.* I-II. 6. 2, vol. VI, p. 57.
42. Cf. "Praeterea, in parte intellectiva intellectus practicus comparatur ad speculativum, sicut aestimativa ad imaginativam in parte sensitiva. Sed aestimativa differt ab imaginativa sicut potentia a potentia, ut supra dictum est. Ergo et intellectus practicus a speculativo. — Ad tertium dicendum quod multae differentiae diversificant sensitivas potentias, quae non diversificant potentias intellectivas, ut supra dictum est," *S.T.* I. 79. 11 obj. 3 and ad 3, vol. V, pp. 278, 279.

so forth, which obviously correspond to the objects of the practical intellect.

A consequence of this is that in its ultimate direction animal sensibility is purely practical. In other words, on the animal level, knowledge is not an end in itself.

> Sensitive cognition has two ends. In one way, as well in men as in other animals, its purpose is the sustaining of the body, because by such a knowledge, men and other animals avoid harmful things, and seek those which are necessary for the sustaining of the body. In a second way, in man it is especially directed to intellectual knowledge, both speculative and practical.[43]

Though there may be certain animal cognitions, which are not immediately practical, it remains true that ultimately all sense cognition for the animal is orientated toward its individual and specific life and well-being.

THE COGITATIVA VIRTUS

MEANING OF THE TERM

It seems that the term *cogitativa virtus* is once used in the

---

43. *S. T.* II-II. 167. 2, vol. X, p. 347. Cf. "Sensus sunt dati homini non solum ad vitae necessaria procuranda, sicut aliis animalibus, sed etiam ad cognoscendum," I. 91. 3 ad 3, vol. V, p. 394; "Sensus autem, ut dicitur I *Metaph.* [920a21], propter duo diliguntur: scilicet propter cognitionem et propter utilitatem. Unde et utroque modo contingit esse delectationem secundum sensum. Sed quia apprehendere ipsam cognitionem tanquam bonum quoddam proprium est hominis, ideo primae delectationes sensuum, quae scilicet sunt secundum cognitionem, sunt propriae hominum; delectationes autem sensuum inquantum diliguntur propter utilitatem, sunt communes omnibus animalibus. . . . Et propter hoc etiam alia animalia, quae non habent delectationem secundum sensum nisi ratione utilitatis, non delectantur secundum alios sensus, nisi in ordine ad sensibilia tactus; 'neque enim odoribus leporum canes gaudent, sed cibatione; neque leo voce bovis, sed comestione', ut dicitur in III *Ethic.* [118a-18]," I-II. 31. 6, vol. VI, p. 220; cf. also I-II. 35. 2 ad 3, vol. VI, p. 241; III. 11. 2, arg. 3 and ad 3, vol. XI, pp. 159, 160; *Contra Gentiles,* III. 33.

Summa as a synonym for reason.[44] For the most part, however, the term in this work means "the human estimative, as acting discursively."[45]

THE HUMAN AND THE ANIMAL ESTIMATIVE

Man, as everyone knows, is not born with a fully developed set of instincts. There are a very few primitive reactions which are innately determined, and this we know from the behavior of children[46] and completely insane persons.[47] But, for the most part, man has to learn what is good for him concretely by instruction and experience. From this point of view, the human estimative is incomplete, and needs the activity of reason to help it to arrive at its own judgments.

To understand how a sensory potency can have a discursive movement analogous to that of reason, we must remember that this movement takes place under reason. Generally speaking, in all movement the power of the mover is to be seen in that which is moved.[48] When the mover is reason, the order of reason will ap-

---

44. "Ad secundum dicendum quod daemones non possunt immittere cogitationes, interius eas causando; cum usus cogitativae virtutis subiaceat voluntati," *S. T.* I. 111. 2 ad 2, vol. V, p. 517; however, this text is not conclusive, since the *vis cogitativa* likewise is under the control of the will; still, *cogitatio* normally refers to an activity of the intellect, as in II-II. 2. 1 ad 2, vol. VIII, p. 27.

45. Cf. *S. T.* I-II. 77. 1, vol. VII, p. 61; text quoted below in note 81; it is also significant that the key text in I. 78. 4, after discussing the four internal senses in animals, and *cogitativa* and *reminiscentia* in men, concludes by saying that there are *four* internal senses: common sense, imagination, estimative, and memory.

46. See what was said on this point in chapter VI, and compare the texts cited there with *S. T.* I. 99. 1 and 101. 2, vol. V, pp. 440, 447.

47. Cf. "Impeditur enim iudicium et apprehensio rationis propter vehementem et inordinatam apprehensionem imaginationis, et iudicium virtutis aestimativae, ut patet in amentibus," *S. T.* I-II. 77. 1, vol. VII, p. 61.

48. Cf. "Manifestum est autem quod omne quod movetur, necesse est proportionatum esse motori; et haec est perfecto mobilis inquantum est mobile, dispositio qua disponitur ad hoc quod bene moveatur a suo motore," *S. T.* I-II. 68. 1, vol. VI, p. 447; "Respondeo di-

pear in the movement.[49] This is the case even when mover and moved are substantially distinct. It will certainly be much more applicable when mover and moved are two powers of one and the same being, as for instance, reason and will.[50] The dynamic relation between intellect and the discursive power has been studied before, but a further refinement is added here. The *Summa* recalls the three orders among human potencies: the order of their rising from one and the same substance;[51] the order of their hierarchical perfection;[52] and the dynamic order of "contact" or "union."[53]

cendum quod intantum aliquid indiget moveri ab aliquo, inquantum est in potentia ad plura," I-II. 9. 1, p. 74.

49. Cf. "Ad tertiam dicendum quod, sicut dicitur in III *Physic.* [202a-13] 'Motus est actus mobilis a movente.' Et ideo virtus moventis apparet in motu mobilis. Et propter hoc in omnibus quae moventur a ratione, apparet ordo rationis moventis, licet ipsa quae a ratione moventur rationem non habeant," *S. T.* I-II. 13. 2 ad 3, vol. VI, p. 100; *ibid.,* 9. 1, p. 74; "Cum enim proprium rationis sit ordinare et conferre; quandocumque in actu voluntatis apparet aliqua collatio vel ordinatio, talis actus erit voluntatis non absolute, sed in ordine ad rationem," *De Veritate,* XXII. 13, ed. Parma, vol. IX, p. 332.

50. Cf. "Et quia virtus prioris actus remanet in actu sequenti, contingit quandoque quod est aliquis actus voluntatis, secundum quod manet virtute in ipso aliquid de actu rationis, ut dictum est de usu et electione; et e converso aliquis est actus rationis, secundum quod virtute manet in ipso aliquid de actu voluntatis," *S. T.* I-II. 17. 1, vol. VI, p. 118.

51. See *S. T.* I. 77. 7, vol. V, p. 247.

52. See *S. T.* I. 77. 4, vol. V, p. 243; I-II. 74. 3 ad 1, vol. VII, p. 37; *Q. D. De Anima,* a. 11 ad 14, ed. Parma, vol. VIII, p. 500.

53. "Ad quintum dicendum quod illam eminentiam habet cogitativa et memorativa in homine, non per id quod est proprium sensitivae partis; sed per aliquam affinitatem et propinquitatem ad rationem universalem, secundum quandam refluentiam. Et ideo non sunt aliae vires, sed eaedem perfectiores quam sint in aliis animalibus," *S. T.* I. 78. 4 ad 5, vol. V, p. 257. If St. Thomas had meant "inquantum radicantur in eadem anima," he would have said so. But he said "secundum refluentiam," which should simply mean "a returning influence." For reason receives from these interior senses under the causality of the agent intellect, and then in turn moves (in-

This third order is precisely a dynamic or operative order, in which the intellect is the ruler and mover, and the discursive power that which is governed and moved.[54] Lest we fail to see that the operation of intellect and human estimative are really *one* operation, and therefore composite precisely as operations, St. Thomas points out that the first is as form and the second is as matter.[55] In studying the nature of choice, he gives an analysis that is directly applicable to the present situation.

> Whenever two elements concur to constitute one thing, one of them is formal with respect to the other. . . . Now, in the acts of the soul, we must consider that an act which is essentially of one power or habit, receives its form and species from a higher power or habit, to the extent that the lower is ordered by the higher. For if someone practices an act of courage for the love of God, that act will be materially one of courage, but formally one of love. . . . Thus, therefore, the act by which the will tends to something which is proposed as good because it is ordered to an end by reason, is materially one of the will, but formally one of reason. Now, in such cases, the substance of the act is in the relation of matter to the order which is imposed by the higher power. And so choice is not substantially an act of reason, but of the will.[56]

---

fluences) them, in the kind of way referred to in notes 48-50. Incidentally, all interpreters agree that "reminiscence" is to be explained not by some mysterious "ontological influence," but by the motion of the reason. St. Thomas puts both powers on the same plane.

54. See below, texts in notes 58-61.
55. There is a wealth of texts in which St. Thomas discusses or mentions, or applies this theory of the matter-form composition of operation. These texts have been gathered and analyzed in Klubertanz, "The Unity of Human Activity," *The Modern Schoolman*, XXVII (1950), pp. 75-103.
56. *S. T.* I-II. 13. 1, ed. Leon., vol. VI, p. 98.
  With the introductory sentence of this passage, compare the statement of Averroes: "Et omnis actio facta ex congregato duorum diversorum necesse est ut alterum duorum illorum sit quasi materia et instrumentum, et aliud sit quasi forma aut agens," *In III De Anima*, t. c. 36 (Venice: Juntas, 1574), vol. VI. i. 2, fol. 184C. This entire comment of Averroes's is devoted to *"continuatio."* Hence, we have here proof that we are correct in juxtaposing the Thomistic

It is unnecessary to point out that "matter" and "form" are used analogously when applied to accidents such as habits or powers.

An exactly paralled analysis can be made of the (sensory) discursus by which man comes to a knowledge of a particular sensible thing as suitable. The basis of the discussion will be the principle that whenever two elements concur to form one thing, one of them will be like form, the other like matter. Now, the act of the soul in question here receives its form and species from the higher power, to the extent that it is ordered and moved. But essentially, materially, and substantially it is an act of the lower power.

Just as choice is not the simultaneous (much less, successive) presence of two really distinct operations, but is a single, composite operation having the characteristics of both reason and will, so the human discursive estimation is not the simultaneous presence of two really distinct knowledges, but a single, composite knowledge. This knowledge has the characteristics of both sense and intellect; on the one hand, it is a sensory appreciation of a particular good, and on the other, it is arrived at by a discursus, by a kind of reasoning process.

HABITS OF THE DISCURSIVE POWER

Not only does reason guide the discursive sense in its individual operations, it also brings about habits in that power. Prior to this development, there may be varying dispositions in the discursive sense, due to individual variations in organic structure.[57]

---

texts on "contact," principal-instrumental cause, mover-moved relation, and the texts on the matter-form relation.

57. Cf. "Unus alio potest eandem rem melius intelligere. . . . Uno quidem modo ex parte intellectus, qui est perfectior. Manifestum est enim quod quanto corpus est melius dispositum, tanto meliorem sortitur animam. . . . Alio modo contingit hoc ex parte inferiorum virtutum, quibus intellectus indiget ad sui operationem; illi enim in quibus virtus imaginativa et cogitativa et memorativa est melius disposita, sunt melius dispositi ad intelligendum," *S. T.* I. 85. 7, vol. V, p. 344; cf. II-II. 51. 3, vol. VIII, pp. 380-81.

Sense powers, according as they operate from the innate de-
terminations of nature, can have no habits. For this reason, animals
left to themselves have no possibility of acquiring habits.[58] But
the sense powers of man are made to obey reason.[59] This does
not hold of the external senses, nor of the common sense, but it
does hold of the other three internal senses.[60] The basis of this
possibility lies in their order to reason, and in their intrinsic indetermination,[61] which has been discussed in regard to the discursive power.

The habits of the interior senses are generated through the
repetition of their corresponding acts.[62] It follows that the habits

58. Cf. "Ad secundum dicendum quod vires sensitivae in brutis animalibus non operantur ex imperio rationis, sed si sibi relinquantur bruta
animalia, operantur ex instinctu naturae. Et sic in brutis animalibus
non sunt aliqui habitus ordinati ad operationes. Sunt tamen in eis
aliquae dispositiones in ordine ad naturam, ut sanitas et pulchri-
tudo. Sed quia bruta animalia a ratione hominis per quandam
consuetudinem disponuntur ad aliquid operandum sic vel aliter, hoc
modo in brutis animalibus habitus quodammodo poni possunt," *S. T.*
I-II. 50. 3 ad 2, vol. VI, p. 319.
59. "Vires sensitivae natae sunt obedire imperio rationis, et ideo in
eis esse possunt aliqui habitus," *S. T.* I-II 50. 3 ad 1, vol. VI, p. 319.
60. Cf. "Quamvis etiam in ipsis interioribus viribus sensitivis apprehensivis possint poni aliqui habitus secundum quos homo fit bene
memorativus vel cogitativus vel imaginativus; unde etiam Philosophus dicit in cap. *De Memoria* [c. 2, 452a28] quod consuetudo
multum operatur ad bene memorandum, quia etiam istae vires moventur ad operandum ex imperio rationis," *S. T.* I-II. 50. 3 ad 3,
vol. VI, p. 319; I. 115. 4, vol. V, p. 544.
61. Cf. "Respondeo dicendum quod vires sensitivae dupliciter possunt
considerari: uno modo, secundum quod operantur ex instinctu naturae; alio modo, secundum quod operantur ex imperio rationis.
Secundum igitur quod operantur ex instinctu naturae, sic ordinantur ad unum, sicut et natura. Et ideo sicut in potentiis naturalibus
non sunt aliqui habitus, ita etiam nec in potentiis sensitivis, secundum quod ex instinctu naturae operantur. Secundum vero quod
operantur ex imperio rationis, sic ad diversa ordinari possunt. Et
sic possunt in eis esse aliqui habitus, quibus bene aut male ad
aliquid disponuntur," *S. T.* I-II. 50. 3, vol. VI, p. 319.
62. Cf. "In apprehensivis autem potentiis, considerandum est quod duplex
est passivum: unum quidem ipse intellectus possibilis; aliud autem

intellectus quem vocat Aristoteles 'passivum,' qui est ratio particularis, id est vis cogitativa, cum memorativa et imaginativa," *S. T.*
I-II. 51. 3, vol. VI, p. 328.

In this passage, the *intellectus passivus* is said to comprise three
interior senses. This interpretation is the same as the one in the
Commentary on the De Anima, which was noted in the preceding
chapter, pp. 194-195. There seems to be only one other occurrence
of the term in the *Summa*: "Dicendum quod intellectus passivus
secundum quosdam dicitur appetitus sensitivus, in quo sunt animae
passiones; qui etiam in I *Ethic.* [c. 13, 1102 b 25] dicitur 'rationalis per participationem, quia obedit rationi.' Secundum autem
alios intellectus passivus dicitur virtus cogitativa, quae nominatur
ratio particularis," I. 79. 2 ad 2, vol. V, p. 260. Cf. *Q. D. De
Anima,* a. 4.

Here St. Thomas seems to be concerned with managing the *dictum
authenticum* that "passivus intellectus est corruptibilis." He will
not contest the statement; yet he must show that it is not at vari-
ance with his own doctrine. For this purpose, an "authentic" interpretation is as good as an argument, or perhaps better, since
it is so much briefer. The former interpretation seems to be that
of Themistius *via* Averroes; cf. Averroes, *Commentary on Aristotle's De Anima,* III, t. c. 20; Themistius, *in De Anima,* III. c.
5, ed. R. Heinze (*Commentaria in Aristotelem Graeca,* Berlin: 1899),
vol. V, part 3, p. 101, line 5. The latter seems to be that of the
Commentator himself, given in the place cited, cf. above, pp. 118-119,
121. These identifications are in agreement with those of the Reverend
Editors of the "Ottawa Edition" of the *Summa Theologiae* (Institute of Mediaeval Studies, of Ottawa, Garden City Press, 1941-),
in their notes on this passage, col. 481 b.

The term "passive intellect" becomes progressively more unimportant to St. Thomas; cf. above, pp. 194-196. Its final function
seems to be merely historical. At first, St. Thomas thought the
"passive intellect" was the discursive power; later on, it is used
rarely, and in any one or more of three meanings: (1) the discursive power; (2) the complex of powers associated with the phantasm, or the imagination itself; (3) the sense appetite.

To show how interpretations differ, an interesting passage is to
be found in the second revised edition of the English translation
of Etienne Gilson's *Le Thomisme,* 3rd ed. (*The Philosophy of St.
Thomas Aquinas,* authorized translation by Edward Bullough [Saint
Louis: Herder, 1941]. Mr. Gilson, explaining his use of the terms
"passive intellect" and "possible intellect," gives this footnote. "5.
De Anima ibid., [i.e., art. 4]. Following St. Thomas we shall keep

will be good or bad, useful or harmful, like the acts that generated them.

In detail, the habits of the imagination will consist in the development of facility in the presentation and formation of images.[63] In the memory, habits will consist in facility in recalling the past by way of the quasi-discursive process of reminiscence.[64] In the discursive power, habits will consist in the promptness and facility in eliciting the sensory judgments concerning the useful and the harmful.[65]

We have spoken of the development of habits in the interior senses. In the strict sense, they are not really complete habits in themselves, but rather modifications or dispositions corresponding

----

the term 'passive intellect' to describe the faculty of the human composite being which Aristotle indicates by that name, and the term 'possible intellect' to describe that immaterial and immortal faculty which St. Thomas, in distinction to Aristotle, attributes to us." This footnote of Mr. Gilson's is followed by an asterisk, indicating the following note in this edition. "*Censor's* note: This is not St. Thomas's opinion; cf. e.g., *Sum. Theol.* I. 79. 2 ad 2m. The author proceeds to use "passive" where possible should be used in the text." (Both quotations from p. 256 of the edition cited.) The terminology of M. Gilson (taken from *Q. D. De Anima*) is explicitly allowed even by the text urged against him.

63. Cf. *S. T.* I. 85. 7, text cited in note 54.

64. Cf. "Respondeo dicendum, quod in viribus sensitivis apprehensivis interius ponuntur aliqui habitus. Quod patet ex hoc praecipue quod Philosophus dicit in libro *De Memoria,* quod in memorando unum post aliud operatur consuetudo, quae est quasi quaedam natura; . . . in homine tamen id quod ex consuetudine acquiritur in memoria, et in aliis viribus sensitivis, non est habitus per se, sed aliquid annexum habitibus intellectivae partis, ut supra dictum est," *S. T.* I-II. 56. 5, vol. VI, p. 360.

65. Cf. "Ad tertium dicendum quod, sicut Philosophus dicit in VI *Ethic.,* prudentia non consistit in sensu exteriori, quo cognoscimus sensibilia propria, sed in sensu interiori qui perficitur per memoriam et per experimentum ad prompte iudicandum de particularibus expertis. Non tamen ita quod prudentia sit in sensu interiori sicut in subiecto principali, sed principaliter quidem est in ratione, per quandam autem applicationem pertingit ad huiusmodi sensum," *S. T.* II-II. 47. 3 ad 3, vol. VIII, p. 351, and cf. note 64.

to intellectual habits.[66] The relation between these dispositions and the intellectual habits is analogous to that of matter and form.[67] It follows therefore that habits of knowledge, both speculative and practical (as well as moral habits), are partly in reason and partly in the sense powers.[68]

66. Cf. "Ad tertium dicendum quod quia vires apprehensivae interius praeparant intellectui possibili proprium obiectum, ideo ex bona dispositione harum virium, ad quam cooperatur bona dispositio corporis, redditur homo habilis ad intelligendum. Et sic habitus intellectivus secundario potest esse in istis viribus. Principaliter autem est in intellectu possibili," *S. T.* I-II. 50. 4 ad 3, vol. VI, p. 321; also text in note 64 and 51. 3, p. 328, 53. 1, p. 337; I. 75. 3 ad 2, vol. V, p. 200, and from the negative point of view, I-II. 48. 3, vol. VI, p. 306.

67. Cf. "Respondeo dicendum quod quidam posuerunt habitum scientiae non esse in ipso intellectu, sed in viribus sensitivis, scilicet imaginativa, cogitativa et memorativa; et quod species intelligibilis non conservantur in intellectu possibili. Et si haec opinio vera esset, sequeretur quod destructo corpore, totaliter habitus scientiae hic acquisitae destrueretur. — Sed quia scientia est in intellectu, ut dicitur in III *De Anima* [429a27]; oportet quod habitus scientiae hic acquisitae partim sit in praedictis viribus sensitivis et partim in ipso intellectu. Et hoc potest considerare ex ipsis actibus ex quibus habitus scientiae acquiritur, nam habitus sunt similes actibus ex quibus acquiruntur, ut dicitur II *Ethic.* [1103b21]. Actus autem intellectus ex quibus in praesenti vita scientia acquiritur, sunt per conversionem intellectus ad phantasmata, quae sunt in praedictis viribus sensitivis. Unde per tales actus et ipsi intellectui possibili acquiritur facultas quaedam ad considerandum per species susceptas; et in praedictis inferioribus viribus acquiritur quaedam habilitas ut facilius per conversionem ad ipsas intellectus possit intelligibilia speculari. Sed sicut actus intellectus principaliter quidem et formaliter est in ipso intellectu, materialiter autem et dispositive in inferioribus, idem etiam dicendum est de habitu," *S. T.* I. 89. 5, vol. V, p. 380; cf. I. 84. 7, p. 325, 85. 1 ad 5, p. 332.

68. Cf. "Quantum ad ipsa phantasmata, quae sunt quasi materialia in virtutibus intellectualibus, virtutes intellectuales destruuntur destructo corpore; sed quantum ad species intelligibiles, quae sunt in intellectu possibili, virtutes intellectuales manent. Species autem se habent in virtutibus intellectuales sicut formales. Unde intellectuales virtutes manent post hanc vitam quantum ad id quod est formale in eis, non autem quantum ad id quod est materiale, sicut et de moralibus dictum est," *S. T.* I-II. 67. 2, vol. VI, p. 439; a different use of the matter-form analogy can be found in *S. T.* I-II. 67. 1, vol. VI, p. 438.

At this stage of the discussion, we have arrived at the other side of the relation between reason and discursive sense. We began by considering what this sense received from reason, and we saw that this was a completion by way of direction in its own order. We ended by seeing that the discursive sense also in some way completes the work of reason. Let us look at this in greater detail.

UNIVERSAL AND PARTICULAR REASON

Human reason, which is the guiding principle of man, by its nature moves in the realm of the abstract and universal. But the activity of man to be guided moves among concrete, singular, contingent things.[69] To bridge this gap, the discursive power is ready to hand. Its specific field is that of concrete utility or appropriateness and their opposites. Its function is to move the sensitive appetite, which in turn moves the bodily members.[70] Since its very apprehension of these concrete relations takes place through the influence of reason, there is obviously no difficulty in its being moved by reason in the application of the practical syllogism.

This relation, wherein the discursive sense in a way completes the work of reason, has been explained most fully by St. Thomas in connection with prudence.

---

69. See *S. T.* I-II. 77. 2, vol. VII, p. 62-63.
70. Cf. "Rationi quidem obediunt quantum ad ipsos suos actus. Cuius ratio est, quia appetitus sensitivus in aliis quidem animalibus natus est moveri ab aestimativa virtute, sicut ovis aestimans lupum inimicum, timet. Loco autem aestimativae virtutis est in homine, sicut supra dictum est, vis cogitativa quae dicitur a quibusdam ratio particularis, eo quod est collativa intentionum individualium. Unde ab ea natus est moveri in homine appetitus sensitivus. Ipsa autem ratio particularis nata est moveri et dirigi in homine secundum rationem universalem, unde in syllogisticis ex universalibus propositionibus concluduntur conclusiones singulares. Et ideo patet quod ratio universalis imperat appetitui sensitivo. . . . Hoc etiam quilibet experiri potest in seipso; applicando enim aliquas universales considerationes, mitigatur ira aut timor aut aliquid huiusmodi, vel etiam instigatur," *S. T.* I. 81. 3, vol. V, p. 290; cf. 80. 2 ad 3, p. 284; 86. 1 ad 2, p. 347; I. 20. 1 ad 1, vol. IV, p. 252; I-II. 74. 3 ad 1, vol. VII, p. 37.

PRUDENCE AND THE DISCURSIVE POWER

In the first systematic discussion of prudence which St. Thomas
wrote, in the *Scriptum super Libros Sententiarum*, it is treated as
a virtue of the practical intellect, without any reference to any
other power.[71] In the *Commentary on the Ethics*, prudence, though
it is still a virtue of the practical intellect, is said to involve in its
complete notion the discursive sense. In the *Summa* he says explicitly that prudence pertains to reason on the one hand,[72] and
on the other hand that it involves a knowledge of singulars.[73] The
reason for this is obvious: it is because prudence concerns operations, which are always singular.[74]

Now, singulars are known by sense, and the sense which is
operative in the estimation of particulars is an interior sense.[75]

71. *Commentarium Super Tertium Librum Sententiarum,* d. 33, q. 2,
    aa. 2-5 and q. 3, a. 1, ed. Pierre Mandonnet and M. F. Moos, O.P.
    (Paris: Lethielleux), vol, III, pp. 1051-79.
72. Cf. "Unde manifestum est quod prudentia directe pertinet ad vim
    cognoscitivam. Non autem ad vim sensitivam, quia per eam cognos-
    cimus solum ea quae praesto sunt et sensibus offeruntur. Cognos-
    cere autem futura ex praesentibus, vel praeteritis, quod pertinet ad
    prudentiam, proprie rationis est, quia hoc per quandam collationem
    agitur," *S. T.* II-II. 47. 1, vol. VII, p. 348.
73. Cf. "Respondeo dicendum quod, sicut supra dictum est, ad pru-
    dentiam pertinet non solum consideratio rationis, sed etiam appli-
    catio ad opus quod est finis practicae rationis. Nullus autem potest
    convenienter alteri aliquid applicare nisi utrumque cognoscat, scilicet
    et id quod applicandum est, et id cui applicandum est. Operationes
    autem sunt in singularibus. Et ideo necesse est quod prudens et
    cognoscat universalia principia rationis, et cognoscat singularia, circa
    quae sunt operationes," *S. T.* II-II. 47. 3, vol. VIII, p. 350.
74. Cf. "Dicendum quod scientia universalis, quae est certissima, non
    habet principalitatem in operatione, sed magis scientia particularis,
    eo quod operationes sunt circa singularia. Unde non est mirum si
    in operabilibus passio agit contra scientiam universalem, absente
    consideratione in particulari," *S. T.* I-II. 77. 2 ad 1, vol. VII, p. 63.
75. Cf. "Ad tertium dicendum quod ipsa recta aestimatio de fine parti-
    culari et intellectus dicitur, inquantum est alicuius principii; et
    sensus, inquantum est particularis. Et hoc est quod Philosophus dicit
    in VI *Ethic.* [c. 8, 1142a26], 'horum' scilicet singularium 'oportet
    habere sensum; hic autem est intellectus'. Non autem hoc est in-

St. Thomas does not name this sense, but from his references to
the *Ethics*, from expressions like *recta aestimatio* and the practical

---

telligendum de sensu particulari quo cognoscimus propria sensibilia,
sed de sensu interiori quo de particulari iudicamus," *S. T.* II-II. 49.
2 ad 3, vol. VIII, p. 369. Commenting on this text, Professor Harry
Austryn Wolfson says: "Of particular interest is a passage in
Thomas which seems to divest the term 'internal sense' of its generic
meaning as inclusive of several post-sensationary faculties and to
identify it with one particular faculty. He identifies it with the
term αἴσθησις in which, according to Aristotle, prudence, φρόνησις,
resides, referring to *Nichomachean Ethics,* VI, 8, 1142a, 27-30. Inasmuch as by αἴσθησις in that passage Aristotle means common
sense, Thomas is thus identifying internal sense with common sense,
which corresponds to the use made of the term by Augustine,"
"The Internal Senses in Latin, Arabic, and Hebrew Philosophic
Texts," *Harvard Theological Review,* XXVIII (1935), p. 122. This
argument sins against two canons: (*a*) it disregards the law of
context, and (*b*) takes no account of St. Thomas's own previously
given description in q. 47. 3 ad 3 (quoted above, note 65; see also
q. 51. 3, quoted, note 62). According to that text, the internal
sense in question is precisely a group of senses "inclusive of several
post-sensationary faculties," since it is perfected by both *experimentum* and memory. Even if this text were lacking or were
missed, there is also St. Thomas's own interpretation in his *Commentary* on the Ethics, according to which the internal sense involved in prudence is the discursive power.

There is one text in which St. Thomas interprets this Aristotelian text in an Augustinian sense: "Ad similitudinem autem corporalis sensus dicitur etiam circa intelligentiam esse aliquis sensus,
qui est aliquorum primorum et extremorum, ut dicitur in VI *Ethic.*,
sicut etiam sensus est cognoscitivus sensibilium quasi quorundam
principiorum cognitionis," *S. T.* II-II. 15. 2 ad 3, vol. VIII, p. 369.
This interpretation could be of the same type as the usage of the
word *sensus* by the later Augustinians; it is also like that of Averroes, in his paraphrase of the Aristotelian text, quoted above, chapter III.

The *authenticum,* though it rests solidly on Aristotle's prestige,
is still a dark saying. It can be verified in several ways, and so
can be interpreted in any of these meanings. No mediaeval author
would have been conscious of any inconsistency in so doing; cf.
M. D. Chenu, O.P., "Authentica et Magistralia," *Divus Thomas*
(Placentiae) XXVII (1925), pp. 257-85.

syllogism,[76] and from the fact that it is said to be perfected by "experiment" and remembering, we know that "interior sense" is a generic name which includes at least the discursive power and memory.

How can prudence be in several powers? Certainly it could not be in several powers which are unrelated, as one skill cannot be in both hands. In the previous discussions we have seen that the powers stand in an hierarchical order, so that one virtue could be in several powers. St. Thomas himself states this: prudence principally is in reason, but by a kind of application it is also in interior sense.[77]

The situation, where particular knowledge stands under universal knowledge, may be said to be the ideal one. Unfortunately,

---

76. Cf. "Respondeo dicendum quod intellectus non sumitur hic pro potentia intellectiva, sed prout importat quandam rectam aestimationem alicuius extremi principii quod accipitur ut per se notum; sicut et prima demonstrationum principia intelligere dicimur. Omnis autem deductio rationis ab aliquibus procedit quae accipiuntur ut prima. Unde oportet quod omnis processus rationis ab aliquo intellectu procedit. Quia ergo prudentia est recta ratio agibilium, ideo necesse est quod totus processus prudentiae ab intellectu derivetur. Et propter hoc intellectus ponitur pars prudentiae," *S. T.* II-II. 49. 2, vol. VIII, p. 368; "Ad primum ergo dicendum quod ratio prudentiae terminatur, sicut ad conclusionem quandam, ad particulare operabile, ad quod applicat universalem cognitionem, ut ex dictis patet. Conclusio autem singularis syllogizatur ex universali et singulari propositione. Unde oportet quod ratio prudentiae ex duplici intellectu procedat. Quorum unus est cognoscitivus universalium. Quod pertinet ad intellectum qui ponitur virtus intellectualis; quia naturaliter nobis cognita sunt non solum universalia principia speculativa, sed etiam practica, sicut nulli esse malefaciendum, ut ex dictis patet.

Alius autem intellectus est, qui ut dicitur in VI *Ethic.* est cognoscitivus extremi, id est alicuius primi singularis seu principii contingentis operabilis, propositionis scilicet minoris, quam oportet esse singularem in syllogismo prudentiae, ut dictum est. Hoc autem principium singulare est aliquis singularis finis, ut dicitur ibidem. Unde intellectus qui ponitur pars prudentiae est quaedam recta aestimatio de aliquo particulari fine," *ibid.,* ad 1; and see also I-II. 77. 2 ad 4, vol. VII, p. 63; II-II. 49. 1 ad 1, vol. VIII, p. 367.

77. See *S. T.* II-II. 47. 3 ad 3, text quoted in note 65.

it does not always occur. Sometimes, the particular knowledge is simply absent, because of a defect of intention. Sometimes distraction, for example, press of business, impedes the application to the particular. Thirdly, bodily infirmity at times prevents the particular knowledge from being present. The passions of the sense appetite cause defective knowledge of the operable in the latter two ways.[78]

First, passion impedes consideration by way of distraction, in a manner analogous to that in which exterior occupation does. Secondly, by way of contrariety, in that passion usually proposes something contrary to what we know to be right in general. Thirdly, passions sometimes "bind" reason, not permitting it an unhampered exercise;[79] in that case they would bind the will to the same extent.

The fact that passion can bind the reason is proved by the instances of insanity arising from uncontrolled passion.[80] It is

78. Cf. "Quod autem homo non consideret in particulari id quod habitualiter scit, quandoque quidem contingit ex solo defectu intentionis; puta cum homo sciens geometriam, non intendit ad considerandum geometriae conclusiones, quas statim in promptu habet considerare. Quandoque autem homo non considerat id quod habet in habitu, propter aliquod impedimentum superveniens, puta propter aliquam occupationem exteriorem vel propter aliquam infirmitatem corporalem. Et hoc modo ille qui est in passione constitutus, non considerat in particulari id quod scit in universali, inquantum passio impedit talem considerationem.
   Impedit autem tripliciter. Primo quidem, per quandam distractionem, sicut supra expositum est. Secundo per contrarietatem, quia plerumque passio inclinat ad contrarium huius quod scientia universalis habet. Tertio per quandam immutationem corporalem, ex qua ratio quodammodo ligatur, ne libere in actum exeat; sicut etiam somnus vel ebrietas, quadam corporali transmutatione facta, ligant usum rationis. Et quod hoc contingat in passionibus, patet ex hoc quod aliquando, cum passiones multum intenduntur, homo amittit totaliter usum rationis; multi enim propter abundantiam amoris et irae sunt in insaniam conversi. Et per hunc modum passio trahit rationem ad iudicandum in particulari contra scientiam quam habet in universali," *S. T.* I-II. 77. 2, vol. VII, pp. 62-63; *De Malo*, III, a. 9; *S. T.* I-II. 78. 1, vol. VII, p. 71; 94. 6, p. 173.
79. See *S. T.* I-II. 77. 7 ad 2, vol. VII, p. 69.
80. Cf. "Respondeo dicendum quod, sicut supra dictum est [9. 2], passio appetitus sensitivi movet voluntatem ex ea parte qua voluntas movetur ab obiecto; inquantum scilicet homo aliqualiter dispositus per

interesting to see that St. Thomas, on Aristotelian principles, re-
fuses to see in this a purely psychic disturbance; in modern technical language, his explanation is "psychosomatic." The problem is
interesting, and some important things are said in the discussion
of it.

In general, passions affect sense knowledge, and by way of
the latter can affect also intellectual knowledge and will. Even
external sensation is in a way relative, in that its apprehension is
of the object as it affects the sense.[81] The knowledge of both the
estimative and common sense are essentially relative. The estimative knows suitability, a relation which depends on the conditions of both its terms.[82] The common sense knows the sensing

---

passionem, iudicat aliquid esse conveniens et bonum, quod extra passionem existens non iudicaret. Huiusmodi autem immutatio hominis per passionem duobus modis contingit. Uni modo, sic quod
totaliter ratio ligatur, ita quod homo usum rationis non habet; sicut
contingit in his qui propter vehementem iram vel concupiscentiam
furiosi vel amentes fiunt, sicut et propter aliquam aliam perturbationem corporalem; huiusmodi enim passiones non sine corporali
transmutatione accidunt. Et de talibus eadem est ratio sicut et de
animalibus brutis, quae ex necessitate sequuntur impetum passionis;
in his enim non est aliquis rationis motus, et per consequens nec
voluntas. Aliquando autem ratio non totaliter absorbetur a passione, sed remanet quantum ad aliquid iudicium rationis liberum,"
S. T. I-II. 10. 3, vol. VI, p. 87, and supra, note 78.
81. Cf. S. T. I. 17. 2 ad 1, vol. IV, p. 220; also the text in note 82.
82. Cf. "Respondeo dicendum quod, sicut supra dictum est, id quod
apprehenditur sub ratione boni et convenientis, movet voluntatem per
modum obiecti. Quod autem aliquid videatur bonum et conveniens
ex duobus contingit: scilicet ex conditione eius quod proponitur,
et eius cui proponitur. Conveniens enim secundum relationem dicitur, unde ex utroque extremorum dependet. Et inde est quod gustus
diversimode dispositus, non eodem modo accipit aliquid ut conveniens et ut non conveniens. Unde, ut Philosophus dicit in III
Ethic. [c. 5, 1114a32] 'qualis unusquisque est, talis finis videtur ei.'
Manifestum est autem quod secundum passionem appetitus sensitivi immutatur homo ad aliquam dispositionem. Unde secundum
quod est in passione aliqua, videtur sibi aliquid conveniens, quod non
videtur ei extra passionem existenti; sicut irato videtur bonum, quod
non videtur quieto. Et per hunc modum ex parte obiecti appetitus
sensitivus movet voluntatem," S. T. I-II. 9. 3, vol. VI, p. 78.

animal and that which it senses, and so knows the immediate proportion of one to the other.

Now, appetite is in its own way a kind of assimilation to the
appetible.[83] Consequently, through the change introduced in the
sensing subject by the act of appetite, the suitability and proportion increase. Hence, the judgments of the estimative and common
sense are reinforced by the passions which follow from them.

A second way in which passion affects sense knowledge is
this. The image, which aroused the affection of the sense appetite,
is by that very fact hard to displace in sensory awareness.[84] To
this extent, reason is prevented from working out the particular
minor of the practical syllogism. If the difficulty of removing the
image becomes an impossibility (for the time), then reason is bound,
and the will is no longer free. Otherwise, the possibility of right
action remains, and freedom, too, to a more or less limited extent.

Prudence, then, is principally and formally a virtue of practical reason. As in the reason alone, it is incomplete, for it has not
yet been brought down to the singular. The application to the
singular is accomplished by inner sense (discursive power and
memory) under the guidance of reason. The work of inner sense
is an application of the universal in reason; the disposition arising
from this work, and corresponding to the virtue of prudence, is a
kind of material part of prudence. Perfect human action, then,
springs from appetite guided by prudence working through both

---

83. See *S. T.* I-II. 26. 2, vol. VI, p. 189.
84. Cf. "Ex parte obiecti voluntatis, quod est bonum ratione apprehensum. Impeditur enim iudicium et apprehensio rationis propter vehementem et inordinatam apprehensionem imaginationis, et iudicium
virtutis aestimativae, ut patet in amentibus. Manifestum est autem
quod passionem appetitus sensitivi sequitur imaginationis apprehensio, et iudicium aestimativae. . . . Unde per consequens iudicium
rationis plerumque sequitur passionem appetitus sensitivi, et per
consequens motus voluntatis, qui natus est semper sequi iudicium
rationis," *S. T.* I-II. 77. 1, vol. VII, p. 61; "Interior autem somni-
orum causa est duplex. Una quidem animalis, inquantum scilicet
ea occurunt hominis phantasiae in dormiendo circa quae eius cogitatio et affectio fuit immorata in vigilando," II-II. 95. 6, vol. IX,
p. 323; I-II. 10. 3 and ad 3, vol. VI, pp. 87-88.

reason and inner sense. But appetite is capable of breaking out of this harmony, and the most significant break is under the influence of sense pleasure through the common sense.

Vis Cogitativa AND KNOWLEDGE OF THE SINGULAR.

From what has been said, it is obvious that the discursive power is the quasi-instrument by reflection upon which the intellect knows the singular in the practical order. The *Summa* would seem to distinguish between the case of the singular operable, in the indirect intellectual knowledge of which the discursive sense is mentioned,[85] and that of the particular in speculative knowledge, in which only the imagination is mentioned.[86] In the *Quae-*

---

85. Cf. "Ad secundum dicendum quod electio particularis operabilis est quasi conclusio syllogismi intellectus practici, ut dicitur in VII *Ethic.* [c. 3, 1147a28]. Ex universali autem propositione directe non potest concludi singularis, nisi mediante aliqua singulari propositione assumpta. Unde universalis ratio intellectus practici non movet nisi mediante particulari apprehensione sensitivae partis, ut dicitur in III *De Anima,*" *S. T.* I. 86. 1 ad 2, vol. V, p. 347; 80. 2 ad 3, p. 284.

86. Cf. "Indirecte autem et quasi per quandam reflexionem potest cognoscere singulare, quia, sicut supra dictum est, etiam postquam species intelligibiles abstraxerit, non potest secundum eas intelligere nisi convertendo se ad phantasmata, in quibus species intelligibiles intelligit, ut dicitur in III *De Anima* [c. 7, 431b2]. Sic igitur ipsum universale per speciem intelligibilem directe intelligit; indirecte autem singularia, quorum sunt phantasmata. Et hoc modo format hanc propositionem: Socrates est homo," *S. T.* I. 86. 1, vol. V, p. 347; "Respondeo dicendum quod de universali dupliciter contingit loqui: uno modo, secundum quod subest intentioni universalitatis; alio autem modo dicitur de natura cui talis intentio attribuitur. Alia est enim consideratio hominis universalis, et alia hominis in eo quod est homo. Si igitur universale accipiatur primo modo, sic nulla potentia sensitivae partis, neque apprehensiva neque appetitiva, potest in universale, quia universale fit per abstractionem a materia individuali, in qua radicatur omnis virtus sensitiva. Potest tamen aliqua potentia sensitiva, et apprehensiva et appetiva, ferri in aliquid universaliter: Sicut dicimus quod obiectum visus est color secundum genus, non quia visus cognoscat colorem universalem; sed quia quod color sit cognoscibilis a visu non convenit colori inquantum est hic color, sed inquantum est color simpliciter. Sic ergo

stio Disputata de Anima, however, it is said that "this reflection cannot be completed except by the joining [to intellect] of the discursive and imaginative powers."[87] Apparently, then, the question raised in the preceding chapter: "Is the discursive power operative in a special way in all knowledge of the singular, or only in the order of practical knowledge?" is still unanswered. There is, however, one very important text, and one borne out by two texts of the *Summa Contra Gentiles,* which may help to solve this question.

In speaking of the knowledge of Christ, St. Thomas objects to himself that the knowledge of singulars does not belong to the perfection of intellect. He answers by making a distinction between speculative and practical knowledge.

---

odium etiam sensitivae partis potest respicere aliquid in universali, quia ex natura communi aliquid adversatur animali, et non solum ex eo quod est particularis, sicut lupus ovi. Unde ovis odit lupum generaliter," I-II. 29. 6, vol. VI, p. 207; also: I. 40. 3, vol. IV, p. 416; I. 54. 5, ad ea quae in contrarium obiiciuntur, vol. V, pp. 52-53; 85. 3, p. 336; I-II. 29. 6 ad 1, vol. VI, p. 208; II-II. 47. 3 ad 1, vol. VIII, p. 350-51; *Quaestio Disputata de Anima,* a. 20, ed. Parma, vol. VIII, pp. 527-28; *ibid.,* ad 1, 2, 6, and ad 3, in contrar., a. 15, ad 18 and ad 20; *Quodlibetum* VII, a. 8, aa. 11, 12; *De Veritate,* II. 6, XIX. 2; *In V. Metaphysicorum,* lect. 13, ed. R. M. Cathala, O.P. (Turin: Marietti, sec. ed., 1926), no. 947.

The doctrine of *Summa* I. 86. 1, the first text quoted in this note, is very briefly put; however, as long as it is kept in mind that q. 84, a. 7 and q. 79, a. 6 ad 2, have preceded, the doctrine is identical with that which St. Thomas has held throughout.

87. "Ad primum quorum [scilicet argumentorum in contrarium] dicendum est quod anima coniuncta corpori per intellectum cognoscit singulare, non quidem directe, sed per quandam reflexionem; inquantum scilicet ex hoc quod apprehendit suum intelligibile, revertitur ad considerandum suum actum, et speciem intelligibilem quae est principium suae operationis, et eius speciei originem; et sic venit in considerationem phantasmatum, et singularium, quorum sunt phantasmata. Sed haec reflexio compleri non potest nisi per adiunctionem virtutis cogitativae et imaginativae, quae non sunt in anima separata; unde per modum istum anima separata singularia non cognoscit," *Quaestio Disputata De Anima,* a. 20, ad 1 in contrarium, ed. Parma, vol. VIII, p. 529.

To the third argument the answer is that the knowledge of
singulars does not pertain to the perfection of the intellective soul as regards speculative knowledge; but it does, as
regards practical knowledge, which is not perfect without
the knowledge of singulars with which action is concerned,
as is said in the sixth book of the *Ethics*.[88]

The knowledge of singulars belongs to the perfection of the intellect according to practical knowledge, but not according to speculative. It is impossible to suppose that St. Thomas is here denying
that sciences are about things which are singular.[89] In a somewhat
parallel connection in the *Summa Contra Gentiles*, he notes that
in a way the knowledge of singulars does pertain to speculative
knowledge;[90] singulars fall short in regard to necessity and in-
fallibility. Even in this text, however, it is said that the knowledge
of singulars belongs to practical knowledge *a fortiori*.

It seems therefore inevitable to conclude that speculative and
practical knowledge bear on the singular in a different way. In
speculative knowledge, we know, of course, that the things we are

---

88. *S. T.* III. 11, 1 ad 3, vol. XI, p. 158. Cf. "Practica autem cognitio
    non est perfecta nisi ad singularia perveniatur; nam practicae cogni-
    tionis finis est operatio, quae in singularibus est," *Summa Contra
    Gentiles,* I. 65, "Amplius, Divinus Intellectus," vol. XIII, p. 179;
    in IV Sent., d. 49, q. 1, a. 1, q. 3 ad 1, ed. Parma, vol. VII, pt. 2,
    p. 1185.
89. Cf. *S. T.* I. 85. 2, vol. V, p. 334; 85. 1 ad 5, p. 332; 81. 1, p. 288;
    In Boethii de Trinitate, V. 2 ad 4; cf. chapter VI, note 57, and
    above, note 86.
90. Cf. "Adhuc. Haec est differentia inter cognitionem speculativam
    et practicam, quod cognitio speculativa, et ea quae ad ipsam perti-
    nent, perficiuntur in universali; ea vero quae pertinent ad cogni-
    tionem practicam, perficiuntur in particulari; nam finis speculativae
    est veritas, quae primo et per se in immaterialibus consistit et in
    universalibus; finis vero practicae est operatio, quae est circa singu-
    laria. . . .
        Item. Cognitio speculativa magis perficitur in universali quam
    in particulari. . . . Ille vero perfectior est in scientia speculativa qui
    non solum universalem, sed propriam cognitionem de rebus habet. . . .
    Multo igitur magis in scientia practica perfectior est qui non solum
    in universali sed etiam in particulari res disponit ad actum," *Contra
    Gentiles,* III. 75, vol. XIV, p. 221.

dealing with *are* singulars.[91] But is it not in a way irrelevant to speculative knowledge *which* singular we are thinking of, provided that it realizes the universal? In practical knowledge, on the contrary, it is precisely this singular as such that we must know. (An apparent exception occurs in such practical sciences which are only remotely practical, and which may be called "speculative from a certain point of view."[92])

To summarize the textual position. In speaking of the return to sense in connection with practical knowledge, the discursive power is always mentioned. In some other texts whose connotations are clearly those of speculative knowledge, only the imagination is spoken of. In a third group of texts the discursive power is mentioned, and there is no qualification, express or implied, concerning the kind of knowledge.

---

91. Cf. "Respondeo dicendum quod contingentia dupliciter possunt considerari. Uno modo, secundum quod contingentia sunt. Alio modo, secundum quod in eis aliquid necessitatis invenitur; nihil enim est adeo contingens quin in se aliquid necessarium habeat. Sicut hoc ipsum quod est Socratem currere, in se quidem contingens est; sed habitudo cursus ad motum est necessaria; necessarium enim est Socratem moveri, si currit. — Est autem unumquodque contingens ex parte materiae, quia contingens est quod potest esse et non esse; potentia autem pertinet ad materiam. Necessitas autem consequitur rationem formae, quia ea quae consequuntur ad formam, ex necessitate insunt. Materia autem est individuationis principium; ratio autem universalis accipitur secundum abstractionem formae a materia particulari. Dictum autem est supra quod per se et directe intellectus est universalium; sensus autem singularium, quorum etiam indirecte quodammodo est intellectus, ut supra dictum est. Sic igitur contingentia, prout sunt contingentia, cognoscuntur directe quidem sensu, indirecte autem ab intellectu; rationes autem universales et necessariae contingentium cognoscuntur per intellectum. — Unde si attendantur rationes universales scibilium, omnes scientiae sunt de necessariis. Si autem attendantur ipsae res, sic quaedam scientia est de necessariis, quaedam vero de contingentibus," *S. T.* I. 86. 3, vol. V, p. 351.

Professor Gilson has brilliantly explained how the philosophy of St. Thomas is concerned with the concrete. *Le Thomisme,* 5th ed. (Paris, Vrin, 1944), pp. 508-09.

92. Cf. *In Boethii de Trinitate,* V. 1.

There are two textual clues to this group. One clue is afforded by the text just considered, as well as by a text discussed in
the preceding chapter concerning what is meant by the "contingent
particular."[93] According to this, the singular in some texts is to
be considered *as singular,* and therefore as strongly *implying practical* knowledge.[94] The second clue is given us by two texts in the
Contra Gentiles,[95] which show that the reflection upon the imagination and discursive power (as well as memory), is to be understood
disjunctively. By this is meant: the intellect knows singulars by
reflection upon the inner senses; by reflection upon the imagination it knows singulars in the speculative order and without time-
reference; by reflection upon the discursive power it knows singulars
in the practical order; whenever time enters in, both the discursive power and memory will come into special relation with the intellect.[96] By means of this second clue, the remaining texts are
adequately taken care of.[97]

This textual argument, as far as I can see, proves this much
conclusively: that there *is* a textual basis for distinguishing between the intellectual knowledge of the singular in the practical
and the speculative orders; secondly, that St. Thomas never says

---

93. *Commentary on the Ethics,* VI, lect. 2 [text quoted above, p. 213].
94. This will be the case for the text, *Commentary on the De Anima,* II,
    lect. 13 [text quoted above, pp. 198-200], and *In IV Sent.,* d. 49,
    q. 2, a. 2 [quoted, p. 175].

    Compare: "Cognitio autem veritatis in talibus contingentibus singu-
    laribus non habet aliquid magnum, ut per se sit appetibilis, sicut
    cognitio universalium et necessariorum; sed appetitur secundum quod
    est utilis ad operationem, quia actiones sunt circa contingentia singu-
    laria," *S.T.* I-II. 14. 3, vol. VI, pp. 106-07.
95. *Contra Gentiles,* II. 80, 81 [texts quoted above, p. 188-189].
96. On the relation between the discursive power and memory, see the
    section next to be discussed (sec. 4).

    For a fuller treatment of the texts concerning the knowledge of the
    singular, see Klubertanz, "St. Thomas and the Knowledge of the
    Singular," *The New Scholasticism,* XXVI (1952).
97. The disjunctive sense will be the one meant in *Contra Gentiles,* III.
    84 [text quoted above, p. 189], and *Quaestio Disputata de Anima,*
    a. 20, ad 1 in contrarium, text cited above, note 87.

that the discursive power is operative in a special way in the indirect intellectual knowledge of the singular in the speculative order.
This textual basis, together with the arguments advanced in the
preceding chapter, is a sufficiently solid ground for using this distinction in the integration and interpretation of the texts.

PREPARATION OF PHANTASMS

St. Thomas tells us that the interior senses prepare for the
possible intellect its proper object.[98] In the context, there is question of those phantasms which correspond to intellectual habits.
In reference to this, we need but refer to what was said above
on habits of the interior senses. In the section treating of prudence, it was also noted that the activity of sense appetite and
estimative power account for a phantasm's remaining in sensory
awareness.

Combining these two ideas, we may say that the preparation
of phantasms by the three interior senses (imagination, discursive
power, and memory) consists in the appropriate combination of
diverse elements into a unified phantasm, in the ready re-presentation of this complex phantasm, and in the maintaining of it within
sense awareness for such length of time as is necessary for the intellect to do its work. St. Thomas does not say it explicitly, but
it seems to be evident that in different cases the relative importance
of the different interior senses will vary. For example, in the preparation of the phantasms of operables, the work of the discursive
power is relatively important, and, as we have seen, is singled out
in many texts.

---

98. "Ad tertium dicendum quod quia vires apprehensivae interius praeparant intellectui possibili proprium obiectum, ideo ex bona dispositione harum virium, ad quam cooperatur bona dispositio corporis,
redditur homo habilis ad intelligendum. Et sic habitus intellectivus
secundario potest esse in istis viribus. Principaliter autem est in
intellectu possibili," *S. T.* I-II. 50. 4 ad 3, vol. VI, p. 321; cf. 51.
3, p. 328; 53. 1, p. 337; I. 75, 3 ad 2, vol. V, p. 200; and from the
negative point of view, I-II. 48. 3, vol. VI, p. 306.

VIS COGITATIVA, MEMORIA, AND MEMORY

In the first chapter, we saw that for Aristotle memory is an actual image known to refer to the past, or, in other words, memory is knowledge of the past as such. In the third chapter, we discovered that in Avicenna and Algazel, *memoria* is the power which retains the intentions discovered by the estimative. In the Latin translations of these authors the word *memoria* would thus be an equivocal term.

Though there may be instances in St. Thomas where this term is used simply according to one or the other of its divergent origins, the general result is a very subtle notion of memory. For an example, let us study briefly the key text of the *Summa*, question 78, article 4.

> For the conservation [of such intentions, there is established] the memorative power, which is a treasury of such intentions. A sign of this is, that the beginning of remembering in animals arises from some such intention, for example, because something is harmful or suitable. And the very note of "pastness," which the memory attends to, is counted among such intentions.

The very use of words here is instructive. The verb *memorari* is evidently used in its original Latin sense, and corresponds to the Latin translations of the Aristotelian terms meaning "to remember." *Vis memorativa*, on the other hand, has in its strict technical sense no immediate reference to remembering. It is simply the power of retaining, conserving the intentions of the estimative. But at once this function is related to remembering, in that the principle of remembering on the sensory level is an intention. And, adds St. Thomas, the very *ratio praeteriti* — "pastness itself" — is such an intention.

It must be likewise noted that mere retention of sensory experience as such is not memory. Nor is the act of again presenting to internal sensation some sensible form the same as remembering. Rather, that is the proper function of imagination. To the actual presence of what is in fact an image there must be added the knowledge that it is in fact an image. This is another way of saying that in memory the phantasm is known as referring to a past experience.

Thus there are two conditions necessary for memory. First, that there is a retention of sensible species, which is a function of the imagination. Second, that there is a sense of time, which seems also to pertain to the imagination. Over and above these, there must be a relation of the sensed object to the sensing subject. To all appearances this is a function of the estimative.

On the sense level, memory is therefore rather limited. In fact, the animal knows past objects only in so far as they are bound up with past experience.

> To the second argument the answer is that "pastness" can be referred to two things: that is, to the object which is known, and to the act of knowledge. These two are simultaneously joined in the sensitive part, which can know something by means of its being changed by a present sensible thing. And so the animal simultaneously remembers that it previously sensed in the past, and that it sensed some past sensible object.[99]

The fact that for the animal "pastness" is first of all a function of its own activity in past time, and secondly of a past object, is based on the kind of knowledge an animal has. If we apply to this text the doctrine of the *Commentary on the De Anima* dealing with the estimative and knowledge of the individual, this conclusion would seem to follow: something sensed by the animal, which for that animal is not an individual object, would not be remembered.

In man, even on the sensory level, there is a possibility of extending the scope of memory. The field of the discursive power is not completely determined by nature, but is to a great extent under the control of reason. Hence, the sensory memory of man can take in a great variety of objects, provided only that they are referrable somehow to man. St. Thomas, after explaining various methods of improving the memory (that is, of developing habits in the memory), adds this significant comment:

> Thirdly, it is necessary that a man be concerned, and use his emotions on that which he wishes to remember, because,

---

99. *S. T.* I. 79. 6 ad 2, vol. V, p. 271.

the more something is impressed on the soul, the less it will slip away.[100]

Directly, this text reminds us that the sensory appetite in man is under the control of reason by way of the discursive power, so that there is a possibility of arousing and directing its acts to a very great number of objects.[101] Indirectly, the text implies that memory occurs, to a certain extent at least, in partial dependence on the sensory passions. Again, with respect to all sensible objects which are not immediately gratifying to the senses, the passions depend on a judgment of the estimative (or discursive power).

Briefly, memory is in direct relation to sensory passion and estimative power. In animals, it is primarily memory of past experience, and is limited in scope to the field of their specific estimative power. In men, the field of sense memory is much larger, because the human estimative, under the guidance of reason, is limited only in so far as it is incapable of passing beyond material things.

CONCLUSION OF THIS CHAPTER

We are concerned here particularly, not with the doctrine of St. Thomas as a whole, for that is the task of the next chapter, but with what is peculiar to the *Summa*. Practically, this amounts to pointing out the differences between the *Summa* and the other works.

(1) The most significant development is in the treatment of prudence. At first, it was handled solely as a virtue of the practical intellect. In the *Commentary on the Ethics*, the discursive power was added as complementary to practical reason. In the *Summa*, memory (and perhaps imagination) is added. Moreover, the relations between intellectual prudence and the corresponding sensory dispositions are clarified: the intellectual virtue is formal and principal; the sensory disposition is material and dispositive or applicative.

---

100. *S. T.* II-II. 49. 1 ad 2, vol. VIII, p. 367.
101. Cf. *S. T.* I. 81. 3, text quoted above in note 70.

(2) The relations between intellectual habits and the interior senses in general constitute a clearly expressed background for the special relation of prudence and the discursive power with memory.

(3) The notion of the estimative judgment is expressed much more fully in the *Summa* than elsewhere.

(4) The *"continuatio"* of the earlier works gives way to a variety of terms: *coniunctio, unio, refluentia,* and *motus mobilis;* St. Thomas adds a refinement, stressing the composite nature of the sensory discursus, in saying that the operation of intellect is as form and that of the discursive power is as matter. The interest in the *Summa* turns rather to habits of the interior senses, and their relation to intellectual habits.

(5) The practical character of estimative knowledge and consequently of animal cognition in general is more explicitly stated and is insisted on.

(6) The connection between practical knowledge, knowledge of the singular, and the discursive power is brought out more clearly than before, though it is still not expressly stated. To reach a much higher degree of probability, arguments drawn from other aspects of St. Thomas's doctrine can be made use of. In the preceding chapter, three arguments were advanced. Briefly, these are the following. (1) In some cases, St. Thomas does make use of the discursive power in the explanation of the intellectual knowledge of the singular in the practical order, while he omits this power when speaking of the speculative order. (2) There is one text in which the singular, with which the discursive power is concerned, is said to be the operable. (3) The discursive is the power man has in place of the estimative. Now the estimative is strictly concerned with practical knowledge, and that alone. If the discursive power is to be the power man has, and its main difference from the animal estimative is to lie in its *mode* of operation, it should be likewise concerned with practical knowledge.

From the *Summa,* two more arguments can be drawn. In I. 78. 4, the discursive power is formally said to be the human estimative, not merely to replace it. Thus the third argument is strongly reinforced. Finally, it has been demonstrated repeatedly in the course of this study that the "influence" (*continuatio, unio, motio, etc.*) which the discursive power receives from reason is precisely an instrumental motion or direction. It is the constant and very explicit doctrine of St. Thomas that the function of something as an instrument is limited by the possible extension of its own proper operation.[102] Now, the function of apprehending specifically determined sensible goods can understandably be extended under the influence of reason to cover all the goods of man as a composite being.[103]

For these reasons, textual and theoretical, it can safely be concluded that the discursive power is operative in a special way in the intellectual knowledge of the singular only in the practical order.

---

102. See *Contra Gentiles,* II. 21; *S.T.* I, 45. 5; III. 19. 1; 62. 4 ad 2.
103. The human good can be extended to include even speculative knowledge, in so far as the latter is a perfection for man; cf. "Ad primum ergo dicendum, quod ex hoc ipso quod veritas est fines contemplationis, habet rationem boni appetibilis et amabilis et delectantis. Et secundum hoc pertinet ad vim appetitivam," *S.T.* II-II. 180. 1 ad 1, vol. X, p. 424.

PART III

CHAPTER 9

A SYNOPSIS OF THE DOCTRINE OF ST. THOMAS IN ITS HISTORICAL SETTING

It is possible, by means of a judicious selection and arrangement of texts, to present St. Thomas's account of man in the guise of a deductive system of propositions. This possibility arises from the interplay of two types of demonstration: the *demonstrationes quia* and *propter quid*.[1] But such a one-sided presentation will be an implicit falsification. To remain faithful to the spirit as well as the letter of the Thomistic texts it will be necessary to follow his method as well: to see the facts which need to be explained, and then to give the explanation which will be in necessary relation with them.

The facts which serve as St. Thomas's starting-point are not discovered by him. Others had used them before; generally they were of a kind that could be verified by almost anyone.

What is new in St. Thomas is the significance he attached to certain facts, and the interpretation he gave of them. Unfortunately for us, on points like the estimative, he has given no complete systematic treatment. Yet such a presentation is necessary if we are to understand his doctrine and compare it with that of others. Hence, this attempt will be made, with the full realization that there is something of a danger of subjective interpretation in the very juxtaposition of two texts.

The order of treatment will be the following. First, there will be a discussion of the estimative power on the level of sensibility as such, with attention to animals, whose sensibility is unaffected by intellect. Secondly, the human estimative will be con-

---

1. Cf. St. Thomas, *Commentary on the Posterior Analytics* I, lect. 13, ed. Leon., vol. I, p. 189; lect. 14, no. 7, p. 195; lect. 23, nos. 4-9, pp. 230-32.

sidered, as far as possible, on its own level. Thirdly, the relation between reason and the discursive sense will be handled from
the viewpoint of the way in which the latter is the complement
of reason.

ESTIMATION AS A POWER OF SENSIBILITY *TOUT COURT*

The explanations of animal activity given by his predecessors
and contemporaries presented themselves to St. Thomas in quite
literally a bewildering variety. To classify or characterize them
accurately is almost impossible. But in a rough kind of way, the
various explanations can be arranged in a series proceeding from
the simpler to the more complex.

The simplest explanation known to St. Thomas was perhaps
the one which held that animals were guided by nature in their
actions. This presented itself under the patronage of Seneca[2] and
some passages of Aristotle.[3] In a way, this explanation is true
enough;[4] and yet it is only generic. After all, the activities of
inanimate things and of plants receive precisely the same explanation.[5]

---

2. See especially *Letter* 121. [Texts quoted above, ch. 2, notes 17-18].
3. *Physics,* II, ch. 8, 199 a 20-30. [discussion above, pp. 34-35].
4. Cf. *Summa Theologiae* I. 81. 2; 83. 1; I-II. 1. 2; 12. 5; 13. 2;
   15. 2; 16. 2 ad 2; 46. 4 ad 2. [Cf. texts quoted above p. 235 and
   ch. 8, note 15].
5. Cf. St. Thomas, *Commentary on the Physics,* II, lect. 13. [Text
   quoted above, ch. 7, note 33].
   Modern equivalents of this position tend to stress mechanical and
   materialistic aspects. Cross mechanical explanations use the terminology of "reflex action" and interpret this in a purely mechanical
   or electro- and chemico-mechanical way. It is true that St. Thomas
   did not formally have the concept of reflex action, but philosophi-
   cally he had an equivalent in the "natural inclination" which every
   form has; cf. *S. T.* I. 80. 1 ad 3; 78. 1 ad 3; and *De Motu Cordis.*
   "Soft" materialistic explanations add the hormones, etc., to their
   list of factors. The hormones, too, were unknown to St. Thomas.
   But fundamentally all this does not change the evident fact that
   "instinctive" activity involves sensory cognition. All explanations
   which overlook this point are to that extent incomplete.

A slightly more involved explanation takes account of the fact that an animal has cognition. St. Augustine said that animals are guided by an inner sense.[6] William of St. Thierry expressed it thus: animals have a greater power of sense.[7] Isaac Israeli presented a picture of animal nature which is characterized by a kind of a vacuum: the absence of reason.[8] These doctrines, too, are on the right track,[9] but they do not advance the solution very far. To say: animals act as they do, because that is the way in which they experience things, is true as far as it goes. Yet the external sensation of at least some animals is quite like that of men.[10] The difference must therefore lie in internal sense.[11] If, however, nothing more than this is said, the statement is lacking in analytic precision.

By analyzing the notion of internal sense, a more complex explanation can be arrived at. Aristotle found that the common source of the proper senses manifested itself in imagination and memory.[12] In imagination, together with appetite, he saw the explanation of all animal activity.[13] Maimonides based his explanation on the imagination also, and he thought of this as a power in a Galenic fashion.[14] Averroes insisted that the animal was

---

On reflex activity, cf. Robert S. Woodworth, *Psychology*, 12th ed. (London: Methuen, 1940), pp. 255-59; on instinctive or "unlearned" activity, cf. *ibid.*, pp. 268-70.

6. St. Augustine, *De Libero Arbitrio*, II, c. 3. [Text quoted, ch. 2, note 58].

7. William of St. Thierry, *De Natura Corporis et Animae*, I. [Text quoted above, ch. 2, note 132].

8. Isaac Israeli, *Liber de Diffinitionibus*. [Texts quoted above, pp. 80-83 and ch. 3, notes 4-7; discussion, pp. 80-83].

9. Cf. *Summa Theologiae* I. 78. 1 ad 3; I-II. 58. 1. [Text quoted above, ch. 8, note 14].

10. Cf. *S. T.* I. 78. 4. [Text quoted above, pp. 221-223].

11. *De Potentia*, II. 2; III. 11 ad 1. [Texts quoted above, ch. 6, note 67].

12. See discussion, above, pp. 24-25.

13. Aristotle, *De Anima*, II, c. 3, 414 b 1-5; III, c. 11, 434 a 1-5; c. 9, 432 b 10-15. [cf. discussion above, pp. 30-32].

14. See p. 84; texts in Harry Austryn Wolfson, "Maimonides on the Internal Senses," *Jewish Quarterly Review*, new series, XXV (1935), pp. 441-42.

guided by the power of imagination and by innate arts.[15] These
solutions, it is true, are an advance in precision. But have they
really solved the problem? Imagination, in all these authors, is
understood as the retention and re-presentation of objects as they
appear to the external senses. Now, if the external senses cannot
account for all animal activity, how can the images of their experiences explain it?[16] Averroes, with his notion of innate arts,

---

15. *Destructio Destructionum,* in physicis, disputatio 2, [text quoted
    above, p. 110]; *Commentary on the Posterior Analytics (Post.
    Resolutor.),* comm. on bk. II, c. 11, t. c. 103 [above, p. 115].
16. Aristotle, *De Anima* III, c. 3, 427 b 20-25; St. Thomas *S.T.* I. 81. 3
    ad 2.
    Modern equivalents of this position are of two types: by asso-
    ciation of phantasms or by innate phantasms. Association may enter
    into all those activities where learning enters in, and to some ex-
    tent learning enters into almost all animal activity; cf. Robert S.
    Woodworth, *Psychology,* p. 371, 268, 270. But at best it is a minor
    element, and it is quite probable that it is not a basic one; cf. "Les
    phénomènes associatifs sensoriels n'agissent que dans le mesure ou
    ils entraînent des conséquenses affectives," Louis Copelam, "L'-
    Élément affectif à la base du reflex psycho-galvanique," p. 136,
    L'Année Psychologique (119-136) XXXVI (1936), quoting with
    approval H. Piéron, "Sur les variations de résistance des corps
    d'origin affectives," *Société de biologie,* 1914, LXXVII, pp. 232-34.
    Domet de Vorges, who attempted a very sketchy and somewhat
    inaccurate history of the *vis aestimativa,* thought that animal ac-
    tivity was to be explained by "association of ideas"; cf. "L'Esti-
    mative," *Revue Neo-Scolastique,* XI (1904), pp. 433-54.
    The theory of innate phantasms or images is held by Cardinal
    Mercier, *Manual of Modern Scholastic Psychology,* tr. by T. L.
    Parker and S. A. Parker (London: Kegan Paul, 1928), vol, I, p.
    216; Joseph Froebes, S.J., *Psychologia Speculativa* (Friburg: Her-
    der, 1927: 2 vols.), vol. I, pp. 32, 34, 174, 176-77; and Michael
    Maher, S.J. *Psychology,* 9th ed. (London: Longmans, 1925), pp.
    92-96, 587; among others. A subtly nuanced theory of physiological
    innatism is held by Mark A. Gaffney, S.J., *The Psychology of the
    Interior Senses* (St. Louis: Herder, 1942), pp. 241-42. The sup-
    position of innate images or patterns is valid only if no simpler
    theory is available.
    All theories which base themselves on images have two defi-
    ciencies; first, they overlook the affective and appetitive elements
    so prominent in instinctive activity; secondly, these clements cannot

would seem to be in a better position. And yet in a way innate arts (or phantasms, as modern writers call them) complicate the problem without really solving it. These innate arts may explain how a bird may *know* a nest, and how to build one. But they still do not explain why it builds a nest, or much less why it builds one in spring.

In Avicenna and Algazel the doctrine reaches its greatest complexity. Avicenna developed a theory of powers, distinguished by their objects.[17] Among the inner or hidden powers he placed the estimative. The function of this power was to perceive in the objects of external sensation some aspect which the external senses did not know: namely, the sensory goodness or suitability of those objects. This kind of knowledge explained the purposive or quasi-intelligent activity of brutes.[18] Here at last was a doctrine which explained precisely the finality, the means-to-end relation which needed explanation.

That the Avicenna theory was at least to some extent satisfactory is seen in this, that it was quite readily adopted by the Latin writers. Gundissalinus simply borrowed whole passages of Avicenna;[19] William of Auvergne used the doctrine slightly, but without change.[20] In a short time, however, some dissatisfaction must have been felt. Avicenna, at least in one passage, seems to have said that the intentions of the estimative were infused into the animal from the separate intelligences. Christian writers soon saw that explanations of this type were inacceptable, and therefore attempted to replace them with others. The *Summa Theologica* (ascribed to Alexander of Hales) decided that these intentions were innate.[21] Jean de la Rochelle and the *Isagoge* (*Philosophia Pau-*

---

be brought into their system without some further element to link them, since images as such do not lead to action, as Aristotle and St. Thomas after him have pointed out; cf. supra, pp. 148, 269-270.

17. *De Anima,* part I, c. 5. [Text quoted above, pp. 93-94].

18. *De Anima,* part IV, c. 3. [Text quoted above, pp. 101-103].

19. *De Anima,* c. 9, section 3, discussed above, pp. 124-126.

20. See discussion, pp. 130-131, and texts quoted in ch. 4, notes 15-23.

21. *Summa Theologica,* Prima Pars secundi Libri, ed. Quaracchi, vol. II, no. 359. [Text quoted above, ch. 4, note 27].

perum) thought that the estimative was a transcendent sense, somehow dealing with immaterial knowledge.[22] St. Albert seems to tend toward making the intentions innate,[23] and explains that the phantasy (compositive imagination) joins the knowledge of the estimative with the sensed or imagined object.[24] Thus, the school of Avicenna breaks up into a number of divergent and irreconcilable theories.

Faced with this welter of conflicting doctrine, St. Thomas chose that of Avicenna.[25] He did not simply take it on authority, however; he studied Avicenna's arguments and made them his own with some modifications. Thus, he sharpened the argumentation.[26] He put it into a broader context, that of natural finality.[27] He explained the mode of operation of the estimative in a way that accorded with the Aristotelian notion of *nature* (as something complete in its being and capable of performing its necessary activities).[28] Hence, he could disregard the variant attempts of others.[29]

---

22. *Summa de Anima* [text quoted above, p. 133].
    Isagoge, ch. 18 [quoted, ch. 4, note 93].
23. *Libri Tres de Anima,* II, tract. 4, c. 7. [Text quoted above, ch. 4, note 44].
24. *Ibid.,* [texts quoted above, ch. 4, notes 45, 49], and also c. 14 [quoted, ch. 4, note 50].
25. See discussion, pp. 158-160.
26. Particularly in *S. T.* I. 78. 4. The logical framework of this article is discussed above, pp. 224-225. St. Thomas likewise omitted the biological data of his contemporaries; for his reasons, cf. *S. T.* I. 75; 78; 78. 3, and the discussion, p. 226.
    On the present status of knowledge concerning the physiological link between sensation and emotion, cf. Robert S. Woodworth, *Psychology,* pp. 274-81, 420.
27. Cf. *S. T.* I. 18. 3; I. 80. 1, and ad obj.; 103. 8; I. 6. 1 ad 2; I-II. 26. 1; discussion of this point, above, p. 230.
28. Cf. discussion, pp. 160-161, 235-237.
29. This is obvious for Alexander of Hales and Jean de la Rochelle, for in St. Thomas there is no reference to innate intentions nor to the estimative as a transcendent power. For St. Albert the case may not be so clear. Fr. George C. Reilly, O.P., *The Psychology of St. Albert the Great* (Washington: Catholic University, 1934), p. 34, says that fundamentally the greatest difference between St. Albert and St. Thomas was one of approach. That this difference

To see how thoroughly the estimative in St. Thomas is an Avicennan doctrine, and yet how completely it is his own, integrated with his metaphysics, it will be useful to present a very brief summary of that doctrine.

The facts that need to be explained are commonly accepted facts. Animals act with respect to objects that are neither gratifying nor unpleasant to the external senses.[30] Their actions concerning such objects show a notable, complex finality, a relation of means to end, a kind of prudence.[31] Such actions, moreover, show a certain specific uniformity.[32]

What precisely needs to be explained about these facts? Not the individual components of the complex series. These components are either simply natural movements of the members involved,[33] or they have been learned. Since the bits of the activity can be thus explained, there is no need for postulating innate phantasms. What does need explanation is precisely the concatenation, the order of the series of actions.

We know, both by observation and by analogy, that such

---

existed is quite true. But there is also an important difference in doctrines, namely, that concerning the highest sense power. For St. Albert, the highest sense power was the phantasy, cf. above pp. 138-139, 116. In St. Thomas there is no reference to such a doctrine; the estimative is simply the highest sense power; cf. pp. 155, 237-238.

Another important point of difference between the two lies in the relation of the potencies to each other and to the soul. This difference is analyzed by Étienne Gilson, "L'Ame raisonnable chez Albert le Grand," *Archives d'Histoire Doctrinale et Littéraire du Moyen Age*, XVIII (1943), pp. 51-58.

30. *In III Sent.*, d. 26, q. 1, a. 1 [text quoted, p. 159]; *De Veritate*, XXV. 2; XV. 1 [text quoted, ch. 6, notes 59, 60]; *Contra Gentiles*, III. 131; *Commentary on the Ethics*, VI. lect. 7 [quoted pp. 215-16]; *S. T.* I. 78. 4 [pp. 221-223].

31. *S. T.* I-II. 3. 6; II-II. 72. 1 ad 2 and 3; I-II. 40. 3 and ad 1; *Commentary on the Metaphysics*, I, lect. 1, [text. quoted above, p. 206-207].

32. *De Veritate*, XXIV. 1; XXIV. 2 [texts quoted above, ch. 6, notes 63, 64]; *S. T.* I-II. 17. 2 ad 3; 13. 2 ad 2 and 3.

33. St. Thomas had at least a generic knowledge of this; cf. above, note 5.

activities flow from cognition and appetite.[34] Any determinate explanation will therefore have to take account of these two factors.

In its broadest terms, instinctive activity has the same general line of explanation as that of the final causality of inanimate things.[35] Ultimately, all such finality is due to the Divine Intellect.[36] More proximately, it is due to the determinate tendency of the thing itself.[37]

The specific tendency of an animal is precisely the sense appetite. Now, sense appetite is a potency which is put into act by a *known* good.[38] The good to which the animal reacts in instinctive activity is its good as a whole (either as individual or as

---

34. *In III Sent.*, d. 27, q. 1, a. 2 [text quoted above, ch. 6, note 6]; *De Virtutibus in Communi*, q. 1, a. 6[ch. 8, note 35]; *S. T.* I. 83. 1 [p. 235].

35. *De Veritate*, XXIV. 1 [text quoted above, ch. 6, note 63]; *S. T.* I-II. 17. 2 ad 3 [ch. 8, note 19; cf. note 13].

36. *De Veritate*, XXIV. 1 [text quoted above, ch. 6, note 63]; *S. T.* I-II. 40. 3 [ch. 8, note 9], and ad 1.

37. *In II Sent.*, d. 25, q. 1, a. 1 ad 7 [text quoted above, p. 160]; *De Veritate*, XXIV. 2. [ch. 6, note 64]; *ibid.*, XVIII. 7 ad 7 [ch. 6, note 62]; *S. T.* I-II. 3. 6; 172. 1 ad 2 ad 3 [ch. 8, note 13].

In recent years, modern psychologists are again beginning to recognize the importance of appetite or "drive" in the explanation of animal activity. Words like "drive," "trend," "tendency," or "motive" all stress the fact that instinctive activity cannot be considered to be merely a matter of ("speculative") cognition or association.

Dr. Schuetz, in an article, "Die *vis aestimativa* s. *cogitativa* des h. Thomas von Aquin," *Goerres-Gesellschaft zur Pflege der Wissenschaft* (Jahresbericht der Section fuer Philosophie fuer das Jahr 1883, Koeln; J. P. Bachem, 1884), pp. 38-62, thinks he can stop the explanation at the level of determinate appetite. To his mind the estimative and discursive powers are superfluous and self-contradictory. The latter charge will be dealt with below, pp. 287-288 and note 108. The charge that they are unnecessary need not delay us long. Appetite, according to the analysis of St. Thomas, always presupposes a corresponding cognition; cf. among many passages, the one quoted above, pp. 152-153, and the subsequent discussion.

38. *In II Sent.*, d. 20, q. 2 ad 5 [text quoted above, p. 159]; *S. T.* I. 78. 1 and ad 1.

member of a species).[39] Such knowledge is not that of the external senses, and consequently neither that of common sense nor of imagination.[40] There must therefore be a distinct internal sense power, capable of apprehending concrete usefulness and the like.

In the animal, the estimative must be specifically determined by the nature of the animal in question, in order that we may account for the specific "zonal" uniformity of action.[41] In other words, what is innate is precisely the structure of the estimative as a potency.

What is the value of this explanation? It allows for the specific uniformity of animal activity, in that the kind of knowledge of any animal estimative is determined by the nature of that animal. It explains the instinctive "drive" in that the moving force is sensory appetite. It also allows for the experimentally verified plasticity of instinctive activity, in that the external operations are not predetermined, but only the kind of judgment of suitability.

In so far as suitability is a relation, the apprehension of it will vary with the change of either term. Hence, organic conditions and changes in the animal (known by propriosensation), as well as the presence of the right object or its absence (known by external sensation), will account for the actual presence or absence of the estimative judgment.[42]

The instinctive judgment is conserved or stored away in a manner similar to that in which the sensible qualities are conserved in the imagination. This conserving power is called memory, and it is the storehouse of all the intentions not received from external

---

39. *In III Sent.*, d. 26, q. 1, a. 2 [text quoted above, pp. 153-154]; *in II Sent.*, d. 24, q. 2, a. 1 [pp. 154-155]; *S. T.* I. 78. 4 [pp. 221-223].
40. *In III Sent.*, d. 17, q. 1, q. 2 ad 2 [text quoted above, p. 157]; *De Veritate*, XXV. 2 [chapter 6, note 59]; *S. T.* I. 78. 4 [pp. 221-223]; *Q. D. De Anima*, a. 13 [chapter 8, note 1].
41. *De Veritate*, XXIV. 1; XXIV. 2 ad 7 [texts quoted above, ch. 6, notes 63, 65]; *De Virtutibus in Communi*, q. 1, a. 6 [ch. 8, note 35]; *Q. D. De Anima*, a. 13 [ch. 8, note 1].
42. *In III Sent.*, d. 27, q. 1, a. 2 [text quoted above, ch. 6, note 6]; *S. T.* I-II. 9. 3 [ch. 8, note 82].

sense. Among these are the intentions of the estimative and "past-ness" itself.[43]

Are these simply two groups of unrelated knowledge? The fact that they are not is seen in this, that for animals the starting-point of recall and recognition of the past is in many instances evidently an estimative judgment.[44]

Why should this be so? One reason is seen in this, that sense cognition in the last analysis is purely practical. Though all sensation is retained, only that which has practical value can be spontaneously recalled.[45] This can be considered from another point of view. Does not the recognition of the past involve some kind of opposition between knower and known? It seems so; and it seems also that this opposition is presupposed by memory and not set up by it. This implies that the animal must know what it knows as somehow other than itself. Now, the merely relative otherness of suitability, leading to appetite and action, is just within the limits of sensibility.[46] Hence, only an object known in this way (that is, by the estimative) is able to be spontaneously recalled.

Because the estimative is the highest power of the animal, it follows that all purely sense cognition will *ultimately* be practical.[47] In other words, the final limit, the highest type of purely animal

---

43. *S. T.* I. 78. 4 [text quoted above, pp. 221-223].

44. *Ibid.*

45. By spontaneous recall is meant such recall of a given sensible object as takes place in the absence of the same or similar object in external sensation.

46. *Commentary on the De Anima,* II. lect. 13; text quoted and discussed above, pp. 198-200, 201-203.

47. *S. T.* II-II. 167. 2; I. 91. 3 ad 3; I-II. 31. 6 [texts quoted above, ch. 8, note 43].

    Robert S. Woodworth, *Psychology,* p. 368, says that animals have an "exploring drive," "a tendency to get acquainted with the environment." This is an item to be added to the account given by St. Thomas. Yet this does not conflict with the ultimately practical character of animal knowledge; R. S. Woodworth himself suggests that this function takes place in view of future action.

knowledge is the apprehension of the individual in so far as the latter is the term of material action or passion.[48]

Thus, St. Thomas's explanation of instinctive activity by way of the estimative power is exactly on the animal level: namely, in terms of sense cognition and sense appetite.

THE HUMAN ESTIMATIVE

In Avicenna and the authors who follow him, the estimative power is to be found in man as well as in animals. Avicenna does have a passing suggestion that there is a difference between the two cases, but in general he and his followers treat it as one power.[49] On the other hand, Averroes says that man has a *virtus cogitativa* instead of an estimative,[50] and shows that human activity is pre-

---

48. *Commentary on the De Anima*, II, lect 13 [text quoted above, pp. 198-200].

   That there is a level of knowledge of objects which is constituted by the relations of actions and passions, is borne out by a related idea of Heidegger and Sartre. Heidegger says that the "world" comes into being inasmuch as it is a tool or instrument for us (*Sein und Zeit* [Halle: Niemeyer, 5th ed., 1941], pp. 68, 353); Sartre (*L'etre et le néant* [Paris: Gallimard, 1943], p. 680), that we "make" or "create" things. Of course, neither of these thinkers are speaking of sense knowledge as such; but the point they make in their analysis corresponds to the point St. Thomas has made concerning the highest form of sense knowledge as such, and to that extent is an illuminating corroboration.

49. Avicenna does indeed remark that "the powers of man, because of the presence of reason, have something which makes his interior powers different from the powers of an animal," *De Anima*, part *IV, c.* 3 [text quoted above, p. 102]. But this is just a passing remark, and applications are made to imagination, the compositive imagination, and memory. Nothing is said about estimative power. In the followers of Avicenna, such a general remark does not occur, as far as present evidence enables us to judge. Cf. the statements of Algazel, *Metaphysics*, part 2, tract. 4 [text quoted, ch. 3, notes 50-52]; St. Albert, *Libri Tres de Anima*, III, tract. 1, c. 2 [ch. 4, notes 49-50]; *Summa de Homine,* q. 39, a. 2 [ch. 4, note 60].

50. Averroes, *Paraphrasis de Memoria et Reminiscentia* [text quoted above, p. 113]; *Collegit,* II, c. 20 [p. 111]; *Destructio Destructionum,* in physicis, disputatio 2 [pp. 109-110].

ceded by a kind of "parade of images" which might perhaps be called a discursive operation.[51] It is, however, essential to remember that for the Commentator the estimative is really the simple imagination,[52] and the *virtus cogitativa* practically only a composing-and-dividing imagination.[53] As they stand, then, these two doctrines are simply in different orders, without any common ground.

As far as can be judged, the followers of Avicenna likewise held that man has an estimative specifically identical with that of the animal. But since man was also endowed with reason, his estimative power became unimportant, and, once mentioned, was not used in the further explanation of human activity.

St. Thomas here makes a radical departure. Alone among all the Avicennans whose works are at present available, he maintains that in man the estimative power is discursive.[54] His language in places suggests that he derived this idea from Averroes.[55] This relationship needs to be very carefully stated to avoid the danger of both historical and doctrinal errors.[56]

---

51. Averroes, *Commentary on the De Anima,* III, t. c. 57 [text quoted above, p. 119].

52. *Paraphrasis de Memoria et Reminiscentia* [text quoted above, p. 113]; *Commentary on the Posterior Analytics (Post. Resolutor.),* II, c. 11, t. c. 103 [p. 115].

53. *Commentary on the De Anima,* bk. II, t. c. 63 [text quoted above, p. 120] and discussion, pp. 120-122.

54. *S. T.* I. 78. 4 [text quoted above, pp. 221-223], and discussion, pp. 242-247.

55. *In IV Sent.,* d. 50, q. 1, a. 1 ad 3 [text quoted above, p. 165]; *in III Sent.,* d. 23, q. 2, a. 2, q. 1 ad 3 [pp. 162-163]; *De Veritate,* XIV. 1 [pp. 181-182].

56. By "historical mistakes" I mean errors made concerning historical relations, for example, concerning dependence in terminology, doctrine, and so forth. Several different mistakes can be made here. For example, Harry Austryn Wolfson says that St. Thomas's view in *Summa* I. 78. 4 "is also meant by him to represent the view of Averroes," "The Internal Senses in Latin, Arabic, and Hebrew Philosophic Texts," *Harvard Theological Review,* XXVIII (1935), p. 121, note 37; again, on the same page, he says that St. Thomas "takes *cogitativa* in the Averroian sense of reason in man and correlates it with the Avicennian *aestimativa* in animals." But before such conclusions are reached, it should be asked: what was St.

In chapter 7, it was noted that St. Thomas's *Commentaries* frequently follow the order and disposition used by Averroes. At times Aquinas will borrow a happy phrase from his predecessor,

---

Thomas taking from Averroes in this passage? was he writing history here or citing an authority? The textual study made in the course of these chapters shows that *cogitativa* in St. Thomas and Averroes is by no means the same power, even though it has some similar functions in the two cases. If St. Thomas took Averroes's doctrine over without profoundly changing it, this can be said only on the supposition that St. Thomas misread Averroes. This supposition is, I believe, rendered extremely improbable by the critique of Averroes made in the *Summa Contra Gentiles*.

The same mistake is made by G. Quadri, *La philosophie Arabe dans l'Europe médiévale,* tr. by Roland Huret (Paris: Payot, 1947), p. 187, note 3.

A different historical mistake is made by Cornelio Fabro. C. Fabro says: "It is necessary to note, however, that the Latin (Thomistic) theory of the *cogitativa* differs from the Arabic (Averroistic) on two important points: in having freed the *cogitativa* from the connections it had with the controversy about the 'unity' of the separated intellect, and in having raised it above the memory, which for the Arabs was the most noble of the senses," 'Knowledge and Perception in Aristotelic-Thomistic Psychology," *The New Scholasticism,* XII (1938), p. 355, note 31. Such a statement implies that *cogitativa* was the same faculty in the two authors. But if *cogitativa* in St. Thomas is the discursive estimative, and in Averroes is the human compositive imagination (or the human reason, according to Professor Wolfson), then the implication is false. C. Fabro goes on to illustrate St. Thomas's doctrine by quoting Averroes. This of course can be done, provided the one making such a comparison knows what he is doing and allows for the fundamental differences in the two conceptions.

By a mistake in doctrine I mean a philosophical conclusion or interpretation, which, in this case, rests on a supposed historical identity. For example, Cardinal Cajetan, commenting on *Summa Theologiae,* III. 76. 7, interprets St. Thomas's doctrine there by reference to the *De Principio Individuationis* and Averroes (ed. Leon., vol. XII, p. 189). The historical mistake here goes the other way. Cardinal Cajetan interprets St. Thomas as if he were Averroes. One might even hazard a guess that Cardinal Cajetan's preference for the *De Principio Individuationis* as a key text to explain all others rests at least partly on his Averroistic interpretation of St. Thomas in this matter.

or follow his lead in the interpretation of an Aristotelian text.[57]
These dependencies and similarities must be admitted, and St.
Thomas himself was quite ready to acknowledge his indebtedness.

And yet, as was mentioned above, the doctrines of Averroes
and St. Thomas are fundamentally different on our point. In
Averroes, the *virtus cogitativa* is a kind of abstractive and compositive imagination, concerned with the singulars corresponding
to intellectual knowledge (singular substance, singular accidents,
individual substantial differences and so forth).[58] In St. Thomas,

---

57. Cf. discussion, pp. 196-198, 200-202.
58. By reference to the texts presented in parallel columns on pp. 198-200,
the following table of differences is readily drawn up.

AVERROES	ST. THOMAS
1. No relation to the estimative power.	1. The estimative knows the individual as the term of action and passion; the discursive power has a wider extent.
2. Difference between sense and intellect is expressed in terms of universal and particular *only*.	2. (In general: in terms of universal and particular, or: accident and substance or essence) Here: term of action and passion for estimative; individual as standing under a common nature for discursive power.
3. Mode of operation of *cogitativa* is abstraction in a higher degree than that of imagination.	3. Mode of operation of the discursive power is discursive (*collativa*) because of *union* with the intellectual soul.
4. Object of the *cogitativa*: intention of an individual substance, individual substantial differences.	4. Object of the discursive power: the individual as standing under a common nature; this man as this man.
5. *Cogitativa* is the reason for the separated intellect coming into union with man.	5. The estimative becomes the discursive because of union with man's own intellect.

The conclusion is inescapable that the Averroistic and Thomistic
cogitativa are two quite different powers, even though they have
this similarity, that they each have a special ordering to the knowledge of the individual (in all kinds of knowledge for Averroes; in
practical knowledge for St. Thomas).

the *vis cogitativa* is the human estimative, concerned with the singulars of action (*operabilia*) as standing under the intelligible light of reason.[59]

Hence, we must conclude that St. Thomas's notion of a discursive estimative in man had an occasional cause in a passing phrase of Averroes. Apart from this, there is no discernible historical ancestry. Having reached this negative conclusion, we may pass on to consider the Thomistic doctrine in itself.

Man is an animal, and has thus the essentials of sensitive nature in a generic sense.[60] Considered simply in itself, this sense nature has an indetermination, an incompleteness, a potentiality about it. We can see this sense nature, as it were in a kind of pure state, in the very young infant or the complete moron. In these cases, the human estimative manifests itself as a sense power.[61] On this level, the human estimative shows itself to have only a very few innately determined judgments, and even these lead only to a kind of generic activity.[62] The same indeterminate end result can be seen in adults, when sensory reaction escapes the bonds of reason and habit: there is a violent upsurge of activity which is not channelled to a definite result.[63]

Thus, considered in itself, in abstraction from the rest of man, the human estimative is a very imperfect power. But when we consider human sensibility together with its specific difference which is reason, we come to an altogether different result. If, indeed, the human estimative were completely determined in itself, the scope of reason as the supreme immanent guide of human

---

59. See discussion, pp. 202-204, 205-206, 213, 254-257.
60. This is the basis for such discussions of human appetite and "sensuality" which begin by a consideration of animals, for example: *in III Sent.*, d. 26, q. 1, a. 2; *in II Sent.*, d. 24, q. 2, a. 1 [texts quoted above, pp. 152-155]; it is explicitly stated in *in II Sent.*, d. 18, q. 2, a. 3 ad 4 [p. 156] and *S. T.* I. 78. 4 [pp. 221-223], as well as *De Potentia*, III. 11 ad 1 [ch. 6, note 67].
61. *S. T.* I-II. 77. 1 [text quoted above, ch. 8, note 84]; *De Veritate*, 18. 8 and ad 5 [ch. 6, note 66].
62. *S. T.* I. 99. 1 and 101. 2.
63. *S. T.* I-II. 77. 1 [text quoted above, ch. 8, note 84]; 77. 2 [note 78]; 10. 3 [note 80].

life would be limited almost to the vanishing point. But as it is, the guiding influence of reason penetrates into all the innumerable fields of human activity.[64]

The human estimative-under-the-guidance-of-reason receives a special name: it is called the discursive power, *vis cogitativa*.[65] It is important to see just what is being done here. When pure sensibility was under discussion, an analysis was carried on in the light of the formal objects discoverable in animal activity, thereby to arrive at the number and kind of internal powers.[66] By this method we arrived at an ordered multiplicity of such powers.[67]

This method carries us only a certain distance in the investigation of human sensibility and its operations. If we look at perception only from the formal point of view, if we consider it as composed of a number of coexisting, distinct operations, difficulties arise. First of all, we thereby miss the given unity of perception.[68] Secondly, there are areas which simply will not handle in this fashion. If, for example, the axe and the woodcutter are considered separately, there is no possibility of understanding how a tree is chopped down. The blended operation of the principal and the instrumental cause partakes of the nature of both, and yet it is not two separate operations occurring at the same time.[69]

This problem can be stated from a different point of view. If we were to extract a definition of the discursive sense, for example, in terms of its supposed formal object, it would probably be worded something like this: "the suitable (and the unsuitable) known through a comparison." Now, St. Thomas has expressed himself very clearly; he says that a potency is specified by the *ratio* of

---

64. Especially *De Virtutibus in Communi,* q. I, a. 6 [text quoted above, ch. 8, note 35].

    Modern experimentalists stress the peculiar character of "instinct" in man, which is such that every activity of man is partly unlearned and partly learned; cf. Robert S. Woodworth, *Psychology,* p. 371.
65. On the meaning of this term, see *in III Sent.,* d. 23, q. 2, a. 2, q. 1 ad 3 [text quoted above, pp. 162-163] and the discussion, pp. 163-164.
66. *S. T.* I. 77. 3; *Q. D. De Anima,* a. 13.
67. *S. T.* I. 77. 5, 6, 8; and the discussion, pp. 170-172.
68. Discussion, pp. 164-170.
69. *S. T.* I. 45. 5; III. 19. 1; 62. 4 ad 2.

its object (by its object precisely and essentially as such).[70] The supposed formal object mentioned above is partly a designation of the object, partly an indication of the way in which the potency acts. The definition is accurate enough, but it is not a definition in terms of formal object.

No, the unity of the adult's apprehension of the sensible good, the indefinite variability of that act, its being penetrated with reason (not always, unfortunately, *right* reason), can be adequately explained from the dynamic point of view alone. Human instinctive activity is the activity of sensibility-under-the-influence-of-reason.[71]

Not all the powers of the sensitive part of the soul are under the guidance of reason. The external senses and common sense receive no direct influence from reason.[72] (Voluntarily acquired keenness of observation is apparently a function of "attention.") Imagination does come under the influence of reason, as Aristotle already noted.[73] Yet, as St. Thomas points out, this influence does not result in a radically different kind of operation.[74] There is simply question of joining or separating images *ad libitum,* and the imagination by itself can combine them according to the laws of association.

But in respect of the estimative and memorative powers the guidance of reason results in a radically different type of activity. Animal estimative and animal memory are characterized by the immediacy of their operation, by uniformity, and by limitation.[75]

---

70. *S. T.* I. 59. 4; 77. 3.
71. Discussion, pp. 172, 247 and notes 53-56.
72. *S. T.* I-II. 50. 3 ad 3 [text quoted above, ch. 8, note 60].
73. Cf. *De Anima,* III, c. 10, 433b29-30.
74. *S. T.* I. 78. 4 [text quoted above, pp. 221-223].
75. (a) Texts on immediacy:

> *S. T.* I. 83. 1 [text quoted above, ch. 8, p. 235];
> *De Veritate* XXIV. 2 [ch. 6, note 64].

    (b) Uniformity:

> *S. T.* I-II. 50, 3 [ch. 8, note 61]; *Commentary on the Physics,* II, lect. 13 [ch. 7, note 33]; *in II Sent.,* d. 25, q. 1, a. 1 ad 7 [p. 160].

    (c) Limitation:

> *Q. D. De Virtutibus in Communi,* q. I, a. 6 [text quoted above,

The discursive sense and reminiscence, on the contrary, are characterized by their quasi-syllogistic processes, their flexibility, their almost limitless applicability.[76]

The very characteristics of the activity of the discursive power and of reminiscence show that they are composite operations. Intellect is the moving or principal cause, and its share (namely, the *order* of the process) is the formal part of the operation. The discursive power (and reminiscence, *a pari*) is that which is moved, the instrument; and its share (the sensory characteristics) is the material part of the operation.

Because of this radical dependence of the discursive sense upon reason it is possible that habits be developed in it. But because these habits are complementary to certain intellectual habits, they are best considered from the point of view of the latter.[77]

There remains one consideration of the function of the discursive sense in the sensory order: the relation between it and memory. We have seen above that the operation of the estimative is the condition of spontaneous recall in the sense order. So, too, in human sensibility, the operation of the discursive sense is required. But since the discursive sense is open to the guidance of reason so that its object extends to the whole field of concrete suitability, so the range of human sense memory extends, at least potentially, to all material objects and all knowledge of them. The significance of this conclusion will become apparent later.

---

ch. 8, note 35]; *S. T.* I-II. 13. 2 ad 2, 15. 2 [ch. 8, note 16]; I. 82. 2 ad 3 [ch. 8, note 17]; *De Veritate* XXIV. 1 [ch. 6, note 63]. On these three characteristics of "instinct," excellent examples and brief summaries can be found in the work of Mark Gaffney, *The Psychology of the Interior Senses,* already referred to.

76. Most of the references in note 75 also treat of the contrasting characteristics of human knowledge. In addition, cf. *Commentary on the De Anima,* II, lect. 13, text and discussion, pp. 198-200, 200-202; *S. T.* I-II. 9. 1 [ch. 8, note 48], 51. 3 [note 62], 56. 5 [note 64].

77. A point that needs to be developed is the relation of the discursive power to the moral virtues. The proper context for such a discussion would be that of the relation of prudence to those virtues.

REASON AND THE DISCURSIVE POWER

So far we have been considering the way in which the human estimative is completed even in its own order by the guidance of reason. The question that will now interest us is that of the opposite relation. Is the operation of reason or intellect completed in any way by that of the discursive power?

Here the historical situation is a bit clearer. There are, as we have seen, several indications in Aristotle. In the *De Anima*, we read that the universal reason (or proposition, opinion) does not lead to action without the particular,[78] and that appetite does not occur without imagination.[79] In the *Ethics*, he tells us that a part of the soul, which is not the speculative part, but rather the "reasonable" (λογιστικόν), is concerned with operable things,[80] and that the virtue of this part, prudence, is in sense.[81] Whatever may be the precise import of these various propositions, their general bearing is clear. Aristotle means that intellect as such does not lead to action, but that the conjunction of sense is somehow required.

According to Averroes, intellect does not seem to lead to action at all. The whole process is a purely sensory one. Deliberation consists in a parade of images; choice in this, that one of these images affects the sense appetite.[82]

In a quite different context and for quite different reasons, an analogous situation arises in the later Augustinians. According to them, the soul is somehow one in itself, in its powers, and in its operations.[83] Why then does one act of knowledge differ so noticeably from another? The reason for these differences lies in

---

78. Aristotle, *De Anima*, III, c. 11, 434a15-20; cf. discussion, pp. 33-34.
79. *De Anima*, III, c. 10; 433b29-30.
80. *Ethics*, VI, c. 1, 1113a13-16; cf. p. 34.
81. *Ethics*, VI, c. 11, 1143b.
82. *Commentary on the De Anima*, t. c. 57 [text quoted above, p. 119] and discussion, pp. 119-120.
83. Claudianus Mamertus, *De Statu Animae*, I, c. 24 [text quoted above, ch. 2, notes 71-73]; *De Spiritu et Anima*, c. 4; Isaac of Stella, *Epistola ad Alcherum de Anima* [ch. 2, note 95]; John of Salisbury, *De Septem Septenis*, section 4 [text quoted above, ch. 2, note 113].

this, that the soul uses different instruments to produce different kinds of knowledge.[84] A more subtle instrument will account for a clearer, more perfect type of knowledge. The particular applications of this principle do not interest us here, but the principle itself needs to be kept in mind.

Let us look at the Aristotelian problem. The practical principles of reason itself deal with the universal.[85] These universal objects are outside the field of operation — they are abstracted from space and time, immobile in themselves. "Children must honor their parents," says the universal reason. This proposition is universal and necessary, and as such it cannot immediately lead to operation, which is always in the realm of the particular.[86] Yet a transition must be made, if reason is to be the guide of human action.[87]

The discursive power stands ready to hand. Its field is precisely the concrete particular, the *bonum sensibile*. Seeing the particular good in the apprehension of the discursive power, reason can relate it to its own universal apprehensions. It can then draw the conclusion: "This good thing is to be done thus and so."[88] This proposition, as conclusion, is both permeated with the intel-

---

84. John of Salisbury, *De Septem Septenis,* section 4, [text quoted above, ch. 2, notes 114-115]. Thierry of Chartres, *Librum Hunc* [ch. 2, note 118]. Clarenbaldus of Arras, *Commentary on Boethius's De Trinitate* [ch. 2, note 120]. Alfred of Sareshel, *De Motu Cordis,* c. 2, 10 [ch. 2, notes 123-125]. William of St. Thierry, *De Natura Corporis et Animae* [ch. 2, note 131]. Richard of St. Victor, *Benjamin Minor,* c. 18 [ch. 2, note 148]. St. Bonaventure, *in II Sent.,* d. 25, p. 2, q. 6.

85. *In II De Anima,* lect. 16 [text quoted above, ch. 7, note 26]; *In Ethic.,* VI, lect. 2, [p. 213]; *S. T.* II-II. 47. 1 [ch. 8, note 72]; I-II. 77. 2 ad 1 [note 74].

86. *In Ethic.,* VI, lect 7 [text quoted above, pp. 215-216]; VII, lect. 3 [pp. 218-219]; *S. T.* II-II. 47. 3 [ch. 8, note 73].

87. *De Veritate,* X. 5 and ad 2 and 4; X. 2 ad 4 [text quoted above, ch. 6, note 56 and pp. 206-207]; *Contra Gentiles* II. 60; III. 26, 37; *In I Metaphys.,* lect. 1 [p. 207].

88. *In Ethic.,* VI, lect. 7 [text quoted above, pp. 215-216]; lect. 9, [pp. 217-218]; VII, lect. 3 [p. 218]; *S. T.* II-II. 47. 3 and ad obj. [ch. 8, note 73]; *De Veritate* X. 5 [ch. 6. pp. 176-177].

ligibility of reason, and limited by the particularity of sense. It is further an object which can be chosen by the will, desired by the sense appetite, and carried into execution in the physical world.

This analysis is an essential prerequisite for the proper understanding of the will and its functions, from the viewpoint of psychology as well as that of ethics.

Presented only in the general terms of the summary given above, the solution of St. Thomas seems to raise as difficult a question as the one it answers. Granted that by a conjunction of intellect and sense the singular is understood, just what is this conjunction, and how does it take place?

Fundamentally, both intellect and sense are powers of one and the same man.[89] Furthermore, both these powers flow from one and the same rational soul, in such a way that in the order of form and perfection intellect is prior to sense, and is the ultimate reason for sense.[90] Thirdly, they form a kind of unity, in so far as both are analogously cognitive powers.[91] Fourthly, they stand in multiple dynamic relations.[92]

The first dynamic relation between intellect and sense consists in this, that the intellect receives from the interior senses the forms which put it into act.[93] The second, known variously as "contact" or "reflection," is that operative relation wherein intellect is as principal cause and formal component, and the interior sense is as instrument and material component.[94] The third is the situation where the intellect is as mover, and the interior sense is as the thing moved.[95]

With regard to intellect and the discursive power, these relations work out something like this. First, the intellect receives from

---

89. *S. T.* I. 76. 1; 79. 4.
90. *S. T.* I. 77. 5, 6. 7.
91. Discussion, p. 172.
92. Discussion, pp. 167-169; *De Veritate* X. 5 [text quoted above, pp. 176-177].
93. *S. T.* I. 84. 6; 86. 1.
94. *De Veritate* X. 5 ad 3 [text quoted above, ch. 6, note 57]; II. 6 and ad 3; discussion, pp. 172-173.
95. *S. T.* I-II. 50. 3 and ad 2 and 3 [texts quoted above, ch. 8, notes 55-58, 70, 61].

estimative-and-imagination the conjoined sensible form-and-knowl-
edge of sensible goods which the estimative apprehends of itself.[96]
Secondly, under the guidance of reason (the mover-moved relation), the discursive power constructs in the imagination the images
of those sensible objects or acts which are to be made or done in
accord with the universal principles of reason.[97] Thirdly (and as
far as time is concerned, simultaneously with the second), the
reason, standing to the discursive power as principal cause to instrument and as form to matter, knows the operable throughout
its construction and in its finished state of image.[98]

PRUDENCE

    In this way it is possible to come to a practical conclusion
which is illumined by reason. But this is a difficult and time-
consuming process. Men simply cannot afford to repeat the same
process every time it is needed, and fortunately this is not necessary, because potencies can be determined toward specific objects
by way of habits.[99]
    Of all natural habits, surely the most important is that of
prudence, for it is the habit of right judgment concerning means
to our end.[100] Prudence is developed by repeated right judgments
made in particular instances.[101]
    We have just seen that practical reason must be dynamically
joined with the discursive power in order to be an adequate source
of action. Thus, too, with respect to the habit: corresponding to
prudence strictly so called, which is in the intellect,[102] there is a

---

96. *S. T.* I-II. 77. 1 [text quoted above, ch. 8, note 84].
97. *S. T.* I. 81. 3 [text quoted above, ch. 8, note 70]. Cf. "In specula-
    tivis scientiis nihil aliud quaeritur quam cognitio generis subiecti;
    in practicis autem scientiis intenditur quasi finis constructio ipsius
    subiecti," *In Posteriora Analytica,* I. lect. 41, no. 7, ed. Leon., vol.
    I. p. 305.
98. Discussion, pp. 192, 248-254.
99. *S. T.* I-II. 49. 3, 4.
100. *S. T.* I-II. 57. 4 and ad 3.
101. *S. T* II-II. 47. 15, 16.
102. *S. T.* II-II. 57. 4; 47. 1, 2; *In Ethic.,* VI, lect. 4. [text quoted above,
    ch. 7, note 50].

disposition of interior sense.[103]

Taken by itself, prudence as a virtue of reason is incapable of moving to action. A man who possessed only this much would indeed be able to give prudent advice, but would not be able to act prudently himself.

The disposition of the internal sense (which in this case comprises both the discursive power and memory[104]) is then no neglible part of prudence. The existence and importance of this complementary part of prudence can be seen from the following fact. Just as an act of intellectual knowledge can be interfered with by a bodily lesion or a bodily indisposition, so too a whole science or art can be made inoperative in the same way.[105] And if the use of such a science or art can be rapidly re-acquired, this strengthens the conclusion that it is principally and formally in the intellect, materially and dispositively in the internal sense.[106]

PREPARATION OF PHANTASMS: *I*

So far we have been dealing with what might well be called the simple relations between the reason and the discursive sense. The points that remain for discussion are both more subtle and less fully developed. Thus, the preparation of phantasms is barely more than mentioned.[107]

It has been alleged that this function of the discursive power

---

103. *In Ethic.,* VI, lect. 7 [text quoted above, pp. 215-216]; lect 9 [pp. 217-218]; *S.T.* II-II. 47. 3 [ch. 8, note 73]; 49. 2 ad 3 [note 75].

104. *S.T.* II-II. 47. 3 ad 3 [text quoted above, ch. 8, note 78].

105. *S.T.* I-II. 77. 2 [text quoted above, ch. 8, note 78].

In virtue of such facts, together with other experiments, modern scientists have succeeded in localizing the sensory and motor areas of the brain; cf. Robert S. Woodworth, *Psychology,* pp. 259-74; see also Ch. Journet "Les maladies de sens internes," *Revue Thomiste,* XXIX (1924), 35-50.

106. *S.T.* I. 89. 5 [text quoted above, ch. 8, note 67]; I-II. 67. 2 [note 68].

107. *S.T.* I-II. 50. 4 ad 3 [text quoted above, ch. 8, note 66]; *Contra Gentiles* II. 80, 81 (texts quoted pp. 188-189].

is incompatible with the one just spoken of.[108] This is true if the
two functions are conceived of as designating formal objects. Otherwise there is no *a priori* difficulty. Thus, the imagination retains
the images of sense, and presents them to intellect. There is no
conflict between these two functions, for the latter derives from
the former. If a similar case can be discovered in the preparation
of phantasms by the discursive power, the difficulty falls to the
ground.

The discursive power discovers sensible good or evil under
the guidance of reason. Precisely in doing this, it presents to reason
the material for the particular premise of the practical syllogism.
In other words, the discursive power prepares phantasms of operables for the practical intellect.

We have also seen that memory on the sense level involves
a preceding judgment of the estimative or discursive sense. Now,
some phantasms need, in their preparation, the action of memory
formally so called. In this way, too, the discursive power prepares phantasms for the intellect.

Does the action of the discursive power concern all phantasms without exception? To answer this question, it is necessary
to consider an even more subtle point, namely, attention.

ATTENTION

The easiest way to see how attention works is to consider
what may be called extreme cases, where the facts will stand out.
Thus, passion can blind reason.[109] Where passion is intensely fixed
on one object, other objects cannot come into sensory awareness.
Now, passion is an act of the sense appetite, and so depends on

---

108. Dr. Schuetz, "Die *vis aestimativa* s. *cogitativa* des h. Thomas von
Aquin," pp. 45-49.
109. *S. T.* I-II. 77. 2; 9. 3; 77. 1 [texts quoted above, ch. 8, notes 78,
82, 85].
On facts uncovered by modern workers in this field, cf. Edmund
S. Conklin, *Principles of Abnormal Psychology* (New York: Holt,
1927), p. 63.

a judgment of common sense or of the estimative and discursive power.[110]

It is obvious that in man there will be two levels of attention. Voluntary attention will not be considered here; the attention we are concerned with is on the level of internal sensation.

To a certain extent, attention on this level is object-determined.[111] In the first instance, this is necessarily so, since there is nothing in internal sense except what has come through the external senses. But once experience has been garnered in the storehouses of imagination and memory, the possibility arises that a phantasm can evoke the judgment of the estimative, and conversely that an intention of the memory can arouse a phantasm.[112]

The tendency of a man or animal is limited. When one object is intensively attended to, there is nothing left for others which may perchance strike the external senses, or be sought for by reason.[113] When the whole tendency is not thus concentrated, other objects of imagination or sense can also be attended to.

Intellectual operations, particularly reasonings, are not instantaneous; they have a duration. Thus it is necessary that a phantasm remain in sensory awareness for at least a minimal time, if the intellect is to grasp anything at all.

The laws of the imagination are of themselves laws concerned with the flux of images.[114] The very definition of phantasm proposed by Aristotle and expressed by St. Thomas in these words: "a motion caused by sense in act,"[115] implies that images are of themselves unstable. It seems therefore that imagination by it-

---

110. *S. T.* I. 81. 3 [text quoted above, ch. 8, note 70]; *in III Sent.*, d. 26, q. 1, a. 2; *in II Sent.*, 24, q. 2, a. 1 [pp. 152-154].

111. *In III Sent.*, d. 27, q. 1, a. 2 [text quoted above, ch. 6, note 6].

On the varieties of attention, and the factors involved in them, cf. Robert S. Woodworth, *Psychology*, pp. 50-51, T. Bartolomei, O.S.M. "L'Attenzione sensitiva," *Divus Thomas* (Placentiae) XLVII-XLIX (1944-1946), pp. 8-10.

112. *S. T.* I. 78. 4 [text quoted above, pp. 221-223].

113. *S. T.* I-II. 77. 2 [text quoted above, ch. 8, note 78].

114. *Commentary on De Memoria et Reminiscentia*, lect. 5.

115. *In III De Anima*, lect. 6, ed. Angelo Pirotta, O.P., (Rome, Marietti, 1924), no. 659, quoting Aristotle, *De Anima*, III, ch. 3, 429a1-2.

self can account for images being in motion, but not for their being at rest.

On the other hand, the thing that is loved tends to remain in the actual apprehension of the lover.[116] It seems reasonable to extend this doctrine to all the acts of the sensory appetite, particularly as the same effect is at times ascribed to anger.[117]

Attention, therefore, in the sensory order is a function of sense appetite, which is determined by the judgments of the estimative or discursive power. In man, the discursive power is of its nature subject to reason and will. Voluntary attention on the sense level is thus brought about in that reason and will direct the discursive power in its judgments.

PREPARATION OF PHANTASMS: *II*

Some degree of attention is necessary in order that the intellect be able to work at all. This must then be true as well of the phantasms leading to speculative knowledge as of others. It follows therefore that the discursive power (or, in the first instance, the estimative) is concerned in the preparation of all phantasms for the intellect.[118]

As far as practical knowledge is concerned, we have seen that this function derives easily and naturally from the proper act of the discursive sense. How does this sense prepare phantasms for speculative knowledge? There is obviously a difference in this that the objects of practical knowledge are more or less immediately sensible goods. The same cannot be said for the objects of speculative knowledge.

Mathematics, for example, in itself is a speculative knowl-

116. *S. T.* I-II. 28. 1-3; II-II. 173. 3 ad 2; 175. 2.
117. *S. T.* I-II. 77. 2 [text quoted above, ch. 8, note 78]; I-II. 10. 3 [ch. 8, note 80]; cf. 'Manifestum est quod delectatio applicat intentionem ad ea in quibus aliquis delectatur; unde Philosophus dicit in X *Ethic* [1175a30] quod unusquisque ea in quibus delectatur optime operatur, contraria vero nequamquam vel debiliter," II-II. 15. 3, ed. Leon., vol. VIII, p. 120.
118. This seems to be what is meant in *in IV Sent.,* d. 50, q. 1, a. 1, ad 3 [text quoted above, p. 161].

edge. It deals with abstractions which neither exist as such nor are good as such. What is there here for the discursive sense to grasp?

The experience of all teachers comes to our rescue. They have found that interest is the key to all learning. But fundamentally there are two kinds of interest. There is interest which flows immediately from the object, because it is known to be sensibly good or useful. There is another form of interest, whose source is interior; it consists in this, that the knowledge of an object which as such is outside the field of value is looked on as the good and perfection of the knower.[119]

---

119. Modern experimentalists have devoted a great deal of their investigations to the learning process, yet have not succeeded in arriving at a universally accepted theory; cf. Robert S. Woodworth, *Psychology,* p. 318. Nevertheless, several conclusions pertinent here seem to be well established.

(1) Learning is of two kinds: affective and intellectual, cf. Harold S. Tuttle, "Two Kinds of Learning," *Journal of Psychology,* XXII (1946), pp. 267-77.

(2) "Value-judgments" and general opinions vary according to various emotions and general attitudes; cf. Selden C. Menefee and Audrey G. Granneberg, "Propaganda and Opinions on Foreign Policy," *Journal of Social Psychology,* XI (1940), p. 404; S. E. Asch, "Studies in the Principles of Judgments and Attitudes: II. Determination of Judgments by Group and by Ego Standards," *ibid.,* XII (1940), p. 463; Allan L. Edwards, "Studies of Stereotypes: I. The Directionality and Uniformity of Responses to Stereotypes," *ibid.,* p. 365.

(3) In all learning, reward and punishment (taken in a very general sense) are real partial factors; cf. Robert S. Woodworth, *Psychology,* p. 319; John A. McGeoch, *The Psychology of Human Learning* (New York: Longmans, 1942), p. 528; there is also an interesting article on the influence of attitudes like that of confidence; cf. Robert L. Thorndike, "The effect of discussion upon the correctness of group decisions, when the factor of majority influence is allowed for," *Journal of Social Psychology,* IX (1938), pp. 358-60.

(4) Motives or incentives act by orienting or directing perception, cf. John A. McGeoch, *The Psychology of Human Learning,* p. 282.

In this way the preparation of phantasms for speculative knowledge falls within the scope of the discursive power.[120] But

---

(5) Acts of appetite can act as standards, defining the satisfactoriness of responses, cf. John A. McGeoch, *The Psychology of Human Learning,* pp. 284-85; this can influence learning by way of the so-called "law of effect," so that desirable or indifferent acts become fixed as habits, while acts which arouse opposition are eliminated, cf. *ibid.,* p. 574.

Approximately the same doctrine is expressed by the psychoanalysts, when they say that repression and memory are functions of the unconscious (that is, of hidden drives, instincts, wishes); cf. James Grier Miller, *Unconsciousness* (New York: Wiley, 1942), pp. 234-35.

More detailed references on the points raised in this and the following note can be found in "The Psychologists and the Nature of Man," *Proceedings of the American Catholic Philosophical Association,* XXV (1951), 66-88.

120. A counter-proof of all this is afforded by some facts of abnormal psychology. For example, distortion of thought can occur under the influence of a particular emotion, cf. Edmund S. Conklin, *Principles of Abnormal Psychology* (New York: Holt, 1927), p. 63. Some peculiarities of behavior are found to depend on some highly emotional past experience, *ibid.,* pp. 65-66. Self-deception (that is, ignorance of one's own character) correlates with bad social adjustment, cf. Else Frenkel-Brunswik, "Mechanisms of Self-Deception," *Journal of Social Psychology,* X (1939), p. 419.

Dr. Sigmund Freud put clinical data into relation with the facts of memory, of association by unconscious links, and with the phenomena of post-hypnotic suggestion; cf. his paper, "The Unconscious," *Collected Papers,* authorized translaton under supervision of Joan Riviere (London: The International Psychoanalytic Press, 1924-1925: 4 vols.), vol. IV, p. 101. On the basis of these juxta-posed facts, he considered his assumption of the unconscious both legitimate and necessary, *ibid.,* p. 99. The kernel of this system "Ucs" consists of instinct-presentations, *ibid.,* pp. 118-19; its nucleus is something analogous to animal instinct, *ibid.,* p. 127. In man, this "Ucs" is capable of development; it acts on the preconscious and can be acted upon by the latter, *ibid.,* p. 122, and even by the conscious system, *ibid.,* p. 126.

These remarks are not intended as a blanket approval of psychoanalysis; even as psychology, this system is affected by a strange dualism, (cf. S. Freud's expression of this in "The Unconscious," *ed. cit.,* p. 107), and is encumbered with a whole family of reified

· let us note that it cannot fall within the scope of the estimative as such.

KNOWLEDGE OF THE MATERIAL SINGULAR

Knowledge of the material singular in the practical order depends on the discursive power in four ways: (1) in so far as that object involves something to be done, the discursive power apprehends the concrete operability and similar intentions; (2) that power directs attention; (3) and grounds the operation of memory; (4) and, in so far as judgment is concerned, it deals with the concrete elements of time and motion involved in every verb.[121] Knowledge of the material singular in the speculative order depends on the discursive power only in the last three ways. The first function (of materially limiting and particularizing universal knowledge) in the speculative knowledge of the material singular is replaced by the act of the imagination.

THE DISCURSIVE POWER AND THE GRASP OF EXISTENCE

In the preceding sections the letter of St. Thomas has become progressively less explicit. At this point no formal statement has been found. Yet the problem of the relation of the discursive power to the knowledge of existence is not devoid of interest, and is capable of at least a tentative solution in the light of other explicit teachings.

---

functions (cf. Rudolf Allers, *The Successful Error* [New York: Sheed and Ward, 1940]).

In less controversial terms, this doctrine says that there are in man unlearned drives which react with his cognitive powers. Ideally, these drives should be guided and developed by reason; in fact, they can be developed by unreasonable habits; when this second type of "habit" is in conflict with the real environment and at the same time strong enough to initiate and control external activity, a state of mental abnormality has been reached. Instead of the division of psychic activities into conscious and unconscious, it may be more advantageous to use the concept of many levels of consciousness which do not always intercommunicate; cf. Joseph Nuttin, *Psychanalyse et Conception Spiritualiste de l'Homme* (Louvain: Publications Universitaires, 1950), pp. 270-75.

121. See discussion, p. 204, and ch. 7, note 30.

The problem is surrounded by a number of points which are very clear in St.Thomas's doctrine. No sense, external or internal, can itself grasp existence; this is a function of intellectual judgment. On the other hand, existence cannot be grasped apart from actual sensation. Thirdly, the judgment that any thing exists is grounded on experience, either mediately or immediately, and if the former is the case, is grounded on experience either through memory or through reasoning. Again, only particulars exist. Finally, the existence we know directly is that of material things in space and time, and therefore in motion.

These are the clues. We have seen that in the animal, and in man as well before the awakening of his intellect, the individual is known to be such only in terms of activity and passion. We have also seen that this apprehension is due to the estimative. We can therefore conclude that the first judgment of existence requires, as a necessary antecedent condition, the judgment of the estimative.

What about later judgments of existence? It would seem that the discursive power functions here as giving the subjective unity of perception by way of interest and attention, as well as bearing on the verb, in so far as action, time, and motion are concerned.

CONCLUSIONS

Etienne Gilson, referring briefly to the internal senses and especially the discursive sense, says very justly:

> Ce qui nous importe, c'est le fait lui-même : l'osmose qui se produit entre l'entendement et la sensibilité dans l'unité du sujet connaissant humain.[122]

St. Thomas, as we all know, considers it of primary importance to maintain inviolate the substantial unity of man. This study of the discursive power shows that he is also concerned with maintaining the dynamic unity of human perception. The position is a subtle blend of analytic distinctness and synthetic unity. The very words

---

122. Étienne Gilson, *Réalisme Thomiste et Critique de la Connaissance* (Paris: Vrin, 1939), p. 207.

he uses as names of the discursive sense expresses "la communication de fonctions distinctes dans l'unité d'un meme sujet."[123]

The same truth can be put from another point of view. St. Thomas is vividly aware of the full implications of the phrase "human sensibility." So too he is aware of the full implications of the term "human knowledge." Human knowledge is not one simple thing; it is analogously one, at the same time one and many. The unity of human knowing is a unity of order, a dynamic unity, in which many distinct faculties work together.

Analysis shows us that there are ten distinct powers of knowing, and three appetites. If these thirteen powers are looked on as if they were so many material organs, the merely material multiplicity would be irreducible. But through the cooperation of powers which stand in multiple relations of order to each other, man experiences that unique and complex unity known as human perception.

Man is a rational animal. Because in him intellect is not self-sufficient for knowing, but needs the body and the sense powers, the human intellect is characterized as *reason;* in other words, as an intellect whose specific trait it is to come to know through a process involving a multiplicity of terms.[124] In St. Thomas's profoundly synthetic view, this same trait of working through a discursive process affects even human sensibility. So much is this true, that man's highest sense power is called, by a significant appropriation of language, the discursive power.

---

123. *Ibid.*
124. *S. T.* I. 58. 4; 85. 5.

APPENDIX I

THE *DE PRINCIPIO INDIVIDUATIONIS*

An *opusculum* with this name is found among the printed works of St. Thomas. According to P. Mandonnet[1] and Roland-Gosselin,[2] this is a spurious work; according to M. Grabmann,[3] it is authentic. It contains a very short paragraph on the *ratio particularis*. We will give the text from the Parma edition, inserting in brackets the variant readings according to the text established by J. Perrier, O.P.[4]

> Quidditas autem rei particularis in particulari non spectat ut per se objectum ad illos [istos] sensus exteriores, cum quidditas ista [ipsa quidditas] substantia sit et non accidens, nec ad intellectum pertinet ut per se objectum ejus propter suam materialitatem. Ideo quidditas rei materialis in ipsa sua particularitate est objectum rationis particularis, cujus est conferre de intentionibus particularibus, loco cujus in brutis aestimativa naturalis est; quae [Haec enim] potentia per [propter] sui conjunctionem cum intellectu, ubi est ratio ipsa quae confert de universalibus, participat vim collativam; sed quia pars sensitivae est, non abstrahit omnino a materia. Unde objectum suum proprium manet quidditas [rei] particularis materialis. Illud ergo quod cadit sub ratione particulari, est hoc aliquid per naturam materiae; quod

1. Pierre Mandonnet, O.P., *Des Ecrits Authentiques de S. Thomas d'Aquin,* 2ème ed. (Fribourg: L'Oeuvre de Saint-Paul, 1910), p. 151, no. 104; *idem, Opuscula* (Paris: Lethielleux, 1927: 5 vols.), V, pp. 193-96.
2. M. D. Roland-Gosselin, O.P., *Le "De Ente et essentia de s. Thomas d'Aquin* (Kain: Le Saulchoir, 1926), pp. 132-34.
3. Martin Grabmann, *Die Werke des heiligen Thomas von Aquin* (Beitraege, Baeumker, Muenster: Aschendorff, 1931, Band XX, Heft 1-2), pp. 301-02. It is to be noted, however, that this work is treated as one of a group of *opuscula* whose authenticity is established as a group. In the third edition (1949), p. 342, Msgr. Grabmann takes the same stand.
4. *Opuscula Omnia necnon Opera Minora,* ed. J. Perrier, O.P., vol. I, *Opuscula Philosophica* (Paris: Lethielleux, 1949).

autem cadit sub sensu exteriori est per quantitatem. [*whole last sentence omitted*].⁵

As far as terminology is concerned, the older reading contains some expressions not usual to St. Thomas. The doctrine of the passage has some similarities to that of his *Commentary on the De Anima.* More striking similarities exist between the quoted passage and the doctrine of Averroes, in as much as both talk about singular *substance.*

Cardinal Cajetan, who does not question the authenticity of the *opusculum,* felt it necessary to reconcile its doctrine with that of *Summa Theologiae* III. 76. 7.⁶ This article of St. Thomas clearly says that substance can be apprehended by the intellect alone. Cardinal Cajetan distinguishes: substance, even singular substance, as having the mode of being of substance, is apprehended by intellect alone; singular substance according to quantified matter is known by the *vis cogitativa.*

It must be granted that St. Thomas very often does distinguish sense from intellect by saying that the former is of singulars, while the latter is of universals.⁷ But even here there is not a mere difference of extension; the universal known by intellect is not merely a sum of particulars; it is that which is known to be *per se.*⁸ Moreover, St. Thomas assigns other differences: sense is

---

5. Ch. 2, ed. Parma, XVI, p. 529; ed. Perrier, p. 575.
6. Cf. "Substantiam particularem percipi a cogitativa, hic vero dicit a solo intellectu substantiam cognosci. Nec loquitur de substantia in communi, sed de substantia singulari. . . . Utrumque siquidem est verum: illud quidem de substantia individuali secundum materiam signatam quantitate; hoc autem de substantia ut habet modum essendi purae substantiae," *In tertiam partem Summae,* q. 76, a. 7, ed. Leon., XII, p. 189.
7. Cf. among many passages, *S. T.* I. 59. 1 ad 1; 80. 2, obj. 2; 85. 3; *Contra Gentiles,* I. 44.
8. Cf. "sensus est singularium, scientia autem consistit in hoc quod universale cognoscimus. . . . Ponamus ergo quod aliquis esset in ipsa luna . . . , sed non propter hoc sciret totaliter causam eclipsis. Illud enim est per se causa eclipsis, quod causat universaliter eclipsim," *In Posteriora Analytica,* bk. I, lect. 42, no. 7, ed. Leon., I, p. 312.

of the external accidents, while intellect penetrates to the interior of a thing, and attains the essence.[9]

These differences are not adequately taken care of by what is said in the *De Principio Individuationis*. Consequently, on internal criteria of terminology and doctrine, the work does not seem to be authentic.[10]

However, internal arguments of this nature are not decisive. Considering the present state of our knowledge, we can only conclude that the work is doubtfully authentic.[11] If it would be proved to be authentic, it should then be considered as an experiment of St. Thomas's in the direction of Averroes; as a temporary adoption of a doctrine which he does not hold in any other work.

---

9. Cf. "Intimior quidem est [coniunctio]; quia sensus sistit circa exteriora accidentia rei; intellectus vero penetrat usque ad rei essentiam; obiectum enim intellectus est quod quid est," *S. T.* I-II. 31. 5, ed. Leon., VI, p. 219; "Ad secundum dicendum quod sensus non apprehendit essentias rerum, sed exteriora accidentia tantum. Similiter neque imaginatio, sed apprehendit solas similitudines corporum. Intellectus autem solus apprehendit essentias rerum. Unde in 3. *De Anima* [430b28] dicitur quod obiectum intellectus est quod quid est," I. 57. 1 ad 2, ed. Leon, V, p. 69; "Sensus autem non cognoscit esse nisi sub hic et hunc, sed intellectus apprehendit esse absolute, et secundum omne tempus," I, 75. 6, V, p. 204; "Nulla virtus cognoscitiva cognoscit rem aliquam nisi secundum rationem proprii obiecti: non enim visu cognoscimus nisi inquantum est coloratum," *Contra Gentiles,* III. 56, ed. Leon., XIV, p. 155.

10. Other unusual expressions in this same *opusculum* are: "figitur acies," the distinction between "essentia materiae" and "ratio materiae," the doctrine on the "potentialitas" and the "actualitas animae."

11. F. Pelster, S.J., reviewing the edition of Perrier (referred to *supra,* note 4), notes that we are as yet not sure of the authenticity of most of the *opuscula in individuo* (*Gregorianum* XXXI [1950], p. 294). It is to be hoped that the edition planned by the Société philosophique de Fribourg (to be edited by John J. Pauson) will bring further clarifications.

APPENDIX II

TEXTS TRANSLATED IN THE BODY OF THIS BOOK

(chapters I to VII)

1

«... ἡ λοιπὴ δὲ ἐνέργεια τῆς ψυχῆς ἡ κατ' αὐτὸ τὸ ἡγεμονικὸν εἰς τὲ τὸ φανταστικὸν καὶ διανοητικὸν καὶ μνημονευτικὸν διαιρεῖται,» Galen, *De Symptomatum Differentiis*, c. 3, ed. Carolus Gottlob Kuehn, *Opera Omnia* (Leipzig: 1823: 20 vols.), vol. VII, p. 56. Translated above, page 45.

2

"Iudicationes et depositiones et fugae et impetus actus, specialiter vero intelligentiae intelligibilium et virtutes et disciplinae et artium rationes et consiliativum et electivum," *De Natura Hominis*, c. 11, Gregorii Nysseni (Nemesii Emeseni) Περὶ φύσεως ἀνθρώπου *Liber a Burgundione in Latinum Translatus*, ed. Carolus J. Burkhard (Vienna: 1896-1902), part 3, p. 15. Translated above, p. 47.

3

"Tres tamquam ventriculi cerebri constituti sunt: unus anterior ad faciem, a quo sensus omnis; alter posterior ad cervicem, a quo motus omnis; tertius inter utrumque, in quo memoria vigere demonstratur, ne, cum sensum sequitur motus, non connectet homo quod faciendum est, si fuerit oblitus quod fecit," St. Augustine, *De Genesi ad Litteram*, VII, c. 18, PL XXXIV. 364. Translated above, p. 52.

4

"Ipsum quoque hominem aliter sensus, aliter imaginatio, aliter ratio, aliter intelligentia contuetur. Sensus enim figuram in subjecta materia constitutam; imaginatio vero solam sine materia iudicat figuram. Ratio vero hanc quoque transcendit, speciemque ipsam, quae singularibus inest, universali consideratione perpendit.

Intelligentiae vero celsior oculus existit. Supergressa namque uni-versitatis ambitum ipsam illam simplicem formam pura mentis acie contuetur," Boethius, *De Consolatione Philosophiae*, V. prosa 4, nos. 18-20, ed. Adrian Fortescue (London: Burns Oates and Washburn, 1925), p. 150. Translated above, p. 54.

5

"Prima est in utraque parte sensibilis, quae nobis tribuit intelli-gentiae sensu, per quam [*variant*: quem] omnia incorporalia varia imaginatione sentimus; facit etiam corporales vigere sensus," Cas-siodorus, *De Anima*, c. 6, PL LXX. 1291. Translated above, p. 55.

6

"Tertia, principalis, cum ab omni actu remoti, in otium reponimur, et corporalibus sensibus quietis profundius aliquid firmiusque trac-tamus," Cassiodorus, *De Anima*, c. 6, PL LXX. 1921. Translated above, p. 56.

7

"In capite sunt tres cellulae, in prora, in medio, in puppi. Prima vero cellula est calida et sicca, et dicitur phantastica, id est visua-lis vel imaginativa, quia in ea vis videndi est et intelligendi; sed ideo calida et sicca est, ut formas rerum et colores attrahat. Media vero dicitur λογιστικόν, id est rationalis; quia in ea est vis discer-nendi. Quod enim phantastica trahit, ad hanc transit, ibique ani-ma discernit. Est calida et humida ut melius discernendo proprie-tatibus rerum se conformet. Tertia vero memorialis dicitur quia in ea est vis retinendi aliquid in memoria. Quod enim in logistica cella discretum est transit ad memorialem, per quoddam foramen, quod claudit quidam panniculus, donec aperiatur quando aliquid tradere volumus vel ad memoriam reducere. Ista est frigida et sicca, ut melius retinet. Frigidi enim et sicci est constringere. Sed dicet aliquis: quomodo hoc in quoquam potuit probari? Dicimus, per vulnera illis partibus accepta," William of Conches, *De Philosophia Mundi*, IV, c. 24, PL CLXXII. 95. The first sentence is corrected according to the reading of Περί διδάξεων *sive Elementorum Philosophiae Libri Quattuor* (among the works of Bede), PL XC. 1174C. Translated above, p. 63.

8

"Cogitatio est, cum mens notione rerum transitorie tangitur cum ipsa res sua imagine animo subito praesentatur, vel per sensum ingrediens, vel a memoria exsurgens," Hugh of St. Victor, *Homiliae* 19 *in Ecclesiasten,* hom. 1, PL CLXXV. 116D. Translated above, p. 73.

9

"In cogitatione evagatio, in meditatione investigatio, in contemplatione admiratio. Ex imaginatione cogitatio, ex ratione meditatio; ex intelligentia contemplatio. . . . Cogitatio semper vago motu de uno ad aliud transit, meditatio circa unum aliquid perseveranter intendit, contemplatio sub uno visionis medio ad innumera se diffundit," Richard of St. Victor, *Benjamin Minor,* c. 3, PL CXCVI. 76A-C. Translated above, p. 76.

10

"In anima enim sunt virtutes multae apprehensivae: sensitiva, imaginativa, aestimativa, intellectiva, et omnes oportet relinquere," St. Bonaventure, *Collationes in Hexaemeron,* coll. 2, no. 27, *Opera Omnia* (Quaracchi: 1882-1902: 10 vols.), vol. V, p. 341. Translated above, p. 77.

11

"Per sensitivum apprehendit sensibilia, retinet apprehensa, componit et dividit retenta: apprehendit quidem per sensitivam exteriorem quinquepartitam secundum correspondentiam ad quinque mundi corpora principalia; retinet per memoriam, componit et dividit per phantasiam, quae est prima virtus collativa," St. Bonaventure, *Breviloquium,* part 2, c. 9, *Opera Omnia* (Quaracchi: 1882-1902: 10 vols.), vol. V, p. 227. Translated above, p. 78.

12

"Et inferior quidem anima racionali in claritate et sublimitate ordinis est anima bestialis quoniam ipsa ex anima racionali generata est et propter hoc elongatur a splendore intelligenciae et acquirit umbram et tenebras et privatur perscrutacione et discrecione et facta est aestimativa secundum veritatem et meditativa secundum transposicionem. Iudicat enim de re ex eo quod apparet, non ex eo ubi est veritas. Et ex proprietate eius sunt sensus et motus et permutacio in locis, et propter hoc factae sunt bestiae presumptuosae multae audaciae quaerentes victoriam et principatum sicut leo qui quaerit dominium super alias bestias absque investigacione et discrecione et cognicione eius quod facit; significat autem quod bestiae sunt aestimantes et non discernentes, illud quod in asino invenimus. . . . Privata sunt investigacione et discrecione et percepcione veritatum rerum et . . . appropriata sunt cum aestimacione et meditacione," Isaac Israeli *Liber de Definicionibus*, "Sermo de Anima," ed. J. T. Muckle, C.S.B., *Archives d'Histoire Doctrinale et Littéraire du Moyen Age*, XI (1937-1938), p. 314, lines 4-16, line 26; p. 315, line 2. Translated above, p. 82.

13

"Definicio aestimacionis; aestimacio est virtus incedens in impossibilibus, et dicitur quod aestimacio sit iudicium de re ex apparacione non ex eo ubi est veritas. Et propter hoc factae sunt bestiae existimantes non meditantes nisi illud dicatur de eis secundum accomodacionem et transposicionem," Isaac Israeli *Liber de Definicionibus*, ed. J. T. Muckle, C.S.B., *Archives d'Histoire Dictrinale et Littéraire de Moyen Age*, XI (1937-1938), p. 324, lines 9-14. Translated above, p. 82.

14

"Cerebrum vero dividitur in suas divisiones, quarum una est anterior, quae est major, et altera, quae est posterior, et in illa anteriori sunt duo ventriculi habentes introitum ad commune spatium, quod est in medio cerebri," Costa-ben-Luca, *De Differentia Animae et Spiritus*, tr. a Johanne Hispalensi, ed. by Carl Sigmund Barach

(Innsbruck: Wagner, 1878, "Bibliotheca Philosophorum Mediae
Aetatis"), c. 2, p. 124. Translated above, p. 84.

15

"Et in ipso transitu et meatu, id est in ipso introitu, per quem
vadit spiritus, habetur quoddam spatium et quaedam particula de
corpore cerebri, similis vermi, quae elevatur et deponitur in ipso
itinere. Cumque fuerit haec particula elevata, aperitur foramen. . . .
Cum ergo apertum fuerit foramen, transit spiritus de anteriori cerebro ad posterius, et hoc non fit nisi cum necesse fuit recordari
alicujus rei, quae tradita est oblivioni in tempore, quo fit cogitatio de praeteritis," Costa-ben-Luca, *De Differentia Animae et
Spiritus*, tr. a Johanne Hispalensi, ed. by Carl Sigmund Barach,
(Innsbruck: Wagner, 1878, "Bibliotheca Philosophorum Mediae
Aetatis"), 2, p. 125. Translated above, p. 84.

16

"Ille spiritus qui est in anterioribus ventriculis operatur sensus, id
est, visus, auditus, gustus, tactus et olfactus, et cum hic operatur
acagum quem Graeci phantasiam vocant; et quod spiritus qui est
in ventriculo medio, operatur cogitationem atque cognitionem atque providentiam; et spiritus qui est in posteriori ventriculo, operatur memoriam atque motum," Costa-ben-Luca, *De Differentia
Animae et Spiritus*, tr. a Johanne Hispalensi, ed. by Carl Sigmund
Barach (Innsbruck: Wagner, 1878, "Bibliotheca Philosophorum
Mediae Aetatis"), c. 2, p. 130. Translated above, p. 85.

17

"Sed vis apprehendens duplex est. Alia enim est vis quae apprehendit ab intus. Apprehendens a foris aut sunt quinque sensus aut
octo," Avicenna, *De Anima*, part I, c. 5 (Venice: 1508), ed. Klubertanz, p. 20. Translation, p. 93.

18

"Sed virium apprehendentium ab intus quaedam apprehendunt formas sensibiles; quaedam vero apprehendunt intentiones sensibilium.

Apprehendentium autem quaedam sunt quae apprehendunt et operantur simul; quaedam vero apprehendunt et non operantur; quaedam apprehendunt principaliter et quaedam sencundario. Differentia autem inter apprehendere formas et apprehendere intentionem haec est: quod forma est illa quam apprehendit sensus interior et sensus exterior simul. Sed sensus exterior primo apprehendit eam, et postea reddit eam sensui interiori. Sicut cum ovis apprehendit formam lupi, scilicet figuram eius, et affectionem et colorem. Sed sensus exterior ovis primo apprehendit eam, et deinde sensus interior. Intentio autem est id quod apprehendit anima de sensibili, quamvis non prius apprehendit illud sensus exterior, sicut ovis apprehendit intentionem quam habet de lupo, quae scilicet est quare debeat eum timere et fugere; quamvis hoc sensus non apprehendit ullo modo. Id autem quod de lupo apprehendit sensus exterior primo et postea interior vocatur hic proprie nomine formae; quod autem apprehendunt vires occultae absque sensu vocatur in hoc loco proprie nomine intentionis. Differentia autem quae est inter apprehendere operando, et apprehendere non operando haec est: quod de actionibus alicuius virium interiorum est componere aliquas formarum et intentionum apprehensarum cum aliis, et separare ab aliquibus. Habet ergo apprehendere et operari etiam in eo quod apprehendit. Sed apprehendere non operando hoc est: cum forma aut intentio describitur in vi tantum, ita ut non possit agere in eam aliquid ullo modo. Differentia autem inter apprehendere principaliter et apprehendere secundario haec est: quod apprehendere principaliter est cum forma acquiritur aliquo modo acquisitionis quod accidit rei per se; apprehendere secundario est acquisitio rei ex alio quod eam induxerit," Avicenna, *De Anima*, part I, c. 5, (Venice: 1508), fol. 5ra-b, ed. Klubertanz, pp. 20-21. Translation, p. 94.

19

"Virium autem apprehendentium occultarum vitalium prima est fantasia quae est sensus communis, quae est vis ordinata in prima concavitate cerebri recipiens per seipsam formas omnes quae imprimuntur quinque sensibus et redduntur ei. Post hanc est imaginatio, vel quae est etiam formans; quae est vis ordinata in extremo anterioris concavitatis cerebri retinens quod recipit sensus communis a quinque sensibus, et remanet in ea post remotionem illorum sensibilium. Debes autem scire quod recipere est ex una vi, quae est alia ab ea ex qua est retinere, et hoc considera in aqua quae habet potentiam recipiendi insculptiones et depictiones et omnino figuram, et non habet potentiam retinendi; quamvis postea etiam addemus certitudinem huius. . . . Post hanc est vis quae vocatur imaginativa comparatione animae vitalis, et cogitativa comparatione animae humanae, quae est vis ordinata in media concavitate cerebri ubi est nervus, et solet componere aliquid de eo quod est in imaginatione cum alio et deinde aliquid ab alio secundum quod vult. Deinde est vis extimativa, quae est vis ordinata in summo mediae concavitatis cerebri, apprehendens intentiones non sensatas, quae sunt in singulis sensibilibus, sicut vis quae est in ove diiudicans quod ab hoc lupo est fugiendum, et quod huius agni est miserendum. Videtur etiam haec vis operari in imaginatis compositionem et divisionem. Deinde est vis memoralis, et reminiscibilis, quae est vis ordinata in posteriore concavitate cerebri, retinens quod apprehendit vis extimationis de intentionibus non sensatis singulorum sensibilium. Comparatio autem virtutis memorialis ad virtutem extimationis talis est qualis comparatio virtutis quae vocatur imaginatio ad sensum communem. Et comparatio huius virtutis ad intentiones est qualis comparatio illius virtutis ad formas sensibiles. Hae sunt vires animae vitalis vel sensibilis. Sed animae rationalis humanae vires dividuntur in virtute sciendi et virtute agendi; et unaquaeque istarum virium vocatur intellectus equivoce aut propter similitudinem," Avicenna, *De Anima,* part I, c. 5 (Venice: 1508), fol. 5rb, ed. Klubertanz, pp. 21-22. Translation, p. 95.

20

"Sensus autem qui est communis alius est ab eo quem tenet illi qui putaverunt quod sensibilia communia haberent sensum communem. Nam sensus communis est vis cui redduntur omnia sensata," Avicenna, *De Anima,* part IV, c. 1 (Venice: 1508), fol. 17rb, ed. **Klubertanz, p. 81.** Translation, p. 98.

21

"Et haec virtus est quae vocatur sensus communis, quae est centrum commune omnium sensuum, et a qua derivantur nervi, et cui
redduntur sensus, et ipsa est vere quae sentit. Sed retinere ea quae
haec apprehendit est illius virtutis quae vocatur imaginatio, et
vocatur formalis, et vocatur fantasia, et fortassis distinguunt inter
imaginationem et fantasiam ad placitum, et nos sumus de illis qui
hoc faciunt. Formae autem quae sunt in sensu communi, et sensus
communis et imaginatio et fantasia sunt quasi una virtus, et quasi
non diversificantur in subiecto, sed in forma: hoc est, quia quod
recipit non est quod retinet. Formam enim sensibilem retinet illa
quae vocatur formalis, fantasia et imaginatio; et non discernit illam
ullo modo, nisi quia tantum retinet. Sensus enim communis et
sensus exteriores discernunt aliquo modo et diiudicant. Dicunt
enim hoc mobile esse nigrum, et hoc rubicundum esse accidit. Per
hanc autem retinentem nihil discernitur de omni quod est nisi tantum de eo quod est in ipsa, scilicet quod habet hanc vel illam
formam. Iam autem scimus verissime in nostra natura esse, ut
componamus sensibilia inter se et dividamus ea inter se secundum
formam quam vidimus extra, quamvis non credamus ea esse vel
non esse. Oportet ergo ut in nobis sit virtus quae hoc operatur,
et haec est virtus quae cum intellectus ei imperat vocatur cogitans,
sed cum virtus animalis illi imperat vocatur imaginativa. Deinde
aliquando diiudicamus de sensibilibus per intentiones quas non sentimus; aut ideo quod in natura sua non sunt sensibiles ullo modo,
aut ideo quia sunt sensibiles, sed nos non sentimus in hora iudicii.
Sed quae non sunt sensibiles ex natura sua sunt sicut inimicitiae
et malitiae, et quae se diffugiunt. Quam apprehendit ovis de forma
lupi, et omnino intentio quae facit eam fugere ab illo; et concordia
quam apprehendit de sua socia, et omnino intentio quae gratulatur
cum illa; sunt res quas apprehendit anima sensibilis ita quod sensus non doceat eam aliquid de eis. Ergo virtus qua haec apprehenduntur est alia virtus et vocatur extimativa. — Aut sunt sensibiles
sic, exempli gratia, cum videmus aliquid ceruleum, iudicamus esse
mel et dulce. Hoc enim non reddit nobis sensus in ipsa hora, cum
ipsum sit de genere sensatorum, quamvis iudicium eius non sentiatur
ullo modo; et quamvis partes eius sunt de genere sensati; non ta-

men apprehendit in praesenti; sed est iudicium quod iudicat quod forte est in eo; et ipsum etiam fit ex alia virtute. Extimatio autem operatur in homine iudicia propria, ex quibus est illud, cum anima pertinaciter negat esse res quae non imaginantur neque describuntur in ea, et omnino non vult eas credere esse. Et haec virtus sine dubio consistit in nobis, quae est diiudicans in animali iudicium non diffinitum, sicut est iudicium intellectuale, immo iudicium imaginabile coniunctum cum singularitate et forma sensibili, et ex hac emanant quamplures actiones animalium. Visus [*sic* - usus] autem est ut id quod apprehendit sensus vocetur forma, et quod apprehendit extimatio vocetur intentio. Sed unaquaeque istarum habet thesaurum suum. Thesaurus autem eius quod apprehendit sensus est virtus imaginativa, cuius locus est anterior pars cerebri, et ideo cum contingit in ea infirmitas corrumpitur hic modus formalis, aut ex imaginatione formarum quae non sunt, aut quod est difficile ei stabilire id quod est in illa. Thesaurus vero apprehendentis intentionem est virtus custoditiva, cuius locus est posterior pars cerebri, et ideo cum contingit infirmitas corrumpitur id cuius proprium est custodire has intentiones; quae virtus vocatur etiam memorialis, et etiam retinens. Sed retinens ob hoc quod id quod est in ea haeret firmiter, et memorialis, propter velocitatem suae aptitudinis ad recordandum; per quod formatur cum memoratur post oblivionem. Quod fit cum extimatio convertitur ad suam virtutem estimativam et repraesentat unamquamque formarum quae sunt in imaginatione, ita ut quasi modo videat quod ipsae sint formae eius. Cum vero ostensa fuerit forma quae apprehendit intentionem quae deleta erat, apparebit ei intentio sicut apparuerat extra, et stabiliet eam virtus memorialis in se, sicut stabilierat prius, et fiet memoria." Avicenna, *De Anima,* part IV, c. 1 (Venice: 1508), fol. 17va-b, ed. Klubertanz, pp. 82-84. Translation, pp. 98-100.

22

"Agemus prius de virtute formali, dicentes quod virtus formalis quae est imaginatio et ipsa est ultima in qua resident formae sensibilium, et facies eius quam ad sensibilia habet est sensus communis," Avicenna, *De Anima,* part IV, c. 2 (Venice: 1508), fol. 184a-b, ed. Klubertanz, p. 85. Translation, p. 101.

23

"Postquam iam perscrutati sumus dictionem de dispositione imaginativae et formalis, debemus nunc loqui de dispositione memorialis, et quid intersit inter ipsam et cogitativam in hora extimandi.
Dicemus ergo quia extimatio est excellentior iudex in animalibus,
quae iudicat ad modum adinventae imaginationis cum non est
certa. Et hoc est sicut id quod accidit homini cum putat mel esse
sordidum quia est simile stercori. Estimatio iudicat ita esse, et
anima sequitur ipsam extimationem, quamvis intellectus prohibet.
Animalia autem, et qui assimilantur eis homines, non sequuntur
in suis actionibus nisi hoc iudicium extimationis, quod non habet
descriptionem rationalem, sed ad modum adinventionis quae est in
eius animo tantum, quamvis virtutibus hominis propter consortium
rationis accidat aliquid propter quod virtutes eius interiores differunt a virtutibus animalium. Unde ex utilitatibus sonorum compositorum et colorum et odorum et saporum compositorum et spei
et desiderii habet quaedam quae non habent cetera animalia. Et
eius virtus imaginativa interior cuiusmodi est quod valet ad scientias, et praecipue virtus suae memoriae valet multum ad scientias,
eo quod confert nobis experimenta quae retinet memoria et considerationes singulorum et cetera huiusmodi. Redeamus autem ad agendum de estimatione dicentes quia oportet inquirere rationes con-
siderandi estimationem in quibus non coniicet intellectus in hora
extimandi, scilicet qualiter apprehendat intentiones quae sunt in
sensibilibus statim ut sensus apprehendit formas, ita ut aliquid de
illis intentionibus non sentiatur, et ita ut plures ex illis neque pro-
sunt post neque in ipsa hora. Dicemus igitur quod ipsa extimatio
fit multis modis. Unus ex illis est cautela proveniens in esse quod
est a divina clementia, sicut dispositio infantis qui cum nascitur
mox pendet ab uberibus, et dispositio infantis qui cum elevatur ad
standum et vult cadere statim currit ad adhaerendum alicui, vel
ad custodiendum se per aliquid; et cum quis oculum eius purgare
voluerit a lippitudine, ipse statim claudit antequam intelligat quid
sibi accidet ex illo, et quid debeat facere super illud, quasi sit
natura animae eius, et non habeat hoc per electionem. Propter hoc
etiam animalia habent suas cautelas naturales. Cuius rei causa
sunt comparationes quae habent esse inter has animas et earum

principia, quae sunt duces incessantes praeter comparationes quas
contingit aliquando esse et aliquando non esse, sicut considerare
cum intellectu, et quod subito in mente venit. Omnia etenim ve-
niunt et per istas cautelas apprehendit estimatio intentiones quae
sunt commixtae cum sensibus de eo quod obest vel prodest, unde
ovis pavet lupum, etsi numquam viderit illum, neque aliquid mali
pertulerit ab illo; leonem quoque multa animalia pavent; sed acci-
pitres pavent aliae aves, et conveniunt cum aliis absque discretione.
Hic est unus modus. Alius autem modus est sicut hoc quod fit per
experientiam. Animal etenim, cum habuit dolorem aut delicias aut
pervenerit ad illud utilitas sensibilis aut nocumentum sensibile adiunctum cum forma sensibili, et descripta fuerit in formali forma
huius rei et forma eius quod adiunctum est illi, et descripta fuerit in
memoria intentio operationis quae est inter illas, et iudicium de
illa, scilicet quod memoria per seipsam naturaliter apprehendit hoc;
et deinde cum apparuerit extra imaginativam forma ipsa, tunc
movebitur per formam, et movebitur cum illa id quod adiunctum
fuerit illi de intentionibus utilibus aut nocivis, et omnino procedet
in memoria ad modum motus et perquisitionis qui est in natura
virtutis imaginativae. Sed estimatio hoc totum sentiet simul, et
videbit intentionem per formam illam. Et hic est modus qui accidit
per experientiam, unde canes terrentur lapidibus et fustibus et similia. Aliquando autem ab estimatione adveniunt alia iudicia ad
modum similitudinis. Cum enim res habuerit aliquam formam coniunctam cum intentione estimationis in aliquo sensibilium quae coniuncta est semper cum omnibus illis, cum visa fuerit forma eius,
videbitur intentio. Aliquando autem animalia differunt in iudice
qui eget in suis actionibus ut istae virtutes obediant. Id autem
quo magis eget est memoria et sensus. Sed forma opus est propter
recordationem et memoriam. Memoria autem est etiam animalibus.
Sed recordatio quae est ingenium recordandi quod oblitum est, non
invenitur, ut puto, nisi in solo homine. Cognoscere etenim aliquid
sibi fuisse quod postea deletum est non est nisi virtutis rationalis;
si autem fuerit alterius praeter rationalem, poterit esse estimationis,
sed quae decoratur rationalitate. Si vero non memorant, memorare
non desiderant neque cogitant inde," Avicenna, *De Anima,* part IV,

c. 3 (Venice: 1508), fol. 19ra-va; ed. Klubertanz, pp. 91-93. Translation, pp. 101-103.

24

"Ferner ist in dem lebenden Wesen eine Kraft die ueber einen Gegenstand bestimmt utheilt, er sei so oder anders. Durch sie engeht das Thier dem, was es zu fuerchten hat, und erstrebt das Wuenschenswerthe. Nun ist klar, dass diese Kraft mit dem Gemeinsinn nicht identisch sein kann, da der sich die Sonne, wie die Sinne es ihm mittheilen, in der Groesse ihrer Scheihe vorstellt, waehrend diese zu einem ganz anderen Resultat gelangt. Ebenso sieht der Loewe aus der Ferne den Gegenstand seiner Jagd in dem Umfang eines kleinen Vogels, ihm bleibt aber kein Zweifel ueber dessen Form und Groesse, sondern er geht darauf los. Nicht weniger klar ist, dass diese Kraft mit der Phantasie nicht identisch ist, denn die letztere wirkt, ohne dass man von ihr glaubt dass die Dinge getreu nach ihren Vorstellungen sind. Diese Kraft nennt mann die Meinung aussprechende, die urthielende (existimativa et opinativa [sic: *perhaps better iudicativa*])," Avicenna, *Psychology*, tr. by S. Landauer, "Die Psychologie des Ibn Sînâ," *Zeitschrift der deutschen Morgenlaendischen Gesellschaft* (Leipzig) XXIX (1875), pp. 400-402. Translated above, p. 105.

25

"Intrinsicae vero sunt tres virtutes: quarum una est virtus imaginativa, et est in parte anteriori cerebri post virtutem visivam. Et in ea quidem est remanentia formarum rerum, quae videntur post clausuram oculi in eo, quod imprimitur in ea id quod deferunt ad eam sensus quinque, et congregantur, at appellatur sensus communis, et nisi esset ipse, is quidem qui videt mel album, non apprehenderet dulcedinem eius, nisi gustu, et cum viderit id secundo, non apprehenderet dulcedinem eius quotienscumque non gustaverit id sicut fecit primo. Attamen in eo non est aliquid quo iudicat quod hac album [sic] sit dulce. Et non est dubium quod erit apud eum iudex, apud quem congregata sunt ambo, scilicet color et dulcedo ita quod determinabit cum presentia unius eorum quod sit presens etiam alterum.

Secunda vero est virtus cogitativa: et est ea quae apprehendit intentiones: prima vero virtus apprehendebat formas. Et intelligimus per formas id quod imposibile est ut sit sine materia, scilicet corpus, et intelligimus per intentionem id quod non requirit esse eius corpus, evenit tamen ei ut sit in corpore, sicut amicitia et odium, nam agnus apprehendit de lupo colorem et figuram et dispositionem eius: et hoc quidem non est nisi in corpore; et apprehendit etiam quod sit eius inimicus, et apprehendit de pecude figuram matris et colorem eius, deinde apprehendit amicitiam eius; quare non appropinquatur lupo, et deambulat post matrem. Diversitas autem et convenientia non est de necessitate earum ut sint in corporibus, sicut est de necessitate figurae et coloris, nisi quod accidit odio et amicitiae etiam ut sint in corporibus. Et haec virtus est distincta a prima virtute; et locus eius est ventriculus ultima [*sic*] cerebri.

Tertia vero virtus est virtus, quae appellatur in animalibus imaginativa, et in homine extimativa, et natura eius est componere formas sensibiles adinvicem, et componere intentiones cum formis: et est in ventriculo medio cerebri inter conservatorem formarum et conservatorem intentionem. Quare poterit homo imaginari equum volantem et hominem cuius caput est caput hominis et corpus eius corpus equi, et alias compositiones licet non viderit talia. Et dignius est ut attribuatur haec virtus virtutibus motivis quam sit in virtutibus apprehensivis. Sciuntur autem loca harum virtutum in arte Medicinae. Nam laesio in capite cum fuerit in his ventriculis involvuntur hae quae appellantur virtutes.

Deinde existimaverunt quod virtus in qua imprimuntur formae sensibiles in quinque sensibus conservat illas formas, adeo quod non amittat receptionem. Et res quidem conservat rem non cum virtute qua eam recipit. Nam aqua recipit figuram et non conservat eam, et cera recipit figuram cum humiditate sua, et conservat eam cum siccitate sua, aliter quam aqua. Igitur conservator hac consyderatione est diversus a recipiente, et appellatur haec virtus conservativa. Et sic intentiones imprimuntur in cogitativa, et conservat eas virtus quae appellatur memorativa. Et erunt apprehensiones intrinsicae hac consyderatione cum coniunguntur cum eis imaginativa, quinque.

312   APPENDIX II

Ait Averroes. Hoc totum non est in eo nisi recitatio opinionis Philosophorum de his virtutibus et attributis earum, nisi quod sequitur in hoc Avicenna," Averroes, *Destructio Destructionum*, in physicis, disputatio secunda (a principio locutionis Algazelis) (Venice: Juntas, 1574), IX, fol. 135I — 136C. Translated above, p. 109.

26

"Differt tamen a Philosophis in eo quod ponit in animali virtutem praeter virtutem imaginativam quam appellat cogitativam loco cogitativae in homine et dicit quod nomen imaginativae praeferunt id Antiqui pro hac virtute. Et cum id proferant, erit imaginativa in animali, loco cogitativae, et erit in ventriculo medio cerebri. Et cum prolatum fuerit nomen imaginativae pro ea quae includit figuram dicitur de ea quod est in anteriori parte cerebri. Et nulla est discordia quod conservativa et memorativa sunt in posteriori, nam conservatio et memoratio sunt duae in actu, una vero in subiecto. Attamen quod apparet ex opinione Antiquorum est quod imaginativa in animali est ea quae iudicat quod lupus sit inimicus agno et quod pecus sit amica. Nam imaginativa est virtus apprehensionis et iudicat necessario absque eo quod indigeat ingressu alterius virtutis praeter virtutem imaginativam. Esset autem possibile id quod dixit Avicenna, si virtus imaginativa non esset apprehendens; igitur nihil est addere virtutem praeter virtutem imaginativam in animali, et praecipue in animali cui sunt multae artes naturaliter. Nam imaginationes in istis non apprehendentur sensu: et quasi sunt apprehensiones mediae inter formas intellectas et imaginatas. Et iam declarata est dispositio huius formae in De Sensu et Sensato, quod dimittimus in hoc loco," Averroes, *Destructio Destructionum*, in physicis, disputatio secunda, (Venice: Juntas, 1574), IX, fol. 136L — 137B. Translated above, p. 110.

27

"Et virtutes cerebri, scilicet imaginativa et cogitativa et reminiscibilis et conservativa, quamvis non habeant membra vel instrumenta, ipsa tamen habent propria loca in cerebro, in quibus manifestantur operationes earum, et propterea de eis dicendum est. Et dicimus quod virtus imaginativa stat in prora cerebri, et illa est quae retinet figuram rei, postquam separata est a sensu communi. Sed cogitativa plus manifestatur in media camera, et per hanc virtutem cogitet homo in rebus quibus pertinet cogitatio et electio quousque apprehenderit quod convenientius est. Propterea non invenitur haec virtus nisi in homine, et animali bruto concessa fuit aestimativa loco istius. Et locus virtutis reminiscibilis et conservativae est puppis sive pars posterior capitis. Et inter conservativam et reminiscibilem non est differentia nisi quia conservativa est conservatio continua, et reminiscibilis est conservatio interrupta. . . . Et in loco in quo est imaginativa, de necessitate est cogitativa, quia cogitatio non est nisi compositio rerum imaginativarum et dissolutio earum. . . . Locus et radix habitationis sensus communis est cor," Averroes, *Collegit*, II, c. 20 (Venice: Juntas, 1574), X, fol. 30FG, K, L. Translated above, p. 111.

28

"Apparet ab his virtutibus, ut non compleantur suae operationes nisi in cerebro, et propterea quia cerebrum aptum est pati, eo quod est frigidum et humidum, ob hoc maior pars causarum istarum virtutum provenit a passionibus cerebri: aut quod sit primum in hac causa, aut hoc fit propter communitatem illorum membrorum. Et si causa erit in toto cerebro, erunt tunc laesae omnes virtutes. Et si fuerint in loco proprio, erit tunc laesa virtus illius loci proprii. Et quando fuerit causa in prora cerebri, tunc erit laesa imaginatio. Et quando fuerit in parte media, tunc erit laesa ratio et cogitatio, et quando fuerit in parte posteriori, tunc erit laesa memoria et conservatio," Averroes, *Collegit*, III, c. 40 (Venice: Juntas, 1574), X, fol. 56 BC. Translated above, p. 112.

29

"Primus est corporalis magni corticis, et est forma sensibilis extra animam. Secundus autem est esse istius formae in sensu communi et est primus ordinum spiritualium. Tertius est esse eius in virtute imaginativa, et est magis spiritualis. Quartus est in virtute distinctiva. Quintus autem est esse eius in virtute rememorativa," Averroes, *Paraphrasis de Memoria et Reminiscentia* (Venice: Juntas, 1574), vol. VI, part 2, fol. 22B. Translated above, p. 112.

30

"Sunt igitur tres actiones trium virtutum, quarum duae sunt fixae
per duas res simplices ex quibus componitur forma composita ex
eis, quarum scilicet rerum una est imago rei, et secunda intentio
imaginis rei, tertia autem est virtus componens has duas intentiones
ad invicem," Averroes, *Paraphrasis De Memoria et Reminiscentia*
(Venice: Juntas, 1574), VI, part 2, fol. 21H. Translated above,
p. 113.

31

"Virtutis rememorativae est facere praesentare post eius absentiam
intentionem rei imaginatae, et iudicare ipsam esse illam intentionem
quam ante sensit et imaginabatur," Averroes, *Paraphrasis de Memoria et Reminiscentia* (Venice: Juntas, 1574), VI, part 2, fol.
21 EF. Translated above, p. 113.

32

"Iudicare autem quod ista intentio est istius imaginati est in homine in intellectu, quia iudicat in eo secundum affirmationem et
negationem, et in animalibus rememorativis est simile actioni: ista
enim virtus est in homine per cognitionem et ideo investigat per
rememorationem; in aliis autem est natura, et ideo rememorant animalia sed non investigant per rememorationem. Et ista virtus in
animalibus non habet nomen; et est ista, quam Avicenna vocat
existimationem, et per hanc virtutem fugit animal naturaliter noci-
tura licet numquam senserit ipsa," Averroes, *Paraphrasis de Memoria et Reminiscentia* (Venice: Juntas, 1574), VI, part 2, fol. 21
GH. (On the reading of this text, cf. chapter 3, note 64). Translated above, pp. 113-114.

33

"Natum est de animalis dispositione, quod eius sit virtus, qua dig-
noscit utile a noxio, quae vocatur virtus sensitiva," Averroes, *Commentary on the Posterior Analytics* (*Post. Resolutionum libri*)
(Venice: Juntas, 1574), comm. on bk. 2, c. 11, t. c. 103 [i.e., tex-

tus commentum 103], I, part 2, fol. 562c. Translated above, p. 115.

34

"Potest intelligi per partem cogitativam, intellectus speculativus, et per partem quae dicitur intellectus, intellectus operativus," Averroes, *In Librum Tertium de Anima*, t. c. 46 (Venice: Juntas, 1574), VI.i.2, fol. 192B. Translated above, p. 115.

35

"Apprehensio, quae appropriatur entibus quorum principia non sunt in nobis, nominatur scientia speculativa, et apprehensio quae appropriatur entibus quorum causae in nobis sunt, nominatur cognitiva operativa: intendo eam, in qua est cogitatio propter operationem. Non enim meditamur neque cogitemus ad operandum res quarum operationem impossibile est esse in nobis, sed est penes natura. Et utitur quidem homo cogitatione operativa in rebus, quas possibile est esse a voluntate. Cumque sic sit, cogitativa est una ex partibus animae rationalis quae recipit rationem; et altera est pars speculativa," Averroes, *Aristotelis Stagiritae libri moralem totam philosophiam complectentes cum Averrois Cordubensis* comm., on bk. 6, c. 1; III, fol. 81M-82A. Translated above, p. 116.

36

"Et ideo non oportet obiicere huic argumento ex eo quod accidit in intellectu de transmutatione propter transmutationem virtutum imaginationis et maxime cogitatione [*sic*]; in intellectu enim existimatur accidere fatigatio hoc modo. Et non est ita nisi accidentaliter. Virtus enim cogitativa est de genere virtutum sensibilium. Imaginativa autem et cogitativa et rememorativa non sunt nisi in loco virtutis sensibilis, et ideo indigetur eis nisi in absentia sensibilis, et omnes iuvent se ad representandum imaginem rei sensibilis, ut aspiciat eam virtus rationalis abstracta, et extrahat intentionem universalem, et postea recipiat eam, id est comprehendat eam," Averroes, *In Lib. III De Anima*, t. c. 7 (Venice: Juntas, 1574), VI.i.2, fol. 155B. Translated above p. 116.

37

"Dicitur, quod virtus imaginativa est in anteriori cerebri, et cogitativa in medio, et rememorativa in posteriori. Et hoc non tantum dictum est a Medicis, sed dictum est in Sensu et Sensato: Galenus autem et alii Medici ratiocinantur super hoc, quod istae virtutes sunt in istis locis per locum concomitantiae, et est locus faciens existimare et non verus. Sed declaratum est in libro De Sensu et Sensato, quod talis est ordo istarum virtutum in cerebro per demonstrationem dantem esse et causam. Sed istud non contradicit illi quod dictum est hic. Virtus enim cogitativa apud Aristotelem est virtus distinctiva individualis, scilicet quod non distinguit nisi individualiter, non universaliter. Declaratum est enim illic quod virtus cogitativa non est nisi virtus quae distinguit intentionem rei sensibilis a suo idolo imaginato. Et ista virtus est illa, cuius proportio ad has duas intentiones, scilicet ad idolum rei, et ad intentionem sui idoli, est sicut proportio sensus communis ad intentiones quinque sensuum. Virtus enim cogitativa est de genere virtutum existentium in corpore. Et hoc aperte dixit Aristoteles in illo libro, cum posuit virtutes individuales distinctas in quatuor ordinibus. In primo posuit sensum communem, deinde virtutem imaginativam, deinde cogitativam et postea rememorativam. . . . Licet igitur homo proprie habet virtutem cogitativam, tamen non facit hanc virtutem esse rationabilem distinctivam. . . . Galenus existimavit quod virtus cogitativa est rationalis materialis," Averroes, *In Lib. III De Anima,* t. c. 6 (Venice: Juntas, 1574), VI.i.2, fol. 154A-C. (On the reading of this text, cf. ch. 3, note 73). Translated above, p. 117.

38

"Sunt tres virtutes in homine, quarum esse declaratum est in Sensu et Sensato, scilicet, imaginativa, et cogitativa, et rememorativa. Istae enim tres virtutes sunt in homine ad praesentandam formam rei imaginatae, quando sensus fuerit absens. Et ideo dictum fuit illic quod, cum istae tres virtutes adiuverint se ad invicem, forte repraesentabunt individuum rei, licet non sentiamus ipsum.

Et intendebat hic per intellectum passibilem formas imaginationis secundum quod in eas agit virtus cogitativa propria homini. Ista enim virtus est aliqua ratio, et actio eius nihil est aliud quam ponere intentionem formae imaginationis cum suo individuo apud rememorationem, aut distinguere eam ab eo apud formationem. Et manifestum est quod intellectus qui dicitur materialis recipit intentiones imaginatas post hanc distinctionem," Averroes, *In Lib. III De Anima,* t. c. 20 (Venice: Juntas, 1574), VI.i.2, fol. 164C. Translated above, p. 118.

39

"Dicit et imaginatio existit in aliis animalibus, cogitatio autem in rationalibus. Eligere enim facere hoc imaginatum et non hoc, est de actione cogitationis, non de actione imaginationis. Iudicans enim quod hoc imaginatum est magis amabile quam hoc, debet esse eadem virtus de necessitate quae numerat imaginationes et in quibusdam iudicat magis delectabilius. . . . Similiter cogitatio numerat imagines, et componit inter eas, donec possit pati ab imaginatione alicuius earum. Et hoc est causa quare animal rationale habet existimationem, existimatio enim est consensus, qui provenit a cogitatione," Averroes, *In Lib. III De Anima,* t. c. 57, (Venice: Juntas, 1574), VI.i.2, fol. 198BC. Translated above, p. 119.

40

"Possibile est ut homo cogitet in alia re, adeo quod invenit ex eo aliquod individuum quod ante non sensit, sed sensit ei simile, non ipsum idem," *In III De Anima,* t. c. 33 (Venice: Juntas, 1574), VI.i.2, fol. 173B. Translated above, p. 120.

41

"Non intendebat quod sensus comprehendit essentias rerum, sicut quidam existimaverunt: hoc enim est alterius potentiae quae diditur intellectus; sed intendebat quod sensus cum quod comprehendunt sua sensibilia propria, comprehendunt intentiones individuales diversas in generibus et in speciebus. Comprehendunt igitur intentionem huius hominis individualis, et universaliter intentionem uniuscuiusque decem praedicamentorum individualium, et hoc vide-

tur esse proprium sensibus hominis. Unde dicit Aristoteles in
libro De Sensu et Sensato, quod sensus aliorum animalium non
sunt sicut sensus hominis, aut simile huic sermoni. Et ista intentio individualis est illa quam distinguit virtus cogitativa a forma
imaginativa et expoliat eam ab eis quae sunt adiuncta cum ea ex
istis sensibilibus communibus et propriis, et reponit ea in memorativa. Et haec eadem est illa, quam comprehendit imaginativa, sed
imaginativa comprehendit eam coniunctam istis sensibilibus, licet
eius comprehensio sit magis spiritualis," Averroes, *In lib. II De
Anima*, t. c. 63 (Venice: Juntas, 1574) VI.i.2, fol. 82EF. Translated above, p. 120.

42

"Virtus cogitativa non est intellectus materialis . . . sed est virtus
particularis materialis. . . . Non debet aliquis dicere quod virtus
cogitativa componit intelligibilia singularia. . . . Cogitatio enim non
est, nisi in distinguendo individuum illorum intelligibilium et praesentare ea in actu, quasi essent apud sensum. Et ideo, quando
fuerint praesentia apud sensum, tunc cadet cogitatio, et remane-
bit actio intellectus in eis. Et ex hoc declarabitur quod actio intellectus est alia ab actione virtutis cogitativae, quam Aristoteles
vocat intellectum possibilem, et dixit eam esse generabilem et cor-
ruptibilem . . . cum habeat instrumentum terminatum, scilicet medium ventriculum cerebri; et homo non est generabilis et corruptibilis nisi per hanc virtutem," Averroes, *In Lib. III De Anima*,
t. c. 33 (Venice: Juntas, 1574), VI.i.2, fol 173C. Translated
above, p. 120-121.

43

"Abstraccio est forme rei qualiscumque apprehensio. Hanc autem
formam aliter apprehendit sensus, aliter ymaginacio, aliter estimacio,
aliter intellectus. . . .

Estimacio vero transcendit hunc ordinem abstraccionis quoniam apprehendit intenciones materiales que non sunt in suis materiis quamvis accidat eis esse in materia," Gundissalinus, *De Divisione Philosophiae*, ed. Ludwig Baur, (Beitraege, Baeumker, Muen-

ster: Aschendorff, 1903, Band IV, Heft 2-3), pp. 28-29. Translated above, p. 124-125.

44

"Eius [*sc.* intellectus] operationem solam inde aut impediri aut destrui, quae illi deorsum est, hoc est a parte sensibilium. Est enim velut alter liber eius descriptio formarum sensibilium, quem librum offert vel exhibet eidem imaginativa," *Des Dominicus Gundissalinus Schrift von der Unsterblichkeit der Seele* (Beitraege, Baeumker, Muenster: Aschendorff, 1897, Band II, Heft 3), pp. 20-21. Translated above, p. 126.

45

"Ad hoc dicendum quod, secundum quod dicit Avicenna, haec vis duo sortitur vocabula, ut dicatur quandoque imaginativa, quandoque cogitativa. In hoc autem est differentia, quod cum imperaverit aestimativa animalis, tunc dicitur imaginativa; si vero virtus rationalis imperaverit ei, et reduxerit eam ad id quod ei prodest, dicitur cogitativa. Sive ergo imperet aestimativa sive rationalis, semper est computata in parte sensitiva, sicut ipse dicit," Alexander of Hales, *Summa Theologica,* prima pars secundi libri (ed. Quaracchi: 1928: 3 vols.), (Inq. 4, tract. 1, sect. 2, q. 2, tit. 1), membr. 2, c. 1, no. 357, p. 435. Translated above, p. 130.

46

"Est autem virtus transcendens, quia apprehensio sua est non solum formas sensibilium et materialium, sed immaterialium; bonitas enim et malitia, conveniens et inconveniens, utile et nocivum in se sunt formae . . . non materiales, non cadentes in sensu exteriori," Jean de la Rochelle, *Summa de Anima,* from a microfilm of Ms. Bruges, 515, fol. 26 r a-b. Translated above, p. 133.

47

"Respondeo dicendum, quod potentiae passivae variantur, secundum quod natae sunt moveri a diversis activis, per se loquendo.

Proprium autem motivum appetitivae virtutis est bonum apprehensum; unde oportet quod secundum diversas virtutes apprehendentes sint etiam diversi appetitus: scilicet appetitus rationis, qui est de bono apprehenso secundum rationem vel intellectum, unde est de bono apprehenso simpliciter et in universali; et appetitus sensitivus, qui est de bono apprehenso secundum vires sensitivas, unde est de bono particulari, et ut nunc. Sed quia potentia passiva non extendit se ad plura quam virtus sui activi, secundum quod dicit Commentator in Nono *Metaphysicorum,* quod nulla potentia passiva est in natura, cui non respondeat sua potentia activa naturalis; ideo appetitus sensitivus ad illa tantum bona se extendit, ad quae se extendit apprehensio sensitiva.

Quia autem, ut dicit Dionysius, septimo capite *De Divinis Nominibus,* divina sapientia conjungit fines primorum principiis secundorum, quia omnis natura inferior in sui supremo attingit ad infimum naturae superioris, secundum quod participat aliquid de natura superioris, quamvis deficienter; ideo tam in apprehensione quam in appetitu sensitivo invenitur aliquid in quo sensitivum rationem attingit.

Quod enim animal imaginetur formas apprehensas per sensum, hoc est de naturae sensitivae apprehensionis secundum se; sed quod apprehendat illas intentiones quae non cadunt sub sensu, sicut amicitiam, odium et hujusmodi, hoc est sensitivae partis secundum quod attingit rationem. Unde pars illa in hominibus, in quibus est perfectior propter conjunctionem ad animam rationalem, dicitur ratio particularis, quia confert de intentionibus particularibus; in aliis autem animalibus, quia non confert, sed ex instinctu naturali habet hujusmodi intentiones apprehendere, non dicitur ratio, sed aestimatio.

Similiter etiam ex parte appetitus, quod animal appetat ea quae sunt convenientia sensui, delectationem facientia, secundum naturam sensitivam est, et pertinet ad vim concupiscibilem; sed quod tendat in aliquod bonum quod non facit delectationem in sensu . . . hoc est in appetitu sensitivo secundum quod natura sensitiva attingit intellectivam; et hoc pertinet ad irascibilem. Et ideo sicut aestimatio est alia vis quam imaginatio, ita irascibilis est alia vis quam concupiscibilis. Objectum enim concupiscibilis est bonum quod natum est facere delectationem in sensu; irascibilis autem bonum quod difficultatem habet. Et quia id quod est difficile non est appetibile inquantum hujusmodi, sed vel in ordine ad aliud delectabile vel ratione bonitatis quae difficultati admiscetur — conferre autem unum ad aliud et discernere intentionem difficultatis et bonitatis in uno et eodem est rationis — ideo proprie istud bonum appetere est rationalis appetitus; sed convenit sensitivae, secundum quod attingit per quamdam imperfectam participationem ad rationalem, non quidem conferendo vel discernendo, sed naturali instinctu movendo se in illud, sicut dictum est de aestimatione," St. Thomas Aquinas, *Scriptum super tertium librum Sententiarum,* d. 26, q. 1, a. 2, sol., ed. Pierre Mandonnet, O.P., and M.F. Moos, O.P., (Paris: Lethielleux, 1929-1933), III, pp. 816-17. Translated above, pp. 152-154.

48

"Respondeo dicendum, quod differt sensualitas et sensibilitas. Sensibilitas enim omnes vires sensitivae partis comprehendit, tam apprehensivas de foris, quam apprehensivas de intus, quam etiam appetitivas. Sensualitas autem magis proprie illam tantum partem nominat per quam movetur animal in aliquod appetendum vel fugiendum. Sicut autem est in intelligibilibus, quod illud quod est apprehensum non movet voluntatem nisi apprehendatur sub ratione boni vel mali, propter quod intellectus speculativus nihil dicit de imitando vel fugiendo, ut in tertio *de Anima* dicitur [text. 46]; ita etiam est in parte sensitiva, quod apprehensio sensibilis non causat motum aliquem nisi apprehendatur sub ratione convenientis vel inconvenientis. Et ideo dicitur in secundo *de Anima* [text. 14], ad ea quae sunt in imaginatione hoc modo nos habemus ac si essemus considerantes aliqua terribilia in picturis, quae passionem non excitarent vel timoris vel alicujus hujusmodi.

Vis autem apprehendens hujusmodi rationes convenientis et non convenientis videtur virtus aestimativa, per quam agnus fugit lupum et sequitur matrem; quae hoc modo se habet ad appetitum partis sensibilis, sicut se habet intellectus practicus ad appetitum voluntatis. Unde, proprie loquendo, sensualitas incipit ex confinio aestimativae et appetitivae consequentis; ut hoc modo se

habet sensualitas ad partem sensitivam, sicut se habet voluntas
et liberum arbitrium ad partem intellectivam.

Hoc autem conveniens quod sensualitatem movet, aut ratio
suae convenientae, aut est apprehensa a sensu, sicut sunt delectabilia secundum singulos sensus quae animalia persequuntur; aut
est non apprehensa a sensu, sicut inimicitiam lupi neque videndo
neque audiendo ovis percipit, sed aestimando tantum. Et ideo motus sensualitatis in duo tendit: in ea scilicet quae secundum exteriores sensus delectabilia sunt, et hoc est quod dicitur, quod ex sensualitate est motus qui intenditur in corporis sensus; aut ad ea
quae nociva vel convenientia secundum solam aestimationem cognoscuntur, et sic ex sensualitate dicitur esse appetitus rerum ad
corpus pertinentium," St. Thomas Aquinas, *in II Sent.*, d. 24,
q. 2, a. 1, sol.; ed. Mandonnet-Moos, II, pp. 601-02. Translated
above, pp, 154-155.

49

"Ad quartum dicendum, quod quamvis homo et equus in hoc con-
veniant quod est sensibile, non tamen oportet quod anima sensibilis sit unius rationis in homine et equo: quia homo et equus
non sunt unum animal in specie; unde in homine anima sensibilis
est multo nobilior quam in aliis animalibus quantum ad principales
actus, ut patet in actibus interiorum sensuum, et in operatione tactus, qui est principalis sensus. In omni enim toto potestativo potentia inferior superiori coniuncta perfectior invenitur, ut potestas
praepositi multo excellentior est in rege. Anima enim sensibilis in
homine per essentiam coniungitur animae rationali; et ideo totum
est per creationem," St. Thomas Aquinas, *in II Sent.*, d. 18, q. 2,
a. 3, ad 4, ed. Mandonnet-Moos, II, p. 471. Translated above,
p. 156.

50

"Ad secundum dicendum, quod sicut appetitus rationis non sequitur quamlibet apprehensionem rationis, sed quando aliquid apprehenditur ut bonum, ita et appetitus sensibilis non surgit nisi
quando apprehenditur ut conveniens. Hoc autem non fit per ex-

teriorem sensum, qui apprehendit formas sensibiles, sed per aestimationem, quae apprehendit rationes convenientis et nocivi quas
sensus exterior non apprehendit. Et ideo in parte sensitiva non est
nisi unus appetitus secundum genus, qui tamen dividitur, sicut in
species, in irascibilem et concupiscibilem, quarum utraque sub
sensualitate computatur," St. Thomas Aquinas, *in III Sent.*, d.
17, q. 1, a. 1, q. 2, ad 2, ed. Mandonnet-Moos, III, p. 531. Translated above, p. 157.

51

"Aestimativa proprie se habet ad eam [sensualitatem] sicut ratio
practica ad liberum arbitrium; quae etiam est movens. Imaginatio
autem simplex et vires praecedentes magis se habent remote, sicut
ratio speculativa ad voluntatem," St. Thomas Aquinas, *in II Sent.*,
d. 24, q. 2, a. 1, ad 2, ed. Mandonnet-Moos, II, p. 603. Translated
above, p. 157.

52

"Invenitur autem [spes] non solum in hominibus, sed etiam in aliis
animalibus, quod patet, quia inveniuntur animalia operari propter
aliquod bonum futurum aestimatum possible, sicut aves faciunt
nidum propter filiorum educationem," St. Thomas Aquinas, *in III
Sent.*, d. 26, q. 1, a. 1, sol., ed. Mandonnet-Moos, III, p. 814.
Translated above, p. 159.

53

"Ad quintum dicendum, quod alia animalia non prosequuntur conveniens et fugiunt nocivum per rationis deliberationem, sed per naturalem instinctum aestimativae virtutis, et talis naturalis instinctus est etiam in pueris; unde etiam mamillas accipiunt, et alia eis
convenientia etiam sine hoc quod ab aliis doceantur," St. Thomas
Aquinas, *in II Sent.*, d. 20, q. 2, a. 2, ad 5, ed. Mandonnet-Moos
II, p. 515. Translated above, p. 159.

54

"Ad septimum dicendum, quod animalia non apprehendunt rationem convenientis per collationem, sed per quemdam naturalem in-

324 APPENDIX II

stinctum; et ideo animalia habent aestimationem, sed non cognitionem; sicut etiam habent memoriam, sed non reminiscentiam, quamvis omnia haec partis sensitivae sint: et ideo ex determinatione naturae actus suos exercent, non autem ex propria determinatione. Unde omnia eiusdem speciei similes actiones faciunt, sicut omnis aranea similem facit telam, quod non esset si ex seipsis quasi per artem operantem sua opera disponerent; et propter hoc in eis non est liberum arbitrium," St. Thomas Aquinas, *in II Sent.*, d. 25, q. 1, a. 1, ad 7, ed. Mandonnet-Moos, II, p. 647. Translated above, p. 160.

55

"Ad tertium dicendum, quod passivus intellectus, de quo Philosophus loquitur, non est intellectus possibilis, sed ratio particularis, quae dicitur vis cogitativa, habens determinatum organum in corpore, scilicet mediam cellulam capitis, ut Commentator ibidem dicit; et sine hoc anima nihil modo intelligit; intelliget autem in futuro, quando a phantasmatibus abstrahere non indigebit," St. Thomas Aquinas, *in IV Sent.*, d. 50, q. 1, a. 1, ad 3, ed. Parma, VII, part 2, p. 1248. Translated above, p. 161.

56

"Ad tertium dicendum, quod illa potentia, quae a philosophis dicitur cogitativa, est in confinio sensitivae et intellectivae partis, ubi pars sensitiva intellectivam attingit. Habet enim aliquid a parte sensitiva, scilicet quod considerat formas particulares; et habet aliquid ab intellectiva, scilicet quod confert; unde et in solis hominibus est. Et quia pars sensitiva notior est quam intellectiva, ideo, sicut determinatio intellectivae partis a sensu denominatur, ut dictum est, ita collatio omnis intellectus a cogitatione nominatur," St. Thomas Aquinas, *in III Sent.*, d. 23, q. 2, a. 2, q. 1, ad 3, ed. Mandonnet-Moos, III, p. 727. Translated above, pp. 162-163.

57

"Alterius naturae est delectatio quae sequitur operationem appetitivae virtutis et delectatio quae sequitur operationem cogitativae.

Sicut enim cogitatio de homicidio vel luxuria, sine appetitu aliquo, non reducitur nisi inordinata sit, ad genus luxuriae vel homicidii, sed ad aliud genus, quod est curiositas vel vanitas, ita etiam delectatio consequens talem cogitationem non pertinet ad genus homicidii," St. Thomas Aquinas, *in II Sent.*, d. 24, q. 3, a. 4, ad 5, ed. Mandonnet-Moos, II, p. 627. Translated above, p. 164.

58

"Ad tertium dicendum quod intellectus practicus ad hoc quod de singularibus disponit, ut dicitur tertio *de Anima* [Text. 47] indiget ratione particulari qua mediante opinio quae est universalis, quae est in intellectu, ad particulare opus applicetur; ut sic fiat syllogismus cuius maior est universalis, quae est opinio intellectus practici; minor vero singularis, quae est aestimatio rationis particularis, quae alio nomine dicitur cogitativa; conclusio vero consistit in electione operis," St. Thomas Aquinas, *in IV Sent.*, d. 50, q. 1, a. 3, ad 3 in contrarium, ed. Parma, VII, part 2, p. 1251. Translated above, p. 165.

59

"Ad secundum dicendum quod intellectus noster in statu viae utitur singularibus, componendo propositiones et formando syllogismos, inquantum reflectitur ad potentias sensitivae partis ut dictum est, et quodamodo continuatur cum eis, secundum quod earum motus et operationes ad intellectum terminantur, prout intellectus ab eis accipit," St. Thomas Aquinas, *in IV Sent.*, d. 50, q. 1, a. 3, ad 2 in contrarium, ed. Parma, VII, part 2, p. 1251. Translated above, pp. 165-166.

60

"Per accidens autem sentitur illud quod non infert passionem sensui neque inquantum est sensus, neque inquantum est hic sensus; sed coniungitur his quae per se sensui inferunt passionem, sicut Socrates, et filius Diaris, et amicus, et alia huiusmodi; quae per se cognoscuntur in universali intellectu; in particulari autem a virtute cogitativa in homine, aestimativa autem in aliis animalibus.

Huiusmodi autem tunc sensus exterior dicitur sentire, quamvis per
accidens, quando ex eo quod per se sentitur, vis apprehensiva cuius
est illud cognitum per se cognoscere statim sine dubitatione et
discursu apprehendit; sicut videmus aliquem vivere ex hoc quod
loquitur," St. Thomas Aquinas, *in IV Sent.*, d. 49, q. 2, a. 2, ed.
Parma, VII, part 2, pp. 1201-1202. Translated above, p. 175.

61

"Sicut autem omnis forma, quantum est de se, est universalis, ita
habitudo ad formam non facit cognoscere materiam nisi cognitione
universali. . . .

Unde patet quod mens nostra singulare directe cognoscere
non potest; sed directe cognoscitur a nobis singulare per virtutes
sensitivas, quae recipiunt formas a rebus in organo corporali; et sic
recipiunt eas sub determinatis dimensionibus, et secundum quod
ducunt in cognitionem materiae singularis. Sicut enim forma universalis ducit in cognitionem materiae universalis, ita forma individualis ducit in cognitionem materiae signatae, quae est individuationis principium.

Sed tamen mens per accidens singularibus se immiscet, inquantum continuatur viribus sensitivis, quae circa particularia ver-
santur. Quae quidem continuatio est dupliciter. Uno modo inquantum motus sensitivae partis terminatur ad mentem, sicut accidit in motu qui est a rebus ad animam; et sic mens singulare cognoscit per quamdam reflexionem, prout scilicet mens cognoscendo
objectum suum, quod est aliqua natura universalis, redit in cognitionem sui actus, et ulterius in speciem quae est actus sui principium, et ulterius in phantasma a quo species est abstracta; et sic
aliquam cognitionem de singulari accipit.

Alio modo secundum quod motus qui est ab anima ad res, incipit a mente, et procedit in partem sensitivam, prout mens regit
inferiores vires; et sic singularibus se immiscet mediante ratione
particulari, quae est potentia quaedam sensitivae partis componens
et dividens intentiones individuales quae alio nomine dicitur cogitativa, et habet determinatum organum in corpore, scilicet mediam
cellulam capitis. Universalem vero sententiam quam mens habet
de operabilibus non est possibile applicari ad particularem actum

nisi per aliquam potentiam mediam apprehendentem singulare, ut sic fiat quidam syllogismus, cuius maior est universalis quae est sententia mentis; minor autem singularis quae est applicatio particularis rationis; conclusio vero electio singularis operis, ut patet per id quod habetur tertio *De Anima,* [text. 68 and 77]," St. Thomas Aquinas, *De Veritate* X.5, ed. Parma, IX, p. 162. Translated above, pp. 176-177.

62

"Ad nonum dicendum quod potentia cogitativa est quod est altissimum in parte sensitiva, ubi attingit quodammodo ad partem intellectivam ut aliquid participet eius quod est in intellectiva parte infimum, scilicet rationis discursum, secundum regulam Dionysii, c. 7, *De Divinis Nominibus,* quod principia secundorum coniunguntur finibus primorum. Unde ipsa vis cogitativa vocatur particularis ratio, ut patet a Commentatore in tertio *De Anima* [t. c. 58], nec est nisi in homine, loco cuius in aliis brutis est aestimatio naturalis. Et ideo ipsa etiam universalis ratio, quae est in parte intellectiva, propter similitudinem operationis, a cogitatione nominatur," St. Thomas Aquinas, *De Veritate* XIV. 1 ad 9, ed. Parma, IX, p. 228. Translated above, pp. 181-182.

63

"Et comprehensio intentionis individualis, licet sit actio sensus communis, et ideo pluries indigetur in comprehensione intentionis individui uti pluribus uno sensu, (ut utantur medici in sciendo vitam eius qui existimatur habere repletionem venarum pluribus uno sensu), tamen videtur quod ista actio est sensus communis, non secundum quod est sensus communis, sed secundum quod est sensus alicuius animalis, verbi gratia, animalis intelligentis. Iste igitur est alius modus modorum secundum accidens, scilicet, quod accidit sensibus comprehendere differentias individuorum secundum quod sunt individua, non secundum quod sunt sensus simplices, sed secundum quod sunt humani, et praecipue differentiae substantiales. Videtur enim quod comprehensio intentionum individualium substantiarum de quibus intellectus considerat est propria sensibus hominis. Et debes scire quod comprehensio intentionis individui est sen-

suum; et comprehensio intentionis universalis est intellectus. Et
universalitas et individualitas comprehenduntur per intellectum,
scilicet definitio universalis et individui. Deinde dicit, 'et ideo non
patitur, etc.' id est visus non patitur ab intentione sensibile per
accidens, quoniam, si pateretur ab aliquo individuo, secundum quod
est illud individuum, non debet pati ab alio individuo," Averroes,
in II De Anima, t. c. 65 (Venice: Juntas, 1574), vol. VI.i.2, fol.
83D-F. Translated above, pp. 199-200.

64

"Viso igitur quomodo dicantur per se sensibila, et communia et propria, restat videndum, qua ratione dicatur aliquid sensibile per accidens. Sciendum est igitur, quod ad
hoc quod aliquid sit sensibile per accidens, primo requiritur
5 quod accidat ei quod per se est sensibile, sicut albo esse
hominem, et accidit ei esse dulce. Secundo requiritur,
quod sit apprehensum a sentiente; si enim accideret sensibili,
quod lateret sentientem, non diceretur per accidens sentiri.
Oportet igitur quod per se cognoscatur ab aliqua alia po-
10 tentia cognoscitiva sentientis. Et hoc quidem vel est
alius sensus, vel est intellectus, vel vis cogitativa, aut
vis aestimativa. . . .
      Quod ergo sensu proprio non cognoscitur, si sit aliquid
universale, apprehenditur intellectu; non tamen omne quod
15 intellectu apprehendi potest in re sensibili potest dici
sensibile per accidens, sed statim quod ad occursum rei
sensatae apprehenditur intellectu. Sicut statim cum video
aliquem loquentem vel movere seipsum, apprehendo per intellectum vitam eius, unde possum dicere quod video eum
20 vivere. Si vero apprehendatur in singulari, utputa cum
video coloratum, percipio hunc hominem vel hoc animal,
huiusmodi quidem apprehensio in homine fit per vim cogitativam, quae dicitur etiam ratio particularis, eo quod
est collativa intentionum individualium, sicut ratio uni-
25 versalis est collativa rationum universalium.
      Nihilominus tamen haec vis est in parte sensitiva, quia
vis sensitiva in sui supremo participat aliquid de vi in-

tellectiva in homine, in quo sensus intellectui coniungitur.
In animali vero irrationali fit apprehensio intentionis in-
30 dividualis per aestimativam naturalem, secundum quod ovis
per auditum vel visum cognoscit filium, vel aliquid huiusmodi.
Differentur tamen circa hoc se habet cogitativa et
aestimativa. Nam cogitativa apprehendit individuum, ut
existens sub natura communi; quod contingit ei, inquantum
35 unitur intellectivae in eodem subiecto; unde cognoscit hunc
hominem prout est hic homo, et hoc lignum prout est hoc
lignum. Aestimativa autem non apprehendit aliquod individuum secundum quod est sub natura communi, sed solum
secundum quod est terminus aut principium alicuius actionis
40 vel passionis, sicut ovis cognoscit hunc agnum, non inquantum
est hic agnus, sed inquantum est ab ea lactabilis, et hanc
herbam, inquantum est eius cibus. Unde alia individua ad
quae se non extendit eius actio vel passio nullo modo
apprehendit sua aestimativa naturali. Naturalis enim aesti-
45 mativa datur animalibus, ut per eam ordinentur in actiones
proprias vel passiones prosequendas vel fugiendas,"
St. Thomas Aquinas, *in II De Anima*, lect. 13, ed. Angelo
Pirotta, O.P. (Turin: Marietti, 1924), nos. 395-98. Translated above, pp. 198-200.

Variants taken from ms. Vat. Latin 762, where the passage
in question occurs on fol. 79va line 54 to b line 25. The form "extimativa" occurs throughout. Other variants, with line references
to the text above:

5 quod est per se sensibile, sicut albo accidit
6 *omit* ei.
7 accideret aliquid sensibili
8 *omit* per accidens
9 Igitur oportet
10 *omit* quidem
11 vel vis cognoscitiva vel
15 in re sensata
16 quod statim
23 etiam dicitur

24 collectiva *for* collativa, as also in line 25
25 *omit* rationum
27-28 intellectu
28 *add* quodammodo at end of line
34 *omit* ei.
42 *omit* eius; illa *for* alia
43 non se
45 inest *for* datur

BIBLIOGRAPHY

I

PRIMARY SOURCES

Adelard of Bath, *Quaestiones Naturales,* ed. Dr. Martin Mueller, Beitraege, Baeumker, Muenster: Aschendorff, Band XXXI, Heft 2, 1934; Hans Willner, *Des Adelard von Bath Traktat de Eodem et Diverso,* Beitraege, Baeumker, Muenster: Aschendorff, Band IV, Heft 1, 1903.

St. Albert the Great, *Opera Omnia,* ed. August Borgnet, Paris: Vives, 1890: 36 vols: *In De Memoria et Reminiscentia, Libri Tres De Anima,* vol. V; *Summa De Homine,* vol. XXXV; *De Animalibus,* ed. Dr. Hermann Stadler, Beitraege, Baeumker, Muenster: Aschendorff, Band XV-XVI, 1916, 1921.

St. Albert the Great (?), *Liber de Apprehensione,* ed. August Borgnet, Paris: Vives, 1890, vol. V; *Isagoge in Libros De Anima* (*Philosophia Pauperum*), vol. V.

Alcher of Clairvaux (?), *De Spiritu et Anima,* PL (Patrologia Latina, Migne) XL.

Alcuin, *De Ratione Animae, Ad Eulaliam Virginem,* PL CI.

Alexander of Aphrodisia, *De Anima Liber, Supplementum Aristotelicum,* ed. I. Bruns, Berlin: 1887.

Alexander of Hales, *Summa Theologica,* Quaracchi: 1928: 3 vols.

Alfarabi, *Die Petschafte der Weisheitslehre, Die Hauptfragen von Abu Nasr Alfarabi,* tr. Friederich Dieterici, *Alfarabi's Philosophische Abhandlungen,* Leiden: Brill, 1892; Max Horten, *Das Buch der Ringsteine* Alfarabi's, Beitraege, Baeumker, Muenster: Aschendorff, Band V, Heft 3, 1906; August Schmoelders, *Documenta Philosophia Arabum,* Bonn: Baaden, 1836.

Alfred of Sareshel, *De Motu Cordis,* ed. Clemens Baeumker, Beitraege Baeumker, Muenster: Aschendorff, Band XXIII, Heft 1, 1923.

Algazel's Metaphysics, ed. J. T. Muckle, C.S.B., Toronto: St. Michael's College, 1933.

Apuleius, *De Dogmate Platonis,* ed. G. F. Hildebrand, *Opera Omnia,* Leipzig: Knobloch, 1842: 2 vols.

Aristotle, *De Anima; De Sensu et Sensato; De Juventute et Senectute; De Vita et Morte; De Memoria et Reminiscentia; Ethica Nicomachea; Metaphysica; Physica; Analytica Posteriora.* Special editions: R. D. Hicks, *Aristotle De Anima,* Cambridge: University Press, 1907; G. Rodier, *Aristote, Traité de l'Ame,* Paris: Leroux, 1900: 2 vols.; J. A. Smith, *De Anima,* Oxford: Clarendon Press, 1931.

331

Asclepias, *In Metaphysicam,* ed. Michael Hayduck, *Commentaria in Aristotelem Graeca,* Berlin: 1888, vol. VI, part 2.

St. Augustine, *Confessions,* CSEL, Vienna, vol. XXXIII; *De Libero Arbitrio,* PL XXXII; *De Trinitate,* PL XLII; *Libri Retractationum,* PL XXXII; *De Genesi ad Litteram,* PL XXXIV.

Averroes (Ibn-Rouschd), *Opera Omnia Aristotelis cum Averrois Commentariis,* Venice: Apud Juntas, 1574: *Destructio Destructionum,* vol. IX; *Posteriorum Resolutorium libri duo cum Averrois Cordubensis magnis Commentariis,* vol. I; *Collegit,* vol. X; *Paraphrasis De Memoria et Reminiscentia,* vol. VI, part ii; *Libri moralem totam philosophiam complectentes cum Averrois Cordubensis Commentariis,* vol. III; *In De Anima,* vol. VI, part i, section 2; Max Horten, *Die Metaphysic des Averroes,* Halle: Niemeyer, 1912; *Die Hauptlehren des Averroes,* Bonne: Marcus und Weber, 1913.

Avicenna (Ibn Sina), *Liber Canonis,* Venice: Juntas, 1582; *De Anima,* Padua: Antonius Carcanus [c. 1485], also in *Avicenne perhypatetici philosophi ac medicorum facile primi opera in lucem redacta* [Venice: 1508], the *De Anima* of this latter edition has been transcribed and edited by George P. Klubertanz, S.J. (St. Louis: School of Philosophy and Science of St. Louis University, 1949); S. Landauer, "Die Psychologie des Ibn Sina," *Zeitschrift der deutschen Morgenlaendischen Gesellschaft* (Leipzig), XXIX (1875); *Risalah fi'l 'ishq,* tr. by Emil L. Fackenheim, "A Treatise on Love," *Mediaeval Studies* VII (1945).

Roger Bacon, *Opus Maius,* ed. John Henry Bridges, Oxford: Clarendon Press, 1897: 2 vols.

Boethius, *Commentaria in Porphyrium a se Translatum,* CSEL XLVIII; *De Consolatione Philosophiae,* PL LXIII, LXIV, critical edition by Adrian Fortescue, London: Burns Oates and Washburn, 1925.

Cassiodorus, *De Anima,* PL LXX.

Chalcidius, *Platonis Timeus, interprete Chalcidio, cum ejusdem commentario,* ed. Joannes Wrobel, Leipzig: Teubner, 1876.

Clarenbaldus of Arras, Wilhelm Jansen, *Der Kommentar des Clarenbaldus von Arras zu Boethius de Trinitate,* Breslau: Mueller und Seiffert, 1926.

Claudianus Mamertus, *De Statu Animae,* ed. Augustus Engelbrecht, *Opera Omnia,* CSEL, 1885.

Costa-ben-Luca, De Differentia Animae et Spiritus, tr. a Johanne Hispalensi, ed. by Carl Sigmund Barach, Innsbruck: Wagner, 1878, "Bibliotheca Philosophorum Mediae Aetatis."

Diogenes Laertius, *Lives and Opinions of Eminent Philosophers,* tr. by R. D. Hicks, London: Heinemann, 1925: 2 vols.

Eustratius, *In Ethica Nicomachea,* ed. Gustav Heylbut, *Commentaria in Aristotelem Graeca,* Berlin: vol. XX, 1893.

Galen, *Opera Omnia,* ed. Carolus Gottlob Kuehn, Leipzig: 1823: 20 vols.

Gennadius, *De Ecclesiasticis Dogmatibus,* PL LVIII.

Gregory the Great, *Libri Moralium,* PL LXXV.

Gundissalinus, *De Divisione Philosophiae,* ed. Ludwig Baur, Beitraege, Baeumker, Muenster: Aschendorff, Band IV, Heft 2-3, 1903; *De Immoralitate Animae,* ed. Georg Buelow, *Des Dominicus Gundissalinus Schrift von der Unsterblichkeit der Seele,* Beitraege, Baeumker, Muenster: Aschendorff, Band II, Heft 3, 1897; *De Anima,* ed. J. T. Muckle, C.S.B., "The Treatise *De Anima* of Dominicus Gundissalinus," *Mediaeval Studies* II, (1940).

Hugh of St. Victor, *Homiliae* 19. *in Ecclesiasten, Expositio in Hierarchiam Caelestem S. Dionysii,* PL CLXXV; *De Sacramentis,* PL CLXXVI; *De Unione Corporis et Spiritus,* PL CLXXVII; *Didascalion,* ed. Brother Charles H. Buttimer, F.S.C., Washington: Catholic University Press, 1939.

Isaac Israeli, *Liber de Definicionibus,* ed. J. T. Muckle, C.S.B., *Archives d'Histoire Doctrinale et Littéraire du Moyen Age, XI* (1937-1938).

Isaac of Stella, *Epistola ad Alcherum de Anima,* PL CXCIV.

Isidore of Seville, *Libri Differentiarum,* PL LXXXIII.

Jean de la Rochelle, *Summa de Anima* (microfilm of Ms. Bruges, 515).

St. John Damascene, *De Fide Orthodoxa,* PG XCIV.

John Philoponus, *In Physica,* ed. Hieronymus Vitelli, *Commentaria in Aristotelem Graeca,* Berlin: 1887, vol. XVI; *Le Commentaire de Jean Philopon sur le troisième livre du "traité de l'âme" d'Aristote,* ed. Marcel DeCorte, Paris: Droz, 1934.

John Philoponus (?), *In De Anima,* ed. Michael Hayduck, *Commentaria in Aristotelem Graeca,* Berlin: 1897, vol. XV.

John of Salisbury, *De Septem Septenis,* PL CXCIX.

Lactantius, *De Opificio Dei,* ed. Samuel Brandt and Georg Laubmann, *Opera Omnia,* CSEL, Vienna: 1893.

Macrobius, *In Somnium Scipionis,* ed. Franciscus Eyssenhardt, Leipzig: Teubner, 1893.

Marcus Aurelius, *The Meditations of the Emperor Marcus Aurelius Antoninus,* ed. and tr. by A. S. L. Farquharson, Oxford: Clarendon Press, 1944: 2 vols.

Moses Maimonides, *The Teachings of Maimonides,* tr. by A. Cohen, London: Routledge, 1927.

Nemesius, *De Natura Hominis,* ed. Carolus J. Burkhard, *Gregorii Nysseni (Nemesii Emesini)* Περὶ Φύσεως Ἀνθρώπου *Liber a Burgundione in Latinum translatus,* Vienna: 1896-1902.

Philo of Alexandria, *Legum Allegoriae,* tr. by Colson and Whitaker, New York: Putnam, 1929: 10 vols.

Plotinus, *Enneads,* ed. Emile Bréhier, Paris: Les Belles Lettres, Budé, 1924: 6 vols.

Plutarch, *De Virtute Morali,* ed. Gregory Bernardakis, *Moralia,* Leipzig: Teubner: 3 vols.

Pseudo-Grosseteste, *Summa Philosophiae,* ed. Ludwig Baur, Beitraege, Baeumker, Muenster: Aschendorff, Band IX, 1912.

Rabanus Maurus, *Tractatus de Anima,* PL CX.

Richard of St. Victor, *De Statu Interioris Hominis; De Emmanuele Libri Duo; Adnotationes Mysticae in Psalmos; Nonnullae Allegoriae Tabernaculi Foederis; Benjamin Minor; Benjamin Major,* PL CXCVI.

Seneca, *Epistolae,* tr. by Richard M. Grummere, New York: Putnam, 1917-1925: 3 vols.

Sextus Empiricus, *Outlines of Pyrrhonism,* tr. by R. G. Bury, New York: Putnam, 1933-1936: 3 vols.

Simplicius, *In Libros De Anima,* ed. Michael Hayduck, *Commentaria in Aristotelem Graeca,* Berlin: 1882, vol. XI; *In Physica,* ed. Hermann Diels, 1882, vol. IX.

Sophonias, *Paraphrasis de Anima,* ed. Michael Hayduck, *Commentaria in Aristotelem Graeca,* Berlin: vol. XXIII, part 1.

Tertullian, *De Anima,* PL II. A better edition: J. H. Waszink, Amsterdam, Meulenhoff, 1947.

Themistius, *Paraphrasis peri psyches,* ed. Leonardus Spengel, *Themistii Paraphrases Aristotelis,* Leipzig: Teubner, 1886, 2 vols., vol. II; *In Analytica Posteriora,* ed. Maximilian Wallies, *Commentaria in Aristotelem Graeca,* Berlin: 1900, vol. V, part 1.

Thierry of Chartres (?), *Librum Hunc,* in W. Jansen, *Der Kommentar des Clarenbaldus von Arras zu Boethius de Trinitate,* Breslau: Mueller und Seifert, 1926.

St. Thomas Aquinas, *Opera Omnia,* Parma, 1852-1873: 25 vols.; Rome: editio Leonina, 1882 ——; *Scriptum super Libros Sententiarum,* ed. Pierre Mandonnet, O.P., and M. F. Moos, O.P., Paris: Lethielleux, 1929-1933; *Le 'De Ente et Essentia' de S. Thomas d'Aquin,* ed. M. D. Roland-Gosselin, Kain: Le Saulchoir, 1926; *In Librum Boethii de Trinitate,* qq. V & VI, ed. Paul Wyser, O.P., Fribourg: Société Philosophique, 1948; *Commentarium in Aristotelis Libros De Anima,* ed. Angelo Pirotta, O.P., Turin: Marietti, 1924; *Commentarium in Libros Ethicorum,* ed. Angelo Pirotta, O.P., Turin: Marietti, 1934; *Commentarium in Metaphysicam Aristotelis,* ed. M. R. Cathala, O.P., Turin: Marietti, 1926; *Summa Theologiae,* ed. Institute of Mediaeval Studies, Ottawa: Garden City Press, 1941 ——; *De Unitate Intellectus Contra Averroistas,* ed. Leo W. Keeler, S.J., Rome: Gregorian Univ. Press, 1936.

William of Auvergne, *Opera Omnia,* Orleans: 1674: *De Anima,* vol. II, supplement; *De Virtutibus; De Legibus,* vol. I.

William of Conches, *De Philosophia Mundi*, among the works of Honorius Augustodunensis, PL CLXXII; this is identical with the Περὶ Διδάξεων *sive Elementorum Philosophiae libri quattuor*, among the works of Venerable Bede, PL XC.

William of St. Thierry, *De Natura Corporis et Animae*, PL CLXXX.

II

GENERAL SECONDARY SOURCES

Mortimer J. Adler, *What Man Has Made of Man*, New York: Longmans, 1937.

Rudolf Allers, "The Intellectual Cognition of Particulars," *The Thomist* III (1941); "The Vis Cogitativa and Evaluation," *The New Scholasticism* XV (1941).

Emile Bréhier, *La Philosophie du Moyen Age*, Paris: Michel, 1937.

George Sidney Brett, *History of Philosophy*, London: Allen and Unwin, 1921: 3 vols.

M. D. Chenu, O.P., "Authentica et Magistralia," *Divus Thomas* (Placentiae) XXVIII (1925), 257-58.

Edmund S. Conklin, *Principles of Abnormal Psychology*, New York: Holt, 1927.

Pierre Duhem, *Le Système du Mond*, Paris: Hermann, 1913.

Cornelio Fabro, "Knowledge and Perception in Aristotelic-Thomistic Psychology," *The New Scholasticism* XII (1938); "L'Organizzazione della persezione sensioriale," *Bolletino Filosofico* IV (1938).

Mark Gaffney, S.J., *The Psychology of the Interior Senses*, St. Louis: Herder, 1942.

Étienne Gilson, *La Philosophie au Moyen Age*, 2nd ed. Paris: Payot, 1944; *Le Thomisme*, 5th ed., Paris: Vrin, 1944; *Etudes sur le rôle de la Pensée Médiévale dans la formation du système Cartésien*, Paris: Vrin, 1930; *The Unity of Philosophical Experience*, New York: Scribners, 1937; *The Spirit of Medieval Philosophy*, New York: Scribners, 1940; "Pourquoi S. Thomas a critiqué S. Augustin," *Archives d'Histoire Doctrinale et Littéraire du Moyen-Age*, I, (1926).

Martin Grabman, *Die Geschichte der Scholastische Methode*, Freiburg: Herder, 1909-1911: 2 vols.

Rodolphe Hain, O.M.I., "De vi aestimativa et de instinctu animalium," *Revue de l'Université d'Ottawa* II (1932); "De vi cogitativa et de instinctu hominis," *ibid.*, III.

André Hayen, S.J., *L'Intentionnel dans la philosophie de Saint Thomas*, Bruxelles: L'Edition Universelle — Paris: Desclée, 1942.

L. B. Geiger, *La Participation*, Paris: Vrin, 1942.

P. Glorieux, *La Littérature quodlibétique de* 1260 *à* 1320, Le Saulchoir —
Paris: Vrin, 1925; "De quelques 'emprunts' de S. Thomas," *Recherches de Théologie Ancienne et Médiévale* VIII (1936), 155-68.

Martin Grabmann, *Einfuehrung in die Summa Theologiae des hl. Thomas
von Aquin,* 2nd ed., Freiburg: Herder, 1928; "De Methodo Historica
in Studiis Scholasticis adhibenda," *Ciencia Tomista* XXVII (1923),
194-209; "Commentatio Historica," *Angelicum* III (1926), 146-65.

P. Goudrault, O.P., "L'Influence des études médiévales sur le progrès de
la philosophie et de la théologie," *Revue Dominicaine* XXXIX (1933),
65-79.

Joseph Gredt, O.S.B., *Elementa Philosophiae Aristotelico-Thomisticae,*
3rd ed., Friburg: Herder, 1921: 2 vols., vol. I.

E. Hocedez, S.J., *Aegidii Romani Theoremata de esse et essentia,* Louvain: Museum Lessianum, 1930.

Eduard Hugon, O.P., *Philosophia Naturalis,* pars. 2, 3rd. ed., Paris:
Lethielleux, 1922.

H. L. Janssens, O.S.B., "St. Thomas et St. Anselme," *Xenia Thomistica,* III (1925), 289-96.

John of St. Thomas, *Cursus Philosophicus Thomisticus,* ed. Beatus
Reiser, O.S.B., Turin: Marietti, 1930-1937: 3 vols.

David Kaufmann, *Die Sinne,* Leipzig: Brockhaus, 1884.

Michael Maher, S.J., *Psychology,* 9th ed., London: Longmans, 1925.

Joseph Maréchal, S.J., *Le Point de Départ de la Métaphysique,* Paris:
Alcan, 1923.

Cardinal Mercier, *Manual of Modern Scholastic Psychology,* tr. by T. L.
Parker and S. A. Parker, London: Kegan Paul, 1928.

H. Noble, O.P., *Les Passions dans la Vie Morale,* Paris: Lethielleux,
1931; translator and editor of *Summa Theologiae,* II-II qq. 47-56,
"Editions de la Revue des Jeunes," Paris: Desclée, 1925.

Julien Peghaire, C.S.Sp., "A Forgotten Sense, the Cogitative, according
to St. Thomas Aquinas," *The Modern Schoolman* XX (1943). This
article appears in French, as chapter 8 of *Regards sur le connaître,*
Montréal: Fides, 1949.

George Sarton, *Introduction to the History of Science,* Washington:
Carnegie Institute, 1927: 2 vols.

Dr. Schuetz, "Die *vis aestimativa s. cogitativa* des hl. Thomas von Aquin,"
Goerres-Gesellschaft zur Pflege der Wissenschaft, Jahresberichte der
Section fuer Philosophie fuer das Jahr 1883.

Hermann Siebeck, *Geschichte der Psychologie,* Gotha: Perthes, 1880:
1 vol., 2 parts; "Zur Psychologie der Scholastik," *Archiv fuer Geschichte der Philosophie* I (1888), 375-90, 518-33; II (1889) 22-28,
180-92, 414-25, 517-25; III (1890), 177-91.

H. D. Simonin, O.P., "La Notion D' *'Intentio'* dans l'oeuvre de S. Thomas
d'Aquin," *Revue des Sciences Philosophiques et Théologiques* XIX
(1930), 445-63.

Lynn Thorndike, *History of Magic and Experimental Science,* New York: Macmillan, 1927: 6 vols.

Domet de Vorges, "L'Estimative," *Revue Néo-Scholastique* XI (1904).

Karl Werner, *Der Entwickelungsgang der mittelalterlichen Psychologie von Alcuin bis Albertus Magnus,* Vienna: Gerold, 1876. Separatabdruck aus dem xxv Band der Denkschriften der philosophisch-historischen Klasse der kaiserlichen Akademie der Wissenschaften.

Harry Austryn Wolfson, "The Internal Senses in Latin, Arabic, and Hebrew Philosophic Texts," *Harvard Theological Review* XXVIII (1935), 69-133.

Robert S. Woodworth, *Psychology,* 12th ed., London: Methuen, 1940; *Experimental Psychology,* New York: Holt, 1938.

Maurice de Wulf, *Histoire de la Philosophie Médiévale,* 6th ed. Paris: Vrin, 1934-1937: 3 vols.

III

SECONDARY SOURCES ACCORDING TO CHAPTERS

INTRODUCTION

J. D'Albi, *S. Bonaventure et les luttes doctrinales de* 1267-1277, Tamines: Duculot-Roulin, 1922.

L. Baur, "Thomas von Aquin als Philosoph," *Theologische Quartalschrift* CVI (1925), 249-66, CVII (1926), 8-38.

C. Boyer, *Essais sur la Doctrine de S. Augustin,* Paris: Beauchesne, 1932.

André Brémond, S.J., "La synthèse thomiste de l'Acte et de l'Idée," *Gregorianum* XII (1931), 267-83.

F. Blanche, "Sur la langue technique de s. Thomas," *Revue de Philosophie* XXX (1930), 7-28.

Robert Edward Brennan, O.P., *General Psychology,* New York: Macmillan, 1937; *Thomistic Psychology,* New York: Macmillan, 1941.

Thomas de Vio Cardinal Cajetan, *Commentary on the Summa Theologiae,* in the Leonine edition of the works of St. Thomas Aquinas.

Joannis Capreoli Defensiones Theologiae, ed. Ceslaus Paban, O.P., and Thomas Pègues, O.P., Turin: Cattier, 1900-1908: 7 vols.

M. D. Chenu, O.P., "Notes de Travail. I. La surnaturalisation des vertus. II. L'amour dans la foi," *Bulletin Thomiste* IV (1931-1933), 93*-99*; "Les réponses de s. Thomas et de Kilwardby à la consultation de Jean de Verceil," *Mélanges Mandonnet,* Paris: Vrin, 1930: 2 vols., vol. I, pp. 191-222; "Pour l'histoire de la philosophie médiévale," *The New Scholasticism* III (1939), 65-74; "Apres dix ans," *Bulletin Thomiste* XI (1934), 1-3.

J. E. Combes, *La Psychologie de Saint Thomas d'Aquin,* Montpellier: Grollier, 1860.

I. T. Eschmann, O.P., "Bonum Commune melius est quam bonum unius. Eine Studie ueber den Wertvorrang des Personalen bei Thomas von Aquin," *Mediaeval Studies* VI (1944), 62-104.

Franz Cardinal Ehrle, *Die Scholastik und ihre Aufgaben in unseren Zeit,* zweite, vermehrte Auflage von Fr. Pelster, S.J., Freiburg: Herder, 1933.

A. Forest, *La Structure métaphysique du concret selon S. Thomas D'Aquin,* Paris: Vrin, 1931.

Joseph Froebes, S.J., *Psychologia Speculativa,* Freiburg: Herder, 1927: 2 vols.

Ch. Journet, "Les maladies de sens internes," *Revue Thomiste* XXIX (1924), 35-50.

Jean Paulus, *Henri de Gand,* Paris: Vrin, 1938.

Anton C. Pegis, *St. Thomas and the Greeks,* Milwaukee: Marquette University Press, 1939; *St. Thomas and the Problem of the Soul in the Thirteenth Century,* Toronto: Institute of Mediaeval Studies, 1934.

Tilman Pesch, S.J., *Institutiones Psychologiae,* Freiburg: Herder, 1897: 3 vols.

Gerald B. Phelan, "Presidential Address," *Proceedings of the Seventh Annual Meeting of the American Catholic Philosophical Association,* 1931, pp. 27-40.

G. Rabeau, *Species, Verbum,* Paris: Vrin, 1938.

Vincentius Remer, S.J., *Psychologia,* 5a ed. a Paulo Geny, S.J., Rome: Gregorian University Press, 1925.

Pierre Rousselot, S.J., *The Intellectualism of St. Thomas,* tr. by J. E. O'Mahony, London: Sheed and Ward, 1935.

Paul Siwek, S.J., *Psychologia Speculativa,* Rome: Gregorian University Press, 1932.

Charles Spearman, *Psychology Down the Ages,* London: Macmillan, 1937: 2 vols.; *The Nature of 'Intelligence' and the Principles of Cognition,* London: Macmillan, 1932.

Francis Suarez, S.J., *De Anima,* in *Opera Omnia,* Paris: Vives, 1856: 24 vols., vol. III.

L. P. Thurstone, *Vectors of Mind,* Chicago: University of Chicago Press, 1935.

John Joseph Urraburu, *Psychologia,* Paris: Lethielleux, 1896.

Fernand Van Steenberghen, *Aristote en Occident,* Louvain: Editions de l'Institut Supérieur de Philosophie, 1946.

J. Wébert, O.P., translator and editor of *Summa Theologiae I,* qq. 75-78, "Editions de la Revue des Jeunes," Paris: Desclée, 1928.

CHAPTER I

Clemens Baeumker, *Des Aristoteles Lehre von den auessern und innern Sinnesvermoegen,* Leipzig: Hunderstund und Pries, 1877.

John I. Beare, *Greek Theories of Elementary Cognition,* Oxford: Clarendon Press, 1906.

Hermann Bonitz, *Index Aristotelicus,* Berlin: 1870.

Franz Brentano, *Die Psychologie des Aristoteles,* Mainz: Kirchlein, 1867.

Stanislas Cantin, "L'âme et ses puissances selon Aristote," *Laval Théologique et Philosophique* II (1946), no. 1, 184-205.

Anthelme Edouard Chaignet, *Essai sur la Psychologie d'Aristote,* Paris: Hachette, 1883.

Francis Macdonald Cornford, *Plato's Theory of Knowledge,* London: Kegan Paul, 1935.

Paul Czaja, "Welche Bedeutung hat bei Aristoteles die sinnliche Wahrnehmung und das innere Anschauungsbild fuer die Bildung des Begriffes," *Philosophisches Jahrbuch* XVII (1904).

Marcel DeCorte, *La Doctrine de l'Intelligence chez Aristote,* Paris: Vrin, 1934; "Notes Exégetiques sur la Theorie Aristotélicienne du Sensus Communis," *The New Scholasticism* VI (1932).

Joannes Dembowski, *Quaestiones Aristotelicae Diversae,* Regensburg: Dalkowski, 1881.

Jacob Freudenthal, *Ueber den Begriff des Wortes* ΦΑΝΤΑΣΙΑ *bie Aristoteles,* Goettingen: Rente, 1863.

Joseph Geyser, *Die Erkenntnisstheorie des Aristoteles,* Muenster: Schoenigh, 1917.

Arthur Kent Griffin, *Aristotle's Psychology of Conduct,* London: Williams and Norgate, 1931.

George Grote, *Aristotle,* ed. by Bain and Robertson, London: Murray, 1872: 2 vols.

Octave Hamelin, *Le Système d'Aristote,* publié par Leon Robin, Paris: Alcan, 1920.

Friederich Ferdinand Kampe, *Die Erkenntnistheorie des Aristoteles,* Leipzig: Fues, 1870.

Ludwig Keller, *Aristoteles und die moderne Psychologie,* Freiburg: Mors und Singler, 1927.

J. M. Le Blond, *Logique et Méthode chez Aristote,* Paris: Vrin, 1939.

G. A. G. Mure, *Aristotle,* London: Benn, 1932.

J. Neuhaeuser, *Aristoteles' Lehre von dem sinnlichen Erkenntnisvermoegen und seinen Organen,* Leipzig: Koshey, 1878.

Clodius Piat, *Aristote,* Paris: Alcan, 1903.

Louis-Marie Régis, O.P., *L'Opinion selon Aristote,* Paris: Vrin — Ottawa: Institut d'études Médiévales, 1935.

W. D. Ross, *Aristotle,* 2nd ed., London: Methuen, 1930.

Hermann Siebeck, *Aristoteles,* 4th ed., Stuttgart: Frohman, 1922.

Eulalie Evan Spicer, *Aristotle's Conception of the Soul,* London: 1934.
Edward Zeller, *Aristotle and the earlier Peripatetics,* tr. by Costelloe and Muirhead, London: Longmans, 1897: 2 vols.

CHAPTER II

Clemens Baeumker, *Die Stellung des Alfred von Sareshel (Alfredus Anglicus) und seiner Schrift de Motu Cordis in der Wissenschaft des beginnenden* 13 *Jahrhunderts,* Munich: Sitzungsbericht der koeniglichen Bayerischen Akademie der Wissenschaften, philosophisch-philologische und historische Klasse, 1913; *Witelo, ein Philosoph und Naturforscher des XII. Jahrhunderts,* Beitraege, Baeumker, Muenster: Aschendorff, Band III, Heft 2, 1908.

Charles Boyer, S.J., *Essais sur la doctrine de S. Augustin,* Paris: Beauchesne, 1932.

Emile Bréhier, *La Théorie des Incorporels dan l'ancien Stoicisme,* 2nd ed., Paris: Vrin, 1928; *Chrysippe,* Paris: Alcan, 1910.

Victor Brochard, *Les Sceptiques Grecs,* Paris: Imprimerie National, 1887.

Anthelme Edouard Chaignet, *Histoire de la Psychologie des Grecs,* Paris: Hachette, 1887-1893; 5 vols.

M. D. Chenu, O.P., "Notes de Lexicographie philosophique: Disciplina," *Revue des Sciences Philosophiques et Théologiques* XXV (1936).

B. Domanski, *Die Psychologie des Nemesius,* Beitraege, Baeumker, Muenster: Aschendorff, Band III, Heft 1, 1900.

J. Ebner, *Die Erkenntnislehre Richards von St. Viktor,* Beitraege, Baeumker, Muenster: Aschendorff, Band XIX, Heft 4, 1916.

Heinrich Flatten, *Die Philosophie des Wilhelm von Conches,* Koblenz: Goerres-Druckerei, 1929.

Robert G. Gassert, S.J., "The Meaning of *Cogitatio* in St. Augustine," *The Modern Schoolman* XXV (1948), 238-45.

Étienne Gilson, *Introduction à l'Etude de Saint Augustin,* 2nd ed., Paris: Vrin, 1943; "Pourquoi S. Thomas a critiqué S. Augustin," *Archives d'Histoire Doctrinale et Littéraire du Moyen-Age* I (1926).

Charles Homer Haskins, *Studies in the History of Mediaeval Science,* Cambridge: Harvard University Press, 1924.

B. Hauréau, *Singularités Historiques et Littéraires,* Paris: Calmann-Lévy, 1894.

R. D. Hicks, *Stoic and Epicurean,* New York: Scribners, 1910.

Werner Wilhelm Jaeger, *Nemesios von Emesa,* Berlin: Weidmann, 1914.

Bernard Kaelin, *Die Erkenntnislehre des hl. Augustinus,* Sarnen: Ehrli, 1921.

John P. Kleinz, *The Theory of Knowledge of Hugh of St. Victor,* Washington: Catholic University Press, 1944.

Josef Kroll, *Die Lehre des Hermes Trismegistos,* Beitraege, Baeumker, Muenster: Aschendorff, Band XII, Heft 2-4, 1914.

E. Lutz, *Die Psychologie Bonaventuras,* Muenster: 1909.

Henri-Irénée Marrou, *Saint Augustin et la fin de la culture antique,* Paris: Bibliothèque des écoles Françaises, 1938.

Wilhelm Meuser, *Die Erkenntnislehre des Isaak von Stella,* Bottrop: Postberg, 1934.

J. T. Muckle, C.S.B., "The De Officiis Ministrorum of St. Ambrose," *Mediaeval Studies* I (1939).

F. Ogereau, *Le Système philosophique des Stoiciens,* Paris: Alcan, 1885.

Heinrich Ostler, *Die Psychologie des Hugo von St. Viktor,* Beitraege, Baeumker, Muenster: Aschendorff, Band VI, Heft 1, 1906.

W. Ott, "Des hl. Augustinus Lehre über die Sinneserkenntniss," *Philosophisches Jahrbuch* XIII (1900).

Carmelo Ottaviano, *Un Brano Inedito Della "Philosophia" di Guglielmo di Conches,* Naples: Morano, 1935.

J. M. Parent, O.P., *La Doctrine de Creation dans l'Ecole de Chartres,* Ottawa: Institut d'Etudes Médiévales, 1938.

Julien Peghaire, C.S.Sp., "Le Couple Augustinien 'Ratio superior et ratio inferior'," *Revue des science philosophiques et théologiques* XXII (1934).

Anton C. Pegis, "The Mind of St. Augustine," *Mediaeval Studies* VI (1944).

Reginald Lane Poole, *Illustrations of the History of Medieval Thought and Learning,* revised edition, London: Society for Promoting Christian Knowledge, 1920.

E. Portalié, "St. Augustin," "Augustinisme," *Dictionnaire de Théologie Catholique,* ed. A. Vacant and E. Mangenot, tome I.

Georges Rodier, *Etudes de Philosophie Grecque,* Paris: Vrin, 1926.

Phil. M. Schedler, *Die Philosophie des Macrobius, und ihr Einfluss auf die Wissenschaft des christlichen Mittelalters,* Beitraege, Baeumker, Muenster: Aschendorff, Band XIII, Heft 1, 1916.

Michael Schmaus, *Die psychologische Trinitaetslehre des hl. Augustinus,* Muenster: Aschendorff, 1937.

A. Schmekel, *Die Philosophie der mittleren Stoa,* Berlin: Weidmann, 1892.

Artur Schneider, *Die Erkenntnislehre des Johannes Eriugena,* Berlin: De Guyter, 1921-1923.

Hermann Siebeck, *Untersuchungen zur Philosophie der Griechen,* Halle: Barthel, 1873.

Ludwig Stein, *Psychologie der Stoa,* Berlin: Calvary, 1886-1889: 2 vols.

B. W. Switalski, *Der Chalcidius-Kommentar zu Plato's Timeus,* Beitraege, Baeumker, Muenster: Aschendorff, Band III, Heft 6, 1902.

Karl Werner, *Die Kosmologie und Naturlehre des scholastischen Mittelalters mit spezieller Beziehung auf Wilhelm von Conches,* Vienna: 1873. Sitzungsberichte der kaiserlichen Wiener Akademie der Wissenschaften, philosophische-historische Klasse.

Dom A. Wilmart, O.S.B., *Auteurs Spirituels et Textes Dévots,* Paris: Bloud et Gay, 1932.

Edward Zeller, *Stoics, Epicureans and Sceptics,* tr. by Reichel, London: Longmans, 1892.

CHAPTER III

H. Bédoret, S.J., "Les premières Traductions Tolédanes de Philosophie: Oeuvres d'Alfarabi," *Revue néoscolastique* LXI (1938).

Nematallah Carame, *Avicennae Metaphysices Compendium,* Rome: Pont. Institutum Orientalium Studiorum, 1926.

Baron Carra de Vaux, *Avicenne,* Paris, Alcan, 1900; *Gazali,* Paris: Alcan, 1902.

A. M. Goichon, *Lexique de la Langue Philosophique d'Ibn Sînâ,* Paris: Desclée, 1938; *Vocabulaires Comparés d'Aristote et d'Ibn Sînâ,* Paris: Desclée, 1931; *Introduction à Avicenne: Son Epitre des Définitions,* Paris: Declée, 1933; *La Philosophie d'Avicenne,* Paris: Adrien-Maisonneuve, 1944.

O. Cameron Gruner, *A Treatise on the Canon of Medicine of Avicenna,* London: Luzae, 1930.

M. M. Gorce, "Averroisme," *Dictionnaire d'Histoire et de Géographie Ecclésiatique,* vol. III.

J. Guttman, *Die Scholastik des dreizehnten Jahrhunderts in ihrem Beziehungen zum Judenthum und zur juedischen Literatur,* Breslau: Marcus, 1902.

Robert Hanui, O.F.M., *Alfarabi's Philosophy and its Influence on Scholasticism,* Sidney: Pellegrini, 1928.

S. Horovitz, *Die Psychologie bei den juedischen Religionsphilosophen des Mittelalters,* Breslau: Schatzky, 1912.

Max Horten, *Die philosophischen Systeme der spekulativen Theologen im Islam,* Bonn: Cohen, 1912.

David Kaufman, *Die Sinne,* Leipzig: Brockhaus, 1884.

Josef Koch, *Giles of Rome, Errores Philosophorum,* tr. by John O. Riedl, Milwaukee: Marquette University Press, 1944.

Ibrahim Madkour, *La Place d'al Fârâbi dans l'école philosophique musulmane,* Paris: Librairie d'Amérique et d'Orient, 1934.

Pierre Mandonnet, O.P., *Siger de Brabant et l'Averroisme latin au XIIIe Siècle,* Fribourg: University, 1899.

S. Munk, *Mélanges de philosophie Juive et Arabe,* Paris: Vrin, 1927.

David Neumark, *Geschichte der juedischen Philosophie des Mittelalters,* Berlin: Reimer, 1907: 2 vols.

G. Quadri, *La philosophie Arabe dans l'Europe médiévale*, tr. by Roland Huret, Paris: Payot, 1947.

Beatrice H. Zedler, "Averroes on the Possible Intellect," *Proceedings of the American Catholic Philosophical Association* XXV (1951), 164-78.

CHAPTER IV

Josef Bach, *Des Albertus Magnus Verhaeltniss zu der Erkenntnisslehre der Griechen, Lateiner, Araber und Juden*, Vienna: Braumueller, 1881.

Matthias Baumgartner, *Die Erkenntnisslehre des Wilhelm von Auvergne*, Beitraege, Baeumker, Muenster: Aschendorff, Band II, Heft 1, 1893.

Jacob Bonné, *Die Erkenntnisslehre Alberts des Grossen*, Bonn: Stodieck, 1935.

Ulrich Daehnert, *Die Erkenntnislehre des Albertus Magnus*, Leipzig: Gerhardt, 1933.

Joseph Art. Endres, "Des Alexander von Hales Leben und psychologische Lehren," *Philosophisches Jahrbuch* I (1888).

J. N. Espenberger, *Die Philosophie des Petrus Lombardus und ihre Stellung in zwoelften Jahrhundert*, Beitraege, Baeumker, Muenster: Aschendorff, Band III, Heft 5, 1901.

Étienne Gilson, "L'Ame raisonnable chez Albert de Grand," *Archives d'Histoire Doctrinale et Littéraire du Moyen Age* XVIII (1943).

Pearl Kibre, "A Fourteenth Century Scholastic Miscellany," *The New Scholasticism* XV (1941).

Dom O. Lottin, "L'Authenticité du de Potentiis Animae d'Albert le Grand," *Revue néoscolastique de philosophie* XXXII (1930).

G. M. Manser, O.P., "Johann von Rupella," *Jahrbuch fuer Philosophie und spekulative Theologie* XXVI (1912).

Amato Masnovo, *Da Guglielmo d'Auvergne a san Tomaso d'Aquino*, Milan: Vita e Pensiero, 1930-1934: 2 vols.

P. G. Meersseman, O.P., *Introductio in Opera Omnia B. Alberti Magni, O.P.*, Bruges: Beyaert, 1931.

Ernest Renan, *Averroès et l'Averroisme*, Paris: Calmann-Lévy, 1869.

Djémil Saliba, *Etude sur la Métaphysique d'Avicenne*, Paris: Les Presses Universitaires, 1926.

Simon B. Scheyer, *Das psychologische System des Maimonides*, Frankfurt: Kessler, 1845.

Auguste Schmoelders, *Essai sur les Ecoles philosophiques chez les Arabes*, Paris: Didot, 1842.

Sociedad Hebraica Argentina, *Maimonides*, Buenos Aires: 1935.

Julius S. Spiegler, *Geschichte der Philosophie des Judenthums*, Leipzig: Friedrich, 1890.

Fernand Van Steenberghen, *Aristote en Occident*, Louvain: Institut Supérieur de Philosophie, 1946.

Moritz Steinschneider, *Allgemeine Einleitung in die juedische Literatur des Mittelalters,* Jerusalem: Bamberger and Wahrmann, 1938.

Josef Strulovici, *Der Einfluss Moses Maimonides' in der Schrift "De Veritate" des Thomas von Aquin,* Kallmuenz: Lassleben, 1936.

Gabriel Théry, *Tolède,* Oran: Heintz-Frères, 1944.

R. De Vaux, *Notes et Textes sur l'Avicennisme Latin,* Paris: Vrin, 1934.

Karl Werner, *Der Averroismus in der Christlich-peripatetischen Psychologie,* Vienna: Gerold, 1881.

Martin Winter, *Ueber Avicennas Opus Egregium de Anima,* "Liber Sextus Naturalium," Munich: Wolf, 1903.

Harry Austryn Wolfson, "Maimonides on the Internal Senses," *Jewish Quarterly Review,* new series XXV, (1935); "Isaac Israeli on the Internal Senses," *Jewish Studies in Memory of George Kohut,* New York: 1935.

P. Minges, "Erkenntnislehre des Jean de la Rochelle," *Philosophisches Jahrbuch* XXVII (1914).

George C. Reilly, *The Psychology of St. Albert the Great,* Washington: Catholic University Press, 1934.

Dr. Arthur Schneider, *Die Abendlaendische Spekulation des zwoelfte Jahrhunderts in ihrem Verhaeltniss zur aristotelischen und juedisch-arabischen Philosophie,* Beitraege, Baeumker, Muenster: Aschendorff, Band XVII, Heft 4, 1915; *Die Psychologie Alberts des Grossen,* Beitraege, Baeumker, Muenster: Aschendorff, Band IV, Heft 5-6, 1903.

Karl Werner, *Die Psychologie des Wilhelm von Auvergne,* Vienna: Karl Gerold's Sohn, 1873. Sonderabdruck aus dem Februarhefte des Jahrganges 1873 der Sitzungsberichte der philosophische-historische Klasse der kaiserlichen Akademie der Wissenschaften.

CHAPTERS V — IX

—— *Dionysiaca,* Paris: Desclée, 1937.

Rudolf Allers, *The Successful Error,* New York: Sheed and Ward, 1940.

S. E. Asch, "Studies in the Principles of Judgments and Attitudes, II. Determination of judgments by group and by ego standards," *Journal of Social Psychology* XII (1940).

T. Bartolomei, O.S.M., "L'Attenzione sensitiva," *Divus Thomas* (Placentiae) XLVII-XLIX (1944-46).

Robert Edward Brennan, "The Thomistic Concept of Imagination," *The New Scholasticism* XV (1941).

Louis Copelam, "L'Élément affectiv à la base du réflex psychogalvanique," *L'Année Psychologique* XXXVI (1936), 119-36,

Marcel DeCorte, "Themistius et s. Thomas D'Aquin, contribution à l'étude des sources et la chronologie du Commentaire de s. Thomas sur le *De Anima*," *Archives d'Histoire Doctrinale et Littéraire du Moyen-Age*, 1932.

Allan L. Edwards, "Studies of stereotypes: I. The directionality and uniformity of responses to stereotypes," *Journal of Social Psychology* XII (1940).

Else Frenkel-Brunswik, "Mechanisms of Self-Deception," *Journal of Social Psychology* X (1939).

Sigmund Freud, *Collected Papers,* authorized translation under supervision of Joan Riviere, London: The International Psychoanalytic Press, 1924-1925: 4 vols.

Étienne Gilson, *Réalisme Thomiste et Critique de la Connaissance,* Paris: Vrin, 1939

Alberto Gómez Izquierdo, O.P., "Valor cognoscitivo de la 'Intentio'," *Ciencia Tomista* XXIX (1924).

Martin Grabmann, *Die Werke des heiligen Thomas von Aquin,* Beitraege, Baeumker, Muenster: Aschendorff, Band 22, Heft 1-2, 1926; 3rd ed., 1949; *Mittelalterliches Geistesleben,* Munich: Hueber, 1926.

George P. Klubertanz, S.J., "The Unity of Human Operation," *The Modern Schoolman* XXVII (1950), 75-103; "The Psychologists and the Nature of Man," *Proceedings of the American Catholic Philosophical Association* XXV (1951), 66-88; "St. Thomas and the Knowledge of the Singular," *The New Scholasticism* XXVI (1952).

Dom Odon Lottin, O.S.B., *Psychologie et Morale aux XIIe et XIIIe siècles* (Louvain: Gembloux, 1942), vol. I.

John A. McGeoch, *The Psychology of Human Learning,* New York: Longmans, 1942.

Pierre Mandonnet, O.P., *Des Ecrits Authentiques de S. Thomas d'Aquin,* 2d ed., Fribourg: L'Oeuvre de Saint-Paul, 1910.

A. Mansion, "Le Commentaire de Saint Thomas sur le 'De Sensu et Sensato' d'Aristote, utilisation d'Alexandre d'Aphrodise," *Mélanges Mandonnet,* Paris: Vrin, 1930: 2 vols., vol. I.

Selden C. Menefee and Audrey G. Granneberg, "Propaganda and opinions on foreign policy," *Journal of Social Psychology* XI (1940).

James Grier Miller, *Unconsciousness,* New York: Wiley, 1942.

Dom Thomas Verner Moore, O.S.B., "The Scholastic Theory of Perception," *The New Scholasticism* VII (1933).

F. Pelster, S.J., review of J. Perrier, O.P., *S. Thomas Aquinatis Opuscula I* (Paris: Lethielleux, 1949), in *Gregorianum* XXXI (1950), 294.

Edmund J. Ryan, C.PP.S., *The Role of the "Sensus Communis" in the Psychology of St. Thomas Aquinas* (Carthagena, Ohio: Messenger Press, 1951).

Gustav Siewerth, "Die menschliche Seele und ihre geistigen und sinn-
    lichen Erkenntnissvermoegen," *Philosophisches Jahrbuch* XIV (1932).
Robert L. Thorndike, "The effect of discussions upon the correctness
    of group decisions, when the factor of majority influence is allowed
    for," *Journal of Social Psychology* IX (1938).
Harold S. Tuttle, "Two Kinds of Learning," *Journal of Psychology* XXII
    (1946).
Two Sisters of Notre Dame, *Aids to Will Training in Christian Educa-
    tion*, New York: Pustet, 1943.
Gérard Verbeke, "Les sources et la chronologie du Commentaire de s.
    Thomas d'Aquin au De anima d'Aristote," *Revue Philosophique de
    Louvain* XLV (1947), 314-38.
Francis A. Walsh, "Phantasm and Phantasy," *The New Scholasticism*
    IX (1935).
J. Wébert, O.P., "Etude sur la 'Reflexio'," *Mélanges Mandonnet,* Paris:
    Vrin, 1930: 2 vols., vol. I.

INDEX OF PROPER NAMES

Abelard 65

Abraham ibn-Daud 83

Adelard of Bath 58-59

Adler 6

St. Albert the Great 19, 134-44, 145, 148, 149, 227, 270, 271

Alcher of Clairvaux 61

Alcuin 57

Alexander of Aphrodisia 33

Alexander of Hales 77, 130, 131, 133, 269, 270

Alfred of Sareshel (Alfredus Anglicus) 68-70, 284

Algazel 106-09, 110, 122, 123, 125, 136, 137, 138, 140, 142, 145, 260, 269, 275

Allers 4, 11

St. Ambrose 44

St. Anselm 77

Apuleius 44

Aristotle 1, 2, 8, 13, 18-36, 37, 47, 53, 62, 70, 80, 81, 83, 84, 85, 89, 105, 109, 110, 115, 136, 139, 149-51, 155, 175, 186, 191-92, 198, 205-06, 212, 214, 219, 220, 228, 260, 266, 267, 269, 283

Aristotelianism 8, 44, 47, 53, 58, 78, 80, 155, 196, 252, 260, 270, 284

Asclepias 35

St. Augustine 37, 48-53, 55, 60, 61, 62, 71, 74, 77, 79, 132, 267

Augustinians 47, 73, 79, 168, 220, 249, 283

Avempace 167

Averroes 1, 7-9, 10, 13, 18, 109-22, 123, 136, 137, 138, 140, 142, 149, 161, 162, 167, 182-88, 194, 195, 223, 225, 241, 244, 268, 275, 276, 278, 283

Avicenna 8, 13, 19, 29, 51, 70, 77, 85, 86, 89-106, 107, 110, 114, 115, 122, 123, 124, 125, 137, 130, 131, 132, 134, 136, 137, 138, 139, 142, 145, 146, 163, 167, 193, 219, 220, 223, 225, 231, 260, 269, 270, 271, 275, 276

Bacon (Roger) 28

St. Bernard of Clairvaux 70

Bihler 17

Boethius 53, 55, 56, 60, 62, 72, 76, 77, 125, 133

St. Bonaventure 77-78, 284

Burgundio 46

Cajetan, 7, 9, 13, 28, 277

Cantin 28

Capreolus 6, 7

Carra de Vaux 106

Cassiodorus 55, 59, 60, 63, 71

Chaignet 39, 40

Chalcidius 44

Chrysippus 41-43

Cicero 43

Clarenbaldus of Arras 67, 284

Claudinus Mamertus 54, 57, 60, 283

Cleanthes 40

Constabulinus, see Costa-ben-Luca

Constabulus, see Costa-ben-Luca

Constantinus Africanus 58, 62, 63

Cornford 19

Costa-ben-Luca 84, 123, 142

De Differentia Animae et Spiritus 63, 84

De Spiritu et Anima 61, 133

DeCorte 39

Dieterici 88

Dionysius 60, 155

347

INDEX OF SUBJECTS